WORDS

in Motion

WORDS

in Motion

TOWARD A GLOBAL LEXICON

Edited by Carol Gluck
and Anna Lowenhaupt Tsing

DUKE UNIVERSITY PRESS
Durham and London
2009

© 2009 Duke University Press
All rights reserved.
Printed in the United States
of America on acid-free paper
Designed by Amy Ruth Buchanan
Typeset in Janson by Keystone
Typesetting, Inc.
Library of Congress Cataloging-
in-Publication Data appear on the
last printed page of this book.

A PROJECT ORGANIZED BY THE
SOCIAL SCIENCE RESEARCH
COUNCIL.

CONTENTS

INTRODUCTION

Words in Motion

As words change, the world changes. This ancient conceit turns on the power of words to make worlds, but the world, we know, also has the power to change words. Words are always in motion, and as they move across space and time, they inscribe the arcs of our past and present. This book considers the relation between words and worlds by tracing the social and political life of words — specific words in specific places at specific times — with an eye to their practical and public effect. We have chosen words that do work in the world, whether organizing, mobilizing, inspiring, excluding, suppressing, or covering up. We then track these words as they cross cultural borders and become embedded in social and political practices, changing their impact and their meaning as they go. "Security," "indigeneity," "conspiracy," "minority," "custom," "sublime" — the particular words matter less than the approach we take in pursuing them. Precisely because of their specificity, these moving words provide methodological entry into social and political experience, often leading in unexpected directions. Following a word in practice — and sticking to that word as it skittered, crawled, and leapt from one context to another — required research strategies at once nimble and daunting. The more closely we pursued each word, the harder it became to rely on received language and disciplinary discourse to do our analytic work for us. The approach acted something like a lever, with a single word at one end conferring an interpretive advantage that lifted a substantial social and political weight at the other. So we began with words and ended with worlds that looked different from those we had imagined when we started.

As anthropologists, sociologists, political scientists, historians, and literary scholars of, and from, different countries, what we have in common is the injunction to follow our word to where it does its work. We also share a disinclination to treat language in isolation from — or as transparently linked to — its social and political context. But we are not linguists, and although most of us deal with the translation from one language, culture, and power to another, we are not engaged in "translation studies" either. There is some etymology and genealogy, but not much, and whatever there is of word-theory is mostly common sense. Nor can we claim more than lateral kinship with such estimable works as the now classic *Keywords* of Raymond Williams; its recent update, *New Keywords*; or the series *Keywords for a Different Kind of Globalization*.[1] Some of our words are also found in these compendia, but the tracking method here is so tightly situated in time, place, and process — "community" in mid- to late twentieth-century Thailand, for example — that the treatment is less cultural or philosophical than social, political, and ethnographic. Some of our words do not at first glance seem "key" at all. "Commission" in the Ottoman Empire, "*ḥijāb*" (Muslim headscarf) in contemporary France, and "injury" in nineteenth-century China — each had powerful political impact in arenas that might appear in the standard political lexicon under such terms as "state," "citizenship," and "empire." For similar reasons, our approach to moving words differs from that of intellectual history or *Begriffsgeschichte* (history of concepts).[2] In fact, we found that the larger the concept, the less productive the word-following of the sort we were after. Important words like "democracy," "tradition," "civilization," and "rights" traveled the globe and appeared in many local and national inflections, but they were often too abstract and discursive — too "big" — to take us into the sometimes less debated but more embedded practices of social life. Tracking the spoor of "democracy" in China, for example, would be too ambitious a goal for an exercise on words in motion of this kind. Ours is a more modest endeavor.

The endeavor of course has a history, which helps to explain why these words and these authors got together in the first place. The idea of "Words in Motion" arose in the aftermath of the Asian Economic Crisis of 1997, when institutions such as the International Monetary Fund (IMF) and the World Bank tightened their already considerable hold on governments that did not meet the "global" standards that they, the rich and powerful, had enunciated for the world. Financial aid and geopolitical bona fides for countries like Thailand and Indonesia depended on their achieving "transparency," the "rule of law," and the rest of the neoliberal litany of the 1990s. Even as the North imposed these words on the South, words like "crony capitalism" traveled within the South, from the Philippines to Indonesia, Malaysia, and beyond. Meanwhile, the expanding vocabulary of globalization brought such terms as "human rights," "civil society," and "the environment" into ever increasing play around the world. Islamic words like "*shari'a*" moved anew across Muslim societies; "terrorism" and other fear words took on expanded global meanings. How could one not be struck by the whirlwind of words in motion?

Southeast Asia provided our first words, soon to be followed by the Middle East and North Africa, East Asia, Europe, the Americas, and had we world enough and time, every other place. For we soon realized that the whoosh of fast-moving words in the 1990s was nothing new. The powerful global words that now moved from North to South — from "developed" to "developing" — had late-nineteenth-century counterparts in the powerful imperial words that moved from West to East — from "civilized" to "backward." If power pushed some words around, others moved by virtue of their own magnetism. "Custom" in Arabic, though incorporated into the colonial glossary, attracted nationalists and reformers from Indonesia to Morocco because of its capacity to create a positive space for local cultures, religious practices, and ethnicities. Words like "responsibility" gained immediate traction in Japan not because they were Western or imposed by the world system, but because they seemed to contain new possibilities for social, political, and moral action. Words also moved fluidly back and forth within the various regions of the world, taking and making meanings across national boundaries. They crossed social lines, too, as they rose from the chants of the powerless into the police orders of the powerful, and sometimes in the opposite direction. In this respect, words often seemed to travel light, at least at first.

Yet in nearly every instance, the initial cross-border transpositions of a word marked only the beginning of its motion. Such imported or imposed words as "secularism" in Morocco, "terrorism" in India, and "good governance" in Thailand subsequently cut their own course through different sectors of society and politics. As they moved, they changed in meaning and practice, at times becoming localized to the point that they no longer resembled the words they once were. Moreover, as they moved — sometimes contentiously, sometimes unnoticed — within a particular society, the words also continued their mobility elsewhere in the world, so that over time new usages looped back to join or counter old ones. There was no end to the trail of words in motion. But one volume can only hold so much, so that what we offer here is a sampling of words chosen for their concreteness, whose movement could be traced first across linguistic and cultural borders, then through social and political processes as these changed across time.

Our choice of words is not random, however, in part because it reflects the origins of the project in thinking about Asian and Middle Eastern societies at the turn of the twenty-first century. But whether our words migrated from Britain to China, Algeria to France, or the United States to Brazil, they are all global, modern, and, above all, political. And although they do not add up to a single "story" — which could be summed up as the postcolonial condition, the nature of the modern state, or the effects of post-Cold War geopolitics — they do link to one another, often in multiple, crisscrossing ways that say a lot about the worlds we live in, the tenor of modern times, and the practices and processes of contemporary politics. Had we been writing in turn-of-the-nineteenth-century revolutionary Europe or turn-of-the-twentieth-century modernizing Asia, the words and the links would have been different. Indeed, a number of our words are new, the products of modernity itself. Some became prominent because they acquired new usages, such as "conspiracy" and "responsibility"; others were neologisms created to meet present needs, which was the case with "good governance" in Thai and "indigenous peoples" in Indonesian. Prince Wan was doubtless in a class by himself as he set out single-handedly to coin official Thai words for foreign terms in the 1930s. Yet even his aristocratic zeal and status could not assure that his new words would stay put and thereby "guarantee the security of the Thai nation."[3] That was too much to ask of words, even official ones. The hundreds of neologisms created in China and Japan in the late nineteenth century merely provided the semantic raw material that was later processed, and reprocessed, into modern ideas and institutions. Most of the words, both old and new, shifted their effects over time, and, like "security," were as much words in process as in motion. Sometimes the words that arrived with the force of imperial or global power behind them either moved into the hands of those resisting that power, who used them for their own political purposes, or the words took on such different connotations in practice that their originators were clearly appalled. In this regard, Turkish "boards" and Thai "good governance" can be said to have reworked the standards of the IMF in the 1990s even as they kept its required words in motion.[4]

We hope that others might wish to continue, and improve on, our experiments in word-and-world-following in various social and historical contexts. The universe of possible words is, of course, immense, and the same word often works differently in different settings. One could imagine, for example, essays that trace the modern word "community" in India, Japan, and the United States or track the Arabic "custom" in societies across its arc from the Mediterranean to the Pacific, including its uses by non-Muslims, and so on. Also, because the kinds of motion within a given society are just as complex as those across national or linguistic borders, there is plenty of opportunity there, too. What we have tried to do here is apply the approach and use it both to shed light on different societies and to derive some sense of the patterns in which words move. To highlight these patterns, we have organized the anthology, roughly, by the kind of word-motion described in the essays, even though singling out only one movement among several has meant flattening the complexity of the individual cases. Like many anthologies, the book may be read in any order, since the links among the essays—both in patterns and in substance—are more salient than any collective argument or plot. (Indeed, this approach lends itself to expansion in digital form, where clicking rather than page turning would bring the links among words into instant motion.)

We begin with "Words with Shadows"—"security" in Brazil and the United States and "indigeneity" in Indonesia—which traveled with their negatives, or their opposites, and were in fact inconceivable without them. "Words That Expand" are "custom" in Indonesia and Morocco and "responsibility" in Japan, which moved away from their doctrinal or legal origins in the direction of defining social practices or creating new social space. "Words That Cover," here "minority" in Egypt and "*ḥijāb*" in France, featured in political and legal debate in a way that covered their discriminatory intent, which identified and excluded by religion or ethnicity. "Words Unspoken"—"secularism" in Morocco and "sublime" in Japan—worked by their silence or absence effectively to shape political institutions and ideologies. "Fear Words"—"injury" in China, "conspiracy" in the Philippines, "terrorism" in India—represented the efforts of imperial powers, in the imperial languages, to control and suppress the political goals and practices of the people they rivaled or ruled. "Words That Set Standards" adopted or imposed from outside—"commission" and "board" in Turkey, "community" and "good governance" in Thailand

— expressed the conditions of acceptance by the world as the powers of the time defined them, only to reveal in the course of their subsequent motion the limits of these allegedly universal terms.

A number of linked patterns appear in the essays. The most obvious perhaps are the mechanisms of transfer: who brought, coined, or transformed the word; who promoted or suppressed it; how it was established in institutions; who "owned" it as its implication shifted over time; how it related to changing domestic and international contexts. Sometimes the initial translation or transposition was the work of a few, but once the word began to travel within a society, the wider its social diffusion, the stronger its effect. And the words seldom traveled alone. The essays attest to the importance of "affinity words" that clustered or hovered around a particular word, constituting a "discourse of injury," for example, or providing a set of "proxy words" that stood in for the word itself, as in the evocations of the unspoken "sublime" in Japanese fascism. The uses, or abuses, of ambiguity figure in several instances. A translated word like "responsibility" traveled for a long time in Japan carrying two different meanings, each depending on the eye of the perceiver. Other ambiguities rested on a meaning "smuggled" in with the word, then repeated to the point that it signified something else, which is what happened to "thug" in India and "barbarian" in China in the British discourse of "injury."

The play of strangeness helped some words move: the Ottoman "*komisyon*" for "commission" or the Japanese "*saburaimu*" for "sublime." Not only did these words possess the allure of the foreign, but they seemed to their proponents to make new institutions and emotions possible. At times multiple choice worked to keep words in motion: in Morocco several words for secularism — " *'ilmaniyya*" and "*laikya*" in Arabic, "*laïcité*" and "*sécularisme*" in French — were all available simultaneously, albeit with separate political and religious histories. In France, a Muslim girl's headscarf could be a *hijāb*, scarf (*foulard*), or veil (*voile*). Although "veil" suggested a covered face and evoked Catholicism (neither of which association accurately described the *hijāb*), its Frenchness and ambiguity gave "*voile*" the edge in political and ideological polemic. Unlikely liaisons between new words and old usages also occurred in several contexts; so it was that Muslim nationalist reformers in Morocco advocated parliamentary government in terms of traditional Islamic "consultation" (*shura*). In some cases, the sound and aesthetics mattered, as in the Thai fondness for doubled and rhyming words; in others, it was the script, as in Chinese and Japanese combinations of existing characters in new compounds and meanings. There were also instances when the word was refused, when some Indonesians did not take to "indigeneity" and Egyptian Copts rejected "minority," which was applied only to them and not to any other group. Certain words shrieked for attention by the power of their very presence: "security" and "terrorism," for example.

But the most common pattern of all may well be the vectors of unpredictability. Authors speak of the "afterlife" of words, of words as points of "transit" where meaning changed direction, of words like balls in a billiard game, where the initial hit sent them scattering every which way. Sometimes their trajectory landed them in situations with unexpected outcomes. The "commissions" and "boards" of the bureaucratic Ottoman and Turkish states, for example, turned out to be sites for increased political participation and negotiation among contending interests, a modern role conventionally assigned to parliaments and other representative institutions. In more than one instance, words imposed on the powerless were turned back on the power that imposed them: "terrorists" in India became "freedom fighters," "conspiracy" in the Philippines sounded a call for revolutionary "freedom."

The travel of words, in short, proved more eventful than suggested either by the standard national narratives of particular countries or by international assertions of global norms the same for all. The moving words both drew the silhouette of a common modernity and filled it with the variegated colors of different cultures and politics. There was no disputing the power of words and its relation to the powers in the world. Yet wielded for ill or good, words made many things possible, few things inevitable. Following words that moved thus ushered us into worlds that are in motion.

Notes

The Words in Motion project began in the late 1990s in discussions of the Regional Advisory Panel on Southeast Asia of the Social Science Research Council (SSRC). A subsequent series of meetings and workshops culminated in a conference in Fez, Morocco, in June 2004, which produced the essays included in this volume. Itty Abraham and Seteney Shami of the SSRC guided and inspired the project throughout. We, as co-editors, and all the participants express our sincere thanks for their insight, enthusiasm, and sheer hard work.

We express our gratitude, too, to the scholars whose lively contributions in the workshops helped so much to develop the ideas and approaches employed here. At the planning meeting in New York, December 2000: Talal Asad, Fred Schaffer, Gayatri Chakravorty Spivak, and Maria Todorova; in the Workshop on "Tradition" in New York, June 2001: Mona Abaza, Mamadou Diouf, Susan Gal, Barbara Kirshenblatt-Gimblett, Hyung-il Pai, and M.S.S. Pandian; at the Southeast Asia workshop in Canberra, October 2002: Penny Edwards, Ariel Heryanto, Resil Mojares, Craig Reynolds, and Kasian Tejapira; and in the Arabic Words in Motion workshop, Montecatini, March, 2004, led and coordinated by Seteney Shami: Mona Abaza, Walid Hamarneh, Driss Maghraoui, Reem Saad, and Fawwaz Traboulsi.

Aziz Isham and Sara Ait Lmoudden offered invaluable assistance at the conference. Later, Peter Sahlins encouraged us to persevere through the editing process. Megan Moodie edited several papers, adding her significant insights to the volume. Craig Reynolds, Kasian Tejapira, and Vince Rafael helped to conceive the original project and the final product. Alan Tansman lent his astute critical eye to this introduction and other parts of the book. Elizabeth H. Lee and Laura Warne lavished care and intelligence on the index and proofing. All of the contributors to the volume deserve special acknowledgment, not only for their extraordinary patience and good will, but also for their willingness to work on the project both individually and collectively over the course of several years.

1. Raymond Williams, *Keywords: A Vocabulary of Culture and Society* (1976), rev. ed. (New York: Oxford University Press, 1983); Tony Bennett, Lawrence Grossberg, and Meaghan Morris, eds., *New Keywords: A Revised Vocabulary of Culture and Society* (Oxford: Blackwell Publishing, 2005); Nadia Tazi, series ed., *Keywords: For a Different Kind of Globalization* (New York: Other Press, 2004–5), with volumes on *Experience, Identity, Truth, Gender, Nature,* each with chapters on Africa, the United States, the Arab world, China, Europe, and India.

2. See the famous "history of concepts": Otto Brunner, Werner Conze, Reinhart Koselleck, eds., *Geschichtliche Grundbegriffe: Historisches Lexikon zur politisch-sozialen Sprache in Deutschland,* 8 vols. (Stuttgart: Klett-Cotta, 1972–97).

3. See the chapter by Kesian Tejapira in this volume.

4. A counter-example is found in one reaction to what the World Bank regarded as a progressive change from the word "women" to "gender" in its development policy in the 1990s. Bangladeshi women regarded this change less as empowerment than as a license for international interference in such intimate relations as marriage. The slogan was "from WID (Women in Development) to GAD (Gender and Development)." See Caroline Moser, *Gender Planning and Development Theory: Theory, Practice and Training* (London: Routledge, 1993). On Bangladesh, see Gayatri Chakravorty Spivak, paper presented at the SSRC workshop on Words in Motion, New York, 8 December 2000.

Worlds in Motion

Words stabilize our understanding. They allow us to insert ourselves into discourses, institutions, and social relations. This volume works against this common sense stability by removing words for a moment from these settings in order to ask how these settings came into being. Our focus is how words and worlds are made at different scales, ranging from particular class niches and political campaigns to transnational realignments of culture and power. This task involves watching words *move* across space and time. Words offer special insight into the remaking of worlds at different scales because they condense past motion in their material form.

Words in Motion explores the question of how scholars might immerse themselves in cultures, nations, and regions without reifying their units of analysis. In the past, such units have lent themselves to stories of self-generation, in which only internal materials make a difference. Cultures, nations, and regions too often have been studied with too clear boundaries and too much coherence. Following words in and out of cosmopolitan discussions, national languages, institutional configurations, and imperial impositions brings out the motion inherent in cultures, nations, and regions. Conversely, *Words in Motion* explores how scholars might study global connections without prematurely homogenizing the globe. A world of global entanglements is not necessarily a uniform world. Tracking words shows where global standards break down as meaning is reinvented.

The essays collected in *Words in Motion* use the travel of words to respond to scholarly questions about the state of the world. To what extent do nations constitute communities? How is politics mobilized within and beyond nations? By following the histories of words of consequence, the authors track shifting political cultures that both form and exceed nations. Our methods are "experimental" in the sense that they use words to try out new approaches to bringing regional, national, and cultural specificity into stories of global connection. The need for such experiments responds, in turn, to challenges in the humanities and social sciences of the past decade signaled, on the one hand, by the multifaceted research object called "globalization," and on the other, by critical assessments of area studies from opponents as diverse as rational-choice theorists and postcolonial critics. The "words-in-motion" response is to explore concrete trajectories through which national-to-global political cultures are formed. Words show us struggles over which scales will matter.

This volume brings together several distinct experimental systems for showing constitutive interactions among nations, regions, and the globe.[1] A series of preliminary workshops and discussions each framed a particular tactic for using words to illuminate the specificity of local-global encounters and exchanges. Each is best introduced in relation to the regional legacies and dilemmas in which it was conceived. Indeed, the volume as a whole testifies to the importance of approaches that themselves derive from the exigencies of regional and transregional situations. Our theories and units of analysis are themselves made in regional-to-global as well as global-to-regional histories.

The first experimental system in our words-in-motion project emerged from a discussion about the effects of neoliberal reform in Southeast Asia.[2] By the late 1990s, terms such as "good governance," "civil society," and "globalization" were everywhere in circulation throughout the region, and the question of how these words were to be rendered in local languages and political cultures occupied many Southeast Asian policymakers and public intellectuals. However, the scholars of Southeast Asia who gathered to discuss these issues never imagined that we were discussing an exclusively Southeast Asian issue; we picked it precisely because it reached out to the world. Questions of whether neoliberalism would succeed in creating the uniform global standards promoters wanted have been important across both the global North and South. The view from Southeast Asia brings heterogeneity immediately into discussion, as scholars are forced to consider different national and local languages as well as political cultures across the region. Furthermore, scholars of Southeast Asian cultures are known for their interest in how foreign influences—religions, languages, ideas, objects—become domesticated. The essays that came out of this discussion highlight the unexpected adventures of globally disseminated terms as they are translated and debated in particular contexts. The volume's two chapters on Thailand — Craig Reynolds's discussion of "community" and Kasian Tejapira's discussion of "good governance" — each show how national debates change the shape of internationally imposed terms and concepts. My own paper on the intersecting trajectories of "indigenous" and *adat* in Indonesia also stresses the contingency of encounter — not only within Indonesia but in unexpected sites of word- and world-making around the world.

Thinking through Indonesian "*adat*," a word derived from the Arabic "*'ada*," brought us to a second region-based set of experiments in which words in motion might show how regional legacies and global encounters became intertwined. What about the circulation of Arabic words through the Islamic world? we asked. Like English, Arabic is an international language. As with English, Arabic words transform localities in the interplay of cosmopolitan encounter. Our project brought together scholars of the Middle East and North Africa.[3] Thinking through the question of cosmopolitanism, each made an interesting choice: Rather than follow keywords in campaigns for Islamic causes, they each chose a term in an awkward relationship to the central currents of Islam. In this volume, Mona Abaza follows " *'ada*" from the Middle East to Indonesia, establishing the broader regional history in which this term was used — and how it shaped social worlds around it. *'Ada* is both inside and outside of Islam, forming a liminal space self-consciously tuned to local-global interactions: where Islamic law and local lifeways meet. Seteney Shami follows "minority" in Egypt; Driss Maghraoui follows "secularism" in Morocco; each offers a counterpoint to Islam. In each case, the space of difference is instructive about the encounter between Islam and its Others. On the one hand, these categories are developed with a hearty dose of public debate. Public intellectuals in contending schools are major figures in each of these stories. On the other hand, words in motion in this space are constantly tugged by the power of contrast and exclusion. The mood here is different from the word play described in Southeast Asia. Here words strain and tug at us as they address repeated dilemmas. Varied schools and institutions work at them, but they come back again and again to face the same cosmopolitan issues.

The issue of stabilized repetition was stronger yet as a theme in a third set of experiments. We tracked words in motion from the most powerful countries of the global North in their imperial relations of difference and exclusion. Here, words are like swords, sometimes becoming so rigid that the words and practices of power can hardly be separated. Lydia Liu offers the case of nineteenth-century British imperialism, which stabilized the translations of "*thug*" in India and "barbarian" (*yi*) in China. When the British claimed they were "injured" by Chinese words, injury became not just a word but a justification for imperial war. Partha Chatterjee traces "terrorism" in British India—and its postcolonial offspring—where the word itself has been an attempt to instill fear. Itty Abraham follows the traces of state exclusions of their own citizens by tracing "security" in the United States and Brazil; in each case, security traveled with its shadow twin "insecurity" in defense against imagined internal and external threats. Vicente Rafael shows how such "fear words" may also open spaces of reversal. The Spanish "*conjuración*" (conspiracy) was deployed in the colonial Philippines to criminalize opposition; in the process, it elevated secret oaths as signs of rebellion. It is sometimes easier to stabilize words than to stabilize audiences, Rafael argues; the Spanish "we" opened frightening possibilities of the Other. Taken together, these papers remind us that histories of empire and state making are informative for understanding contemporary geopolitics. This is a matter of concrete historical connections, not just conceptual parallels; many colonial terms are still in use today. The study of words in motion thus requires us to work back and forth across historical periods as well as regions, and to recognize continuities in how power operates, not just continual change. This, of course, is not the only way to approach the power of the global North. Claudia Koonz's essay on the subject of France and its Others traces the political journey of the Arabic and French words for Muslim women's headscarves, taking us back toward the flexible word play that returns in our fourth set of experiments.

This experimental system treats countries where national political cultures both emulated Western-style projects of modernity and made their way with considerable autonomy. In two essays on Japan, the volume turns to words that, while originating, certainly, from the West, became so transformed within the events and contingencies of national history that they were quickly lost from an easy identification as "the same thing." Carol Gluck follows "responsibility" from nineteenth-century legal texts as it expands in ever widening popular contexts to focus on issues of self, society, and responsibility for the past. Alan Tansman follows "sublime" from a moment when it was named into its voiceless traces in national texts and fascist political ideologies. These words helped to create Japanese understandings of modernity—as these both depended on knowledge of the world and refused any simple mimicry. Both Gluck and Tansman show the importance of a deep understanding of Japanese intellectual and political history to understand how globally circulating terms might be reinvented. Similarly, Huri Islamoglu traces the rise of "commissions" in the Ottoman Empire and the turn to "boards" in contemporary Turkey. These Europe-derived forms almost immediately began to do unexpected national work; commissions, for example, ushered in a new participatory politics. National discussions, dilemmas, and goals transform traveling words. In this experiment, words in motion once again point us toward the instability not just of words but also of the political projects with which they are associated. Words here are tentative moments in processes of changing nations, states, and societies; they shift with public debates, intellectual innovations, and institutional change.

This volume juxtaposes these four related sets of experiments, bringing the papers together to illustrate various approaches to thinking through words in motion. What do we learn from these experiments, read together? First, our project shows the importance of what Lydia Liu calls "translingual practice" — that is, the invention of new meanings as words travel.[4] Most histories of concepts, discourses, ideas, and even words begin with a "civilizational" unit within which to trace the evolution of these things. One of the meanings, indeed, of the word "civilization" is the space within which authorities have tended to trace concepts and discourses. It is that unit so deeply embedded in scholarly legacies and training that an individual scholar is often unself-conscious about using it. Our volume departs from this well-established practice in showing how words — and worlds — are made in cosmopolitan and power-laden encounters at multiple scales. Here, local, national, and regional legacies shape and are shaped by global histories. Words can guide us into these entanglements.

One way to pay attention to both the cosmopolitan and the regional specificity of words in motion is to consider their materiality. Some of the best images in this volume show the materiality of communication. Kasian Tejapura tells us of the musicality of Thai, in which potent translations must rhyme well. Carol Gluck writes of little-used Chinese compounds, retrieved in nineteenth-century Japan, whose component characters carried contradictory meanings in their graphic inscriptions. Vicente Rafael tells of Filipino non-verbal signs, such as handshakes, scars, and drawings, which Spanish colonial language defined as outside its ken. These are not just features "inside" language; they open the borders of language, setting forms for translation and transformation. They anchor us within language as they simultaneously beckon across languages to experience the world. This material aspect of language is good to think with in considering how local and global agendas become entangled in words in motion.

Yet the varied experiments in the volume do not allow us to see all entanglements in the same way. Indeed, our project suggests that *theories* about global and local entanglements are themselves informed by regional legacies. The words that scholars use, like the words we study here, have particular meanings and affinities in particular places. The diversity of approaches in this volume suggests that when we build theories of global process, we need to be self-conscious about the regional points of view we necessarily represent.

Consider, for example, how our words-in-motion experiments differ from one another in relation to questions of continuity and change. Discussions among scholars of Southeast Asia—and of Japan and Turkey— turn on the mutability of words, which cannot be held down, despite the intentions of their sponsors. Discussions of both Arabic and European words about difference focus instead on the stabilization of words as key aspects of relations of power. Both, of course, are important approaches to the question of how words make worlds and vice versa. The contrast, however, speaks to the political dilemmas that inform regionally cogent points of view. This has nothing to do with cultural essences. It has a great deal to do with historically specific scholarly formations in which certain ways of seeing easily come to mind and others must be worked at with greater effort. Some of these may be of marginal interest over the long haul. Still, we only have a chance at cosmopolitan scholarship if we take the alternatives seriously. A place to reopen discussions of theory might be the local, national, and regional situations that make certain kinds of theory useful—not just to regional adherents, but also more generally. This includes theories of words in motion.

One of the reasons the words-in-motion project focused on national and transnational word making was to highlight the contributions of critical public intellectuals who shape ideas and institutions not just in their home nations but also between and beyond national space. Too often, stories of globalization ignore the work of thinkers, writers, scholars, and journalists in the global South. This volume aims to put their work back into the public record. Taking this work seriously, however, moves scholarship beyond a singular global agenda: scholars, like the public intellectuals they recognize, must engage with varied local, regional, and global dilemmas. Ideas that matter emerge from places, even as they traverse, and transform, worlds.

Notes

A full set of acknowledgments is in Carol Gluck's introduction. Itty Abraham, Craig Reynolds, and Seteney Shami generously read earlier drafts of this introduction and offered invaluable suggestions.

1. My use of the term "experimental system" derives from Hans-Jörg Rheinberger, who discusses the formation of research objects in the biological sciences: Hans-Jörg Rheinberger, "Experimental Complexity in Biology: Some Epistemological and Historical Remarks," *Philosophy of Science* 64 (1997): S245–54. Rheinberger shows how self-consciously simplifying research frameworks facilitate the emergence of scientific events, through which new questions are raised. The term is also useful to understanding the social sciences and humanities, where new research objects also come into being within self-consciously simplifying research frames. The workshops of the words-in-motion project, which took place between 2000 and 2004, set up such frames. Each workshop tested the use of a specific set of regional and transregional approaches in understanding diversity, change, and interconnection.

2. Itty Abraham, coordinating the SSRC Regional Advisory Panel on Southeast Asia, initiated this facet of the words-in-motion project.

3. Seteney Shami, coordinating the SSRC Regional Advisory Panel on the Middle East, brought together this facet of the words-in-motion project. Itty Abraham and Seteney Shami worked together to advise and facilitate the next stages.

4. This is a deep simplification. Liu states, "Broadly defined, the study of translingual practice examines the process by which new words, meanings, discourses, and modes of representation arise, circulate, and acquire legitimacy within the host language due to, or in spite of, the latter's contact/collision with the guest language": Lydia Liu, *Translingual Practice: Literature, National Culture, and Translated Modernity —China, 1900–1937* (Stanford, Calif.: Stanford University Press, 1995), 26.

WORDS WITH SHADOWS

ITTY ABRAHAM

Segurança/Security

in Brazil and the United States

Motility is as integral to words, then, as it is to human being. For words also travel and constitute a record of journeys made. . . . Each — the human and the word — possesses a career, describes a history, travels a measure of existence, does more than is knowingly intended and signifies more than they can know.
— Michael Dillon, *The Politics of Security*

There are few words in our modern political lexicon as parasitic as "security." Most commonly preceded by the word "national" (meaning, in fact, the state), this traveling signifier has attached itself to nearly every scale of human activity, from the individual to the international, even to outer space; from comestible (food security), natural (environmental security), financial (security/securities), and territorial (homeland security) to virtual (cyber security); to forms of community, from Social Security to collective security, which is the principle behind the United Nations. The power of the word and its associations is such that even those critical of the emphasis on national security have taken to using the word, joining it, for example, to "human" and "ecological" as a way to say that people and nature, too, are in need of special protection. But this strategy of renaming ultimately fails because it assumes that replacing the modifier will transform the object merely by shifting the scale at which security is applied. The effort to make secure objects other than the state cannot succeed without examining "security" itself — what the word means and what it does.

Here I explore some of the meanings, movements, and practices associated with one of the most powerful words of our time between and within two countries: the United States and Brazil. To understand what makes "security" move with such abandon, the word will first be laid bare to show that it travels with an inseparable shadow, "insecurity," a word that may do more to explain its better-known modifier, *national* security, than is generally recognized. The weight of national security as an unimpeachable reason of state makes the extraction of the shadow word, "insecurity," both difficult and necessary. This is an act of salvage, restoring to the foreground a shadow that most often impels the movement of its better-known traveling companion. I then follow the word and its shadow as they move from the United States to Brazil and conclude with an exploration of the lateral movement of national security within each country, both outward and inward.

Michael Dillon argues for a "radical ambivalence" embedded in the meaning of "security."[1] He notes that the highest state of security is defined in negative terms, as an *absence* of *insecurity*. In other words, the expression of security always brings with it insecurity, contained in its very meaning. Dillon reminds us that this simultaneously doubled articulation comes from the Latin origins of the word — "*sine cura*," in its root form, or more familiarly, "*securitas*" (freedom from doubt or without concern) — which is the common root of the English "security," the French "*sécurité*," and the Portuguese "*seguridade*." The doubled meaning of security, with the negative conditions of doubt and concern incorporated from the beginning, provides a direct link to the ambivalence of the word today. The duality of meaning embedded in "security" is not, as Dillon points out, a dialectical struggle, leading to the emergence of one meaning over the other (and not an equal struggle, either). Rather, both are always simultaneously present, locked in a clumsy *pas de deux*, each circling the other, taking turns to lead and to follow. This describes a "conflict of unequal opposites which are rooted and routed together."[2] Fear and threat, danger and uncertainty are embedded in — and are byproducts of — the process of securing the object of (in)security. "Security" is, in that sense, not a noun but a verb; not a steady state or stable condition of being safe, but a continuous process of securing safety. What we now call "national security," a desired outcome, is produced by the securing, the fixing or grounding, of the sources of national (in)security.

A number of implications flow from this — in particular, the *absence of limits* once the process of securing is under way. It has long been recognized in international relations that new insecurities are automatically generated by the reflexivity of security work in a world filled with nation-states, the so-called security dilemma. This is the process whereby securing one nation leads to another's insecurity and so on in an endless spiral.[3] The security dilemma also arises from the realization that, with every new threat that is identified and secured, uncertainty persists about the extent of danger that has been contained. This leads to what might be called an "excess" of insecurity, because the process of securing can never be known to be complete. Notwithstanding the official anxiety that such a process generates, this excess of insecurity produces its own form of perversity: The most advanced national-security apparatus eventually takes pride in —and is defined by—the ability to identify more sources of insecurity than its competitors, even if in the process it makes that state more insecure than any other state. Such a process is reinforced in the nuclear age when, due to the global reach of missiles and the intergenerational effects of harmful radiation, familiar distinctions of political space break down. A fetishizing of insecurity forms the basis of security, turning the object on its head, making nuclear weapons—alleged to be the ultimate means of securing the state — the simultaneous source of its ultimate insecurity. The insecurity of security takes these relations to their extreme contradiction —that is, the security of insecurity.

Once "national security" is driven by its shadow, "national insecurity," it expands effortlessly into all domains of life, making any object and person a potential threat. If danger and threat are everywhere and can come from anywhere, insecurity has no obvious or material origin. Recognition that insecurity connotes ever present danger prevents us from falling back on familiar distinctions between a safe "home" and a dangerous "abroad."[4] As has been pointed out, it is not just that foreign policy is necessary to secure the home. Rather, we may need foreign policy to know where *is* home.[5] As David Campbell puts it, "The boundaries of a state's identity are secured by the representation of danger integral to foreign policy"[6] Since insecurity respects no limits, the process of national security making fixates on the need for firm and stable boundaries between us and them. As a result, the most insidious threat for national-security agents is the idea of the internal enemy—seditious fifth columnists or subversives passing for loyal citizens. Such imagined insecurities tend to gravitate to the marginal and illegible elements of the national body, especially those distanced by race, class, geography, origin, faith, language, or belief. Lack of hard evidence of disloyalty becomes proof that the enemy is even more dangerous than imagined, reinvigorating the search for sources of insecurity.

United States

It is often assumed that the United States invented what we now think of as the regime of national security in the wake of the Second World War: symbolically, with the renaming of the War Department as the Department of Defense, and practically, with the passing of the National Security Act of 26 July 1947, which created the National Security Council, the Pentagon, and the Central Intelligence Agency (CIA). None of these institutions was completely new, of course, but their formal institutionalization through an act of Congress helped to establish a new legal basis through which any discussion of national *defense* would be recast as a problem of national *security*.

But it was not the naming and institutionalization of these departments and organizations that made for the ubiquity of national security, nor was it simply the presence of a global military threat from the Soviet Union. Although Harry Truman was a fervent cold warrior, deeply suspicious of the Soviet Union, during his administration efforts were made to create an international system to control nuclear weapons (the Brodie Plan), military spending dropped substantially, and most of the personnel in the armed forces were demobilized. George Kennan's famous "Long Telegram," and its subsequent publication in *Foreign Affairs* under the pseudonym X, argued for the need for containment but was not a particularly hostile piece. It was more concerned with noting contradictions in the Soviet system and suggesting that the United States could win the Cold War by waiting it out.

In any event, historians of the Cold War are now more likely to see the end of the First World War, rather than the end of the Second World War, as the beginning of the antagonism between the Soviet and American empires in the making, especially in its symbolic component, the alleged struggle between communism and capitalism.[7] A greater surprise, perhaps, is that the National Security Act of 1947 said nothing about the Soviet Union or communism and its putative threat.[8] In fact, the act was a belated congressional response to the debacle at Pearl Harbor, to establish the means by which better intelligence would be available to prevent such attacks from happening again. In this context, the CIA's job was merely to "correlate, evaluate, and disseminate" intelligence and "other functions and duties related to intelligence affecting the national security as the National Security Council might from time to time direct."[9]

Before the Soviet Union could become the prime source of postwar insecurity, popular memories of the alliance between the United States and the U.S.S.R. (Uncle Sam and Uncle Joe, respectively) during the Second World War had to be overcome. The transformation of the U.S.S.R. from military ally to threat to source of insecurity required the ideological foregrounding of communism as a total, insidious, and also seductive alternative to all things American. Anxiety about the ideological power of communism reached an early peak during the Korean War when a number of American prisoners of war refused to be repatriated to the United States.[10] As Ron Robin points out, the easiest way for U.S. elites to understand how American citizens could be seduced by communism was to assume that the Reds had mastered the art of brainwashing.[11] At this point, insecurity took on a whole new meaning, because the primary focus of threat — by the same token, the weakest link — was the unreliable citizen. If national defense was about defending the homeland, that project alone was inadequate to overcome this form of insecurity. And so national security entered to secure the loyalty of the individual faced with dangers beyond the imposition of military force.

The necessary step, in other words, for the U.S.S.R. and communism to become an overwhelming source of insecurity was the weakening of the boundary between the United States and the rest of the world. Although there was no shortage of communists, anarchists, and other leftist radicals visibly present in the political life of the United States during the first half of the twentieth century, they were still *American* communists.[12] The U.S.S.R. and communism became the prime source of insecurity when American communists were redefined as disloyal and unpatriotic, beholden now to the U.S.S.R. rather than to the United States. Immigrant Jews and ethnic minorities, regarded as non-normative and illegible presences in the body politic, had long been stereotyped as vectors of anti-American thought. The U.S. homeland became a threatening source of insecurity when American communists, who included large numbers of white Protestants, came to be considered a fifth column along with suspect minorities. The espionage trial of Alger Hiss, together with Senator Joseph McCarthy's allegations of a grand conspiracy and his list of "205 spies" in the State Department (1950), served to prove that Soviet communism had infiltrated the heartland. It was the totality of the communist threat — not just the U.S.S.R. as a military threat — that required an equally total response from the United States. Finding un-American communists and suspect foreigners *at home* was a necessary step in the remaking of the United States as a national-security state.

A comprehensive "national-security" orientation is most sharply captured in NSC-68, the long-secret and now infamous document of 1950 written largely by Paul Nitze, the Wall Street banker turned State Department analyst and policy planner. Although his hyperbolic document remained classified until 1975, its view of the world offered a totalizing vision both of the Soviet Union and its long-term plans and of the necessary response by the U.S. government across all domains of life. Its paranoid vision drew on support from a variety of sources, not the least of which was the work of the RAND Corporation, a think tank set up in 1946 in Santa Monica, California, with Air Force funds. The mathematician Albert Wohlstetter, his wife, Roberta, and other RAND theoreticians such as Herman Kahn pioneered the use of game theory to model U.S.–Soviet relations and did much to create a strategic mindset that argued for the need to be prepared for the worst-case scenario at all times.[13] This approach to strategic analysis, with its focus on surprise attacks (the strategic legacy of Pearl Harbor) and concomitant marginalization of arms control, frequently became a self-fulfilling prophecy in that it provoked the Soviet Union to react belligerently to U.S. actions. Given the limited understanding of the Soviet system available in U.S. policymaking and intelligence circles for decades, NSC-68, which was completed just as the Korean War broke out, appeared remarkably prescient and helped to reverse the decline in U.S. military budgets up to and in the present.

The domestic front was hardly immune to these developments. Perhaps as important as NSC-68, if not as famous, was another document cowritten by Nitze, NSC-141 (1953), which offered the most expansive meaning of national security yet in circulation, especially in its focus on civil defense. In 1957, based on the growing fear of Soviet intentions and working with inflated estimates of its military strength, a high-level committee was created to consider internal or "civil" defense. H. Rowan Gaither, president of the Ford Foundation and chairman of the board of RAND, which he had helped set up, led the committee. According to Fred Kaplan, although the original mandate of the committee was to give advice on how to prepare the country for an attack from the Soviet Union, following effective lobbying by Wohlstetter and Nitze, the committee's brief expanded to include the consideration of a "second-strike" capability that would allow the United States to respond militarily to a Soviet attack, thereby guaranteeing that all-out nuclear war would take place and devastate the world.[14] President Dwight Eisenhower, notoriously thrifty and a former general, might well have balked at the huge expense implied by this report were it not for Sputnik, which beeped its electronic message over the United States a month before the Gaither committee submitted its report in November 1957. The rest, as we know, is history. That Sputnik might have marked the zenith of Soviet global technological leadership would not be understood for nearly three decades.

In retrospect, it is all too easy to argue that the creation of a national-security state was inevitable. But to understand its emergence in the United States and its incorporation into state policy and institutions, the starting point is the transformation of national defense into national security through the articulation of insecurities that could take root in the unconscious as well as in political and material sources.

Brazil

The corresponding story of national security in Brazil begins with a journey and an institution. The journey is the famed excursion of the Fôrça Expedicionária Brasileira (FEB) to Europe during the Second World War; the institution is the Escola Superior de Guerra (ESG), or the Brazilian Higher War College. The group of military leaders who overthrew the civilian government of João Goulart in 1964, which led to military rule for the next twenty years, were overwhelmingly veterans of the FEB and alumni of the ESG. The coup's leaders were nicknamed the "Sorbonne" group in memory of their common training during the French military mission (1919–39) and their shared experiences at the ESG.

In 1944, Brazil sent a small expeditionary force to fight on the Allied side during the Second World War. The FEB was attached to the U.S. Army's Fourth Corps in Italy, where it participated in the war effort for ten months. The soldiers' experience was ambivalent, to say the least. Brazilian officers were irritated by the dismissive treatment they received at the hands of American staff officers, who ridiculed their military skills even as the U.S. Army provided the FEB with practically all of its food, clothes, and equipment. Making a link between their treatment and that of the segregated units in the U.S. Army, the Brazilian officers noted, as well, the "federally sanctioned racism" in the U.S. forces.[15] Nevertheless, FEB officers returned to Brazil deeply impressed by American military skills and professional attitudes. Following a coup in 1945 to oust the civilian dictator Getulio Vargas, the FEB's artillery officer, General Cordeiro de Farias, was commissioned to write a report on setting up a war college and became the first commander of the ESG in 1950.[16]

The ESG is a complex of buildings on a small military base in the shadow of Paõ de Açucar, Rio de Janeiro's famous Sugar Loaf mountain. At the request of the Brazilian military, a U.S. advisory mission was resident at the college from 1948 to 1960 and helped to shape the courses and curriculum. American training sought to move the Brazilian military away from its French doctrinal antecedents and equipment and to alert it to the threat posed by international communism. In the course of the 1950s, the ESG became known as a place where bold new conceptions of the military and Brazilian society were being put forward. These ideas reached well beyond the military, since advanced extension courses often included doctors, politicians, civil servants, clergy, writers, and other people with no explicit connection to the armed forces.[17] The ESG played an important role in establishing a sense of corporate identity and professional mission for the Brazilian military by creating the intellectual foundations for a new relation between the military and society. This was not necessarily a benign transformation.[18] The military, led by a clique of officers with experience in both the FEB and the ESG, took over state power in 1964 and ruled uninterrupted for the next two decades. In a strikingly new role, the Brazilian military "captured the state."[19] General Castello Branco, commander of the FEB, became president of Brazil following the coup; the American liaison officer between the U.S. Army and the Brazilians during Second World War, Vernon Walters, served as military attaché in Brazil from 1962 to 1967.[20] Among the first acts of the military government (13 June 1964) was the creation of the Serviço Nacional de Informações, the national intelligence service. Its first director was General Golbery do Couto e Silva.[21]

The key ideologue of the transformation of Brazil's military identity from the moderating power to an institution that directly took on the role of social, political, and economic transformation was General Golbery. Author of the *Basic Manual*, a textbook used by all students at the ESG, Golbery had been writing since the 1950s on the need for a totalizing conception of "*segurança nacional*," one that went far beyond the military defense of the country. The Doctrine of National Security and Development developed at the ESG combined a "theory of war, a theory of internal subversion and revolution, a theory of Brazil's role in world politics and its geopolitical potential as a world power, and a particular model of associated dependent economic development that combines Keynesian economics and state capitalism."[22] Cordeiro de Farias, the ESG's founder, would explain that because Brazil was a developing country, its "objective conditions" were different. As a result, the incorporation of national security took on a distinctly Brazilian flavor, summed up in the slogan of the military dictatorship: *"segurança e desenvolvimento"* (security and development).[23] This slogan meant that in a less-developed country such as Brazil, security and development were closely related and had to be addressed simultaneously for positive economic change and political stability to come about. Development, as it was implemented during the military period, was not ideologically neutral. As the now classic study by Fernando H. Cardoso and Enzo Falleto argued, this version of development meant a break with Brazil's transformative policies of protection of infant industries and emphasis on national control over production, replacing it with a "free" market and foreign capital and ownership, usually American in origin.[24]

Golbery's writings did not lead to the coup of 1964. Once in power, however, Golbery's ideas combined with the network of ESG alumni across military and civilian spheres to create a state devoted to the control of fear and danger and the reduction of threats to the nation: a state devoted to the management of national insecurity. These fears appeared to be confirmed by the proliferation of violent resistance to the military coup across social sectors, from middle-class urban guerrillas to the movements of poor and landless peoples. Taking the battle against violent leftist groups to a continental scale, the Brazilian military would secretly ally with colleagues in Argentina, Uruguay, Paraguay, Bolivia, and Chile in Operation Condor to murder suspected leftists and other troublemakers in each other's countries and even in Europe and the United States.

The threat to the Brazilian state, however, went beyond overt violence. Showing clear influence of his American training, Golbery argued that during the Cold War the concept of war was expanded "to the entire territorial space of the belligerent states, thus involving the whole economic, political, cultural, and military capacity of the nation." The communist enemy had infiltrated the domestic sphere on many fronts. Its strategy was to avoid direct confrontation and, instead, work at an invisible, "psychological" level. Golbery warned of this strategy "involving the population of the target country in a gradual slow action — both progressive and continuous — which aims at the conquering of minds. . . . They may also use devious, non-armed tactics."[25]

The origins of national security in Brazil began with the FEB's exposure to American military training and influence during and after the Second World War. "National security" was indigenized as *"segurança nacional"* by military intellectuals based on an analysis of Brazilian circumstances. What was common to both Brazil and the United States was the idea of domestic *insecurity*, driven by the image of a global communist threat. Unlike U.S. national security, however, the content of national security in Brazil also included a concern with economic development, *segurança e desenvolvimento*, which had the net effect of reducing Brazil's control over its economy in favor of foreign capital.

The ambivalent nature of national security is clear in the two countries. The shadow of insecurity accompanied the political conjunctures that produced "national-security" discourses in both the United States and Brazil. Insecurity was constituted as the fear of infiltration of the most intimate of political spaces, the domestic sphere; most ominously, such an infiltration was likely to take forms invisible to the securing eye. This had the effect of making the entire body politic, the putative object to be secured, itself a prime source of danger and threat. National insecurity made national loyalty the most prized national attribute even as such loyalty could never be proved beyond doubt. The resulting state paranoia was pithily expressed by Walt Kelly's cartoon character Pogo: "We have seen the enemy and it is us."

In the first stage of the institutionalization of national security in both countries, the scale of insecurity continued to increase, due to the imagined ability of the global communist threat to cross both material and ideological boundaries. The battle for the "hearts and minds" of the domestic population took the form of loyalty tests and the often violent containment of perceived subversives. Once national security became an unquestioned and self-justifying form of state practice, its invocation could be used to override other objectives of state action. Even as the acknowledged threat from global communism began to recede, national security as a state practice remained institutionalized in bureaucratic repertoires and collective imaginations of national integrity. It could be said that "national security" had begun to settle down.

This relative stasis was not true of its shadow word "insecurity," which by its very nature is a restless word. As a result, "national security" began to move again, driven now by the motive force of insecurities emanating from new sources of perceived threat. Here I examine two forms of this movement. The first is a national-security response to a perceived threat to the territorial heartland of Brazil from global environmentalism. The resulting expansion of national techno-political power is called "*projecão*" in Portuguese. If *projecão* is an expression of national security outward for the domination of national territorial space, the second movement of national security might be described as an interiorization of insecurity. Here the object to be secured is information, and the sources of "information insecurity" are other state agencies and public regulators of state behavior. In the United States, the practice of information insecurity is glossed as "official secrecy."

Projecão (Expansion)

Following years of declining economic performance and an upsurge of protest against the military, the dictatorship ended in 1985 with the *abertura*, or opening. A series of civilian leaders with ever greater levels of popular legitimacy have ruled Brazil since that time. While many of the military's excesses were exposed and their secret projects were closed down, some aspects of national-security thinking that began during the military period continue into the present. A prominent example of the afterlife of the original conception of national security is the effort to extend state control into the interior of Brazil, particularly the vast Amazon region.

The contemporary strand in geopolitical thinking among Brazilian elites began with Mário Travassos's *Projeção Continental do Brasil* (1931).[26] Travassos and others such as Everado Beckhauser articulated the idea of a Brazilian frontier, which involved turning away from Europe and the densely populated Atlantic coast and engaging more intensely with Brazil's mostly unpopulated interior, its northwestern and western boundaries. This geopolitical perspective was picked up in the postwar period by General Golbery do Couto e Silva and General Carlos de Meira Mattos, who cast their arguments for increased control over and expansion into the Amazon basin in terms of the logic of development: the exploitation of new lands, minerals, and other raw materials as resources for rapid economic growth. This was a policy wholly consistent with the prevailing slogan of the dictatorship, "security and development."

A military-led expansion into the interior did not face the problem of political resistance. Those who might make a fuss — indigenous peoples, rubber tappers, gold miners, and small landholders — did not count, and those who did count generally approved of the mission. The military dictatorship began its push into the interior with Operation Amazonia in 1966. Building roads and increasing access to the region were a priority, on the premise that economic development and settlers would follow. Operation Amazonia was followed by the Trans-Amazon Highway project, which included constructing a major transport artery from the impoverished Northeast deep into the interior, increasing efforts to extract minerals and forest resources, and seeking to resettle politically restless, landless peasants in newly cleared areas of the Amazon basin. By the mid-1970s, it was clear that expansion had caused more problems than it had solved, including increased tensions with Brazil's northern and western neighbors.[27]

In 1985, the military returned to its barracks, having suffered a considerable loss of corporate power and political legitimacy, but Amazonian projects continued apace. Fernando Collor de Mello, Brazil's first elected post-military civilian president introduced the initially secret Calha Norte (Northern Trench) project in the 1980s. While Operation Amazonia and other military-led projects of expansion had been framed in terms of their development goals, Amazonian expansion was a distinctly military effort under the new civilian leadership. Even if Calha Norte was initially intended as a sop to the military, keeping it busy and away from civilian politics, the Amazon continued to be identified as a major strategic project requiring close military attention under the presidency of Fernando Henrique Cardoso a decade later. This attention led to the System for Vigilance over the Amazon (SIVAM) and the System for Protection of the Amazon (SIMPAM) projects — massive techno-political enterprises dedicated to "vigilance" and "protection," respectively.[28] As the SIMPAM website says, this "system" was created to "integrate information and generate knowledge . . . for the protection and . . . sustainable development of this region." The means to do so were highly capital-intensive, "composed of integrated subsystems of remote sensing, radar, meteorological stations, and data platforms," and included fleets of planes and boats and a network of military bases.

If, under military rule, the desire to domesticate the Amazon derived from a long tradition of geopolitical thinking together with a search for raw materials to sustain economic development, the Amazonian insecurities of the new civilian leadership were externally driven. Their fears crystallized during the Earth Summit in Rio de Janeiro in 1992. Transnational movements brought increased international attention to the plight of the indigenous people of the region and led to growing discussion of the global ecological importance of the Amazon. Protecting the Amazon's ecology became the focus of efforts by international environmental non-governmental organizations (NGOs) and foreign governments because of concerns about global climate change, even as indigenous people allied with media-savvy rubber tappers and Western celebrities to become the leading edge of a new rights-based "Fourth World" international movement. This global attention to the Amazon was interpreted in Brasilia as a transnational penetration of the Brazilian geopolitical heartland, tantamount to hostile external intervention. The "internationalization of Amazonia" was interpreted as a major national-security threat, implying the loss of Brazilian sovereignty over its own territory.[29] Civilian political leaders agreed that enormous investments in "vigilance" and "protection" and a greater presence of the state in these remote areas was the correct response to this threat.

This territorialization of national security in Brazil coincided with, and was a reaction to, the increasing transnationalization of economic and political forces in the last decades of the twentieth century. From the initial geopolitical instinct to fill "empty" land and transform it for economic exploitation, the Amazon now became defined as the weakest link in the Brazilian national security-scape, exposed under the gaze of satellites and scientific measurements and reinforced by the presence of unwanted foreigners and disloyal indigenous citizens. Rather than focus on the military's role in transforming the region, the historical mistreatment of Amazonian residents, and indiscriminate land and resource use that resulted in harmful environmental outcomes, invoking the Amazon as a national-security problem offered Brazilian military and civilian elites a defensive and defensible response to unwanted international attention. As the word "security" moved across four decades, the object of national security shifted from anticommunism to economic development to territorial control, with new insecurities leading at each step of the way.

Secrecy

The rise of a national-security state in the United States can be described in euphemistic terms as the shifting distribution of power between different branches of government: the rise of the executive branch at the expense of Congress and the courts. This alludes to the ability of the U.S. presidency to act with few restraints and constrain the actions of other branches of government when "national security" is held to be at stake. If national security were limited to the defense of the state, such a development would not come as much of a surprise. But the impossibility of limiting the definition of national security because of the inevitable expansion of potential insecurities makes national-security planning and actions far more political than technocratic.

One specific national-security practice owes its roots to the Manhattan Project, the U.S. effort to build an atomic bomb during the Second World War. The success of the Manhattan Project — which, strictly speaking, was about building a bomb, not winning a war or thinking about what these weapons might mean — established a tendency to view expert knowledge deployed for state ends as a supremely successful means to national security. The heavy shroud of secrecy that surrounded this project was justified by the need to keep privileged knowledge from the enemy. What was kept secret was not only that the weapon was being built, but also that the weapon *could* be built. After giving due credit to the brilliance of the scientists and the organizational abilities of the military, the success of the project was, in retrospect, also attributed to the official secrecy that surrounded it from its inception.[30] This lesson was quickly absorbed by interested bureaucracies: From being a means to protect state knowledge from evildoers, official secrecy became a boundary condition, both within the state and between the specialized state security apparatus and the public. With insecurities looming on every side during the Cold War, national security defined a totalizing condition of state behavior. As a result, "secrecy" became an affinity word closely tied to "security." Now all agencies of the state could legitimately participate in official secrecy. Rather than bemoan with the philosopher Sissela Bok that "there is little that national security cannot come to envelop in secrecy," it may be more accurate to say that there is little that secrecy cannot come to envelop in national security.[31]

As early as 1906, Georg Simmel recognized the power of information as a currency of power.[32] The intertwined nature of official secrecy and information insecurity as everyday practice is reflected in many settings, whether in the everyday use of terms like "need to know," leaks from unnamed government sources that seek to influence internal bureaucratic struggles, the transformation of the Federal Bureau of Investigation (FBI) into a mechanism for establishing the loyalty of American citizens and for carrying out covert operations against its citizens (e.g., COINTELPRO), the failed efforts by the U.S. government to tap personal computers (the Clipper chip), the short-lived Total Information Awareness initiative, or in the struggle of the National Security Agency to monitor electronic and wireless communications around the world. Typical of this tendency is the argument that even the gross budget of the U.S. intelligence community should be kept secret (revealed in 2003 to be between $26 billion and $30 billion annually). Under these conditions, official secrecy has become a self-referential reason and a low-risk way to protect institutional interests from unwelcome public attention.[33] Little wonder that when information about "national-security" activities does become public, as in the Church and Pike Commission reports from the 1970s, Iran–Contra in the 1980s, or more recently via the 9/11 Commission report, the extent of state illegality, malfeasance, and ineptitude is perceived as staggering.

The simplest technique for making the state's work publicly invisible is the over-classification of state knowledge. No one, as Senator Patrick Moynihan pointed out, has ever been held accountable for over-protection. When secrecy and hierarchy fed off each other, with differential access to knowledge becoming the measure of the relative importance of bureaucrats and politicians, it became easier to classify information as "secret" rather than "confidential" and as "top secret" rather than "secret." The original three-tier classificatory mechanism had been borrowed from the British empire, which by the nineteenth century could legitimately claim to have raised "mandarin culture" to its highest levels.[34] Bureaucracies across the U.S. government found in increasing layers of officially sanctioned secrecy a perfect way to keep their own failings under wraps and to block or deny access to their work to public representatives. Other techniques included denying the existence of relevant information, foot dragging by delaying the release of information well after the statutory time period for information protection had passed, and reclassifying information at higher levels to block release.[35]

The skill of bureaucrats in denying access to state knowledge is reflected in changes made to the Freedom of Information Act (FOIA), first passed in 1966 with help from Donald Rumsfeld, then a U.S. congressman. This pattern repeated itself in 1974 (over a presidential veto) and then again in 1976, 1978, and 1984. In 1986, the act was reformed substantially by Congress and added to in 1996 to reflect the growing quantities of electronic records. In 2001, Attorney-General John Ashcroft issued a memorandum explaining how the act would work in practice. According to the Department of Justice website:

> The Ashcroft FOIA Memorandum emphasizes the Bush Administration's commitment to full compliance with the FOIA as an important means of maintaining an open and accountable system of government. At the same time, it recognizes the importance of protecting the sensitive institutional, commercial, and personal interests that can be implicated in government records — *such as the need to safeguard national security, to enhance law enforcement effectiveness, to respect business confidentiality, to protect internal agency deliberations, and to preserve personal privacy* [emphasis added].

National security, law enforcement, business secrets, government confidentiality, and personal privacy: There can be no clearer statement of the rank-ordering of U.S. national interests today. In short, not all revisions to the act moved in the direction of greater openness.

Secrecy can no longer be considered an aberration to be tolerated within a liberal political system for justifiable reasons of state. It belongs to a larger family of state practices relating to information insecurity, including surveillance, intelligence gathering, espionage, and counter-terrorism and has become a distinctive cultural expression of the modern state.[36] We are now at a point where what is secret must be kept secret for reasons of national security. The ability of officially sanctioned secrecy to expand effortlessly is a product of the limitless capacity of insecurity to see threats coming from anywhere and everywhere all the time. Under these conditions, officially sanctioned secrecy becomes the form of knowledge management most compatible with national security. This condition leads to perverse outcomes. For instance, the unwillingness to pool information about threats across agencies prevents the full extent of danger facing the state from being either fully known or acknowledged. This resulted in catastrophe when the CIA did not share its knowledge of 9/11 conspirators with the FBI. Counter-intuitively, however, such compartmentalization might be a necessary response to the pervasiveness of insecurity today. It could be argued, in other words, that secrecy now exists to protect the state from full knowledge of potential threats. Official secrecy and inter-agency compartmentalization becomes a rheostat protecting the national-security system from collapsing due to information overload.

Conclusion

By tracing the course of "national security" and "*segurança nacional*" across and within two political spaces, this essay underlines the importance of insecurity as a driver of modern statecraft. Such an approach exposes intimate connections between seemingly discrete aspects of state policy. Territorial expansion and official secrecy are examples of state actions with very different effects arising from the same source.

Modern national-security regimes are built around insecurity, the shadow presence of a word legitimized around the world as a necessary and obvious attribute of state power. The porosity of national borders always raises the possibility of unknown internal enemies, leading to ever expanding techniques of domestic monitoring and control. Because se-curity is built on scaffolding grounded in insecurity, efforts to secure can never be complete. If danger and threat are ubiquitous and unending, national security will always be inadequate to its appointed task of securing the state. A discourse of (in)security leads inevitably to the expansion of the state security apparatus as new historical junctures produce percep-tions of new threats that must be responded to: Witness the U.S. Depart-ment of Homeland Security.

Recognizing the difference between the *process* of securing and the *con-dition* of safety helps us to understand why contemporary efforts by activ-ists and critics to expand the object(s) of security are misplaced. Calling for human security and ecological security to be treated as equal partners in the state's work of protection — which is the definition of "national secu-rity" — does not offer greater protection to humans and nature. Rather, it sets into motion new vectors of insecurity. Security practices work by identifying and controlling sources of insecurity, and the link between these practices and greater safety can rarely be known in advance. If we seek freedom from fear and want, we have to begin by defining the positive attributes of both conditions rather than do battle with shadows that de-fine them only in absentia. Security exists because we are made insecure. Since insecurity takes the form of radical doubt about the possibility of a collective future, for us to be genuinely safer and more confident requires a different word and set of state practices altogether.

Notes

1. Michael Dillon, *Politics of Security: Towards a Political Philosophy of Continental Thought* (London: Routledge, 1996), 116.

2. Ibid., 120.

3. Faced with the modern "dread of unreason," the process of identifying sources of insecurity, which is the first step in securing, is always inadequate to the potential extent of danger or threat. Even as threats are contingently defined in distinct form, they are never adequate to account for the prevalence of danger, which Michel Foucault understands as an expression of radical doubt associated with modernity: Michel Foucault, *Madness and Civilization: An Exploration of Insanity in the Age of Reason*, trans. Richard Howard (New York: Vintage, 1988), 205.

4. R. B. J. Walker, *Inside/Outside: International Relations as Political Theory* (Cambridge: Cambridge University Press, 1993).

5. Sankaran Krishna, *Postcolonial Insecurities: India, Sri Lanka and the Question of Eelam* (Minneapolis: University of Minnesota Press, 1999).

6. David Campbell, *Writing Security: United States Foreign Policy and the Politics of Identity* (Minneapolis: University of Minnesota Press, 1992), 3.

7. John Lewis Gaddis, *We Now Know: Rethinking Cold War History* (New York: Oxford University Press, 1997).

8. Rhodri Jeffreys-Jones, *Cloak and Dollar: A History of American Secret Intelligence* (New Haven, Conn.: Yale University Press, 2002), 156–58.

9. Ibid., 159.

10. Ron Robin, *The Making of the Cold War Enemy: Culture and Politics in the Military-Intellectual Complex* (Princeton: Princeton University Press, 2001), 162. The most vivid expression of this fear in popular culture was the film *The Manchurian Candidate*.

11. Robin, *The Making of the Cold War Enemy*, 175.

12. See Maurice Isserman, *"If I Had a Hammer...": The Death of the Old Left and the Birth of the New Left* (New York: Basic Books, 1987), 3–34.

13. Fred Kaplan, *The Wizards of Armageddon* (Stanford, Calif.: Stanford University Press, 1983).

14. Ibid., 125–43.

15. Alfred Stepan, *The Military in Politics: Changing Patterns in Brazil* (Princeton: Princeton University Press, 1971), 242–43; Alain Rouquié, *The Military and the State in Latin America* (Berkeley: University of California Press, 1987), 282–83.

16. Stepan, *The Military in Politics*, 245.

17. Maria Helena Moreira Alves, *State and Opposition in Military Brazil* (Austin: University of Texas Press, 1985), 7.

18. During the first half of the twentieth century, the military's self-defined role in Brazilian politics was of a social regulator, the "moderating power" of an unruly,

unstable society as it saw it. The *poder moderador* did not mean distance from politics: The military carried out coups in 1930, 1937, 1945, 1954, 1955, and 1961. What it did mean was that once the military High Command decided that a change in civilian leadership was necessary, it installed a new regime and then voluntarily withdrew to the barracks to await the next journey to the Presidential Palace: Eliézer Rizzo de Oliveira, "Forças Armadas: Pensamento e ação política," in *Inteligência Brasileira*, ed. Reginaldo Moraes, Ricardo Antunes, and Vera Ferrante (São Paulo: Editora Brasiliense, 1986).

19. René Dreifuss, *1964: A Conquista do Estado*, 4th ed. (Petrópolis: Editora Vozes, 1986).

20. Stepan, *The Military in Politics*, 128. Walters went on to serve as deputy director of the CIA.

21. Alfred Stepan, *Rethinking Military Politics: Brazil and the Southern Cone* (Princeton: Princeton University Press, 1988), 15–16.

22. Moreira Alves, *State and Opposition in Military Brazil*, 8.

23. The resonance of this slogan, rhetorically and ideologically, with the official motto of Brazil, "*ordem e progreso*" (order and progress), is too obvious not to mention.

24. Fernando H. Cardoso and Enzo Falleto, *Dependency and Development in Latin America* (1969), repr. ed. (Berkeley: University of California Press, 1979).

25. Quoted in Moreira Alves, *State and Opposition in Military Brazil*, 15, 17.

26. *Projeção Continental do Brasil* (1931), 2nd. ed. (Saul Paulo: Companhia Editora Nacional, 1935).

27. For a longer discussion, see Ronald A. Foresta, "Amazonia and the Politics of Geopolitics," *Geographical Review* 82, no. 2 (April 1992): 128–43.

28. Available online at http://www.sipam.gov.br/ (accessed 30 January 2008).

29. João R. Martins Filho and Daniel Zirker, "Nationalism, National Security and Amazonia: Military Perceptions and Attitudes in Contemporary Brazil," *Armed Forces and Society* 27, no. 1 (Fall 2000): 105–30.

30. Richard Rhodes, *The Making of the Atomic Bomb* (New York: Simon and Schuster, 1986).

31. Sissela Bok, *Secrets: On the Ethics and Concealment and Revelation* (New York: Vintage 1989), 194.

32. Georg Simmel, "The Sociology of Secrecy and Secret Societies," *American Journal of Sociology* 11, no. 4 (1906): 441–98.

33. Edwards Shils, *The Torment of Secrecy: The Background and Consequences of American Security Policies* (Glencoe, Ill.: Free Press, 1956).

34. Daniel Patrick Moynihan, *Secrecy: The American Experience* (New Haven, Conn.: Yale University Press, 1998), 111.

35. Ibid.

36. For a fine discussion of the culture of secrecy and how race and citizenship are implicated in the nuclear complex, see Joseph Masco, "Lie Detectors: On Secrets and Hypersecurity in Los Alamos," *Public Culture* 14, no. 3 (2002): 441–67.

Adat/Indigenous

Indigeneity in Motion

For light, Sirissheh, is the shadow's shadow.
— Somtow Sucharitkul

Words in motion surprise us. Their far-flung antics interrupt conventional intellectual history, with its assumption of stable genealogies of thought. They are spread too far for the boundaries of national history; they ricochet too widely to follow strictly colonial geographies. Words in motion urge us to consider multiple linguistic and cultural legacies in dialogue.

Communal difference and identity are based on demarcating lines: nations, tribes, North and South, traditional and modern, Christian, Muslim, and pagan. Yet notions of difference and identity depend on conquests and mobilizations that cross every one of these lines. No village is too isolated to be touched; no civilization is too powerful to be swayed. World-making projects in Mecca, Bandung, and Wounded Knee call to each other, despite the best attempts of politicians and scholars on every side to keep them apart. Refusing, answering, copying, or transforming imperial genealogies, such world-making projects traverse the global South and move in and out of the Fourth World. Through these projects, words for difference and identity compete, collide, and coalesce, forming new sites for agency and political action. Such words in motion challenge us to learn about world crossings.

This essay tracks a moment of coalescence between two phrases: the Indonesian "*masyarakat adat*" and the English "indigenous peoples." As this century turned, the equivalence of these terms came to be accepted, not only among advocates for indigenous rights, but also among international agencies and within at least some Indonesian government bureaus.

One set of experts concludes: "Self-identification should be a fundamental criterion for defining 'indigenous people.' In Indonesia this term is increasingly used by a self-defined social movement of *masyarakat adat*— communities governed by custom — that includes a very wide number of peoples in Indonesia. These peoples have increasingly begun to refer to themselves as 'indigenous peoples' in international discourse and elements in the reform era government now seem to accept that '*masyarakat adat*' and 'indigenous people' are co-terminous."[1] An Asian Development Bank report has also accepted the equivalence of *masyarakat adat* and indigenous people.[2] Yet this equivalence is most unstable: many officials, intellectuals, and policymakers have argued vociferously against it. The translation highlights the heterogeneity of "global indigeneity," and it raises political questions for all words in motion. To what extent do global categories standardize local cultures? Does cultural difference shape conflict in the twenty-first century? Both homogenizing narratives of globalization and clash-of-civilization models of cultural difference assume answers rather than opening curiosity about such questions. Both blinker our attention by positing that cultural difference and global interconnection cannot coexist.[3] By tracking indigeneity in motion, I offer a model of difference *in* interconnection. Concepts in translation — such as *masyarakat adat* and indigenous people — both refer to something in common and exceed that common reference.

"*Masyarakat*" has been translated into English as "peoples," "communities," "populations," "inhabitants," "public," and "society." One could write a book on the travels and political uses of "*masyarakat*" and "peoples." In this essay, however, I focus on the other part of the phrase: *adat* and indigenous. "*Adat*" and "indigenous" have very different genealogies. *Adat* emerged from the Arabic *'ada*, which refers to ordinary practices or habits that are not addressed in Islamic law. In Southeast Asia, *adat* is translated as "custom" or "tradition." In contrast, "indigenous" emerged from the Latin for "beget" and points in the direction of origins. Sixteenth-century Spanish conquests in the New World offered Europeans the term "*indigena*" as a template with which to classify natives of the places they hoped to settle and civilize.[4] How could it possibly be appropriate to make such different words the same?

"Customs" and "origins": About all the two terms have in common is their respective negativity. *'Ada* is that which cannot be codified into universal law. *Indigenas* are those who stand outside civilization. Each term is a shadow. Each refers to those things that cannot be universalized and cannot be modernized. The particular, the traditional: As civilization moves, these remain unassimilated. The content of a negative term is always hard to specify. Such terms group everything that does not fit. Vulnerabilities of coherence and authenticity are built into them. They are the words others call us. Yet such shadows can become powerful sources of self-identity. As they mobilize adherents, shadows of shadows may take on the charisma of light.

My challenge here is to study the travels of both "*adat*" and "indigeneity." Indonesian uses of "indigeneity" are no simple North–South imposition, and merely to track how "indigeneity" got to Indonesia would be to slight the importance of the travels of "*adat*," with its own contingent history, weight, and influence on world affairs. Might some meanings of *adat* have come to influence international deliberations on indigeneity? The only way to find out is to consider both sets of travels equally important. Such analytic symmetry is the first step in taking South–South and South–North circulations seriously.

Such circulations are poorly documented, and they require knowledge of many different histories. To proceed into this challenging territory, I look for moments of translation and the negotiation of meaning rather than full historical context. I pay special attention to the tropes through which words and concepts are set into context. Tropes are entry points into political histories; they suggest trajectories obscured by standard historical methods.[5] To look for tropes, I bring texts to the front of my analysis. My story emerges from the juxtaposition of three quite different texts: the International Labor Organization's Convention 169 on Indigenous and Tribal Peoples in Independent Countries (1989); C. Snouck Hurgronje's study of custom and law among the Muslim Acehnese during their late-nineteenth-century war against the Dutch, *The Achehnese* (1906 [1893–94]); and Richard Wright's *The Color Curtain: A Report on the Bandung Conference* (1956).[6] Each of these texts tells us about problems of translation and the remaking of words; each marks and manages a key transition in the linked but separate travels of customs and origins. I follow the fragile thread connecting these texts — as I also attend to their massive gaps and mutual interruptions. My story runs in and out of these texts, searching through laws, translations, and accounts of events for the contingent historical conjunctions that make a difference.

To trace the movements of "*adat*" and "indigenous" across place and time, I begin in Indonesia at the turn of the twenty-first century, when "*masyarakat adat*" came to be an accepted translation, at least among internationally minded activists, for "indigenous people." I then move back to discuss how "*adat*" — from an Arabic word for "that which cannot fit into law" — was reshaped in colonial and nationalist Indonesia to refer to native law and, indeed, the spirit of native culture. I dare to offer the suggestion that, indirectly, Indonesian debates over "*adat*" helped forge the forms of cultural nationalism that inspired North American minorities, including Native Americans, in the 1960s. Such cultural nationalism gave a heady charge to the possibilities for indigenous organizing that took off in the 1970s.

Indigenous mobilizations only came to affect international law, however, because the dramas of U.S. radicalism in the 1960s were channeled along another route. Imperial and missionary legacies gave the emergent indigenous movement its British empire-wide shape, and international institutions gave it further impetus. Canadian, Australo-Pacific, and Northern European struggles over land rights took the lead. The new organizations were self-conscious, however, about their inability to touch South America, the *ur*-site of indigeneity.

Only the contingent emergence of new developments in Brazil changed the balance. In the late 1980s, international conservationists and progressive Brazilians joined rubber tappers and indigenous leaders in coalition to protect the Amazon. The expanded transnational force that emerged propelled indigenous rights into international forums in the late 1980s and 1990s. In this enriched transnational form, the indigenous-rights cause came to Indonesia to add legitimacy and resources to the struggle against state and corporate rip-offs of rural people under Indonesia's New Order regime — and beyond. The translation introduced causes such as human rights, environmental advocacy, and democratic opposition to authoritarianism to the task of bringing citizenship to marginalized minorities in Indonesia. At the intersection of "*adat*" and "indigeneity," however, new wrinkles developed, which had to be worked through both at home and abroad.

How did "*adat*" and "indigeneity" take on new meanings in their travels, even as they dragged old ones with them? I can address this question only through attention to shadows — that is, the negative images through which these terms were formed. The story of the shadow's shadow tells how these terms became forces in their own right. In each of the following sections, I present that shadow space in which some version of these terms came into its own, and in each section title, the shadow-space term appears after the more powerful term from which it had been excluded.

Negara/Adat: Making Room for the Dispossessed

Kalau negara tidak mengakui kami, kami pun tidak akan mengakui Negara.
If the state does not recognize us, we will not recognize the state.
—Aliansi Adat Masyarakat Nusantara, Archipelago-wide Alliance of
Indigenous People, Jakarta, 1999

Negara is the state. Between 1966 and 1998, Indonesia was ruled by the authoritarian New Order regime under General Suharto. *Adat* was revived as an activist concept in the 1980s and 1990s to oppose the New Order's non-recognition of the rights of rural citizens. The state expanded and flourished by claiming the lands and resources of rural communities in the name of "national development." Forests and minerals were sacrificed to global capital accumulation; the residents who depended on these lands were displaced. Activist campaigns for *adat* rights addressed these policies; the state, they said, should stop operating as a resource thief.[7] *Adat* campaigns thus articulated concerns for democracy and the rule of law. Ironically, opponents of the recognition of *adat* cited the absence of such modern political concepts as the major reason to reject the call to revive "tradition"; critics argued that democracy and *adat* were incompatible. In the midst of these quarrels and in the shadow of the state, the equivalence between "*masyarakat adat*" and "indigenous people" came of age.

The New Order bred a rising class of transnationally savvy professionals, especially lawyers, engineers, and business managers, who could mediate between global capital and the national development program. Environmental activists emerged from this class niche, forging a politics that could squeak by the regime's political repression through appeals to the anticommunist valence of science and modernity. Activists were also influenced by national legacies of populism and rural romance to look for political partners in the countryside. In and beyond *adat*, they spoke of rural social justice in the languages of law and international standards.

The Indonesian translation of ILO Convention 169 on Indigenous and Tribal Peoples in Independent Countries appeared in 1994 under the imprint of ELSAM, an important human-rights institute in Jakarta, and the LBBT, a Dayak-rights NGO in West Kalimantan.[8] The translation was the brainchild of Sandra Moniaga and Stepanus Djuweng. Moniaga is a lawyer who has devoted her career to environmental, human-rights, and legal advocacy for rural victims of national development. Convinced that activism must emerge directly from the countryside, not Jakarta, she moved to West Kalimantan for several years to start the Institute of Dayakology with the Dayak spokesman Djuweng. When Moniaga returned to Jakarta to further human-rights initiatives through ELSAM, she continued her focus on advocacy for *adat* rights as rural social justice.

The ILO Convention 169 of 1989 is an awkward document, bristling with unhappy compromises. No direct or continuous participation of indigenous representatives went into the preparation of the document, which, furthermore, had been ratified by only fourteen states as of December 2001.[9] Debates over self-determination left their traces in ambiguous and defensive language. Some three hundred indigenous representatives walked out of the hall in protest of the document's weaknesses at the United Nations Working Group on Indigenous Populations.[10] Yet Convention 169 is better than the ILO document of 1957 (Convention 107), which it replaced. It is the only internationally recognized "hard law" on indigenous rights, and as such it is a key resource for activists. Most important for my argument, the debates about and within the document marked a moment of transnational translations and betrayals that are not erased from the text. Words are still very much in motion here.

Who is covered by the convention? International disputes are registered in the use of both "indigenous" and "tribal" peoples in the title. Government representatives from Asia had refused to acknowledge the relevance of "indigenous" concerns to their countries, arguing that, after all, their majority populations could claim indigeneity. In the 1980s, the Indonesian government told the United Nations Working Group on Indigenous Populations that "indigenous peoples" did not apply to Indonesia.[11] The governments of India and Bangladesh have made similar statements.[12] The term "tribal" intervenes in this argument, but African representatives have very much resented the use of the word "tribe." ILO Convention 169 is a halfway point in this argument. In the 1990s, international documents dropped "tribal" in favor of "indigenous peoples" as a global constituency.

Indonesian translation further wobbles the document's already unsteady gait. Forced to find separate words to translate "indigenous" and "tribal," ELSAM and the LBBT choose "*pribumi*" for the former and "*mas-*

yarakat adat" for the latter. Yet "*pribumi*" (native) is its own can of worms. Its major use has been to discriminate against Indonesians of Chinese descent, who cannot be "natives," despite generations of residence. The verb "*pribumisasi*" (to make native) refers to the nationally promoted practice of offering privileged access to business or educational opportunities to non-Chinese Indonesians.

The translation uses this term without comment, but Djuweng and Moniaga do their best to salvage a different agenda in their introduction. While accepting that the majority of Indonesians are *pribumi*, they also criticize Indonesian authorities for denying the relevance of indigeneity—for example, in changing the word "indigenous" to alternatives such as "vulnerable" or "backward" in applying international standards. The introduction mainly ignores the *pribumi* issue to describe the complaints of *masyarakat adat* facing callous state development. Occasionally, however, the authors use the *pribumi* and *masyarakat adat* combination to their advantage. They pay tribute to the Javanese farmers who resisted the building of the Kedung Ombo hydroelectric dam without mentioning that these peasants of the national heartlands are not ordinarily recognized as either tribal or indigenous in English or as *masyarakat adat* in Indonesian. They identify East Timorese as *pribumi*, thus making a case against the Indonesian occupation of the island.[13] Meanwhile, they urge their readers to press for Indonesia's ratification of the convention, to follow international best practices and affirm that Indonesia is a "*Negara Hukum*," a state that recognizes the rule of law.

In 1998, the New Order fell. Politics blossomed across the country. *Masyarakat adat* came out of the shadows to seize mines and timber camps, besiege the courts with cases, hold conventions, and make bold demands. In 1999, Aliansi Masyarakat Adat Nusantara (AMAN), or the Archipelago-wide Alliance of Indigenous People, held its first conference.[14] By this time, there was no messing around with other translations, at least for these activists, whose challenge to state authority opened this section: "If the state does not recognize us, we will not recognize the state." AMAN's first demand, indeed, was to refuse other names, such as *suku terpencil* (isolated tribes), *masyarakat/suku terasing* (more versions of "isolated tribes"), and *peladang liar* (illegal slash-and-burn farmers). The members of the alliance would be recognized only as *masyarakat adat*. Their tenth demand was for Indonesia to join the international community of nations by ratifying ILO Convention 169 and taking an active part in United Nations negotiations on indigenous peoples. Here the translation is most explicit: Indigenous peoples are *masyarakat adat*.

The AMAN convention of 1999 kicked up a storm of controversy. Much of the national intelligentsia opposed the revitalization of *adat* as mere political romance. Foreign donors worried that "identity politics" would lead to ethnic cleansing. International scholars criticized the resort to communal logic. Within the organization, arguments began about who would be considered *masyarakat adat*. While activists had built the core network to link rural communities fighting state and corporate theft of resources, other *masyarakat adat* had also joined. *Adat* politics diverged. In West Papua, for example, identification with *adat* was conservative compared with demands for independence. The term *"adat"* itself drew adherents from many directions: state-supported communal leaders; aristocrats remembering lost privilege; the children of headmen and sultans who had made colonial treaties; cultural entrepreneurs who sold tradition. *Masyarakat adat* conventions were held across the country. Empowered by its identification with the internationally recognized "indigenous," *"adat"* had come to offer something new.[15] Just what this will be remains open. Yet one thing is clear: It is impossible to make *"masyarakat adat"* just mean "indigenous people" for the transnational struggle. *Masyarakat adat* have been shaped by a longer genealogy.

Shari'a/'Ada: Universality and Its Others

Hukom ngon adat han jeuet chre, lagee dat ngon sipheuet.
Law and *adat* are inseparable, even as God's essence and his attributes.
—Acehnese proverb

Islam first spread in insular Southeast Asia as mysticism and philosophy. By the sixteenth century, Muslim teachers and religious texts were widely regarded as sources of wisdom. Associated with knowledge itself, Arabic words were adopted into Malayic languages across the Indonesian archipelago.

Shari'a, the law, traveled with Islam. *Shari'a* is a universal framework for evaluating human conduct; it does not attempt to incorporate local practices within the law. It is self-consciously transcendent, creating unity among believers. Islamic practice makes this possible by allowing local usages to remain in force if they do not contradict the law. In Arabic-speaking countries, such usages are generally called " *'urf*." Muslims outside Arabic lands tend to use the term " *'ada.*" The Arab diaspora scholar Engseng Ho has explained the distinction as follows: "In Arabic, *'ada* has the sense of something normal, regular, repeated, and can be used for a person's habits, as well as common practices. The more specific sense of custom tends to be labeled *'urf*, where it's classically 'tribal law' as opposed to Islamic, and is the kind of contrastive category jurists would use to label what is not kosher to them. Literally, [*'ada*] would be something like 'that which is known, common knowledge.' "[16] *'Ada* is common sense; it is routine. Because it is outside the discipline of world religion as civilization, " *'ada*" does not travel with the universal. It is embedded in particular local situations. It is not in itself law, because it cannot travel. Yet it thrives only in the shadow of law.

Versions of the term " *'ada,*" particularly "*adat,*" are known throughout Malayic Southeast Asia. In Malaysia, with its heritage of British-established Islamic courts, *adat* is recognized but rarely considered of much political significance. In Indonesia, in contrast, Dutch colonial authorities gave new life to *adat* by transforming it into what was known in Dutch as *Adatrecht* (*adat* law). Dutch *adat* scholars were committed to preserving Indonesian traditions, but their efforts to do so entailed a major shift in what *adat* could do. From the shadow of law, Dutch scholars created law itself.

Dutch efforts to find "native law" in *adat* cannot be separated from the long struggle of Europeans to contain the spread of Islam. Dutch *adat* advocates imagined *adat* as an indigenous articulation of Indonesian beliefs and customs that a foreign religion (Islam) should not be allowed to overrun. At the same time, these advocates were arguing against other Dutchmen who wanted to modernize the Indies by imposing European standards, displacing local authority and customary-access rights by state decree.

The ethical contradictions of this position were particularly well developed in the "discovery of *adat* law" in late nineteenth-century Aceh.[17] The Acehnese sultanate controlled the western tip of Sumatra, where it was excellently situated as a node in east–west traffic between the archipelago and the Indian Ocean. Muslim scholars from India and the Middle East visited, and—basking in the admiration accorded them for their cosmopolitan knowledge—they often stayed. Indonesian pilgrims stopped there on their way to the *hajj*. The location offered ideal opportunities for trade. Yet by the late nineteenth century, Aceh was embroiled in war. The Dutch spent forty bloody years subduing Aceh. The Aceh War became a test for

Dutch colonialism — and for transnational Islam. Indeed, the discussions of terrorism and civilization of those times sound very familiar today.

In the midst of this situation, the Arabic scholar Christiaan Snouck Hurgronje went to Aceh at the behest of the Netherlands Indies government. The book he produced, translated into English as *The Achehnese*, is best known for its attempts to disentangle Islam and *adat*.[18] Since in his estimate Acehnese resistance was led by Muslim religious leaders, segregating and strengthening *adat* leadership could promote Dutch interests.

But Snouck, as he is known, is not remembered only as a colonial chauvinist. The nationalist novelist Pramoedya Ananta Toer includes Snouck in the first volume of his *Buru Quartet* as the most progressive Dutchman of the late nineteenth century.[19] Pramoedya reminds us that Snouck argued against colonial arrogance and imagined Europeans and natives working together to lead the Indies. Snouck continually stresses that the point of his scholarship is to oppose European ignorance and racism. Embracing ambiguous motives that mixed love and science, he disguised himself as a Muslim to live in Mecca and tell the European world its human stories.[20] His accounts of life in Mecca — and in Aceh — are full of appreciation for local learning and the arts, and his stories reflect the friendships he shared with particular individuals. Reading Snouck's lively accounts, it is hard to know whether to laugh in appreciation or cry in shame.

Such contradictory reactions point to the anxiety of the translations Snouck attempted to manage in his writing. For "*adat*" this is a moment of transformative truth. Snouck tells us that Acehnese are both committed Muslims and committed traditionalists. It does not subtract from their piety that they also have *adat*; this is how Islam works. "In the course of its victorious progress through the world, the Mohammedan religion has been compelled to adopt a vast quantity of new matter which was originally quite alien to it, but which appeared indispensable to the majority of its adherents, and all of which has now been exalted to be law and doctrine. Many old customs too, deep-rooted from ancient times in certain parts of the Mohammedan world, have had to receive the sanction of the newer creed, and these now constitute the local peculiarities of Islam in different countries."[21]

Acehnese need not throw off Islam to embrace *adat*; they can be Europe's "good Muslims."[22] Snouck describes the rich legacy of written texts on Islamic law and theology available in Aceh. But this law, precisely because of its universality, is not intended to regulate everyday customary behavior, he explains. This is the domain of *adat*.[23] "As a general rule we do not sufficiently reflect that in countries of the standard of civilization reached by the Malayan races, *the most important laws are those which are not set down in writing*, but find their expression, sometimes in proverbs and familiar sayings, but always and above all in the actual occurrences of daily life which appeal to the comprehension of all."[24]

Superficial European observers have missed the importance of *adat*, he explains, because "they are nowhere to be found set down in black and white. We arrive at them only after painstaking and scientific research."[25] Indeed — and here is the key transformation such research offers — these customs turn out themselves to be a form of law. For Acehnese chiefs, he says, "*adat* (custom law) and *hokum* (religious law) should take their places side by side in a good Mohammedan country" and, indeed, "in such a way that a very great portion of their lives is governed by *adat* and only a small part by *hokum*."[26]

This insight did not in fact become a turning point in the Aceh War. Snouck quickly found himself at odds with aggressive colonial policy. However, it set a precedent for Dutch efforts to respect Indonesian traditions and protect an indigenous third space from the demands of radical Islam, on the one hand, and European modernity, on the other. In the early twentieth century, the legal scholar Cornelis van Vollenhoven codified *adat* law and established a system of *adat* law regions across the archipelago.[27] *Adat* law entered key pieces of colonial legislation, although it never gained more than an embattled presence as an issue of debate in colonial policy. In only a few regions of the Indies did colonially reconstructed *adat* law become institutionalized, although in many areas considerations of *adat* entered formal and informal negotiations of European–native relationships. *Adat* also became a popular topic for colonial scholarship, which used the idea of *adat* to respect the particularity of places and their customs across the archipelago.

Indonesian nationalism drew heavily on European and Islamic ideas of modernity, to which *adat* seemed anathema. Yet *adat* haunted nationalist discussions, precisely because colonial authority had made it the essence of native distinctiveness. What did Indonesia have that was not just a repetition of Europe except *adat*? The idea of *adat* as national spirit was best expressed by the nationalist *adat* scholar Mohammed Koesnoe, who argued that *adat* law could be the foundation of a distinctive and dynamic national law. "*Adat* is the path of life of the Indonesian people welling up from its sense of ethics," wrote Koesnoe.[28] As national ethics, *adat* could inform Indonesian nation making without trapping it in past tradition. Yet this also required a transformation. *Adat* was no longer called on to be the local and the particular; *adat* would now be a flexible cultural framework. "*Adat* law provides the principles only, and as such does not dwell on detailed prescriptions."[29]

Although this perspective was only one within a great debate about Indonesian nationalism and development, it left its mark, not only in early postcolonial legislation (which recognized the spirit if not the content of *adat*), but also in public enthusiasm for a culturally inflected national spirit. The new elites of the postcolonial period insisted that Indonesia would carve its own cultural path to international politics. It is not by chance that the two best-known U.S. scholars of the *cultural* path to nationalism and development—Benedict Anderson and Clifford Geertz—both developed their ideas in early postcolonial Indonesia.[30] It is from this postcolonial Indonesian vantage point that the spirit of *adat* spoke to the world about possibility, difference—and freedom.

Rationality/Race: Cultural Nationalism at a Time of Freedom

[Indians in the United States] had watched nations in Africa and Asia assert and fight for their independence and freedom and wished something of the same for themselves.
—Paul Chaat Smith (Comanche) and Robert Warrior (Osage), chroniclers of American Indian activism

The victory of anticolonial struggles in the 1950s and 1960s spread excitement about freedom around the world. For one intense moment, that excitement emanated from the collected humanity gathered in one Indonesian town: Bandung, the site of the 1955 Asia–Africa Conference.

There are many stories to tell about Bandung. Indian scholars remember Nehru's agenda: The creation of a neutral zone between communism and anticommunism.[31] Chinese remember the statesmanship of Zhou Enlai. New Order repression encouraged Indonesians to forget Sukarno's charisma—and cultural nationalism. Yet another of Bandung's legacies revives this cultural element in the global North in struggles of U.S. minorities against racism. The cultural nationalism of U.S. minority politics in the 1960s was self-consciously modeled on anticolonial struggles in the emergent Third World. Until the mid-1980s, when the term "people of color" became prevalent, U.S. minorities used the term "Third World" as a collective term of self-identification and solidarity. Black Power — and Red Power — emerged from this moment of identification.

It would be silly to claim that Indonesian discussions about nationalism and development played more than a bit part in influencing U.S. cultural nationalism. Yet that bit part was there, and to acknowledge it is important. Storytelling about U.S. politics almost never offers genealogies outside the global North, thus reinforcing the sense that the United States gets to invent global politics entirely through its own perverse fantasies. Even a bit part for Indonesia challenges that premise.

Richard Wright's *The Color Curtain: A Report on the Bandung Conference* is a key node of translation for this connective thread. Wright was already well known as a cosmopolitan African American novelist when he went to Bandung. Bandung was his opportunity to experience the thrill of colored humanity in common conversation.

What might all those colored people have in common? his acquaintances ask before he leaves for the conference. He moves toward the answer in a series of interviews, each suggesting more than the last the angry shadow of European racism. Thus Wright speaks to an elite Indonesian in Paris, and finds him very modern. "He feels that Western contact has had an emancipating effect upon him and his people, smashing the irrational ties of custom and tradition."[32] But the man concludes, "I'm alone in my country."[33] The next Indonesian he finds to interview in Paris, in contrast, is "more typical." "His contacts with the West have left scars."[34] "Of Western values he wanted none."[35] "He was willing and ready to die for what he felt to be the value of himself, that is, his sense of dignity."[36] By the time he arrives at the conference, Wright is ready to consider the convergence of race and religion as a newly united force in world history. "And, as I sat listening, I began to sense a deep and organic relation here in Bandung between race and religion, *two of the most powerful and irrational forces in human nature*. . . . [A] racial consciousness, evoked by the attitudes and practices of the West, had slowly blended with a defensive religious feeling; here, in Bandung, the two had combined into one: *a racial and religious system of identification manifesting itself in an emotional nationalism which was now leaping state boundaries and melting and merging, one into the other*."[37]

Wright's report was written for a progressive Western audience. He warned his readers of the force of racial and religious irrationalism: It could easily turn to violence, reverse discrimination, or communism. Yet it could also be channeled through the kind of modern nationalist internationalism he saw in Bandung toward a better future. Race — constructed in the shadows of European colonialism and racial hatred — would be a force for further racial hatred if it was not transformed through opportunities to make modern partnerships. Westerners had better start paying attention. "To have an ordered, rational world in which we all can share, I suppose that the average white Westerner will have to accept this ultimately; either he accepts it or he will have to seek for ways and means of resubjugating these newly freed hundreds of millions of brown and yellow and black people."[38]

Furthermore, these people are not all found outside the West. Wright told of the African Americans who, like himself but with rather less knowledge of the world, had flocked to the conference "to feel a fleeting sense of identity, of solidarity, a religious oneness with the others who shared [their] outcaste state."[39] "At the very moment when the United States was trying to iron out the brutal kinks of its race problem, a world event came along that reawakened in the hearts of its "23,000,000 colored citizens the feeling of *race*, a feeling which the racial mores of American whites had induced deep in [African American] hearts."[40]

Wright's report is seductively lucid — and yet confusingly unfamiliar, a product not only of a time before our own but also of a set of only partially coherent transnational translations. Anticolonialism becomes race-consciousness here. Each forms in the productive border zone between the rational (modern, cosmopolitan) and the irrational (customary, emotional). The irrational poses the threat of violence and reverse discrimination against the lazy and thoughtless West. The call is to capture the passion of the irrational — to guide it toward a cosmopolitan modern progress.

By the 1960s, the threat and promise of race as the irrational had become a main theme of black mobilization in the United States, moving the liberal critique of civil-rights campaigns into the cultural drama of "Black Power's Gon' Get Your Mama." U.S. interpretations of the spirit of anticolonialism encouraged activists to mix threats of violence and demonstrations of cultural pride. Precolonial custom — for example, an idealized Africa — took on a new role as the source of community. The drama of such mixing was effective in moving liberal audiences and forging multicultural alliances. Educated Native American youth, forced into the cities by U.S. assimilation policies of the 1950s and 1960s, took notice.

The activist Clyde Warrior spoke out in 1966: "What it amounts to is that the Indians are getting fed up. It's just a question of how long the Indians are going to put up with being took every day. How long will Indians tolerate this? Negroes, Mexican Americans, and Puerto Ricans could only take colonialism, exploitation, and abuse for so long, then they did something about it. Will American Indians wait until their reservations and lands are eroded away, and they are forced into urban ghettoes, before they start raising hell with their oppressors?"[41]

In 1969, Native Americans staged their first spectacular Red Power drama: the occupation of the prison island of Alcatraz in San Francisco Bay. The occupation was so successful, not only in bringing together an Indian campaign but also in drawing white allies, that it energized an emergent movement. One spectacle led to the next. In 1970, the American Indian Movement (AIM) occupied the building of the Bureau of American Indians in Washington, D.C. Then in 1973, AIM occupied the settlement of Wounded Knee in South Dakota, declaring the independent Oglala Nation. Firefights and negotiations finally ended the occupation, and the legal costs of criminal charges wore down AIM's energy and resources, putting an end to this moment in Indian history. The movement's chroniclers Paul Chaat Smith and Robert Warrior wrote: "That a few thousand who fought to bring power and visibility to the most ignored population in the United States failed to win all they dreamed can be hardly surprising. That they came so close is the miracle."[42]

Population/Peoples: Indigeneity on the Move

"The [Working Group on Indigenous Populations] meeting makes a vivid impression. . . . The indigenous crowd the chamber, often donning the costume of their people, contrasting with the sober attire of the diplomats. . . . In U.N. fashion, people come and go constantly. Meetings are often commenced by prayers. . . . The WGIP has been described as 'politics', 'performance', 'social drama', 'where the sublime meets the ridiculous'—the latter perhaps including the international lawyers who 'preen themselves,' 'resplendent in the latest theories of self-determination.'"
—Patrick Thornberry, international lawyer

Red Power caught the world's attention.[43] Urban aborigines in Australia and urban Indians in Canada were inspired to use cultural drama to call attention to the plight of their peoples. However, another legacy of protest connected them to more traditional rural leaders. Imperial, Christian, and internationalist activism beckoned with a transnational notion of indigeneity. While Red Power offered the movement its unprecedented new energy, it was the history of world-crossing petitions that brought the concept of indigeneity to the international organizations that became the next arena for indigenous rights.

Native peoples within the British empire had long petitioned the crown for justice. Even when the crown ignored them, the history of petitions connected New Zealand Maori, Australian aborigines, and Canadian Indians. In the early 1970s, the Canadian government reassessed its native policy in commonwealth-wide comparison. Native Canadians traveled to Australia and New Zealand, forming a sense of common purpose. The network was further expanded through contacts with Christian and betterment organizations, such as the Anti-Slavery Society in London. These organizations put the nascent indigenous leaders in touch with the United Nations, as well as with their counterparts among the Sami of northern Scandinavia. In 1974, the National Indian Brotherhood of Canada was granted status as a United Nations NGO with the understanding that it would start an international organization. In 1975, an international conference of indigenous people was held in Port Alberni, British Columbia, hosted by the Sheshaht Band of Nootka Indians. Native peoples from twenty countries attended. The conference formed the World Council of Indigenous Peoples, one of the earliest transnational indigenous organizations.[44]

Legacies of imperial, missionary, anthropological, and internationalist contact have contributed to both the form and content of indigenous demands. Two conjunctions — neither commented on in the literature — strike me as particularly important. First, notions of native spirituality and "sacred sites" have allowed powerful arguments for land rights and cultural autonomy in an international context in which the notion of "rights" has a genealogy of Christian values at its core. Through the notion of the sacred, Christian assumptions about entitlement and justice have facilitated indigenous claims.

This conjunction emerged in Australia, where anthropologists used the concept of the sacred to imbue aboriginal culture with a dignity that might be understood by the Christian settler culture. "Sacred sites" entered legal discussions in the 1970s, when anthropologists mediated between aborigines and legal professionals in the negotiation of land-rights claims. In

1976, the concept entered commonwealth legislation with the Aboriginal Land Rights (Northern Territory) Act, and since then it has increasingly gained in legal significance.[45] Native spirituality is a modernist fetish around the world, yet here, for the first time, native spirituality would have a major material effect on settlement and property rights. The success of aboriginal spiritual claims has ricocheted around the world, and indigenous leaders everywhere now attempt to transform cosmologies into rights. Spirituality has been confirmed as a key feature of the assertion of global indigeneity through this exemplary model.

Second, the transnational petition, formed at the intersection of imperial, missionary, and internationalist legacies, has itself become a goal of indigenous organizing. Indigenous representatives struggle over documents, hoping that these will inspire the intervention of higher powers.[46] In the process, words take on new significance as the proving ground for rights. The rhetoric of sovereignty, so important to the possibility of political negotiation, occupies a central position. But to just what kind of sovereignty can indigenous groups aspire? Because this question has no single, clear answer, indigenous leaders have fought for the words of sovereignty as a precondition to the process of deliberation.[47] It is in this context that indigenous leaders have struggled to be considered "peoples," not "populations." Self-determination begins with language.

Like all traveling legacies, these nodes of articulation solve certain dilemmas — and open others. Spiritual claims and the rhetoric of sovereignty have worked best where powerful national constituencies do not feel threatened by the indigenous presence — either because it has been so thoroughly suppressed or because it adds to national multiculturalism. North America, Australia, New Zealand, and northern Europe led the global indigeneity movement that emerged in the decade after the 1975 international conference.[48] Even in 1975, conference organizers worried about the omission of Latin Americans from this leadership:

> The Sami, the North American Indians, the Inuit, the Maoris and the Australian aborigines could understand each other's situation quite easily. But the relationships between those groups and their national governments were paradoxical, perhaps incomprehensible to the delegates from most of Latin America. Correspondingly, the political tension within which Indian organizations functioned in Latin America was difficult for the other delegates to appreciate. . . . These factors seem to explain why

the initiative for the World Council came from North America and Europe, though the crisis area for indigenous people is clearly in the hinterland of Latin America.[49]

In the second half of the 1980s, however, the international spotlight fell on Brazilian Indians, opening new doors. Brazilian Indians have a long history of struggles for cultural rights and social justice. Yet this history was cast *against* the history of Brazilian national development in the national imagination. Between 1964 and 1985, Brazil was ruled by an authoritarian military regime that regarded advocacy for Indians as subversion. When international organizations engaged in advocacy for Brazilian Indians, the government was able to argue even more strongly that the Indian issue was a foreign effort to undermine Brazilian sovereignty.[50] Official "indigenism" meant only the assimilation of Indians to modern Brazilian lifeways. The Brazilian Left left used indigenous people to present their case against government repression, but this only hardened official antagonism.[51] Thus, although Indian organizations were blossoming during the 1970s and early 1980s, they had difficulty sharing their perspectives in international fora.[52]

The civilian governments of the late 1980s changed the context for Indian organizing. The emergence of the Workers' Party as a national force opened up what might count as Brazilian nationalism. Brazilian environmentalists, in concert with international allies, began to take on the preservation of the Amazon as a *Brazilian* issue. The Forest Alliance that gathered in 1987 around Chico Mendes's defense of the rubber tappers was a node for rethinking the possibilities of Brazilian social and environmental justice. Indians, rural workers, and environmentalists worked together for what was simultaneously a national and a transnational cause.[53] For one intense moment, Brazilian Indians could represent their nation's best interests.

The global indigenous network surged forward as a result of this development. Armed with the support of the global environmental movement and aided by the symbolic valence of the Amazon, indigenous leaders suddenly found themselves with access to all kinds of international "instruments." In 1989, ILO Convention 169 was born.

The ILO is an agency of the United Nations. Made up of representatives of labor, business, and government from each member nation, the organization was a plaything of the Cold War, during which it served as a forum for the United States and the Soviet Union to throw charges of forced labor at each other.[54] Other causes were paraded there, too. The United States quit for two years in 1978 because the organization offered the Palestinian Liberation Organization observer status.[55] The ILO first became interested in indigenous rights in the 1920s, when it was asked to investigate forced labor in Europe's African colonies.[56] Convention 169 of 1989 supersedes Convention 107 of 1957, which stresses the "protection" of indigenous people and their "integration" into national development. Twenty-seven states ratified Convention 107, and it remains in force for all but those that have subsequently ratified Convention 169.[57]

Convention 169 emphasizes indigenous land rights, nondiscrimination, and participation in environmental management: the hard-won rhetorical gains of indigenous organizing. Indigenous organizations are able to pressure countries that have signed it to live up to the terms of the accord. In Mexico, for example, indigenous organizers have been effective in using this international discourse of standards to mobilize both at home and abroad.[58]

Yet these gains are not enough, even at the level of rhetoric. Many of the convention's most engaged readers focus on continuing rhetorical struggles and especially on the use of the terms "populations" and "peoples." One draft used "peoples/populations." Despite many government objections, "peoples" won—but with qualifications. Article 1.3 of the text states: "The use of the term 'peoples' in this Convention shall not be construed as having any implications as regards the rights which may attach to the term under international law."[59] This compromise caused an uproar that has not yet died down. One of its outcomes has been the stronger wording of the United Nations draft Declaration on the Rights of Indigenous Peoples. This emergent global standard contains no reference to ILO Convention 169 because of these objections to the article, and it uses a stronger language of indigenous self-determination. However, commentators speculate that this language will make it difficult for the draft to become an established global standard.[60]

As of 2008, no African states and only one Asian state have ratified Convention 169.[61] This stark fact makes the campaign to bring indigenous rights to Indonesia transnationally important. The barriers between Third Worldism and Fourth World–First Nations advocacy remain very high. But if some understanding is to be reached, where better to begin than this site for the development of cultural nationalism?

Adat/Indigeneity: Living with Contradictions

> To assume a right to define indigenous peoples is to further deny our right of
> self-determination.
> — Cree spokesperson for the International Working Group for
> Indigenous Affairs

In much of the global South, the heritage of cultural nationalism has been harnessed by the development state. The state denies indigenous rights because they stand in the way of national development, the hard won right of independence. Indigenous people are not the "national populace" for whom independence was won. National development is charged with moving indigenous people, materially and symbolically, to transform their subjectivities and their resources for the benefit of elites. National development is the road to that "ordered rational world in which we all can share" of which Richard Wright spoke longingly. As Wright suggested, transnational alliances among cosmopolitan elites have been key to building this road to the future.

At the same time, other alliances have encouraged indigenous leaders and advocates to speak out. The rejection of the violence of development by middle-class critics of military rule in Indonesia — as in Brazil — tied democratic agitation to indigenous rights. Indigenous-rights campaigns, indeed, have only prospered where they have been able to gather national as well as international allies. As long as social protest is channeled by and toward the state, political campaigns of all sorts must capture the national imagination. This is part of the story of how words change "in motion."

Yet national consciousness is always formed in the grip of transnational dialogue. As in the Aceh War, U.S. militarization has promoted a clash between Western civilization and transnational Islam. *Adat* is being drawn into this battle, as Indonesian Christians learn to use *adat* conventions to organize against Muslim neighbors. The cultural essentialism imagined by cosmopolitan critics as a result of traditionalist localism is instead the harvest of global war.

So how can "*masyarakat adat*" be translated as "indigenous peoples"? I have argued that this question can only be answered through a history of shifting commitments and alliances. These ties crosscut continents and confound discriminations between tradition and modernity. "*Adat*" and "indigeneity" have come to life in these sometimes contradictory layers of connection.

Are *adat*/indigenous rights a foreign import? Or do they represent primordial consciousness? The intertwined histories of *adat* and indigenous rights show that they come into being in the "contact zone" of global mobilizations and local concerns.[62] *Adat* and indigenous rights help bring globality and locality into being; they cannot be imagined apart from the making of scales. Are *adat*/indigenous rights a challenge to national sovereignty, an imitation, or an extension of its principles? Again, the histories of identification and alliance from which *adat*/indigenous rights have grown guide us to all answers simultaneously. In this zone of contradiction, new commitments and trajectories are very much in process. As indigenous people insist on self-definition, so, too, must analysts learn to follow the flow.

To appreciate the role of shifting commitments and alliances in producing the trajectories of global history, we need new forms of storytelling. Almost everything we read about the global North presents self-contained Northern histories. Almost everything we read about the global South — if not contained by national historiography — presents only a singular dialogue between colonizer and colonized. Then when we hear about "the global," it is presented to us as a giant, undifferentiated lump. These stories are not enough. An appreciation of the mystery and potential of the history of the world should take us through the contingent connections across villages and continents that give depth and direction to history. Through these connections, words may shift and turn back against the purposes of their original users. Coalitions form, offering unexpected opportunities. Through their very instability, "*adat*" and "indigeneity" remind us of this molten history.

Any history of cultural or political difference is a history of shadows and the shadows of shadows. All communal identities are adopted and adapted in a displaced, defensive, imitative, and parodic spirit. To see why this is not tiring for participants, we need to appreciate the breadth and excitement of the geographic travels of these mobilizing shadows. "*Adat*" and "indigeneity" become charged in that contradictory space of moving dialogue that negotiates the ever changing perils of global power.

Notes

This essay addresses issues of concern in and beyond Indonesia between 2000 and 2004; since then, the word has continued in motion as debates about indigeneity developed in new if not always promising directions.

1. Marcus Colchester, Martua Sirait, and Boehi Wijardjo, *The Application of FSC Principles No. 2 and 3 in Indonesia: Obstacles and Principles* (Jakarta: WALHI and AMAN, 2003), 105–106. See also the website at http://www.walhi.or.id/.

2. Myrna Safitri and Rafael Edy Bosko, *Indigenous Peoples/Ethnic Minorities and Poverty Reduction in Indonesia* (Manila: Asian Development Bank, 2002). See http://www.adb.org/Documents/Reports/Indigenous_Peoples/INO/foreword.pdf.

3. For a more elaborate analysis of this problem, see Anna Lowenhaupt Tsing, *Friction: An Ethnography of Global Connection* (Princeton, N.J.: Princeton University Press, 2005).

4. It would be interesting to consider fifteenth-century Islamic or Arabic influences on Spanish concepts of cultural difference. Global connections are intricate, and there may be a layered history of ties between *'ada* and *indigena*: see n. 23 below.

5. Some historians consider the search for tropes an anthropological deformation of the historical task. At a conference I attended just before writing this essay, a historian threw up his hands at anthropological histories. "Tropes, tropes, tropes!" he said. "I'm so tired of hearing about tropes." In the continuing interdisciplinary dialogue, I suggest that attention to tropes can open critical frames of analysis where more conventional historiography fails us. At the same time, the histories tropes open need further research to establish the relationship between frames and events.

6. International Labor Organization, "Convention 169 on Indigenous and Tribal Peoples in Independent Countries," 1989, available online at http://www.unhchr.ch/html/menu3/b/62.htm. The convention has been translated into Indonesian as *Konvensi ILO 169* (Jakarta: ELSAM and LBBT, 1989). Christiaan Snouck Hurgronje, *The Achehnese* (1893–94), trans. A. W. S. O'Sullivan, repr. ed. (Leiden: E. J. Brill, 1906); Richard Wright, *The Color Curtain: A Report on the Bandung Conference* (Cleveland: World Publishing, 1956).

7. Tsing, *Friction*. Other assessments of *adat* politics include John Bowen, "Should We Have a Universal Concept of 'Indigenous Peoples' Rights?" *Anthropology Today* 16, no. 4 (2000): 12–16; Tania Li, "Masyarakat Adat, Difference, and the Limits of Recognition in Indonesia's Forest Zone," in *Race, Nature and the Politics of Difference*, ed. Donald S. Moore, Jake Kosek, and Anad Pandian (Durham: Duke University Press, 2003), 380–406.

8. ELSAM stands for the Lembaga Studi dan Advocasi Indonesia; LBBT stands for Lembaga Bela Banua Talino. Both organizations are usually referred to by their acronyms.

9. Patrick Thornberry, *Indigenous People and Human Rights* (Manchester: Manchester University Press, 2002), 42.

10. Bradley Reed Howard, *Indigenous Peoples and the State: The Struggle for Native Rights* (DeKalb, Ill.: Northern Illinois University Press, 2003), 124.

11. Colchester et. al., *The Application of FSC Principles No. 2 and 3 in Indonesia*, 103.

12. Thornberry, *Indigenous People and Human Rights*, 56.

13. This is found in the caption of a photograph in *Konvensi ILO 169*, 23. Indonesia occupied East Timor between 1975 and 1999.

14. Aliansi Masyarakat Adat Nusantara (AMAN), *Catatan Hasil Kongres Masyarakat Adat Nusantara* (Jakarta: AMAN, 1999).

15. The information in this paragraph was gleaned from discussions and interviews with Indonesian and foreign participants in the debate over *adat* politics from 1999 to 2003. Sandra Moniaga, "Hak-hak Masyarakat Adat dan Masalah serta Kelestarian Lingkungan Hidup di Indonesia," *Wacana HAM*, no. 10 (2004); Li, "Masyarakat Adat, Difference, and the Limits of Recognition in Indonesia's Forest Zone"; and Bowen, "Should We Have a Universal Concept of 'Indigenous Peoples' Rights?" provide useful accounts of the rise of *adat* and indigenous politics in Indonesia in the late 1990s and early 2000s. Their disagreements with each other show the diversity of opinion on *adat* politics.

16. Engseng Ho, personal communication, 2004.

17. "The discovery of *adat* law" is a translation of the title of Cornelius van Vollenhoven, *De Ondekking van het Adatrecht* (Leiden: E. J. Brill, 1928). Although I have not been able to get my hands on a copy, all sources describe it as van Vollenhoven's account of how Dutch scholars crafted *adat* law from the messy materials of custom.

18. Snouck, *The Achehnese*.

19. Pramoedya Ananta Toer, *This Earth of Mankind*, trans. Max Lane (Victoria: Penguin Books, 1982).

20. Christiaan Snouck Hurgronje, *Mekka in the Latter Part of the 19th Century* (1888–89), trans. J. H. Monahan, repr. ed. (Leiden: E. J. Brill, 1931).

21. Snouck, *The Achehnese*, 2:313.

22. In using this phrase, I am referring to Mahmood Mamdani's account of the more recent history of Cold-War meddling in Islam: Mahmood Mamdani, *Good Muslim, Bad Muslim* (New York: Pantheon, 2004).

23. The idea that Muslims are always already local and particular, despite Islam's attempts at universalization, has a long history in European thought: see, e.g., Clifford Geertz, *Islam Observed* (Chicago: University of Chicago Press, 1971). One might think back to Spain's New World conquests, in which indigenes were imagined not only as a kind of Asian ("Indios") but also as Moors. The dance dramas of Christians conquering the Moors, which Spaniards introduced across the New World, showed a triumphant traveling Christianity subduing the locally rooted superstitions of indigenes imagined as Muslims: Olga Najera-Ramirez, *La Fiesta de los Tastoases* (Albuquerque: University of New Mexico Press, 1997.) Here, indeed, was another moment of intersection of *'ada* and *indigena*.

24. Snouck, *The Achehnese*, 1:10–11.

25. Ibid., 14.

26. Ibid.

27. Cornelis van Vollenhoven, *Van Vollenhoven on Indonesian Adat Law: Selections from Het Adatrecht van Nederlandsche-Indie* (1918), ed. J. F. Holleman, repr. ed. (The Hague: Martinus Nijhoff, 1981).

28. Mohammed Koesnoe, *An Introduction into Indonesian Adat Law* (Nijmegen, Netherlands: Publicaties over Adatrecht van de Katholieke Universiteit te Nijmegen 3, 1971), B8.

29. Ibid., B17. I discuss colonial, nationalist, and New Order meanings of *adat* in more depth in Anna Tsing, "Land as Law: Negotiating the Meaning of Property in Indonesia," in *Land, Property, and the Environment*, ed. John Richards (Oakland, Calif.: Institute for Contemporary Studies, 2002), 94–137.

30. See, e.g., Benedict Anderson, *Imagined Communities* (London: Verso, 1981); Clifford Geertz, *Agricultural Involution: The Process of Ecological Change in Indonesia* (Berkeley: University of California Press, 1963).

31. Aijaz Ahmad offers a cogent analysis of this agenda in "Three Worlds Theory," in *Theory: Classes, Nations, Literatures* (London: Verso, 1992), 287–318.

32. Wright, *The Color Curtain*, 47.

33. Ibid., 53.

34. Ibid., 57.

35. Ibid., 63.

36. Ibid., 62.

37. Ibid., 140.

38. Ibid., 203.

39. Ibid., 177.

40. Ibid., 178–79.

41. Quoted in Paul Chaat Smith and Robert Allen Warrior, *Like a Hurricane: The Indian Movement from Alcatraz to Wounded Knee* (New York: New Press, 1996), 37.

42. Ibid., 279.

43. The influence of Red Power politics was surprisingly wide. Courtney Jung reports that Mexican anthropologists were inspired by AIM to criticize assimilationist *indigenismo* policy, thus beginning the Mexican turn from "peasant" to "indigenous" politics: Courtney Jung, *The Moral Force of Indigenous Politics* (Cambridge: Cambridge University Press, 2008).

44. Douglas Sanders, "The Formation of the World Council of Indigenous Peoples," doc. 29, International Work Group for Indigenous Affairs, 1977.

45. Kenneth Maddock, "Metamorphosing the Sacred in Australia," *Australian Journal of Anthropology* 2, no 2 (1991): 213–32. Kimberly Christen describes the history in which spirituality became the sole basis for aboriginal land rights as well as for the processes of translation and transformation through which this ruling was put into practice in central Australia: Kimberly Christen, "Properly Warumungu," Ph.D. diss., University of California, Santa Cruz, 2004.

46. Annelise Riles analyzes the emergence of documents as a central concern of transnational feminism: see Annelise Riles, *The Network Inside Out* (Ann Arbor: University of Michigan Press, 2000).

47. Eben Kirksey reminds us of the parodic quality of the petition for sovereignty, in which religious and civil authorities mingle in the performative borders between rebellion and subjection. He cites the following prayer offered by a leader of the West Papuan independence movement: "Lord God, Lord God in Heaven. . . . Our purpose

is to have freedom and complete sovereignty like other nations that are free around the world . . . Lord God please pass this along to the higher rulers of humanity, to the U.N., so that they begin to know human rights soon": Eben Kirksey, "Freedom in Entangled Worlds: Experiences of Possibility in West Papua," Ph.D. diss., University of California, Santa Cruz, 2008.

48. Latin American organizations did play important roles during this period, although they were rarely in a position of global leadership. The 1977 International Non-governmental Organization Conference on Discrimination against Indigenous Populations in the Americas was an important beginning for Latin American participation. Jung describes this history, showing how Mexican peasant mobilization was transformed in the 1980s and 1990s into indigenous mobilization: see Jung, *Moral Force of Indigenous Politics*.

49. Sanders, "The Formation of the World Council of Indigenous Peoples," 23–24.

50. See the chapter by Itty Abraham in this volume.

51. Ceylan Cemali, personal communication, 2004, notes that under the military government, Brazilian progressives made those whose legal "incompetence" might render them immune from sanctions into icons of protest. In this context, violence against street children as well as Amazonian Indians made international news — yet without domestic gains for either.

52. Alcida Rita Ramos, *Indigenism: Ethnic Politics in Brazil* (Madison: University of Wisconsin Press, 1998).

53. Susanna Hecht and Alexander Cockburn, *The Fate of the Forest: Developers, Destroyers and Defenders of the Amazon* (New York: Harper Perennial, 1990).

54. Walter Galenson, *The International Labor Organization: An American View* (Madison: University of Wisconsin Press, 1981).

55. Economic Policy Council, *The International Labor Organization and the Global Economy: New Opportunities for the United States in the 1990s* (New York: United Nations Association of the United States of America, 1991).

56. Ronald Niezen, *The Origins of Indigenism* (Berkeley: University of California Press, 2003), 36.

57. Thornberry, *Indigenous People and Human Rights*, chap. 13.

58. Jung, *The Moral Force of Indigenous Politics*.

59. Quoted in Thornberry, *Indigenous People and Human Rights*, 344.

60. Niezen, *The Origins of Indigenism*, 197.

61. Of the twenty countries that had ratified, Nepal was the only Asian state: see, http:www.ilo.org/ilolex/english/convdisp1.htm (accessed on 2 December 2008).

62. Mary Louise Pratt developed the concept of a "contact zone" of cultural emergence in *Imperial Eyes* (London: Routledge, 1992).

WORDS THAT EXPAND

'Ada/Custom

in the Middle East and Southeast Asia

The Arabic term " *'ada*" has traveled — not only across the Middle East but across Asia, Africa, and Central Europe. Today it is found not just in Muslim cultures but also among non-Muslims. Its journey is an extraordinary story, in part because the term refers to the most humble and ubiquitous aspects of human social life: those forgettable habits we call "custom."

A travelogue of " *'ada*" takes us where few studies of cultural encounters venture to go: across the global South, as well as in the North and through relations among widely varying cultures and languages. " *'Ada*" follows the travel routes of law and governance as well as of religious belief. Spread first through respect for Islamic knowledge, it also blossomed in the face of European colonial attempts to contain Islam. " *'Ada*" runs in and out of Islam: It has been reviled by Muslim reformers and embraced by advocates of diversity. It has found its way into many divergent conversations on the borders between formal governance and vernacular communal practice.

Ideas about "custom" are formed in a variety of top-down and bottom-up social processes: in arrangements for legal pluralism, in defenses of community rights, in colonial segregation, in ethnic and religious consolidation, and many others. "Custom" involves public ideas as well as official proclamations. To see the traveling play of meanings of such a word, one must watch for clusters of related terms — tradition, authenticity, law, "native" culture. To track these terms over such a wide terrain requires an open-ended play of associations that acknowledges their many meanings and uses. Eschewing a linear story of semantic imposition from "elsewhere" shows the variety of intellectual and political contexts relevant to the way the word is understood in different settings. Here I track " *'ada*," or custom, in its motion between the Middle East and Southeast Asia by way of its layers of association and meaning. My goal is not to trap " *'ada*" in a single argument: It has traveled too far and escaped too often for that. Instead, I offer a tapestry of *'ada* associations. The tapestry reveals sheaths of interwoven continuity as well as individual threads of connection.

What Is *'Ada*?

The word " *'ada*" is given the following meaning in one Arabic dictionary: "Everything that is habitual so that it is done or (undertaken) without effort. The case or the state of the thing is being repeated in the same pattern, similar to women's menstruation."[1] According to Hans Wehr's Arabic dictionary, the Arabic root means "habit, wont, custom, usage, practice."[2] It is no coincidence that menstruation is the illustrative example, since the same root occurs in both words. *'Ada* involves a cyclical and repetitive act, and it implies a natural cycle. The repetitive act itself becomes so natural a custom that it ceases to raise questions about its nature or the practices surrounding it.

The family of words related to " *'ada*" includes " *'urf*" and "*taqlid,*" which both refer to custom. "*Taqlid*" literally means imitation and suggests manners and customs that derive from imitation or emulation. " *'Urf*" is derived from the verb " *'arafa,*" which means "to know."[3] According to a specialist in Yemen's customary law, " *'urf*" means "the thing known by all, that none is supposed to ignore, according to which one regulates relations with other people."[4]

It is also worth noting the way in which the English word "custom" is translated and understood by Egyptian social scientists. The *Arabic Dictionary of Sociology* translates "custom" in two words (*'ada jama'iyya*), which conveys the meaning of a collective habit, understood as repeated actions in everyday life, together with the rules regulating those actions. Concepts related to custom are given as culture, folkways, mores, norms, and values.[5]

Custom Can Be a Matter of Law: Some Egyptian Examples

In Egypt, there is much discussion about legal pluralism in which customary law and Islamic *shari'a* are seen to operate parallel to Egyptian positive law. Indeed, forms of conflict resolution outside the state and jurisdictions of informal arbitration seem to have proliferated in recent years. Some legal specialists argue that these are successful because they replace the role of the state in dispensing justice. Others claim that these "informal councils" are in fact dependent on state authority for acknowledgment and function practically within its confines. Many of their heads belong to the government party or work closely with the local police.[6] The councils are registered with the government organ that oversees the local services of the Ministry of Interior, including village mayors, and success in the councils can lead to promotion to government positions.[7] In short, these "customary" practices seem not to replace but to complement the legal apparatus of the state.

What has been derogatorily labelled ʿurfi marriage has increased in frequency in recent years. Major press coverage of this phenomenon attests to evolving sexual and social norms in Egyptian society. ʿUrfi marriage, which is a customary matrimonial institution acknowledged by Islamic law, has resisted the centralized registration policies of the modern nation-state by surviving alongside the Personal Status Law that regulates marriage.[8] It requires two witnesses and a third party to oversee the contracting of marriage and normally presents no problem from a legal standpoint.[9] But when even the smallest conflicts arise, ʿurfi marriage leads to social and legal problems, for the reason that neither spouse is able to file a lawsuit because one cannot prove the marriage if the other denies the relationship. This is particularly difficult for women filing for divorce or alimony or claiming such marital rights as inheritance.[10] ʿUrfi marriage has since been acknowledged by the government after much pressure from the media, which stressed the fact that it revealed an acute crisis in the sexual norms of young Egyptians. It is unclear whether the revival of the state-tolerated ʿurf custom in a context of expanded economic pressure is a strategy of younger couples eager to avoid the moral and religious censorship of "illicit" relationships or a plain transgression of socially accepted customs and manners. Press reports place all manner of imported illegal marriage contracts, which are said to be flourishing in Egypt, under the heading of ʿurfi marriage, but they also include new forms of ʿurfi marriage.[11] What matters for the tracking of "custom," however, is the status of semi-legality, which makes such marriages a source of debate and conflicting fatwas (religious advisories) about how to deal with them in contemporary Egyptian society.

Custom and Its Cluster of Affinity Words

The Arabic words " '*ada*" and "*taqlid*" (plural, " '*adat*" and "*taqalid*") are linked in the Arab world to a cluster of related terms. For Arab intellectuals, "tradition" evokes associations with "heritage" (*turath*) and "authenticity" ('*asala*). "Heritage" is related linguistically to "inheritance," while "authenticity" is set in opposition to "modernity." These terms evoke a problem discussed for nearly two hundred years in Arab discourse on the intricate relationship with the Other. Often the words "contemporary" and "contemporaneity" are used interchangeably with "modernism" or "modernity."[12]

The intellectual debates on tradition and authenticity centered on what constitutes heritage and whether it should be restricted to religious knowledge, identified as tradition, or included in the secular sciences, which were linked to modernity. In this regard, Tariq al-Bishri divided Egyptian culture into the inherited Islamic-Arabic heritage and the imported component imposed by modern Western civilization and its institutions, such as the press, parliament, and modern education. He juxtaposed the "inherited," with its implied authenticity, to the "intruded," which suggested an emulated or mimicked import, and he contrasted "renewal" with "imitation" (*tajdid wa taqlid*).[13] The words "heritage" and "renewal" (*turath* and *tajdid*) were similarly used by the Sorbonne-trained Egyptian philosopher Hassan Hanafi, who was known for advocating a progressive leftist Islam in the wake of the Iranian Revolution of 1979. Because Hanafi seemed to reproduce the simplistic binaries of an imagined static encounter between East and West, he was criticized by many Arab intellectuals for mythologizing the past, denying any dialectical understanding for the interaction with the Other, and eliding class, ethnic, and regional differences among Muslims and Arabs. '*Asala* (authenticity) here resides with Islamist ideologies, implying that the opposed secularist position is inauthentic. Indeed, Islamists or Islamicists are designated "authentics" ('*usuliyyun*), an appellation that alludes to a return to "roots" ('*asl*).

How Did "Custom" Travel?

The expansion of Islamic civilization since the early conquests created a cross-border unity within a great cultural variety. What unified all Muslims was the spread of the pillars of faith through the Qur'an. Another unifying element was provided by the cosmopolitan class of well-traveled religious scholars who propagated the scriptural culture from Morocco to the Malay archipelago. It is known that travel in "search of knowledge" began in early Islam with the faithful followers who aspired to compile the Prophet's sayings, even venturing as far as China. *Shari'a*-minded scholars also flourished, but as Islamic law spread throughout the Muslim world, it did not abolish local customary practices. The medium of the transmission of faith was the Arabic language, which over time gained a quasi-sacred status among non-Arabic-speaking Muslims. But the usage of Arabic, too, did not dislodge the local languages of the converts.

In early Islam, the Qur'an, which had been revealed directly to the illiterate Prophet, was taught by heart and transmitted orally from one generation to another. The collection and arrangement of the sacred book occurred during the time of the third Caliph in the mid-seventh century, not long after the death of the Prophet. Soon Islamic civilization was according great significance to the written word. At the same time, the art of chanting and reciting the sacred word according to classical principles became one of the most respected skills among believers, whether they were in Africa, India, or Indonesia. *Itmam al-Qur'an*, the achievement of reciting by heart the entire holy book, remains a cardinal part of outstanding religious education for young people. Indonesians today are proud to excel in Qur'an competitions in the Middle East. The level of comprehension of the recited verses is another matter, although the same might be said for many liturgical texts. Arabic, the sacred language of the Qur'an, traveled with Islam wherever it went, reaching the coast of West Africa. It is thus no surprise to find that the word " *'adat*" is used in several African societies whose Muslims speak no Arabic.[14] Sometimes Arabic traveled together with Islam, so that today, for example, it is one of the most popular languages in *pesantren* (religious boarding schools) of Indonesia. Indeed, when the word " *'adat*" reached the Malay archipelago, it was even taken up by non-Muslim groups such as the Balinese.

During the travels of " *'adat*" to Southeast Asia, a slight change occurred in the pronunciation of the word. In the Malay archipelago, the Arabic letter *'ayn* was replaced by a simple *a*. It thus became "*ada*" (plural, *adat*). The first romanization of the Indonesian language (Bahasa Indonesia) did not include the letter *'ayn*. Yet, "*adat*" in Indonesia carries the same meaning as its Arabic counterpart: "custom" or "tradition." In Hindu Bali, "*adat*" designates local customary practices that differ from those of the Hindu religion. Fred Eiseman defines the word "*adat*" in Balinese usage as "conventional religious law."[15]

In fact, many languages in the Indonesian archipelago picked up the word "*adat*." In Java, "*adat*" is used for all that is customary, including festivities and the preparation of food. In the Minangkabau region of Sumatra, the traditional matriarchal system is called "*adat*." The distinctive Minangkabau architecture, in which the extended family lives in common, is called "*adat* house." Balinese use "*adat*" for traditions other than Hindu religious practices. The word "*adat*" is used in Javanese, Malay, and Acehnese (*ngadat*, Javanese; *odot*, Gayonese). In Minangkabau, the people use a two-word phrase, "*adat limbago*," since "*adat*" alone implies a binding rule of custom, while "*limbago*" means non-obligatory custom.[16] In short, it is possible to argue that "*adat*" in Indonesia operates locally the way " '*urf* " does in the Arab world to mean the familiar, "customary" realm.

How Did "Custom" Become Law in Indonesia?

Colonial rule was responsible for the next crucial motion of "*adat*" in Southeast Asia, when it leapt languages to become part of a new Dutch word "*Adatrecht*," or customary law. This hybrid was a product of the long colonial heritage of Dutch Orientalism in the Malay archipelago, as well as of its purposeful reversal of the nineteenth-century Pan-Islamic reformism that began in the Middle East and had considerable impact in Southeast Asia. In places like Morocco and Indonesia, the colonial interest in customary law was related to the appropriation of land at the expense of the local populations. Although many scholars regard *Adatrecht* as a "myth" invented by Dutch scholars at Leiden University, it is also true that the definition of "*Adatrecht*" proceeded in step with the sharpening dichotomy between *adat* and *shari'a* law.

This story is best told through the careers of two ideologues, Cornelis van Vollenhoven (1874–1933) and Christiaan Snouck Hurgonje (1857–1936), who were responsible for codifying *Adatrecht* in the Netherlands East Indies. Van Vollenhoven invented the word, but only after he had tried other terms, such as "Oriental popular law" in his effort to differentiate between Western law and "Oriental legal institutions." Arguing against using the Dutch term for "customary law," he finally decided on a compound based on "*adat*," the widely known Arabic word for "custom." Hence, in its meaning of "*adat* with legal consequences," *Adatrecht* did not imply a rigid division between matters of law and other customs, or *adat*. The Dutch word "*Recht*" is said to carry "stronger overtones of 'rights' and 'justice' than does the English term 'law.' "[17]

Van Vollenhoven, appointed in 1901 a professor of constitutional and administrative law of the Dutch Overseas territories and of *Adatrecht* of the Dutch East Indies, was the first scholar to elevate *adat* law into a "science."[18] His pleading for the significance of the indigenous law in the colonial territories was part and parcel of his advocating respect for the cultures of the local peoples and their "right of avail" to land. This view in turn was a natural outgrowth of his religious beliefs in an "ethical civilizing mission," whereby the Dutch had no right to impose their own laws on other peoples.[19] Both Snouck Hurgronje and van Vollenhoven were products of the "ethical policy," which was declared official government policy under Queen Wilhemina in 1901. In the first part of his voluminous work, *Het adatrecht van Nederlandsch-Indie* (The *Adat* Law of the Netherlands Indies), published in 1918, van Vollenhoven described *adat* law as "clan law." In its scope he included the Dutch East Indies, Formosa, the Philippines, Malacca, Indochina, and Madagascar and extended his analysis to the *Adatrecht* of "foreign Orientals," by whom he mean Chinese, Arabs, and Indians. He strongly defended local rights over virgin and cultivated lands in Java, arguing against the dismissal by colonial courts of *adat* law and "indigenous municipalities" and "traditional land rights."[20] On the last page of his challengingly entitled *Misconceptions* (1909) one finds van Vollenhoven's credo: "Our objective is not to know *adat* law for the sake of juridical science, still less to impede Indonesia's development by fondly preserving *adat*-curiosa; our aim is to create, not on paper but in reality, good government and a good administration of justice, both of which are unthinkable without a thorough knowledge of indigenous law and indigenous conceptions."[21]

Van Vollenhoven was inspired by Snouck Hurgronje's *The Achehnese* (1893–94), which he repeatedly cited in his own work.[22] Dispatched in 1889 by the Dutch colonial government as an adviser on Islamic affairs to contain the Aceh War, Snouck had described Acehnese *adat* in detail and then advised the Dutch to make a deal with *adat* chiefs to separate them from the Islamic religious leaders whom he blamed for the war. But the distinctive contribution of Snouck Hurgronje was his contention that heterodox Southeast Asian Muslims were not really different from their counterparts in the Middle East. He referred to the Hadhramaut of Yemen to argue that even in the Middle East, religious practices differed from doctrine.

Snouck remains a controversial figure. Because he lived in Arabia for a year in the mid-1880s and spent six months as a disguised Muslim in Mecca, his personal life made him something of a legend. While in Mecca he converted to Islam, and later in Indonesia, as in Mecca, he lived as a Muslim,[23] marrying two Indonesian Muslim women. Indonesians would later remember him under different Muslim names and titles.[24] In some Muslim circles, in both the Middle East and Southeast Asia, Snouck appears in popular discourses as a Dutch "spy'" and Orientalist who promoted policies antagonistic to Muslims. But others see him, with reason, as an enlightened and concerned scholar who advocated humane policies toward the people of the Indies.

While in Mecca, Snouck had become suspicious of the politicized aspects of rising Pan-Islamism, to which he was opposed.[25] He was, however, optimistic about the prospects for an Indonesian educated class. He promoted the idea of a political and national association of Dutchmen and Indonesians "which would find its expression in a Netherlands empire consisting of two geographically distant but spiritually closely allied parts."[26] For this he was criticized by the nationalist Mohammed Natsir, who rejected the association idea à la Snouck, which he saw as leading to repressing one culture by another.[27] Even as he spoke for "association," Snouck took measures to suppress those he considered to be the fanatic Islamists in Aceh. At the same time, he advocated the separation between religion and politics. Snouck's "*Islam-Politik*" in Indonesia is said to have led to the increasing involvement of the colonial government in the daily affairs of the "Islamic church," to the point that the Office for Native Affairs, which he proposed and founded, has been called a predecessor of the Indonesian Ministry of Religious Affairs."[28]

His policies apart, Snouck's vision and pioneering scholarship of Islam became the backbone of the philosophy of *Adatrecht*. As one of the few Orientalists of his time who not only studied but also "lived" Islam, Snouck knew the ways of local communities, children's games, secular literature, and village organization.[29] Comparing his experience in Mecca and Sumatra, he was able to measure the impact of religion in different societies. In this sense, the *Adatrecht* that developed from his ideas owed a lot to lived religions and customs — what one scholar describes as a realist ethnography of lived Islam.[30] In any case, Snouck was the one who formulated the binary opposition between *adat* and Islamic law "as a conflict between the actual (*adat*) and occasionally realized and largely alien ideal (Islam)."[31]

A Moroccan Parallel

There is a parallel here with Morocco, where the issue of customary law has been important for the Berber community. As in Indonesia, colonial administrators were responsible for making custom an object of codification. Snouck Hurgronje himself advised the French government on the codification of Berber customary law in 1931, the same year that Snouck presided over the International Congress of Orientalists in Leiden.[32] What Snouck did to shape modern Islam in Indonesia was done in Morocco by Jacques Berque (1910–95) and others.[33] In both colonies the classification and codification were undertaken to aid the colonial administration in regulating indigenous affairs. Berque and Snouck both made the connection between law and ethnography and understood the social implications of law. In both places, the main issue was land rights and colonial interference.[34] And in both cases, a conflict arose between practices of indigenous tenure and collective communal use of village lands and the impact of foreign colonization, symbolized by the French *colon* in Morocco and the Dutch and Chinese landowners in Java.

Berque responded to the diversity of local practices by arguing that the French word for custom, "*coutume*," was too ambiguous in that it referred not only to custom but also to "folklore" in a general sense. This vagueness led Berque to develop a classifying system that could differentiate between Islamic and customary law.[35] He thus followed the same path as Snouck in setting up '*adat* as a category through which indigenous uses of land might be recognized.

Reformism as a Colonial Mirror Image:
How Custom Became Superstition

The word "*Adatrecht*" raises the question of how its invention served colonial interests. Important in this respect was the growing significance of the reformist movements launched by Islamic leaders in the nineteenth-century Muslim world. These leaders advocated modern education; promoted a modern, scientific, and positivist outlook; and attacked both passive imitation and mystical excesses. But their relation to the colonial authorities was not as clear-cut as it might seem. Some scholars now argue that the famous Egyptian leader of Islamic modernism, Muhammad 'Abdu (1849–1905) was prepared to cooperate with the British in the interest of reform. Indeed, the British proconsul Lord Cromer described him and his group as "the natural allies of the European reformers," and it was Cromer who supported him when the Khedive regime wanted to dismiss him as mufti of Egypt.[36]

For if the reformists were seen to be accommodative rather than disruptive, then the suspicion of colonial powers toward Pan-Islamism might be misplaced. Of course, what the colonial powers overlooked in this picture was the rising force of nationalism in the Islamic world. From 'Abdu's reformist ideology emerged the first generation of anticolonial nationalists and, later, the movement of the Muslim Brotherhood, influenced by 'Abdu's disciple Rashid Rida. In this sense, Islamic reformism and colonial apprehensions about it may be read as mirror images of one another.

In a different register, the Orientalist efforts to codify customary law—in Dutch, *Adatrecht*; in Arabic, *'adat*, *'urf* (plural, *'a'raf*); in Morocco the word used is *'a'raf*—could just as well be regarded as an indirect counter to reformist claims. It is no coincidence that the Wahhabi purists of Saudi Arabia,[37] like Islamic reformists in Indonesia and Morocco, regarded *'adat* (custom) and *bida'* (innovation) as equal evils to be combated. "Innovation" in this context means drifting from orthodoxy toward heterodox practices, such as those manifested in popular forms of Islam, including popular Sufism, visiting shrines, and worshiping saints. These practices were abhorred and combated by Islamists who wanted to return to the original source of Islam. Their aim was to purify religion from the practices manifested in both *'adat* and *bida'*, which they saw as having corrupted the true religion. In Morocco, for example, 'Allal al-Fassi labeled customary law "*jahili*," a "pre-Islamic custom" that had to be abolished, and he seemed to equate *'adat* with *khurafat* (magical beliefs), which he mentioned together as the main obstacles to progress.[38] For al-Fasi, women at the mercy of customary law are humiliated and treated like objects to be bought and sold. They are deprived of the right of inheritance, a right guaranteed by Islamic *shari'a*, and are thus kept in a backward, pre-Islamic state. Al-Fasi tells us that he compared Moroccan customary law with some primitive African tribes and concluded that they were equally horrific.[39] In his view, *'adat* was not the ally but the enemy of reform.

In Southeast Asia, Islamic reformism reflected Middle Eastern influence. Ahmed Khatib Minangkabau (c. 1855–1916) was among the first to be influenced by 'Abdu; he vehemently attacked *adat* and the traditional law of succession in Minangkabau, in Sumatra.[40] Another controversial figure was Sayyid 'Uthman bin Yahaya (1822–1913), a prolific scholar and the mufti of Batavia during Snouck's time.[41] In 1889, he was appointed by the Dutch "Honorary Adviser for Arabian Affairs" at the recommendation of Snouck, and many think that Snouck's policies could not have been implemented without his assistance. While some considered him a respected and influential scholar, others attacked him as a Dutch spy and traitor to Islam. He probably owed this accusation not only to his association with Snouck, but also to his opposition to such episodes in the "holy war" against the Dutch as the Banten Jihad of 1888, whose protagonists he accused of following the Devil. Although Sayyid 'Uthman agreed with some Islamic customary regulations, he is nonetheless considered a reformist because he fought such innovations (*bida'*) in Islamic practice as believing in auspicious days, writing traditional pseudo-historical narratives, having recourse to traditional healers, engaging in competitive Qur'an recitals, and dividing inheritance according to local *adat* rather than Islamic law. Sayyid 'Uthman's main concern was to purify Muslim beliefs of these and other non-Islamic practices. He was, however, an active supporter of the Islamic nationalist movement, the Sarekat Islam, founded in 1912.

There is a parallel between Sayyid 'Uthman and Snouck Hurgronje in the East Indies and Muhammad 'Abdu and Lord Cromer in Egypt. Both Muslim reformers fought to change their societies, and both interacted and cooperated with an important colonial official, even as they supported fledging Islamic nationalist movements in their countries. And both were caught in the cross currents among *adat*, *shari'a*, and colonial law.

An Orthodox Middle East versus a Syncretic Southeast Asia?

The elaboration of alternative indigenous systems by colonial administrators was part of the colonial divide-and-rule policy to counteract political Islam. In 1948, one anthropologist wrote that customary law was a "confusing fiction" and that custom is not law.[42] Others have also concluded that *Adatrecht* cannot be considered law as such and "that the search for original *adat* is futile."[43] Without denying the significance of *adat* in everyday Indonesian life, this view judges the concept of *adat* to have led to a paradox—namely, that it served a different purpose from the one originally intended by its elaborators. It began as a colonial construct but survived and evolved on its own in postcolonial times.[44]

In comparing *'adat* in the Middle East and Southeast Asia, one finds a seemingly unconscious regional stereotyping that perpetuates the notion of a pure, orthodox, scripturalist Islam emanating mainly from the Middle East. This stream of Islam, including reformism and Wahhabism, is seen as flowing from the Middle East toward the heterodox, syncretic, lax, and "oral" Islam of Southeast Asia. Customary law, too, was regarded as hierarchically inferior in legal status. This inferiority seemed to be confirmed by the fact that these unwritten customary practices had to be codified through the anthropological observations of colonial administrators. This view sharpens the dichotomy between Islamic law, constantly revivified from its sources in the Middle East, and the local *adat*, or customary tradition, of Southeast Asia. This binary opposition extends to "Arab puritans" versus "local pagans." Implicit in this logic is the view that the Muslims of the Malay archipelago are recipients or followers, rather than innovators, in Islamic religious matters. Take, for instance, G. W. J. Drewes's vision of Indonesian Islam published in 1955: "Indonesia has shown great receptivity and an amazing faculty for adapting newly acquired ideas to her old basic pattern of thinking, but she has not displayed any creative impulse. In matters of religion the Indonesians have always been good followers: they have never taken the lead."[45] Indonesian Islam is portrayed as receptive and imitative, while innovative streams of thought are derived from elsewhere. Drewes also insists on the fact that Indonesian Islam is different because of its inconspicuousness. "Whoever knows Islam only as it appears in North Africa or in the Near East can, on visiting Indonesia, at first hardly believe himself to be in a Muslim country at all. And not only passing visitors but even people who have been living in the country for a considerable time will tell you first and foremost about Borobudur and Hindu-Javanese temples, about Javanese and Balinese dancing and stage performances. In short, they can inform you about all kinds of non-Muslim aspects of Indonesian life, but most probably they will never have seen the inside of the mosque."[46] Here the Hindu Javanese element adds to the image of "laxity" associated with Indonesian Islam. Drewes stresses the fact that Islamic law is restricted to daily family life, while inheritance is based on customary law, *adat*.[47] In matrilineal Minang-kabau, *adat* is portrayed as struggling against *shari'a*.

Clifford Geertz repeated this often drawn polarity, in his astute comparative anthropological study of two Muslim societies, *Islam Observed*. Critics noted that his distinction between "high" and "popular" Islam presented an image of a dogmatic, rigorous Moroccan Islam compared with a syncretic, reflective Indonesian version.[48] Often this dichotomy stresses the tensions of a rigid "Arab" import that constantly threatens a local brand of "lived Islam." Yet it is clear that networks of orthodoxy and high culture throughout the Muslim world facilitate communication between Indonesian and Egyptian Muslim intellectuals, who share a language and references, whatever the regional, generational, and ideological differences that have always characterized the cosmopolitan class of Islamic religious scholars.

This imagined dichotomy between the Middle East and Southeast Asia was present in the Western interpretations of early-nineteenth-century Islamic reformism, which colonial advisers tried to counteract with the concept of *'adat*. The idea that the Middle East is exporting fundamentalism remains powerful in the global imagination today, as exemplified in press portrayals of the Hadrami Arab community in Indonesia after September 11, 2001. The bombing of a Bali discotheque in October 2002 and the condemnation of Abu Bakar Ba'asyir as a possible suspect with alleged connections to al-Qaeda only reinforced clichés about the association of Indonesia with a harsh, imported "Arab" brand of Islam, so often perceived as a threat to a "local," syncretic religious culture. Many ask whether it is a coincidence that the four major leaders of the Islamic Jihadist groups in Indonesia are—like Osama bin Laden—of Hadhrami Arab descent.[49] Such questions have political and social repercussions for the nearly five million Indonesians who are of Yemeni descent.[50]

But these preconceived ideas about Middle Eastern orthodoxy versus syncretic Southeast Asian Islamic peripheries can be dangerously misleading. As I have shown, it is the links and continuities of thought—both colonial and reformist—that characterize transregional Islam in the modern period. Cosmopolitan networks of religious scholars (*'ulama'*) have long since created a homogenized, scripturalist, high Islamic culture, whether in Indonesia, Morocco, or Egypt. Similarly, the force of the Arabic word "*'ada*" has made itself felt across the Muslim arc from North

Africa to the Pacific, where "*adat*" and its affinity words — "tradition" not the least of them — have succeeded in enshrining indigenous custom in diverse Muslim contexts. Indeed, it is the continuous dialectic between doctrine and practice that keeps the word " '*adat*" forever in motion.

Notes

1. Majma' al-Lugha al-'Arabiyya, *Al-mu'jam al-Wasit*, vol. 2 (Cairo: Matabi', 1982).

2. Hans Wehr, *A Dictionary of Modern Written Arabic* (Ithaca, N.Y.: Cornell University Press, 1961), 654, quoted in Peter Burns, *Concepts of Law in Indonesia* (Leiden: Koninklijk Instituut voor Taal-, Landen Volkenkunde Press, 2004), xvii.

3. Quoted in Sarah Ben Nafissa, Sameh Eid, and Patrick Haenni, "Règlement des conflits et ordre politique urbain au Caire: Les faux semblants des Majalis Orfia," in *Un passeur entre les mondes, le livre des Anthropologues du Droit, disciples et amis du Recteur Michel Alliot*, ed. Etienne and Jacqueline Le Roy (Paris: Publications de la Sorbonne, 2000), 207–26.

4. Ibid.

5. Muhammad 'Ali Muhammad, "Custom," in *Qamus 'ilm al-ijtima'* [The dictionary of sociology], (Cairo: Al-Hay'a al-Misriya al-'ammah lil-kitab, 1979), 115.

6. Informal arbitration forms of jurisdiction are called "*jalsat al-'arab*," "*majlis 'urfi*," or "*majlis al-'arab*": Ben Nafissa et al., "Règlement des conflits et ordre politique urbain au Caire."

7. Sarah Ben Nafissa, "Les Majlis Urfiyya en Egypte entre domination politique et domination sociale," in *Carrefour de justices*, ed. B. Dupret and F. Burgat, *Revue Egypte Monde Arabe*, nos. 7–8 (2005): 1.

8. In Egypt, marriage, divorce, and inheritance are governed not by the Civil Code but by *shari'a*, as progressively "codified" in the 1920 and 1929 Laws of Personal Status, which have since been amended and augmented by additional clauses and decrees. As far as registration of legal marriages is concerned, this is done with the *ma'zun* (Personal Status public notary). The position of Islamic law vis-à-vis *'urfi* marriage is still evolving today.

9. One could argue, as some jurists do, that *'urfi* marriage has no legal status. Other jurists hold that the fact that no legal action can be taken against a couple living publicly as an *'urfi*-wed couple to contest the marriage is proof enough that the marriage possesses legal legitimacy. This legitimacy in the end is conditional, since it is contested as soon as conflicts arise and legal action is taken by one of the parties.

10. Gihan Shahine, "Illegitimate, Illegal or Just Ill-Advised," *Al-Ahram Weekly*, 18–24 February 1999.

11. Ahmad Khalid and Ahmad Farghalli, "Al-halal wa-1 -mubah fi 'uqud al-nikah [The permitted and valid in marriage contract], *Al-Ahram al-'arabi*, 7 April 1997.

12. In Arabic, *mu'asara*, *mu'asir*, and *hadatha*: see 'Aziz al-'Azmah, *Al-'Asala, aw, Siyasat al-hurub min al-waqi'* [Authenticity and the politics of escapism] (London: Dar al-Saqi, 1992), 8.

13. *Taqlid* — imitation or, rather, "blind imitation" — is a theme first raised by the reformist Mohammed 'Abdu, who associated the decadence of the *'umma* with the rise of Turkish powers who encouraged the blind submission to power: see Albert Hourani, *Arabic Thought in the Liberal Age, 1798–1939* (Cambridge: Cambridge University Press, 1983), 150.

14. Mamadou Diouf, " 'Tradition' in Senegal," paper presented at the ssrc Words in Motion Workshop, New York, June 2001.

15. Fred B. Eiseman, *Essays on Religion, Ritual and Art*, vol. 1 (Berkeley, Calif.: Periplus Editions, 1989), 69.

16. H. W. J. Sonius, "Introduction," in *Van Vollenhoven on Indonesian Adat Law*, ed. J. F. Holleman (The Hague: Martinus Nijhoff, 1981), iv.

17. Peter Burns, *Concepts of Law in Indonesia*, xvii.

18. Sonius, "Introduction."

19. Ibid., xxx.

20. Ibid., xxxiv.

21. Ibid., xxxvi.

22. J. M. Otto and S. Pompe, *The Legal Oriental Connection, 1850–1950* (Leiden: Van Vollenhoven Institute for Law, Governance and Development, 1989), 238–39.

23. He was known to have prayed regularly.

24. Names such as "Abdogapha," "Si Gam," and later "Teungkoe Hadji Blanda": see Jean-Jacques Waardenburg, *L'Islam dans le miroir de l' occident*, 3rd ed. (Paris: Mouton, La Haye, 1962), 21.

25. J. Vredenbregt, "The Haddj: Some of Its Features and Functions in Indonesia," *Bijdragen Tot de Taal-, Land- en Volkenkunde* 118, no. 1 (1962): 102.

26. Ibid., 101.

27. Natsir comments that Snouck's theory of association was biased against Islam, since it aimed at "liberating the Moslems from the precepts of their religion": quoted in ibid., 102, n. 39.

28. Karel Steenbrink, *Dutch Colonialism and Indonesian Islam: Contacts and Conflicts, 1596 — 1950*, trans. Jan Steenbrink and Henry Jansen (Amsterdam: Rodopi, 1993), 87–88.

29. Waardenburg, *L'Islam dans le miroir de l'occident*, 246.

30. Ibid., 249.

31. William R. Roff, "Islam Obscured? Some Reflections on Studies of Islam and Society in Southeast Asia," *Archipel* 29 (1985): 10.

32. Ibid.

33. Jacques Berque was born in 1910 in Frenda, Algeria, to a *pied noir* family. His father was an Arabist who likely played a great role in his education. Berque worked in his early career as an agronomist in Morocco and was concerned with improving the life of Moroccan peasants. He was then appointed an administrator of the Seksawa tribe in the Western High Atlas, where he stayed for five years and wrote *Les structures sociales du Haut Atlas*, the work that brought him fame: see Ernest Gellner, "Obituary of Jacques Berque," *Guardian*, 11 July 1995.

34. For the intricate and complex land rights, communal usage, and administration

on the village level in colonial times in Indonesia, see the inspiring article by Frederic Durand, "La question foncière aux Indes Neerlandaises, enjeux économique et lutes politiques (1619–1942)," *Archipel* 58 (1999): 73–88.

35. Jorn Thielmann, "A Critical Survey of Western Law Studies on Arab-Muslim Countries," in *Legal Pluralism in the Arab World*, ed. Baudouin Dupret, Maurits Berger, and Laila al-Zwaini (The Hague: Kluer Law International, 1999), 44–45.

36. Hourani, *Arabic Thought in the Liberal Age*, 158.

37. The founder of Wahhabism was Muhammad ibn Abdul Wahhab (1703–92), who sought to purify Islam of cultural and tribal customs. It has been viewed as an attempt to return to a pristine form of Islam.

38. 'Allal al-Fassi, *Al-naqd al-dhati* (Auto-Critique), 7th ed. (Casablanca: Dar al-thaqafa al-dar al-bayda', 2002), 54–55.

39. Ibid., 231.

40. Steenbrink, *Dutch Colonialism and Indonesian Islam*, 134–35.

41. The following information on Sayyid 'Uthman bin Yahya is summarized from Azyumardi Azra, "A Hadhrami Religious Scholar in Indonesia: Sayyid 'Uthman," in *Hadhrami Traders Scholars and Statesmen in the Indian Ocean, 1750s–1960s*, ed. Ulrike Freitag and William G. Clarence-Smith (Leiden: E. J. Brill, 1997), 249–63.

42. Burns, *Concepts of Law in Indonesia*, 208.

43. Ibid., 254.

44. Ibid., 182.

45. G. W. J. Drewes, "Indonesia: Mysticism and Activism," in *Unity and Variety in Muslim Civilization*, ed. Gustave E. von Grunebaum (Chicago: University of Chicago Press, 1955), 284.

46. Ibid., 285.

47. Ibid.

48. Clifford Geertz, *Islam Observed* (Chicago: University of Chicago Press, 1968).

49. *Al-Hayat*, 18 October 2002; *Far Eastern Economic Review*, 14 November 2002, 16–19.

50. This is an approximate estimate provided by the *Far Eastern Economic Review*. Not all Indonesians with Arab ancestry would readily acknowledge their heritage, especially if they are not *sayyid* in lineage. The emphasis on one's "Arabness" is considered a subjective matter.

Sekinin/**Responsibility**

in Modern Japan

Responsibility is the first step in responsibility.
— W. E. B. du Bois, *John Brown*

As words go, "responsibility" ("*sekinin*" in Japanese) is unprepossessing. Unlike "big words" like democracy or modernity, it often moves within and across societies without calling undue attention to itself. This stealthiness gives it an advantage for an exercise that traces words in motion. For although its ordinariness makes it hard to track, its movements soon lead from lexical thin air into the historical thick of things where politics, society, and the self are debated in modern terms.

Another advantage of tracing this word is its mobility: In the nineteenth and twentieth centuries, it moved across languages and, equally important, across social place and lines of power with promiscuous ease. Compare it to a word like "public," which has long been the subject of debate in Japan. Because "public" in Confucian parlance referred to the state, not the people, it is frequently said that "there is no word for public" in Japanese that would allow for such things as an American-style public library or a Habermasian public sphere. There then follows a stock explanation of how Japanese social relations have stunted the development of public politics, an explanation that is culturally essentialist and also inaccurate. In comparison, the word "responsibility" passed through semantic customs without a declaration; even in translation, it settled quickly into the wordscape. And because of its ordinariness, it moved between intellectual discourse and social vernacular, between public affairs and private life, between international relations and domestic politics without conceptual resistance.

It did so in part because of its ambiguity: Responsibility has many facets, not always sorted out one from the other in actual usage. Moral, legal, political, and social responsibility are sometimes separately conceived or more often conflated. Individual versus collective responsibility remains a matter of argument. And conceptual pairings such as freedom and responsibility, rights and responsibilities, subjectivity and responsibility do not always travel together in different historical settings. But with or without a particular word-partner, "responsibility" itself has made many a global transit in the course and discourse of modernity.

Here I am interested in the transits of responsibility that affect political and social practice. The general historical hypothesis is this: The word "responsibility" is largely modern, dating from sometime in the eighteenth century, swelling in use in the nineteenth century, and reaching a global prominence by the end of the twentieth century that was both striking in language and consequential in practice. In the West, the word spread, probably from England, traveling revolutionary tides to North America and Europe and, later, the sea-surge of international law and nation-state formation, to other parts of the globe, including Japan. Its role in the rhetoric of a world order dominated by the West was primarily legal and often narrowly technical. But "responsibility" soon moved into other domains, encompassing broader meanings within and across different societies. And as its meanings expanded, the word gained markedly in presence and in weight. Corporate social responsibility, responsibility toward the earth, responsibility for the future—by the 1990s it was said that we were living in "a time of responsibility."[1] In Japan, a time of *sekinin*.

To state the obvious, the concept, perception, or action expressed by the word in the nineteenth century was neither new nor modern. People everywhere have always had ways of saying and being what we now call responsible. That is why Oedipus and Antigone are favored examples in Western philosophical literature: They took personal responsibility for acts over which they had no control (the word was "fate"). And that is why Japanese so often evoke the forty-seven righteous retainers of 1703 who took responsibility for avenging their lord, placing faithfulness above the law and dying for it (the word was "loyalty"). So while the word "*sekinin*" was newly present in late-nineteenth-century Japan, the experience of responsibility was not.

Nor—and this is important—was "*sekinin*" strictly speaking a neologism of the sort created to translate Western words for things that did not exist in Japan — national assembly, railroad, and statistics, for example. With those words came not just the name but also the model for the thing itself. This was all the more true of politically and philosophically charged Western words such as "freedom," "rights," and "sovereignty." Although earlier Japanese counterparts may have existed for such concepts, in creating these new words and meanings, nineteenth-century Japanese were consciously "translating the West."[2] The word "*sekinin*," in contrast, did not seem particularly foreign, even when it appeared in translation from Western sources. Naturally, the word had its own mixed baggage, but its career did not resemble the typical transit from West to East of terms borne by European imperial power or civilizational models. The seeming ordinariness of the new word helped in its rather rapid establishment, and once established in several meanings, it changed the way people thought about and acted in politics and society, both in relation to meanings already there and in constant interaction with the changes in the word across time in other parts of the world. The history of "*sekinin*" is in fact part of a global history of the word "responsibility" and its expansion of meaning in modern societies in modern times.

After describing the early transits of the word, I follow four different directions in which it moved — personal responsibility, responsibility in politics, war responsibility, and social responsibility — along the way suggesting some simple propositions about the motion of words in general. Because tracking the presence of a single word is a matter of all haystack and few needles, there is no genealogy or storyline that presumes to trace the history of the word. Instead, I traverse a diffuse social topology across the temporal frame of modernity, during which the meanings and usages of the word "responsibility" proliferated, some for the good and some not.

Early Transits

According to Boethius, a word is a sound that air makes, but most of the new words that rushed into Japan in the mid-nineteenth century made no sound at all. They came on one printed page — in Chinese, Dutch, English, or French — and were translated into written Japanese on another page. From roughly the 1860s through the 1880s, a semantic avalanche of unfamiliar words hit first the universe of print and soon the domain of institutional change. The translations of these terms did more than create new Japanese words for foreign originals. They constituted a wholesale reframing of the world in a different conceptual language. Of course, most belonged to the diaspora of words from the West,[3] but they were also viewed as vehicles of modernity, or "civilization," as Japanese called it, which — one strains now to remember — many Asians of the time believed to be not only Western but universal. Universal and new — these years were a kind of *Sattelzeit*, or temporal watershed, marking a consciously historical transition to "new times" (*Neuzeit*), as the modern period came to be known in German.[4] From the beginning of the Meiji era in 1868, Japanese, too, were acutely conscious of living in new times and thinking about them with new words.

New words such as "society," "politics," "literature," "philosophy," and "objectivity" were fashioned in several ways. Two Chinese characters could be combined into a new compound, attaching "iron" and "path" to get "railroad," for example. Or an old, often obscure, Chinese compound could be resurrected with a new meaning, as happened with "civilization." Or — and this was the method that prevailed after the initial avalanche had been ground into the soil of ordinary language — the Western word could be transliterated in the Japanese syllabary, bypassing Chinese characters altogether, as in *sebiro* (Saville Row) for a Western-style man's suit. The routes of translation varied, too, with some words translated directly from Western texts, others from Chinese translations of Western texts, and some from both.

When it appeared as a Japanese translation of the English word "responsibility" in the mid-nineteenth century, "*sekinin*" was an existing Chinese compound — meaning office or duties of office — known in Japan for centuries but not in common use.[5] It did not figure in early translations from the Dutch, or with any stability in Japanese–English dictionaries until the mid-1880s.[6] Although the compound was unfamiliar to Japanese of the time, it consisted of two characters that were well known separately: *seki*, meaning "charge with" (either as duty or reproach), and *nin*, signifying "office" (the obligations entrusted in a professional connection). Thus, in the 1870s *sekinin* might have seemed, misleadingly perhaps, to mean just what its two component characters had always meant individually: responsibility of office or status.[7]

One of the earliest head-on encounters with "*sekinin*" as a translation word occurred in the mid-1860s and early 1870s when Japanese scholars struggled to render Henry Wheaton's influential *Elements of International Law* of 1836 into Japanese. Most worked from the Chinese translation by the American missionary William Martin, who at times used the compound *sekinin* for the English word "obligation," either legal or contractual. Perhaps because this did not jibe with the Japanese understanding of these characters as a task or office, the translator sometimes substituted the word "duty" or glossed it with a term like "contract." In other places in the text, the word "*sekinin*" appeared in what was in fact a new meaning: that of liability. One could not, for example, "evade responsibility in cases of loss or damages incurred by the government or people of another country." Thus *sekinin* in Japanese acquired the legal meaning of an action requiring compensation or restitution, a definition it retains to this day.[8]

What a muddle, but a typical one in the days of shotgun translation. After Japan signed unequal treaties with the Western powers in 1858, international law — or the "Public Law of All the Nations," as Wheaton's text was titled in Chinese and Japanese — took on surpassing national importance, moving rapidly from the printed page to the diplomatic table. There was no question that "all the nations" referred primarily to Europe, with the United States smuggled in by virtue of its "European origin."[9] Not only did China and Japan have little choice but to join the world the West had made, but strange Western words such as "extraterritoriality" had real bite to them; they ate into the status and sovereignty of the nation.

Sekinin, however, entered legal language in a less threatening register. Its initial translations generated new and sometimes incommensurable meanings of the word as responsibilities, liabilities, and obligations incurred between nations, with the further claim that states had to make good for the consequences of their actions. Similar concepts soon appeared in other translations of Western law under scrutiny in Japan at the time, entrenching the new legal definition of "*sekinin*" in several contexts. In 1880, "*sekinin*" appeared as the definition of the French "*responsabilité*" in the legal dictionary compiled by the government and used by the drafters of the first version of Japan's civil code, modeled after the French.[10] The new word conceived in a muddle of trial-and-error translation of English via Chinese was on its way to becoming a legal term of art.

If the transits of "*sekinin*" had stopped with the law, it might have ended up a technical word like "tort," of little import in daily life. But this word had legs, and quick ones, too, although it is unclear to me how it managed so fleet a passage into the vernacular. Intellectuals began to use it in the 1870s and early 1880s, primarily but not only in translations of Western works. The meaning was usually the familiar responsibilities of office, status, or, in new Christian contexts (such as the ever popular translation of Samuel Smiles' *Self-Help* of 1870), God-given abilities: basically, what one ought to do by virtue of one's place or role. But it was not a galvanizing word like "freedom," which leapt from public debate into popular argot during the 1870s, or a controversial one like "rights," which became central in political discourse.

I would argue that although the word "*sekinin*" appeared as part of the rush to rethink the world in terms of "Euro-American" civilization, translation from the West was not in fact the critical transit for the word "responsibility" that it was for so many other Meiji neologisms. And I would further generalize that although translation from other languages and worlds may be the engine powering the transnational discourse of modernity, it is not necessarily the most important stage in the travels of a word. It is what happens to the word once it puts down roots in new social terrain that determines in practice how it works in the world.

Taking Responsibility

The word "responsibility" put down roots in Japan with remarkable speed. The rapid vernacularization of the word is especially striking for the way in which the meaning of personal responsibility became so quickly embedded in ordinary language. However this happened, it did not depend on translated legal meanings or even on the older sense of responsibility of office. No doubt the circulation of all words, old and new, was greatly expanded by the proliferating media of public discourse that began in the 1870s, the press and popular culture in particular. One can follow the vernacular appearance of "*sekinin*" in the *Yomiuri* newspaper, founded in 1874, which appealed to a general urban audience. By 1877, it was selling 5.5 million copies annually, and in 1885, as many as 15,000 copies daily, considerable numbers for newspapers at that time.[11]

In the 1870s, the compound *sekinin* had not yet appeared in the newspaper, older words doing its work instead. The first use of the word was probably in an 1879 letter arguing that it was the responsibility of parents to provide their children with kimono for festival days — not a legal but a customary responsibility of familial role. *Sekinin* came into its own in the late 1880s, used in a variety of meanings: a report of a newly established "limited liability" company; an editorial lecturing painters about their "heavy responsibilities" to Japanese national art; another urging the abolition of the guarantor system at the Imperial University in order to develop the "individual responsibility" of the students.[12] Other common uses included responsibility — in the sense of liability — for negligence or damage to others' property. Assuming that readers understood the word as "taking responsibility" of one sort or another, "*sekinin*" seemed to settle quickly in these meanings. The timing fit the general chronology of linguistic change, since the canonical moment of semantic and orthographic stabilization for many new Japanese compounds occurred during the 1880s. In the case of *sekinin*, it slipped into the place of earlier words for familiar feelings of social obligation, though it seems to have done so without the overtones of a word translated from a Western language.

Taking responsibility by committing suicide, for example, was nothing new, just that it had earlier occurred without the rhetorical evocation of *sekinin*. Suicide figured frequently in the sensational features favored by the *Yomiuri* from the early days of the paper. A man who accidentally killed two children; a businessman who failed his customer; a soldier who returned late to camp; a babysitter who dropped an infant into a pool of manure, where it drowned; a night watchman on duty when a new elementary school burned down — all these unfortunates, and more, committed suicide to atone for their actions. Their motivations were described with the old words: no excuse, no apology, dishonorable, and so forth. But by the turn of the twentieth century, such suicides were commonly explained in terms of *sekinin*.

In a preachy definition of the word in a middle-school ethics text from 1903, responsibility meant discharging the "vocation" each person has by virtue of his status and duty. One "must not evade responsibility," treat it lightly, or fail to fulfill it. After these moral injunctions came the caution: "In earlier times a samurai apologized to the world for losing his honor by committing suicide; and although one ought not to follow such a custom today, one must nonetheless value one's status and be deeply aware of one's responsibility."[13] Most Japanese at the time agreed that such a samurai custom was long out of date. Yet when General Nogi famously followed the Meiji Emperor to death in 1912 by disemboweling himself, he left a note regretting his loss of the regimental colors in the samurai rebellion thirty-five years before. The newspapers immediately praised his "powerful feeling of responsibility" and his "strong resolve to make his responsibility clear through his death" — a sense of individual responsibility (*jiko no sekinin*), one writer lamented, which was sadly lacking in today's youth.[14] In the ultranationalist 1930s, this lineage of *sekinin*-by-suicide was hailed as a distinctively "Japanese sense of responsibility."[15] Others took a different view. Headlines about "responsibility suicides" in the 1920s led some to criticize the common linkage of "death and responsibility" that claimed young lives needlessly. One editorial writer expressed his "social uneasiness" about this trend, rejecting the notion that death releases a person from responsibility and describing suicide instead as "craven behavior that impedes mutual coexistence in society."[16] In general parlance, however, taking personal "responsibility" had by then become an established—and respected—explanation for suicide.

During the same decades in the early twentieth century, the word "*sekinin*" appeared in frequent exhortations to women to fulfill their responsibility-by-role, to exercise their responsibility in society, to "marry responsibly and take responsibility in 'modern love.'" "Autonomy, responsibility, creativity" were heralded as the three principles necessary for achieving women's suffrage.[17] Mothers were to instruct their children to take care of toys given to them as gifts so they would learn how to "fulfill their responsibilities" to others.[18] Here was another instance of old notions in new words, some parceled out paternalistically by men, others brandished by women seeking equality. As with suicide, it seems that *sekinin* entered the vocabulary of gender expectations without altering them very much.

These usages are relatively easy to track, but the origins of the common colloquial use of the word that peppers Japanese speech today are less clear. It appeared suddenly—or so it seems—in some works of early-twentieth-century fiction. The archetypically modern novelist Natsume Sōseki has his characters use it both to characterize others and to reproach themselves: "That's his fault"; "It's my responsibility, so I'll do it"; "It's a lot of responsibility"; "You can't just be irresponsible (*musekinin*)"; and many more. In the well-known novel *Kokoro* of 1914, the young protagonist praises his mentor's wife, whom he admires, for almost never using the "so-called new words that had begun to be fashionable at that time." Yet a few lines later, the wife says, "You don't think I'm responsible, do you?" Perhaps "*sekinin*" no longer counted as a new (and certainly not fashionable) word. Nonetheless, it does seem that Sōseki's use of it had a great deal to do with his conception of the modern self and its frictions with social convention. In this early stage of self-conscious modernity, *sekinin* possessed a psychological and philosophical valence that it has since lost, at least in colloquial speech. Later, as movies were made about the "re-sponsibility of love," and newfangled radios were advertised as having "responsibility attached" (a guarantee, perhaps), the word moved away from the psychic association with the modern self, even as it remained firmly ensconced in the personal language of everyday life.[19]

Over time, the main motion of the word "*sekinin*" thus lay in the trans-formation and vernacularization of the new meanings of responsibility as something an individual must do and as the obligation to bear the conse-quences of one's actions, responsibility one "could not evade." Although this meaning overlapped with responsibility of status or role, it had been individualized — as in Sōseki's novels — in terms of the relation between modern subjectivity and society, a weight it had not borne before. This occurred by dint of wide circulation, social saturation across class and status, and a polysemic fit with everyday life. Once attached to the obliga-tions of the individual *qua* individual in the context of human relations, *sekinin* entered the core of Japanese social vocabulary. A person either "has responsibility" or he doesn't — a judgment of worth in a single salient phrase. This trajectory suggests the generalization that words move fastest and farthest when they resonate in the vernacular and make sense in dif-ferent social dialects.

Responsibility in Politics

The translingual practices of modernity did not in fact develop smoothly, even with such a low-profile word as "*sekinin*." Unlike its relatively easy vernacularization as personal responsibility, its movement in the political realm shows a pattern in which new and old meanings tangled with awk-ward results. One reason for the tangle was the two characters used to write "*sekinin*." Anyone who saw those characters in the 1870s — even without having encountered the compound before — would think of of-fice, official duties, position, vocation. This visual connotation attached to the characters, no matter the new meaning of the compound. When it came to deciding the shape of the modern polity after 1868 and the con-tent of the constitution to be promulgated in 1889, the notion of office and position stood at the center of political debate.

I think of this as the rabbit-and-duck phase of words in motion. It derives from Wittgenstein's claim that the Jastrow figure of an entwined rabbit-duck gestalt can be perceived either as a duck or as a rabbit, but not both at the same time. So *sekinin* may have appeared to the first generation who used it as a duck—the duck they were familiar with from the days of samurai bureaucracy and hereditary status hierarchy. Others, often younger, saw a rabbit—the rabbit of "responsible cabinets" associated with the British parliamentary system and political parties. Crucial to the word's motion, however, was this double vision, which made it *appear* as if both constituencies understood the same word, an appearance that proved deceiving.

The illusory alignment between new and old meanings characterized many political words during the period of semantic avalanche. Some rabbit–ducks were produced by the neologisms themselves. The compound created to translate European words for "rights" (*kenri*), combined the character for "power" or "authority" with the one for "advantage" or "benefit." The very look of the word might have led Japanese of the time to understand—and in many cases, fear—the demands of the Freedom and Popular Rights Movement as being about "power much more than rights."[20] Of course, this opposition movement was indeed about power, but the duck–rabbit point is that the word for rights itself harbored the character for "power" or "authority" within it. And "authority" in the Japanese political world meant the state, which was perceived as the main obstacle to popular rights. Fox in the henhouse might be an appropriate metaphor in this instance.

In a slightly different but similarly denaturing way, the word for freedom smuggled in an old meaning to the new translation of Western words for liberty. The Chinese compound used for freedom (*jiyū*) meant doing as one was inclined, with the connotation of willfulness.[21] So freedom could be a positive good, as in freedom of the press and of religion, both important issues in the 1870s and 1880s. And it could be the basis for representative government, as expressed in the name of the Liberal, or Freedom, Party, founded in 1881. But freedom also carried the negative freight of selfishness, a term evoked by the government to derogate the partisan politics of the new political parties. In short, the rabbit of political liberty was also the duck of self-interest. And since both "rights" and "freedom," like "responsibility," were vernacularized early, in the 1870s, these duck–rabbits brought their dual meanings with them into political life. To generalize about the duck and the rabbit: When words move, they are often understood in divergent ways; the greater the ambiguity, the greater the appearance of naturalization, an appearance belied by the contradictory meanings carried forward in the words.

For *sekinin*, the duck–rabbit impact animated the debates over the nature of responsibility in the new constitutional system, which went into effect in 1890. The opposition, broadly the Freedom and Popular Rights Movement, wanted "responsible cabinets," its term for party cabinets responsible to the parliament, or Diet. The fierce public debate, much of it in the press, was led by the political generation inspired by the idea of a parliament since the 1870s. In 1885, one man even named his son Sekinai (from "*sekinin naikaku*," something like "Rescab," poor thing) in the hopes that responsible cabinets would soon be realized in Japan.[22]

But the government in power in the 1880s had little use for such an idea, not only because the oligarchs preferred to retain their power, but also because they had decided on Prussian rather than British or French models of representative government. They preferred what they called "transcendental cabinets," where "people who are ministers of state have a duty to assist the Monarch. . . . In no case ought they to assume a responsibility towards other bodies such as the Diet; still less can one see any reason why they should undertake any responsibility towards the people as a whole."[23] There it was: the rabbit of parliamentary government and the duck of a bureaucratic imperial state, both expressed by the same word, "*sekinin*." The opposition understood responsibility in its new parliamentary meaning; the government took responsibility of office to mean something more like the traditional Confucian duty of officials to "advise" their lord. When it came to the constitution, the ducks won, proving "the rights of the state" stronger than "the rights of the people." In the constitution, the emperor was the "sacred and inviolable" head of state, while the "ministers of state serve [advise] the emperor and are responsible (*seki ni ninsu*) to him." The people were accorded "rights and duties," a term that paired rights — the word with "authority" in the midst of it — with the old and unambiguous word for "duty," avoiding any bifocal effect that might have accompanied the newer liberal uses of the word "*sekinin*."

In political practice, however, the parties continued to pursue the goals of parliamentary responsibility. They could do this because the Constitution of 1889 was something of a rabbit–duck itself, establishing both a parliament and the supremacy of imperial authority. In 1924, the first real party cabinet took office, followed in 1925 by universal manhood suffrage. But the hybrid system also enabled bureaucratic cabinets to return in the early 1930s and remain in power as "advisers" to the emperor through the years of aggression and war. Indeed, this conflict constituted the main story of Japanese politics between 1890 and 1945, prompting a further generalization about the way words move: As words conflict with experience, discursive frictions rub institutional abrasions, keeping the word in motion and producing changes both in meaning and in practice.

The institutional abrasion that was the imperial state was removed with Japan's defeat in 1945. The new Constitution of 1947 transformed the emperor from absolute authority into the "symbol of the state" and made the cabinet responsible. "The advice and the approval of the cabinet shall be required for all acts of the emperor in matters of state, and the cabinet shall be responsible therefor (*sono sekinin o ou*)." True enough that Americans wrote the new constitution, but true, too, that the discourse and practices of political responsibility now had a history dating as far back as the 1870s. Japanese voices resumed the old debate within weeks after the war, well before the Americans intervened. The main cause of the defeat, said one politician, was the monopolizing of politics by the military and the bureaucrats, and a "people without responsibility for politics. . . . It is now the proper duty of the people to return to the original form of constitutional responsible politics (*sekinin seiji*)".[24] Political *sekinin*, once a diasporic word from the West, had long since acquired at least oppositional citizenship. In this sense, the postwar political system marked a return of the rabbit, only now under circumstances that reduced or eliminated the double understanding of *sekinin* and thereby altered its political effect.

Some argue that contemporary Japanese politics still has a responsibility problem, posed as the question of whether politicians feel more responsible to their party than to the people. This, combined with the strength of the national bureaucracy, suggests the shadowy outlines of a duck still concealed in the democratic woodwork, but if duck there be, it no longer captures the political meaning of the word "*sekinin*."

War Responsibility

Where Germans once discussed "war guilt," Japanese speak of "war responsibility" (*sensō sekinin*), a term that gained greater import in public discourse around the world over the course of the twentieth century. Appropriately enough for the subject of war, here the motion of "*sekinin*" traced a more transnational path than that of the word as used in domestic politics. It began as a legal term but was transformed over time into both a social and an individual matter, tracing a motion common to the global transits of the word "responsibility" in many of its meanings.

The twentieth-century concept of war responsibility emerged after the First World War in connection with German war guilt. The report of the Commission of Responsibilities at the Paris Peace Conference in 1919 named as culpable acts those "that provoked the world war" and "violations of the laws and customs of war and the laws of humanity."[25] Japanese diplomats participated in the conference as allies of the victors, but at home in Japan the awareness of this new "responsibility for making war" (*kaisen sekinin*) was largely confined to government and legal circles.

Not so the words "war responsibility" after the Second World War. This time, of course, it was Japanese leaders who were charged as "guilty of conspiracy to wage aggressive war" in the Tokyo War Crimes Tribunal of 1946–48. After the defeat, Japanese did not wait for the Allies to debate questions of war responsibility. Even under imperial government and, later, American Occupation censorship, the press carried a stream of editorials, articles, and letters about who was responsible for starting the war or, in some cases, for causing the defeat. The self-serving government slogan "a hundred million repenting as one," prompted some of those hundred million to voice their keen objection. "The government says the Japanese people as a whole should bear responsibility for the defeat. . . . And who was it that made Tōjō the prime minister, and what did our Diet representatives do? Aren't they elected to protect us from the military cliques?" wrote one reader to the *Asahi* newspaper in late September 1945.[26] While most focused on the military and the government who had caused this "reckless war," others suggested that the people, too, had war responsibility, since they had permitted the ascension of these leaders to power.

The Diet debated different drafts of a "Resolution on War Responsibility" throughout the fall of 1945, discussing the responsibility of the cabinet, the Diet, the bureaucracy, the people "one by one," the capitalists, the imperialists, the intellectuals, the press — but not the emperor, who was instead credited with the decision to end the war. It was hard, some said, to pinpoint the locus of responsibility, an insight famously expressed by the scholar Maruyama Masao in his description of the prewar polity. In this "system of irresponsibility," the buck never stopped, referred ever upward toward the emperor who, when it reached him, had been placed "beyond responsibility" by the rabbit–duck Constitution of 1889.[27] The consensus in the postwar Diet debates — which jibed with the views of the Americans and the Tokyo War Crimes Tribunal — was that the individuals "most responsible" were the military and top government leaders who had planned and executed the conspiracy to wage aggressive war.[28] The emperor, protected from prosecution by the Americans, remained on the throne, now the symbol both of the state and of a people victimized by their leaders (in his case, the "advisers" responsible to him). A similar sleight of memory occurred in Germany, France, and other countries, where initial accounts of war responsibility focused on the villains at the top, freeing the people to imagine themselves as their victims.

Victims or not, Japanese soon came to know the phrase "war responsibility," as the meaning of the word "*sekinin*" broadened beyond the narrow confines of war leadership and war crimes to society and the individual. In 1946, the film director Itami Mansaku wrote that "everyone says they were deceived, but no one says 'I deceived people.' . . . The people think they were deceived by the military and the bureaucracy, the military and the bureaucrats say they were deceived by those higher up, and those higher up say they were deceived by those above them, until finally it must come down to one or two individuals." This, he said, is not possible. And anyway, "Being among the deceived doesn't mean one is free of all responsibility. . . . A nation that can say 'we were deceived' and feel fine about it will be deceived again, and no doubt we are already beginning to be deceived by another lie right now."[29] Further debates about war responsibility occurred in every subsequent decade, keeping the now familiar words in motion. At times conservatives reacted against the "victors' justice" of the war crimes trial and sought to re-ascribe war responsibility to the Allies. More often it was the progressives who urged Japanese to confront both their war and their "postwar responsibility," by which they meant the long years of official amnesia about Japan's imperialist past and wartime atrocities in Asia.[30] The thorough diffusion of the term "war responsibility" suggests the generalization that public debate, especially in times of crisis, can create new meanings, which once set in motion become part of the collective social vocabulary.

But knowing words does not mean acting on them, and it took more than common social knowledge to change Japanese attitudes toward their responsibility in the Asia–Pacific War, which began with aggression in Manchuria in 1931, included eight years of total war against China beginning in 1937, and did not end until after the atomic bombings in 1945. The unfreezing of Japanese war memory did not really occur until 1989, when by historical coincidence the Cold War ended and the wartime emperor, Hirohito, died in the same year. The emperor had been gone only days when polls showed that a quarter of the people thought that, "of course," the emperor had war responsibility, and constitutional experts publicly rehashed the distinction between legal responsibility, which the emperor may or may not have had, and moral responsibility, which as the supreme and sacred head of state he surely did possess. New historical inquiries after his death concluded that Hirohito had indeed been an active participant in the events and decisions of the war. But more important for the movement of the words "war responsibility" was the first public statement in 1991 of a former "comfort woman," one of hundreds of thousands of Asian women enslaved as prostitutes by the Imperial Japanese Army. Demands for apology and compensation arose all over Asia, not only from "comfort women" but also from victims of the Nanjing Massacre, Japan's biological warfare, and other wartime atrocities. After nearly half a century, Japanese were brought face to face with both their war and their postwar responsibilities in the harsh spotlight of Asian pressure and international criticism.

Crucially important here is that the words "war responsibility" had continued in motion in other places during the decades of Japan's frozen memory. In West Germany, the finger of responsibility, which had once pointed emphatically at the demonic leadership of Hitler and his henchmen, moved first to implicate large numbers of middle-level participants in crimes of war and the Holocaust, and then widened the arc of responsibility to encompass broad social complicity that included bystanders as well as perpetrators. Similar expansions of meaning occurred in France and Italy as well. From the mid-1980s, Asian, Western, and Japanese critics alike made repeated and unfavorable comparisons between Japan and Germany in respect to public memory of the war. By the time Japanese did come to confront their wartime past in the 1990s, the meaning of "war responsibility" had changed radically from the months after the Second World War, when trying handfuls or hundreds of perpetrators in war crimes tribunals had seemed to settle such questions once and for all.

Now individuals were making claims in court against their own and foreign governments for compensation, restitution, and apology for past injustices. This was not the state-to-state liability of Wheaton's nineteenth-century international law or the reparations exacted by peace treaties but a demand that nations take responsibility for the harm done to individual citizens of their own and other countries. Scholars referred not to collective guilt but to a "potentially new international morality" in which perpetrators willingly acknowledged and chose to compensate their victims or their descendants.[31] The name of the German fund established in 2000 to compensate slave labor — Fund for Memory, Responsibility, and the Future — used words that now widely signified an amplification of the notion of responsibility, which linked the past to the future and made claims on both nations and their citizens. At the same time, since compensation could never be sufficient to the suffering, open and official recognition of responsibility became ever more important. Thus some comfort women rejected Japanese monetary compensation, and others refused the personal letter of apology from Japanese leaders because it did not constitute an official apology from the state.

Much has been written about the current politics of apology, from Australia's national "I'm Sorry Day" to recognize the depredations of aboriginal society to the Vatican's apologizing for two millennia of injustice to Jews, women, minorities, and others. But Marina Warner was surely right in saying that the concern with public apology reflected "an ever deeper investment in concepts such as responsibility, blame, accountability, which search out individual human agents and perpetrators."[32] This deepening of the concept of responsibility changed the understanding of official responsibility, too. As ideas of impunity altered, heads of state — including Chile's Augusto Pinochet — lost their immunity and were brought to trial. Even the notoriously resistant Japanese courts showed signs of change. Although they continued to invoke legal grounds to deny claims for monetary compensation, their rulings increasingly recognized the "responsibility" of the state toward Chinese, Korean, and other victims. The change in language was significant even if it did not mean the end of the long juridical battle over Japan's responsibility for its wartime acts.[33]

The activism of the former comfort women and their supporters made an important contribution to the transnational legal discourse of war responsibility, helping to get rape designated both a war crime and a crime against humanity, a crime tried for the first time at the International Criminal Court for the Former Yugoslavia in The Hague and now included in the statute for the International Criminal Court. In this instance, the words "war responsibility" and their claims moved from Asia to the world, with real outcomes both for women's rights and for the definition of crimes of war. Another generalization, then: Even well-worn words can gain new edge in changing times, with sometimes powerful results.

The transnational expansion of the idea of war responsibility brought new problems and revived old ones — notably, questions of collective and transgenerational responsibility. Most people rejected older concepts of collective guilt, arguing that only individuals could be responsible for actions past or present. The question became: To what extent must individuals answer for the nation, and if so, for how many generations? Was there no escape from the nation, no refuge from the national "we" even in an allegedly global age? In what way were young Germans responsible for the Holocaust or young Japanese for the Nanjing Massacre? Sixty years and several generations later, the answers were likely to be different, but they could not be so different that past injustices remained unredressed. In 2004, the German chancellor commented that "we should talk less of guilt (*Schuld*) and much more of responsibility (*Verantwortung*) in regard to future generations."[34] Guilt, he suggested, belonged to the wartime generation, but responsibility remained for present and future Germans to shoulder.

In Japan, the conservative government and the nationalists short-circuited this discussion, at least on the official level. In the late 1990s, the right wing called for Japan to become a so-called normal nation by ending its "masochistic" obsession with the wartime past. Yet when it came to "war responsibility," the definition of normal was no longer what it used to be. The words had moved. From 2001 to 2006, the prime minister's visits to Yasukuni Shrine — where not only the war dead but convicted war criminals were enshrined — disqualified Japan as a normal nation in the eyes of much of the world. By 2005, Japanese public opinion seemed to agree, with polls showing that 75 percent believed that the debate over Japan's "war responsibility" was "insufficient."[35] One public intellectual suggested redefining "*sekinin*" as "the capacity to respond" in order to introduce the other-directed aspect of the Western words for "response"-ibility. With such a "responsive responsibility," he argued, Japanese could confront both their war and their postwar responsibility — in German terms, both their guilt and their responsibility — and do so in accord with transnational norms.[36] An antinuclear scholar in Nagasaki advocated "peace responsibility" as a way to take responsibility for war in the past and peace in the future.[37] Some Western scholars and critics argued that any individual who took national pride in the good parts of a country's past also had "national responsibility" for the bad things that happened.[38] But this was easier said than practiced, as the debate over reparations for slavery in the United States made quite clear.

"War responsibility" was now part of a widening ambit of something called "responsibility for history," and in this public and political, national and transnational definition, "responsibility" remained a word very much in motion. However it moved in the future, its meaning — while not singular — would not be confined to a single nation or language. In this respect, *sekinin* toward the past (and future) was the Japanese inflection of a large and vexing global issue. This suggests the general proposition that the movement of a word in any given society is affected by the continued movement of the word elsewhere, and that this interaction is more intense in today's world than ever before.

Social Responsibility

The same may be said of other meanings of "*sekinin*" that ramified and spread during the closing decades of the twentieth century. "Responsibility" joined the global jet stream of words and practices swirling about the earth, affecting local rhetorical and social weather. The proliferation of varieties of responsibility was striking in many languages. Japanese spoke now of administrative responsibility, corporate responsibility, managerial responsibility, economic responsibility, social responsibility, medical responsibility, international responsibility, environmental responsibility, product responsibility (liability), and more. In January 2004, the prime minister stated that it was the responsibility of a ruling party "to develop the buds of reform into a large tree." Having mastered that metaphor — though not the reality — he declared that it was Japan's "responsibility as a member of the international community" to provide both financial and human contributions, inseparable "like the two wheels of a cart," by sending troops to America's war in Iraq.[39]

The ubiquity of the word "responsibility" did not go unnoticed. Listing the series of political scandals that plagued Japan for two decades, a 1995 newspaper article parodied the way "politicians love the word *sekinin*: responsible change, responsible opposition party, politics responsible for results. . . . The opposition party says 'take responsibility and resign,' to which the prime minister responds, 'because I am responsible, I cannot resign.'" The writer remarked that in samurai society disembowelment was considered manly, but after the war resignation replaced death. Thinking that "if I resign they won't come after me," politicians take responsibility by putting on a "Resignation Act" when their real responsibility is to tell the people the truth.[40] Taking responsibility in this way could work as a shield against action: Accepting responsibility (in the passive sense), an individual resigned, and for him that might be the end of it. Resignation might "release" the individual from the consequences of his actions, but it was not necessarily socially useful or honorable behavior. The same applied to apologies, which once offered could mean the end of responsibility rather than its fulfillment.

The word "irresponsibility" (*musekinin*) commonly appeared in descriptions of public life, from the irresponsibility of corrupt politicians, corporations that pollute the environment, arrogant bureaucrats, and careless pet owners, to women who refuse to marry and bear children. A series of popular film comedies in the 1960s entitled "Japan's Age of Irresponsibility" featured a man called Taira Hitoshi (the name means "average") who violated the samurai–salaryman work ethic of high-growth Japan and sort of slithered his way to the top, ending up a company president. The phrase "age of irresponsibility" soon entered the language, applied to serious and frivolous matters alike.

Many of these usages were thin, diluting the meaning of the word and depleting its power. Indeed, the law of trivialization affected both the semantic and moral content of responsibility in many societies. Some variants of the word, however, were thicker and suggested a motion that directed "*sekinin*" outward toward society. Rather than responsibility of office, role, or the individual, it was responsibility *toward* rather than *for* something. Medical responsibility, for example, meant that doctors owed their patients the truth about their illness. The Information Disclosure Law of 2001, which had been debated for decades in terms of the "right to know," was now characterized as the "government's responsibility to explain its activities to the people." The law was also associated with a new word for responsibility that entered common usage in the 1990s: "*akauntabiritei*" (accountability), glossed as the "responsibility to explain" (*setsumei sekinin*). In Japan's case, this globally circulating word did not appear because of pressure from the IMF or the World Bank to conform to standards of transparency or accountability. Rather, it was imported from American English to emphasize the responsibility of public institutions toward the people. Its proponents argued that because there was no Japanese word for the "responsibility to explain," the government had felt no pressure to do so. However unpersuasive this claim, the increased emphasis on *akauntabiritei* in public discourse showed that, in general, words can move more readily than practices, but move enough words, and repeat them often enough, and practices — if more slowly — move, too.

A tainted-blood scandal of the late 1990s intensified public outrage at the black box of government and the close relations with business derived from the custom of former bureaucrats retiring — "descending from heaven" — to comfortable jobs in private companies. Three former presidents of a pharmaceutical company (former officials with the Ministry of Health and Welfare) were indicted as "criminally responsible," as was a former director of the ministry. Their responsibility toward the public was upheld with stiffer penalties than expected — stiffer, in fact, than those received by French officials on trial in a similar scandal in 1999, one of whom famously said that she "felt responsible but not guilty" (*responsable mais non coupable*), when in fact she was both.

The expansion of social responsibility in Japan owed a great deal to the thriving networks of domestic and transnational NGOs, which worked tirelessly on behalf of causes from peace to the environment. Many of them fit Václav Havel's description of those "who approach the world with humility, but also with an increased sense of responsibility, who wage a struggle for every good thing."[41] The reorientation of responsibility outward toward society represented a gradual but significant change in the meaning of *sekinin*.

Not to paint too rosy a picture of the state of responsibility in Japan, a public eruption of the word in April 2004 revealed its darker side. Three Japanese civilians were taken hostage in Iraq, with the threat that they would be killed unless Japan withdrew its troops from the country. When they were finally released and returned home, they (and their families) faced a barrage of criticism from their fellow citizens and from members of the government, who accused them of failing in their "individual (or self-) responsibility" (*jiko sekinin*) and "causing trouble to a great many people." This public pillorying of the victims for having put themselves in harm's way for humanitarian or journalistic purposes suggested the opposite of an outward-directed vector of responsibility and cast a petty shadow of social meanness over the word "*sekinin*."

Indeed, the late 1990s was tagged "the age of self-responsibility," referring to neoliberal market-centered policies like the "big bang" of financial deregulation in 1998, when investors were warned that they were now "self-responsible" for their investments. The term spread like an oil slick over the surface of many social policies, choking off measures for a more just society. Patients could be blamed for their diseases by redefining adult-onset diabetes, for example, as a "lifestyle disease."[42] Salarymen restructured out of their jobs were said to be self-responsible for choosing to work for that company in the first place. The poor and less privileged could be held responsible for their condition as the state fled from its social responsibilities.[43] These uses of "self-responsibility" took *sekinin* back to the days when it was easier for society to blame the poor for their poverty than to do something to help alleviate it.

In many so-called advanced societies today, responsibility is repeatedly called for and repeatedly evaded, both by states and by individuals. For this reason, some critics claim that the word is *too* narrowly centered on the individual or the state. Although both are enjoined to "take responsibility" — whether for or toward something — the moral charge is often couched in terms of self- or national interest. These critics call instead for a "relational theory of responsibility," which stresses the fact that humans are social beings and are responsible always — and only — in relation to others.[44] Or, invoking the Zulu concept of *ubuntu* that proved so important in taking responsibility before the Truth and Reconciliation Commission in South Africa: "A person depends on other people to be a person."[45] Levinas said it, too, as did Derrida: Without the other, there is no self. Here, in a word that has not yet moved into many languages, we are called upon to be "co-responsible" for one another.[46]

Global Transits

These meanings of *sekinin* that I have separated for analytic purposes in fact overlapped, blended, sometimes oxymoronically self-contradicted, and otherwise traveled with their ambiguities intact. The Japanese version of the global transit of "responsibility" began as a nineteenth-century Western term of legal liability, a definition the word retains today. But this was followed by an unexpected expansion of meaning that pried open new space between the individual and his role or status, introducing the moral and subjective "feeling of responsibility" (*sekininkan*) associated with the modern self. This ascription of responsibility to a person *as a person* remains the most common vernacular meaning of *sekinin* to this day. The charge to the individual is probably intensified by the fact that responsibility in Japan remains closely conjoined to whatever it is one is supposed to do by virtue of one's position — the old meaning of the two characters *seki* and *nin* before the new word was created. And in Japan, as elsewhere, the ever increasing emphasis on individual, political, and social responsibility, whether for the national past or the collective environmental future, has produced a proliferation of responsibilities articulated — if not fulfilled — in every corner of the globe. For an ordinary word, "responsibility" has moved far and done a lot of work, with a great deal more still to do.

Notes

(Japanese last names first and italicized)

My thanks to *Umezaki* Toru and Alan Tansman for their generous help with this essay.

1. Jean Greisch, "L'amour de monde et la Principe Responsabilité," in *La responsabilité: La condition de notre humanité* (Paris: Éditions Autrement, 1995), 72.

2. Douglas R. Howland, *Translating the West: Language and Political Reason in Nineteenth-Century Japan* (Honolulu: University of Hawaii Press, 2002).

3. Arjun Appadurai, *Modernity at Large: Cultural Dimensions of Globalization* (Minneapolis: University of Minnesota Press, 1996), 36.

4. Reinhart Koselleck, *Futures Past: On the Semantics of Historical Time* (Cambridge, Mass.: MIT Press, 1985), 231–66.

5. The first edition of Shōgakkan's twenty-volume *Nihon kokugo daijiten*, published in the 1970s, carried no examples of "*sekinin*" before the 1870s; the second edition (2000–2002) added two earlier examples but seemingly rare of use: *Nihon kokugo daijiten*, ed. Nihon daijiten kankōkai (Tokyo: Shōgakkan, 1972–76, 2000–2002).

6. "*Sekinin*" does not appear in the famous Hepburn dictionary until the third edition of 1886; the seventh edition of 1903 defined it as "responsibility, obligation, duty, accountability," which by then was accurate: J. C. Hebon, *Eiwa Waei gorin shūsei* (A Japanese–English and English–Japanese Dictionary) (Tokyo: Maruzen, 1886, 1903).

7. *Endō* Sakiko, *Meiji jidaigo no kenkyū — goi to bunshō* (Tokyo: Meiji shoin, 1981), 158 ff.

8. *Matsui* Toshihiko, "Kan'yakugo no Nihongo e no ukeai: Kan'yaku 'Bankoku kōhō no baai,'" *Bunrin* 36 (2002): 21–46.

9. Henry Wheaton, *Elements of International Law*, 8th ed. (Boston: Little, Brown, 1866), 17–18.

10. *Matsui*, "Kan'yakugo no Nihongo e no ukeai," 41.

11. Thanks to electronic databases, I found thousands of appearances of "*sekinin*" in the *Yomiuri shinbun* from 1874 to 1945, and nearly ten thousand in headlines alone in the *Asahi shinbun* from 1945 to 1999: *Yomiuri shinbunsha media senryaku kyoku deeta beesu* (2001–2); *Asahi shinbun sengo midashi deeta beesu* (2000). The circulation figures

are from James Huffman, *Creating a Public: People and Press in Meiji Japan* (Honolulu: University of Hawaii Press, 1997), 60, 93, 142.

12. *Yomiuri shinbun*, 24 December 1886, 22 April 1887, 5 March 1887.

13. *Inoue* Tetsujirō and *Ōshima* Yoshinaga, *Chūgaku shūshin kyōkasho* (Tokyo: Bungakusha, 1903), 44, 46.

14. *Yomiuri shinbun*, 21–22 September 1912.

15. *Hasegawa* Nyozekan, "Nihonteki na sekininkan," *Yomiuri shinbun*, 12 March 1936.

16. *Yomiuri shinbun*, 11 May 1921, 24 July 1922.

17. Ibid., 5 May 1914, 19 May 1914, 11 November 1920, 29 October 1935.

18. *Takashima* Beihō, *Haha no tame* (Tokyo: Gengendō, 1903), 47–48.

19. The movie *Ren'ai no sekinin* (Responsibilities of love; 1936) was advertised as treating the "various problems of love marriage and women's economic livelihood": *Yomiuri shinbun*, 10 October 1936; radio advertisement, 20 January 1927.

20. *Yanabu* Akira, "The Concept of 'Right,'" trans. Joshua A. Fogel, *Sino-Japanese Studies* 13, no. 2 (March 2001): 74.

21. An early and famous mistranslation from the Dutch made this association clear. "The world situation tends toward greater selfishness (*vrijheid*) every year": Howland, *Translating the West*, 102–103.

22. "*Rescab*" from *re*sponsible *cab*inets. *Yomiuri shinbun*, 13 September 1885.

23. *Tsuzuki* Keiroku, "Chôzenshugi" (1892), quoted in Junji *Banno*, *The Establishment of the Japanese Constitutional System* (London: Routledge, 1992), 31–32.

24. Speech in the Diet reported in "Sekinin seiji no kakuritsu," *Asahi shinbun*, 6 September 1945.

25. Michael R. Marrus, *The Nuremberg War Crimes Trial, 1945–46: A Documentary History* (Boston: Bedford/St. Martin's Press, 1997), 1–11.

26. "Koe," *Asahi shinbun*, 25 September 1945.

27. Masao *Maruyama*, "Thought and Behavior Patterns of Japan's Wartime Leaders" (1949), in *Thought and Behavior in Modern Japanese Politics* (Oxford: Oxford University Press, 1969). The phrase is "*musekinin no taikei.*"

28. Diet debates: *Kanpō* (gōgai), 6 September–2 December 1945.

29. *Itami* Mansaku, "Sensō sekininsha no mondai," *Eiga shunjū* (August 1946), in *Itami Mansaku zenshū*, vol. 1 (Tokyo: Chikuma shobō, 1961), 205–10.

30. E.g., *Ōnuma* Yasuaki, *Tokyo saiban kara sengo sekinin no shisō* e (Tokyo: Tōshindō, 1987).

31. Elazar Barkan, *The Guilt of Nations: Restitution and Negotiating Historical Injustices* (New York: W. W. Norton, 2000), ix.

32. Marina Warner, "Amnesty Lecture in Human Rights," *Times Literary Supplement*, 1 August 2003.

33. Since the mid-1990s, suits brought by former comfort women, forced laborers, Chinese victims of exploded gas canisters and biological warfare, and others have been defeated (with some exceptions, which are routinely overturned on appeal) on the grounds of expired statute of limitations and settlement by postwar treaties. But the narratives of the rulings have increasingly acknowledged both the facts of the wartime acts and Japanese "responsibility" for them.

34. Gerhard Schröder in *Le Figaro*, 5 June 2004.

35. *Mainichi shinbun*, 15 August 2005.

36. *Takahashi* Tetsuya, *Sengo sekininron* (Tokyo: Kōdansha, 1999), 17–54.

37. *Takahashi* Shinji, "Heiwa sekinin: heiwa kenpō o mamoru tame ni," *Akebono* (February 2005): 14.

38. Farid Abdel-Nour, "National Responsibility," *Political Theory* 31, no. 5 (October 2003): 693–719.

39. *Koizumi* Junichirō, speech to the Diet, 19 January 2004: *Asahi shinbun*, 20 January 2004.

40. *Asahi shinbun*, 29 November 1995.

41. Václav Havel, "The Responsibility of Intellectuals," *New York Review of Books* 42, no. 11 (22 June 1995): 36–37.

42. "Lifestyle disease," is *"seikatsu shūkan byō."*

43. *Saitō* Takao, *Anshin no fashizumu: Shihai saretagaru hitobito* (Tokyo: Iwanami shinsho, 2004), 17–24.

44. Peter Cane, *Responsibility in Law and Morality* (Oxford: Hart Publishing, 2002).

45. Michael Battle, *Reconciliation: The Ubuntu Theology of Desmond Tutu* (Cleveland: Pilgrim Press, 1997), 39.

46. The German *"Mitverantwortung"* has been used in connection with war responsibility, from Karl Jaspers in 1946 to Günter Grass in 2006, but there is no equivalent Japanese word, and the English counterpart is not standard either.

WORDS UNSPOKEN

DRISS MAGHRAOUI

'Ilmaniyya, Laïcité, Sécularisme/Secularism
in Morocco

What is "secularism" in Morocco today? In January 2008, an editorial in a liberal newspaper put the question: "What does it mean to be modern if *laïcité* (secularism) is not openly debated?"[1] It seems that the gradual opening of the regime under King Mohammed VI since 1999 may have created a space for renewed debate on the subject, which has a long history in modern Morocco. "Secularism" is expressed in the Arabic word " *'ilmaniyya*," as well as in the French "*laïcité*" and "*sécularisme*." The interplay of these terms is not simply a reflection of Morocco's cosmopolitan heritage. Rather, it is the result of fierce debate: Are these words, and the concepts to which they refer, colonial imports? Or are they part of Morocco's national and cultural history? When evangelical Christians from the United States, such as William J. Murray, the chairman of the Religious Freedom Coalition, call for the "secularization of Morocco," secularism seems easily identifiable as part of an "alien" or imperialist agenda.[2] When Islamists, such as Abdessalam Yassine, speak of *laïcité* as a colonial "weapon," we recognize the grain of truth in his contention.[3] Here I argue, however, that the words in use today are also signs of a longer, more contradictory history *within* Morocco itself. Some of the discussions over the years avoided these key words entirely in their active endorsement of many of the concepts condemned today as (colonially defined) "secularism." In contrast to such evasion, by bringing these *words* to the foreground of debate, contemporary political discussion in Morocco — on both the left and the right and among both "secular" and "religious" sectors — has become charged with the need to justify itself in relation to both the *definition* and the *derivation* of " *'ilmaniyya*," "*laïcité*," and "*sécularisme*." I begin by asking why these different words for secularism, which are so important today, were so long absent from public debate in Moroccan history. Only by understanding this absence, I believe, can we comprehend the words in motion in the current debates.

My reading of the history of Morocco suggests a series of ironic twists in regard to both the words and the strategic silences that relate to "secularism" in all its guises. First, despite French commitments to *laïcité* and its evocation of a secular state, France did not establish such a state in colonial Morocco. Second, because Moroccan elites stood outside the debates about secularism going on elsewhere in North Africa and the Middle East, they were able to introduce "secular" ideas into nationalist discourse without mentioning the forbidden words or dealing consistently with their meanings and political implications. That is, nationalist political models from Egypt and Turkey came to Morocco without their "secularism" marked in so many words. In the 1910s and 1920s, Moroccan nationalists carefully maintained their distance from the words for secularism, arguing that the ideas that others might call secularist were in reality Moroccan and Islamic ideas. In the late 1950s, the monarchy further pushed secular models of government, but without abandoning religion; indeed, the monarchy supported a religious rhetoric of government. As the Moroccan state increased secularization at the political and institutional levels, it avoided publicizing changes that might have downplayed its religious legitimacy. Ironically, too, the religious rhetoric endorsed by the monarchy was picked up by its critics and used to denounce the idea of "secularism." The increasing presence of the Islamic movement has now triggered new motion in these words. As a result of this ambiguous history, a number of political thinkers of different ideological stripes are now forced to position themselves in relation to secularism. Most important, they are asked to take a stand on whether "*'ilmaniyya*" is a *translation* in the imperialist and alien sense or a concept that is compatible with an authentic Islam. Different stances are of course possible, but there is little choice but to participate in talking about the *words* — and in doing so, closing off their meaning and history.

Since the entire terrain is grounds for debate, it would be a mistake to take a firm stance from the start on the definitions and differences among "*'ilmaniyya*," "*laïcité*," and "*sécularisme*." The terms are best understood within a cluster of affinity words and related concepts that constitute a discourse on secularity, each word carrying its own constellation of linked words.[4] The scholarly and philosophical term " *'ilmaniyya*" is the word most frequently used for secularism in communication across the Arab world. Reference to *'ilmaniyya* occurs in philosophical debates as well as in discussions of religion, politics, culture, the economy, gender, law, the headscarf, and other issues. Its frequent use in these contexts does not mean that it is well defined or that there is a general agreement on its meaning. Nor does it imply that the word is part of everyday discourse on the popular level. According to some etymologists, " *'ilmaniyya*" comes from " *'ilm*" (science); others derive the word from " *'alam*" (the world). Since worldliness and science continue to hover around the word " *'ilmaniyya*," it is key to current debates that these attributes not be seen as opposed to Islam.

More contentious yet is the French word "*laïcité*," which is perceived, depending on one's ideological position, either as foreign and therefore threatening to an Arab or Islamic cultural heritage or, alternatively, as a universal concept based on reason and a scientific view of the world. Some Moroccan writers use the Arabic word "*laikiya*" as a translation of the French "*laïcité*," sometimes with positive and sometimes with negative connotations. "*Laïcité*" is associated with concepts such as the separation of spiritual and temporal powers, the scientific view of the world, the limitation of religion to the private sphere, or very simply, *'ilhad* (atheism). The last of these is the favored definition of Islamist commentators as well as of the common people who pay attention to these discussions.

The French version, "*sécularisme*," which is not frequently used by scholars, is invoked by the state monarchy in its efforts to rationalize society in the service of economic progress and political control. This interpretation of secularism is closely linked to the word "*hadatha*," or modernity. Thus, the state's version of *sécularisme* highlights social and economic rather than intellectual and cultural change. The Moroccan state's story of *sécularisme* tells of the transition from a rural, agrarian society to one that is urban and industrial. In the view of the state monarchy, the secularization of Moroccan society in no way implies the decline of religion. Indeed, the monarchy promotes a vision of *sécularisme* in which religious rhetoric substitutes for the language of democratization and social rights. In this way religion and *sécularisme* proceed together in state planning. The Moroccan context is obviously very different from that of the French secular state as it was shaped by Republicanism and anticlerical sentiment.

Despite their differences, " *'ilmaniyya*," "*laïcité*," and "*sécularisme*" are often used interchangeably. All of these words travel with other words, such as "constitutionalism," "democracy," "*hurriyya*" (liberty), "*hadatha*" (modernity), or " *'ilm*" (science). For its part " *'ilmaniyya*" is linked to words like "*turath*" (heritage), "Islam," "tradition," "*salafiyya*," and "*shura*" (consultation), which are seen — depending on one's ideological position — as either compatible or incompatible with secularism. Most important, perhaps, neither " *'ilmaniyya*" nor "*sécularisme*" is understood *necessarily* to imply a separate sphere — removed from religion — for science, knowledge, government, or public life. In Morocco, only "*laïcité*" demands such separation. In this mix and match of words and meanings, there is thus a great deal of flexibility for different points of view. And underlying contemporary demands for clear positions concerning "secularism" is a history of flux, evasion, and ironic contradiction. I turn now to this history.

Did the French Colonial Regime Import Secularism?

Contemporary Islamists charge that France wielded *laïcité* as the weapon with which to claim North Africa and that, rather than fostering liberty, *laïcité* was central to the strategy through which the French subjugated their colonial subjects. Although this may have been the case in neighboring Algeria, where secularism was violently introduced as an antidote to Islam, in Morocco, colonial *laïcité* was not asserted to the point that it eroded religious sentiment or reshaped belief. When the colonization process began in 1912, it made no attempt to transform religious and political institutions so thoroughly. The architect of the colonial project, Marshal Lyautey, was a monarchist with nostalgia for the ancien régime and had little interest in spreading ideals of secularism or republicanism in Morocco. Because attempts at "Christianization" were limited, Islam continued to be the fundamental source of religious ideals and political legitimization. In contrast to Algeria, where state-imposed *laïcité* was rejected by Algerians as a sign of their cultural and political resistance to colonial rule, in Morocco, Islam neither retreated nor dominated as a discourse of colonial social and political organization. Instead, religion and secular ideas came to coexist in a continually ambiguous relationship. This ambiguity was made possible, in part, by avoiding discussion of *laïcité*, even as institutions and ideologies elsewhere labeled "secular" came into play in Morocco.

The educational system was one place that maintained the ambiguous coexistence of two intellectual systems. The French made few efforts to interfere with Muslim religious schools. Although Muslim schools were brought under the Direction des Affaires Chérifiennes, their curricula remained largely unchanged, aimed at producing religious scholars, judges (*qadis*), and notaries. Parallel to the Islamic schools, the French established Franco-Muslim schools under the supervision of the Direction Générale de l'Instruction Publique. Under the Franco-Muslim system, primary education prepared Moroccan urban elites for government and professional careers. The École des Fils de Notables, established in 1916, combined education based on Qur'anic studies taught by a *faqih* (religious scholar) and French subjects taught by a French schoolmaster.[5] The latter consisted of language, art, mathematics, humanities, and history of North Africa and France, and were not considered a success.

The students who graduated from the École Franco-Musulmane generally qualified for secondary education at the College Musulman. Their course of study continued the practice of combining Islamic studies with Western science. But there was no attempt to create a synthesis between the two systems. The addition of Western subjects was meant not to transform the ideas and worldviews of the educated elite but only to familiarize them with developments outside their own cultural tradition. The decree of 4 September 1920 is revealing:

> Secondary education designed for the Muslims must prepare the young Moroccans for general cultural background which, without turning them away from their tradition, prepares them to accept, and become interested in the various aspects of modern life. . . . It is not a question of giving to the young Moroccans in the colleges a bookish education foreign to their social milieu, to their intellectual taste, to the needs of their country. . . . On the contrary, it is necessary to form in the young people of these establishments a good Muslim background, and to touch sufficiently upon European civilization in order that they may contribute to the normal development of their country towards its new destiny. . . . In consequence, the fundamental formula of the College Musulman is reduced to this: Muslim culture and French education.[6]

Almost thirty years later, French educators reaffirmed this goal: "to prepare for traditional Muslim life without opening the door to Western culture in general and modern science in particular."[7] Pierre Boyer de

Latour, who became resident-general of Morocco in 1952, expressed his views on education more openly when he stated that "the instructor is supposed to teach the young kids that they are French but will abstain from teaching them much."[8] Meanwhile, the French created the Institut des Hautes Études Marocaines for professional careers. The one exception to the rule of prioritizing Muslim education as the core training was the Institut Scientifique Chérifien, established in 1921 as the only institution that dealt with self-consciously "secular" and scientific subjects.

The historian Charles-André Julien argues that education in colonial Morocco was an instrument of apartheid, not of progress. It kept Moroccans closed off in their own social classes while it excluded them from the possibility of cultural evasion. It was the result of the resident-general's will to stop the emergence of an intelligentsia that is difficult to control and that is inclined to foment a destructive nationalism. Schooling was therefore more informed by the conservatism of the ancien régime than by liberalism.[9]

In contrast to other colonial situations, the French did not create a class of Frenchmen "Moroccan in appearance and French in education," to paraphrase Macauley's famous memorandum on India. Nor did the educational system erode religious authority. The schools introduced a "modern and professional" dimension, but their curricula were not "liberal and secular." The educational system assumed that awakening to *professional* rather than "secular" knowledge would be useful for the emerging Moroccan elite. This policy was closely associated with the politics of indirect rule, and it imposed a clear limit on the transformation of Morocco through education.

Thus, French colonial authorities never intended to create a secular Moroccan elite, and accordingly, "secularism" did not become a key word in the nationalist debates. What elsewhere was spoken of as "secular" came to Morocco in the form of "Pan-Arabism," "republicanism," or "political reform." My historical narrative therefore has now to consider silences to trace how ideas so often labeled "secular" in other contexts became embedded in Moroccan political life precisely because the controversial words remained unspoken in public debate.

Secular Constitutionalism Came to Morocco from the Middle East and Turkey

My contention is that ideas associated elsewhere with secularism emerged in Morocco not only without the words but also without direct coercion — or even translation — from Europe. They arrived instead as a part of a spirit of political reform and revolution that spread through North Africa and the Middle East at the beginning of the twentieth century. Because secularism was not at issue, Moroccans were able to combine ideas that in other political settings would have appeared contradictory. Thus, in my view the period when the words were silent rather than in motion both underlies and explains the layered meanings of contemporary arguments about the words in question. Because "secular" ideas entered Moroccan politics, as it were, sotto voce, they have a life beyond words tagged as imperially motivated translations from European languages.

The first glimmering of what elsewhere was called "secularism" came to Morocco in the early twentieth century when Syrian and Egyptian thinkers began to promote the idea of Pan-Arabism in the Arabic press.[10] One result was the Moroccan "constitutional movement," which, though confined to a small number of religious scholars from Fez who were in contact with a few Syrian intellectuals, nonetheless opened a new era in Moroccan politics. Thus, the new ideas of secular Pan-Arabism reached Morocco via Muslim madrasas and Muslim *'ulama'*, such as Chouaib al-Doukkali and Mohammed ibn Abdekabir al Kettani. And unlike the Pan-Arabists in Egypt and Syria, Moroccans unself-consciously combined secular and religious ideas. For the new educated Moroccan elite, "ideological differences between religious and secular tendencies as they existed in the Middle East were unknown in this part of the Maghreb. Moroccan *'ulama'* accepted Pan-Arab and Pan-Islamic ideas as a whole without being able to discern the ideological differences that reflected a heterogeneous Middle Eastern reality. As a result, many secular ideas were assimilated by a few enlightened individuals."[11]

At the end of 1907, some of these individuals presented the sultan with a liberal constitution that called for freedom of expression, individual liberty, equality, and popular sovereignty based on a parliamentary system of government. Making no reference to Western political thought, they explained that these reforms were inspired by the Islamic concept of *shura*, or consultation. This religious interpretation made little difference to the sultan, who responded by suppressing the reform proposals, a suppression facilitated by the fact that the sultan's French advisers had excluded the *'ulama'* from their traditional role as advisers to the sultan. And even if the reformists had succeeded, their evocation of liberal ideas did not include the separation of religion and the state. Quite the contrary: They thought that it was they, the religious leaders, who could bring needed reforms to the state.[12] Although their words would have been identified with a "secular" discourse in much of the Middle East, these concepts did not have the same resonance in Morocco.

Meanwhile, the experience of the Turkish nation under Mustafa Kemal Atatürk was viewed with admiration. Well-known Moroccan nationalists such as Mohammed ibn Hassan al Ouazzani and Mohammed ibn Abdelkarim al-Khattabi saw the Turkish experience as a model of freedom, progress, and renaissance. Al-Khattabi in particular was receptive to the ideals of republicanism. His "Rifi Republic" in the 1920s, although shortlived, showed the form of his aspirations for a modernizing project attuned to the tribal context of the Rif Mountains. One of al-Khattabi's main objectives was to introduce and institutionalize a concept of collective consciousness based primarily not on religiosity but on national unity (*aljama'iyya al-wataniyya*), which downplayed religious symbolism. The failure of the Rifi Republic was in part due to the opposition that the religious brotherhood created vis-à-vis al-Khattabi's ambitious project. At the same time, his successes show the new political possibilities opening to Moroccan reformists and visionaries — and without abandoning religion.

While the emergence of nationalism in the Middle East was closely connected with ideas of the secular, in Morocco nationalism had a strong religious basis. For Moroccan nationalist leaders, religion was an effective means of political mobilization. The ideas of *watan* (nation) and *wataniyyun* (nationalist) were often articulated with reference to a religious discourse. It is not by coincidence that the first nationalist organization was given the name "*zawiya*" (brotherhood) and that 'Allal al-Fassi, the symbol of urban nationalism in Morocco, was referred to in the 1930s as "*shaykh*." In its initial phase, the discourse and organizational structures of the nationalist movement were closely linked to the Sufi religious orders.[13] The idea of freedom in Moroccan nationalist discourse was predominantly expressed as freedom from French occupation — rather than from religious authority. Freedom was seen through the prism of a power relationship vis-à-vis the colonial occupier, not as an abstract conception of freedom from a repressive form of rule. Furthermore, freedom was considered a matter for the community as a whole, not a principle of individual liberation.

This easy fusion between religiosity and the rhetoric of "freedom" was made possible, I argue, by the lack of a well-established Moroccan secular elite. At the same time, however, discussion about whether or not science, freedom, and modernity were "European," "Islamic," or "universal" had also already begun. This discourse is the precursor to contemporary arguments about the appropriateness of secularism in Morocco, and so I turn to it.

If Islam Contains Science and Democracy, Does Morocco Need "Secularism"?

Nationalist thinkers in Morocco maintained an ambivalent relationship with concepts of secularism and never endorsed any of the terms as such. Many argued that the terms for secularism carried the baggage of the peculiar history of Europe and that this legacy was not needed in Morocco because Islam already had a deliberative tradition that nurtured science. Here I trace some of this discourse, as well as the European "baggage" to which Moroccan thinkers have pointed.

The ideas of the Salafiyya movement constituted part of the founding principles of Moroccan nationalism. Drawn from the word "*salaf*," which means "ancestors," Salafi ideology called for a return to an Islam of the "worthy ancestors" who represented the "authentic" religion from which "obscurantist" practices could be purified. The two key figures who introduced Salafi ideology to Morocco were Shaykh Abdallah al-Sanousi and Shaykh Abou Chouaib al-Doukkali. Shaykh Muhammad Ibn al-Arabi al-Alaoui also propagated Salafi ideas among students at Al-Karawiyyine University in Fez, spreading the nationalist struggle against colonialism. Although it was not clearly presented as such, Salafism was a reaction to the colonial project. Its main objective was to counter the discourse and practices of French colonialism by endorsing a reformist religious discourse that brought together the "true" Islam and science.

The symbol and intellectual source of Salafi nationalism was for many years 'Allal al-Fassi. Al-Fassi presented Islam as a religion that favors science and reason. He wrote, "If our contact with Western culture reveals to us the great battle between religion and science in the eighteenth century, we need to keep in mind that this battle is not ours. From an Islamic perspective, religion can support science."[14] The reference to Islam as a religion in harmony with science was an important claim in the context of nationalist resistance. As al-Fassi put it, "It is a fact that the fusion of Salafi doctrine with the nationalist cause in Morocco was profitable to both Salafiyya and nationalism. We can also deduce that the method followed in Morocco resulted in the success of the Salafiyya to a degree not attained even in the country of Mohammed Abduh and Jamal al-Din al-Afghani."[15]

Al-Fassi also compared secularism as it relates to Christianity versus Islam:

> It is wrong to limit religion only to one aspect of life without the others. . . . A nation has to choose in its private and public life between two things: either atheism and neglect of religious teachings or religiosity. . . . If we look at the great revolution in the world that destroyed the churches, imprisoned religious scholars, and came up with secular freedom (al-tahrir al-laiki), it is important to note that it came in the historical Christian experience. This revolution against the medieval Church is not in contradiction with the pure religion. Islam can only agree with any revolution that opposes the control of the mind and people in the name of religion.[16]

Discussing "laïcité" in translation (al-laiki), al-Fassi argued its European specificity, on the one hand, and the embeddedness of its key concepts in Islam, on the other. To follow this argument, it is worth turning briefly to some of the features of European secularism that stood out for Moroccan thinkers.

In European history, "secularism" was associated with the taking over of church lands by lay owners as well as the process by which priests and nuns left their religious orders.[17] By the nineteenth century, the term started to be used more widely to refer to politics, economics, and culture; it became possible to speak of the "secularization of the European mind."[18] Secularism became associated with scientific understanding and political reform; European thinkers imagined it as a new "stage" of history after the decline of religion. The process of secularization was imagined as universal progress. In this movement, science, education, and politics would be separated from the world of faith.

By the nineteenth century, education and law in Europe took on the new commitment to secular practice, as new policies removed them from religious teachings. In Great Britain, the Education Act of 1870 became the basis of a secular school system. In France, the educational laws of Jules Ferry replaced religious teachings in public schools with civic curricula, while a 1905 law abolished the Napoleonic Concordat and permanently separated the state from the church. The natural sciences, too, required the suppression of religious belief, in some cases affirming atheism.

Philosophers and scientists identified with the secular project because they saw reason as antithetical to religion. The success of the sciences over the church was imagined as an entry in a universal sequence, leading from superstition to knowledge. Furthermore, Europe was seen as the acme of progress, ahead of the backward peoples of Africa, China, India, and the Middle East, whose cultures were based on superstition.[19] Non-Europeans were primitive, mystical, and sentimental; they lacked the knowledge to understand the rational laws of the universe.

Muslim reformist thinkers in Morocco knew — and resented — these distinctions. Thus, for example, Ernest Renan, a proponent of the French Enlightenment, was well known in Morocco. Renan wrote, "The Arab, and in a general sense the Muslim, are further apart from us more than any other time. The Muslim and the European are to one another like two different species, having nothing in common in the manner of thinking and feeling."[20] He continued: "The essential condition for the expansion of European civilization is the destruction of the Semitic thing *par excellence*, the destruction of the theocratic power of Islamism. . . . When we reduce Islamism to its religious and individual state, it will disappear. . . . Islam is the most complete negation of Europe. . . . Islam is fanaticism. . . . Islam is the disdain of science and the suppression of the civil society, restricting the human mind and closing it to rational thinking."[21] Such sentiments shaped the attitudes of Moroccan reformist intellectuals in their understandings of secularism and the European Enlightenment.

On the eve of Moroccan independence, neither the Moroccan elite nor the monarchy was receptive to secularism as such. At the same time, many reformists argued for key components of the "secular" project — particularly science and reason — but as features of a reinvigorated Islam. The Salafiyya movement articulated an Islamic nationalism that would bring about political reform through the critical intervention of the *'ulama'*. And traditional Sharifism (doctrine of prophetic lineage) brought the monarchy and the elite together in a familiar discursive field on which to base political legitimacy. Later, after independence, when the words for secularism did appear in debate, it was within the contours carved out by this legacy. By that time, however, other — now postcolonial — contradictions had already come into play.

Is the Religious State "Secular"?

The postcolonial monarchy has thrived on a contradiction since its inception after independence in 1956. On the one hand, it relied on "secular" economic and administrative policies, overtly employing the language of "*sécularisme*." On the other hand, it leaned heavily on the rhetoric of religious legitimacy to justify its rule. *Sécularisme* became a mechanism for political and social control rather than a conceptual tool for social, political, and economic justice, while the discourse on national identity remained religious.

Many twentieth-century nationalist leaders were attached to the traditional religious school of Malikism, based on Sunni Islam and scripturalist orthodoxy, while popular Islam was closely associated with Maraboutism and the long-established religious brotherhoods known as *zawiyas*. The monarchy drew on both traditions to ground its legitimacy in Islam.[22] Since the early days of independence, the king has managed to create a regime resonant with Islamic traditions while proclaiming an attachment to democracy and modernization.[23] Political Islam in Morocco functioned by preserving all aspects of religion that were conductive to political power and authority.

King Hassan II (1929–99) represented himself as ‘*amir al-mu'minin* (commander of the faithful) and as the supreme representative of the nation: "I received this title at birth, without asking for it. That means I am one of the descendants of the Prophet. . . . This title 'Commander of the Faithful' . . . does not meet with indifference. It is a title that imposes a great deal of humility and, all the same at certain times, great responsibilities."[24]

The king used his religious title to arbitrate a multiparty political system of the sort associated with secular and democratic forms of government. And so "*sécularisme*," now called by this name, is a word that moved to accommodate the rationalization of state institutions without the privatization of religion.[25] The monarch, moreover, monopolized the language of the "secular" nation-state, associating itself with *watan* (nation), *wahda* (unity), and *hawiyya* (identity).[26] Any contradictions that arose between religion and *sécularisme*-as-state-expansion were built into state policy. Thus, the Ministry of the Interior and the Ministry of Education encouraged Islamist ideology to counter the growing popularity of left-wing ideas among high school and university students. At the same time, Hassan II limited the ability of the Islamists to operate in the political field through manipulation, co-optation, and repression. When the Islamists began to create a political threat in the late 1980s, Hassan II as the "commander of the faithful" found no contradiction in saying, "We should resort to what the Christians say: Render unto God what is God's and unto Caesar what is Caesar's."[27]

After the death of Hassan II, in 1999, a new era began in the political history of Morocco. From the beginning of the 1990s, a more open atmosphere developed. Hassan II's successor, Mohammed VI, confirmed the principles of constitutional monarchy, called for a concept of political authority based on accountability, and encouraged greater freedom of expression. Yet this more liberal king maintained the monarchy at the center of political life and refrained from uttering any of the words for "secularism." But with the rise of Islamism, even without the king's speaking, national debate thickened around these words, which changed the very tenor of politics.

On 16 May 2003, a series of suicide bombings by radical religious groups in Casablanca killed more than forty people — and took the monarchy by surprise. For much of its history, the Moroccan monarchy was able to claim a monopoly over the religious field that would prevent the rise of religious radicalism. The terrorist events shattered that claim. They also brought the words for "secular" to the forefront of public debate.[28] The political Party of Justice and Development (PJD) took up the rhetoric of religion against the "secular." In response, some leftist parties asked for a separation between politics and religion and blamed the PJD for the spread of religious politics, which, some say, encouraged the perpetrators of the 16 May bombings. The discourse on secularism had changed to the point that political figures had to position themselves in relation not only to practices but to the words themselves.

Islamists Condemn Secularism

The Islamist movement in Morocco emerged in the 1970s and 1980s as an alternative source of religious legitimacy. As in other Arab Muslim states, the Moroccan state encouraged the Islamists in order to counter the growth of the left. One of the most important Islamist groups was the Muslim Brotherhood, whose main spokesman was Abdessalam Yassine, a former school inspector who founded the movement of Al-Adl wal-Ihsan (Justice and Charity). Yassin was critical of Hassan II's regime, calling for greater social equality; at the same time, he supported the establishment of an Islamic state in which the *shari'a* (Islamic law) would be strictly applied.

The Islamists' reaction to *'ilmaniyya* and *laïcité* in Morocco found its most articulate theoretical formulation in the work of Yassine. In 1989, he published the book *Islam and Secular [*'ilmaniyya*] Nationalism*, which presented his critique of the secular project.[29] He criticized the concept of nationalism as based on a linguistic and ethnic construction of identity that would lead to the fragmentation of the *'umma* (Muslim community). And he identified secularism (*laïcité*) as part of the imperial project: "*Laïcité* is considered by the Muslims as the weapon with which France came to North Africa in order to devastate and destroy their liberty. This *laïcité* that the French colonizer used is now being brandished by some secular Algerians as an ideological tool and as a weapon against Islam and those who claim it as the source of truth."[30] Yassine argued that these ideas resulted in the emergence of conflicting and "dual" identities throughout the Arab world. According to Yassine, submission to Western culture, norms, and philosophy, would threaten the "Muslim mind" and lead to a denial of the role of religion in society. For him, as for some of the earlier nationalist thinkers, *laïcité* made sense in Europe where it liberated society from the hold of the church and its oppressive political power. But where the church opposed political freedom, Islam, on the contrary, called for the liberation of the poor and for progress in Muslim societies. Islam thus did not need a liberating ideology like secularism to promote political and social equality because those ideals were inherent in Islam itself.

While Yassine blamed European colonial powers for the spread of secular ideas, he also singled out Arab intellectuals, both Christian and Muslim, as responsible for the promotion of secularism. He denounced the colonial system of Francophone education for promoting the dual character of the Moroccan society. In contrast to my view, Yassine argued that secularism as such — the word and the practice — did succeed in colonial Morocco and must now be extirpated. In effect, he moved the bar: What once was not considered "secularism" now was.

Liberals and the Left Respond

The strong Islamist reaction against the coupled ills of " *'ilmaniyya*" and "*laïcité*" made it essential for liberal and leftist intellectuals to deal explicitly with these words, something that earlier nationalists were able to avoid because they combined religious and secular values rather than opposing the two.

Contemporary liberal discourse draws heavily on the legacy of Mohammed Hassan al-Wazzani, who participated in the nationalist struggles before independence, though he later departed politically from a Salafi orientation. Educated at the Institut d'Études Politiques in Paris, he represented a more *laïcité*-influenced branch of the nationalist movement and called for the creation of a constitutionalist state in Morocco. Yet he never dissociated himself from religious discourse in his conception of the state. According to him, "Islam is not only a religion, it is a global way of life in the lives of people. It relates to the spirit as well as to matter. It relates to individual consciousness, to the community at large, to individual feelings as well as to the system of state power."[31] While al-Wazzani never dissociated religion from the state, he opposed any form of divine authority. Instead, he relied on the concepts of *shura* (consultation), *hurriyyat al-ta'bir* (freedom of speech), and *'adala* (justice) to conceive a more politically liberal Morocco. According to him, "freedom of expression is the enemy of every personal, oppressive and despotic power."[32] Because al-Wazzani wanted a constitutional government based on *shari'a* and *shura*, a contemporary commentator described him as a "*laïc potential*."[33] In his time, al-Wazzani remained on the margins of the Moroccan political field, but in contemporary political debates, his legacy has been recuperated in defense of his "potential" — and certainly nationalist — *laïcité*.

From a more leftist perspective, *'ilmaniyya* is conceptualized within a broader philosophical *problematique* that reconciled religion and rationalism. In his discussion of the relationship between Islam and *'ilmaniyya*, Mohammed Lambarki assigned a universal dimension to *'ilmaniyya*. He wrote: "Reason is the outcome of a general human knowledge. Reason is the product of all civilizations, and all cultures. . . . That is to say that reason is subject to the scientific experience in its totality."[34] *Al-Ilmanya* in this context is part of human reason or what is called *'aqlaniyya* (rationalism). Lambarki identified *'ilmaniyya* as the "propagation of rationalism into the organization of state affairs and clarifications of social relationships in society. In other words, it is the creation of founding principles based on equality and legality where sovereignty comes from the people . . . where people have equal rights and equal obligations."[35] Lambarki argued that the concepts of reason and rationalism are epistemological while the concept of *'ilmaniyya* is essentially political: " *'Ilmaniyya* is nothing but a democratic political practice in the modern age, it is therefore the objective form that all human societies should eventually take in one way or the other."[36] In short, *'ilmaniyya* is the product of reason in the political field as societies move historically beyond an autocratic state:

> Our reading of *'ilmaniyya* does not limit it to a specific societal experience such as in France . . . because *'ilmaniyya* in its profound meaning is the application of reason to politics and the liberation from dogmatism and ideology. At this level, it is clear that *'ilmaniyya* is not an enemy of religion. Instead it rejects the hegemony of religious ideology in the organization of society and politics. We are therefore aware of the large difference that exists between religion as a faith and religion as a political ideology in order to legitimate an autocracy.[37]

'Ilmaniyya is presented as a political structure in which the state is free from religious ideology, open to political pluralism, and able to protect social democracy. Lambarki identified three poles around which this concept of *'ilmaniyya* evolves. The first pole is respect for religion as faith in the context of individual and collective liberties. From this angle, *'ilmaniyya* does not oppose religion but instead protects it. The second pole of *'ilmaniyya* is its respect for cultural specificity in a way that is compatible with overall civilizational progress. From this perspective it becomes a dynamic factor for enriching the heritage of different cultures, including Arab cultures, while it promotes cross-cultural understanding. The third pole of *'ilmaniyya* is its ability to transform Islamic religious ideology into a political force that is open to cultural diversity and political democracy. In this context, religion complements, rather than opposes, the meaning of *'ilmaniyya*.

The Amazigh Movement Responds

The rise of the Amazigh movement in the last two decades of the twentieth century helped to reshape Moroccan politics. "Amazigh" refers to the cultural identity of the "original" inhabitants of Morocco, and "*Imazi-*

ghen" literally means "free, or noble, people," replacing the term "Berber," now seen as a pejorative, colonial construct.[38] After independence, Amazigh identity was marginalized — if not repressed — by a Moroccan national imaginary that was predominantly Arab Islamic. The Amazigh movement has challenged the adoption of Arabic as the official national language and pressed for diversity within a secular context.

The gradual emergence of civil society during the 1990s gave new life to the Amazigh movement as an expression of identity. Amazigh associations proliferated in Morocco and today number more than one hundred.[39] While these associations have different political agendas, most agree on the necessity of 'ilmaniyya as a way to safeguard Amazigh culture and defend the linguistic and cultural rights of the Amazigh people. In the context of the Amazigh movement, the word "'ilmaniyya" — which has not been translated into Amazigh — has moved to align with discussions of full citizenship, modernity, and democracy.

The most prominent intellectual figure in the movement is Mohamed Chafik, who is identified with the more moderate groups. Chafik, interestingly, argues for secularist views using Islamic discourse. In a letter addressed to Abdessalam Yassine he wrote, "The word democracy is the Latin translation of *shura* [consultation], one of the pillars of the Islamic state. . . . Religious sciences cannot be put above secular sciences, Islam provides a wider interpretation of the word 'science,' this without limiting it to the science of religion."[40] In another context, Chafik straightforwardly stated that "the definition of 'secularism'['ilmaniyya] is wrapped in the Qur'anic text, 'la ikraha fi-al-din' (there is no coercion in religion). . . . Only secularism ['ilmaniyya] can free Islam from religious fanaticism. . . . This is actually an explicit statement that in normative Islam there is no religious coercion. We speak here of freedom of religion and freedom from religion."[41] The clear message is that there is no contradiction between Islam and secularism. In his critique of Arab nationalism and call for a multicultural Morocco, Chafik argued that Arab nationalism made a connection between "Islam and Arabic language, a connection that excluded the Berbers [Amazigh]."[42] Scholars and Amazigh activists such as Chafik, Ahmed Boukous, and Mohamed Atarkin have argued not only that secularism is the way to achieve cultural rights, but that the empowerment of the Amazigh will facilitate the transition to modernity and to a more secular and democratic state in Morocco.

Is "Secularism" in Morocco in Stasis or in Motion?

Moroccan cosmopolitanism allows a mix-and-match of languages and cultures. On the one hand, " *'ilmaniyya*," "*laïcité*," and "*sécularisme*" are used in a fluid, shifting constellation, alive to local debates; on the other hand, they are just as often rejected as foreign. I have argued that these terms provoke lively debate in contemporary Morocco in part because they rest on a history of productive evasions of the secularism question in the twentieth century. The multiple viewpoints of current debates in Morocco draw on this history of contradictions and ironies. Although today's anti-secularists criticize the colonial imposition of the concept, in fact the French colonial administration did *not* create a self-consciously secular Moroccan elite. Dreams of nationalist freedom arrived not from elite colonial schooling but from Pan-Arabism and the Turkish Republic. An earlier generation of nationalists combined religion and freedom, aided by the silence of words for secularism that might have polarized the debate. Now that these words — whether in French or Arabic — pervade political discourse, the earlier option has become impossible. In response to Islamist condemnations of secularism as the enemy of religion, liberals, leftists, and Amazigh activists are forced to defend it, placing "secularism" at the center of political debates that once elided the term by evoking other, less confrontational oppositions, such as consultation versus autocracy or discussion versus dogmatism.

As leftists try to revive "*'ilmaniyya*" as the basis for a diverse national culture, clerics raise the specter of "*laïcité*" as an imperial import to be rejected, while ordinary people are more likely to think of "*sécularisme*" in terms of monarchical state power and government repression. This medley of possibilities and constraints informs contemporary politics to the point that these words sometimes seem to be in stasis — stuck in religious quarrels, colonial history, and state authority — even as they move in ever greater animation through the political culture of contemporary Morocco.

Notes

1. See "Un cri dans la nuit," *Le Journal*, no. 333, 19–25 January 2008, 5.

2. William J. Murray, "Morocco's Future: Secularism or Terrorism," *Religious Freedom Coalition Quarterly* 1, no. 2 (April–June 2004): 1–2.

3. Abdessalam Yassine, *Islamiser la modernité* (Rabat: Al Ofok Impressions, 1998), 70.

4. For a good discussion of the word " '*ilmaniyya*" in contemporary Arab thought, see 'Abd al-Wahab Al-Masiri and 'Aziz Al-'Azma, *Al-'Ilmaniyya Taht al-Mijhar* (Secularism: A dialogue) (Damascus: Dar al-Fikr al-Mu'asir, 2000), 334. A less academic analysis of secularism in Morocco is Jirari Abbes, *Islam and Laicism* (Rabat: Impremerie Omnia, 2003).

5. See Alan Scham, *Lyautey in Morocco: Protectorate Administration, 1912–1925* (Berkeley: University of California Press, 1970).

6. Ibid., 155.

7. Quoted in Ignace Dalle, *Maroc 1961–1999: L'espérance brisée* (Paris: Tarik Editions, 2001), 44.

8. Quoted in Robin Bidwell, *Morocco under Colonial Rule: French Administration of Tribal Areas 1912–1956* (London: Frank Cass, 1973), 249–50.

9. Charles-André Julien, *Le Maroc face aux imperialismes, 1415–1956* (Paris: Éditions jeune Afrique, 1978), 101–102.

10. The first ideas about constitutional government were circulated in newspapers such as *Lisan al-Maghrib* and *Al-Fajr* in the early 1900s. These papers were founded, respectively, by the Syrian brothers Arthur and Faraj Allah Nimur and by the Lebanese Ni'mat Allah al-Dahdah. Self-consciously secular ideas about the organization of Arab society were also articulated in the Egyptian newspapers *Al-Ahram* and *Al-Manar*.

11. Mohamed El Mansour, "Salafis and Modernists in the Moroccan Nationalist Movement," in John Ruedy, *Islamism and Secularism in North Africa* (New York: St. Martin's Press, 1994), 55.

12. Abdallah Laroui, *Les origines sociales et culturelles du nationalisme Marocain, 1830–1912* (Casablanca: Centre culturel Arabe, 1993), 381.

13. See Robert Rezette, *Les parties politiques Marocains* (Paris: Armand Colin, 1955).

14. 'Allal al-Fassi, *Al-Naqd al-dhati*, 7th ed. (Casablanca: Dar al-thaqafa al-bayda, 2002), 96.

15. El Mansour, "Salafis and Modernists in the Moroccan Nationalist Movement," 60.

16. Al-Fasi, *Al-Naqd al-dhati*, 95–96.

17. Alain Gerard, *Permanence de la laïcité en France et dans le monde* (Toulouse: Éditions privat, 2001).

18. Owen Chadwick, *The Secularisation of the European Mind in the Nineteenth Century* (Cambridge: Cambridge University Press, 1975).

19. See Johannes Fabian, *Time and the Other: How Anthropology Makes Its Object* (New York: Columbia University Press, 1983).

20. Ernest Renan, *Oeuvres completes*, vol. 2 (Paris: Calmann-Levy, 1948), 323.

21. Ibid., 333.

22. In terms of Islamic legitimacy, the current Moroccan dynasty, the 'Alawis, have reigned uninterrupted for close to four hundred years. The 'Alawis claim direct lineage from the Prophet Muhammad, and King Hassan II emphasized his role of religious leader through the performance of important rituals. This can be seen also in the use of the "allegiance," an action after the death of the Prophet used for the delegation of power.

23. The constitutional initiative was largely the work of King Hassan II, who

promulgated the constitution of 1962, which was reworked in 1970, 1972, 1992, and 1996. The different stages of the constitutional dynamic reflect the king's attempt to modernize traditional institutions and democratize political life, but only as long as the centrality and powers of the monarchical institution were not called into question.

24. Quoted in Francois Burgat and William Dowell, *The Islamic Movement in North Africa* (Austin: Center for Middle Eastern Studies, University of Texas, 1993), 168.

25. See Mohamed Tozy, *Monarchie et Islam politique au Maroc* (Paris: Presses de Sciences Po, 1999).

26. Mohammed Othman Benjelloun, *Projet national et identité au Maroc: Essai d'anthropologie politique* (Casablanca: Éditions eddif, 2002), 68.

27. Quoted in Dale Eickelman and James Piscatori, *Muslim Politics* (Princeton, N.J.: Princeton University Press, 1996), 52.

28. See "Islamistes/laïcs: le duel," *Telquel*, no. 75, 26 April 2003.

29. Abdessalam Yassine, *Al-Islam wa Qawmiyya al-'Ilmaniyya* (Casablanca: Dar al-Khattabi, 1989).

30. Yassine, *Islamiser la modernité*, 70.

31. Muhammad Hassan Al-Wazzani, *Harb al-Kalam* (Fez: Institut al-Wazzani, 1998), 176.

32. Ibid., 116.

33. Tozy, *Monarchie et Islam politique*, 155.

34. Mohammed Lambarki, *Al-Islam wa al-'Ilmaniyya* (Rabat: Manshurat Ikhtilaf, 1999), 6.

35. Ibid., 12.

36. Ibid.

37. Ibid., 13.

38. When the Romans arrived in North Africa, they met tough resistance and named the inhabitants of the region Barbarians — hence, the word "Berber."

39. Among others, one can cite l'Association Marociane de la recherche et d'échanges culturels and the Association nouvelle pour la culture et les arts populaires. These kinds of associations exist in the countryside and in the cities.

40. Quoted in Samir Ben-Layashi, "Secularism in the Moroccan Amazigh Discourse," *Journal of North African Studies* 12, no. 2 (June 2007): 154.

41. Ibid., 157.

42. Ibid., 158.

ALAN TANSMAN

Saburaimu/**Sublime**

A Japanese Word and Its Political Afterlife

How can we follow the movement of a word across time and place if the power of that word depends less on its semantic content than on the images it sets into motion, images that have an affective appeal and evoke an aesthetic experience that is beyond the reach of cognition and narrative representation? "Sublime" is just such a word. Entering Japanese literary and philosophical discussions in the 1890s through German and British Romanticism, it was left almost as it was, rendered as "*saburaimu,*" even though Japanese equivalents were available in the classical aesthetic vocabulary.[1] Native aesthetic terms were ignored in the 1890s, only to be called on in the 1930s by purveyors of political propaganda, for whom the prestige of native words served as the amorphous but powerfully binding agent of a fascist social imagination. If, in the 1890s, which was early in Japan's modernity, the experience of the *saburaimu* produced an affective aesthetic moment giving birth both to an intensely felt interior self and a socialized self requiring suppression of that interiority, in the 1930s classical renderings of "sublime" suggested a will-less binding to a tradition whose bonds were to be felt but not understood. In the late 1950s and early 1960s, when the word itself was absent, the *feeling* of sublimity provided a language for leftist, antimilitarist critique.

I use "sublime" here to indicate not only evocations of the unnamable, but also the wish for it, in texts that not merely described sublimity but also attempted to harness its affective appeal in order to change people. To quote one of the foundational theorists of the sublime, Edmund Burke, "I know of nothing Sublime which is not some modification of power."[2] I follow the conceptual lineage of the sublime that stretches back to Longinus and moves through Burke and Kant in the eighteenth century and includes recent critics like Neil Hertz. In this lineage, the evocation of the sublime is understood as a process of containing the powerful emotion felt by those who experience it.[3] For Burke (as for Kant) and others in his lineage, the aesthetic of the sublime has a political dimension: It can socialize the individual into political quiescence or lead, as has often been argued, to the "irrationalist, fascist politics" of a Martin Heidegger.[4]

The turn from aesthetic experience to political commitment is what Neil Hertz calls the "sublime turn." I will look at this turn in three Japanese historical moments. In the first, the 1890s, sublimity offered the possibility of both self-individuation and self-sacrifice. In the second, the 1930s, it more narrowly offered only the opportunity for self-abnegation. In the third, the late 1950s and early 1960s, the sublime bound the politics of the antinuclear left to the silent suffering of the victims of Hiroshima. In each of these cases, "sublimity" stood in for other words that it either energized or repressed. These were its shadow words.

I want to propose that the word "sublime" arrived in Japan in the 1890s and became a central part of the poetic and existential projects of important writers and intellectuals but soon after ceased circulating because it was a word that represented an affective experience beyond the capacity of the imagination to fully grasp and beyond the limits of language to express. It was a word whose meaning was best expressed by leaving the word itself behind. Though it did continue to move in arcane academic discussions, its force was most fully felt in the traces it left as it traveled through literary texts and then into the realms of ideology and politics. To follow the word, then, means paying attention to it not as if it represented a concept to be elucidated but, rather, in artistic forms and patterns that evoked what the word designated: Affective aesthetic moments evoking what lies beyond cognitive understanding. To follow the movement of the sublime means following it as a style of thought and representation, embodied in forms that move and that have, in Henri Focillon's words, "a mobile life in a changing world."[5]

By style, I mean the movement of forms that have left their meanings behind as they move across time and space. The sublime is one such style, which is why in the 1890s it did not need to be translated into Japanese as anything other than "*saburaimu*," a word whose semantic value may have been opaque to its first readers but whose affective force certainly enchanted them. In his famous essay on translation, Walter Benjamin wrote that translation must not merely replicate what comes to it from another language, or even strive for beauty, but shock the reader, by the confrontation of incommensurable languages, into an awareness of a "true language" that lies beyond all languages and is always unattainable.[6] Translation, in this sense, produces the thought of a sublime language. We might consider that the word "sublime" itself evoked such a "pure" language as it passed through its form as "*saburaimu*" and then left its semantic content behind, moving readers not through that part of language that describes a reality but through the rhythms of prose that work out its subject matter. The sublime, that is, must be traced through literary texts that perform their meanings because it is the stylistic features of texts, as much as their content, that provoke our emotional involvement with them.[7]

What kind of word is "sublime"? It is a word whose force is released when it itself disappears and whose power depends on its very invisibility. Unnamed, it creates a spell; once named, its spell is broken. When we speak of the sublime, we show that we are already outside its orbit. Our possession of the word guarantees that we will be bystanders to the workings of sublimity. To follow the word requires that we first follow its traces back to its now absent origin.[8]

Mori Ōgai and the Sublime Return from Germany

In Japan of the 1880s and 1890s, the word "sublime" and the epiphany it evoked were happily, even voraciously, consumed by Japanese poets and intellectuals who were fairly drunk with new possibilities of poetic and existential exploration. At least as far back as 1869 the word had begun to appear in Japanese–English dictionaries.[9] In his 1894 essay "What Does It Mean to Traverse Life?" the poet Kitamura Tōkoku, a reader of Coleridge, was explicit about the sublime. The *saburaimu*, he wrote, is reached not through form but through imagination. It is a place of "the absolute thing," of "annihilation" (he used the English word) beyond the capacity to see, arrived at by looking at "the great, great world of emptiness" bathed by the light of the moon. The searcher for the sublime is a hero flashing a sword, striking at the sky, reaching the stars.[10]

To the extent that they were consciously playing with the new term and idea, writers like Tōkoku were, like us, bystanders to the experience. Another of the bystanders was Mori Ōgai (1862–1922), the Japanese intellectual who in his time was perhaps the best read in the aesthetics of German and British Romanticism and one of the central figures in Japan's intellectual, artistic, and political modernization. Ōgai described a white, "sublime" moment in his novella *The Dancing Girl* (*Maihime*; 1890), in which the main character has an epiphany when his mind and body become still as he freezes in the snow.[11] This was an experience unnamed but felt, an experience that moved the newly born modern self toward an affective tie to the nation. His narration of sublimity erased the word but conjured it through literary language. He showed how the process of political identification is a matter of silent, emotional assent to the nation and to one's feeling of devotion to it. In *The Dancing Girl*, the word disappears beneath its evocation. Ōgai's tale asks us to consider what happens politically when the word "sublime" falls below the threshold of perception, when the sublime is sublimated.[12]

The novella tells the story of a young Japanese intellectual sent to Germany by his government to further his studies and take his place among the most elite translators and brokers of European culture and thought, only to fall for a poor dancing girl and then suffer the archetypal modern dilemma of having to choose between his heart and his intellect, his passion and his duty, his lover and his nation. The story, written by one of the progenitors of the modern novel, a man acutely conscious of the demands of modernity, occupies a place in the imagination of Japanese identity akin to Huck Finn's in the imagination of those educated in the United States: It is the first and most encapsulating story of the birth of modernity and of the modern self, of their triumphs and sorrows. Two sublime epiphanies structure the story, each showing the hero blacking out, yet each leading in a different direction: one toward passion and an intensely felt suffering self; the other toward a surrendering of the will to the demands of the state. Together, they yield the modern subject: aware of an inner self that suffers but socialized to the harmony of the state. The story does not "argue" this; it evokes it through its narrative hesitations (the narrator's inability to proceed in a linear fashion) and its evocations of sublime moments that rely on the rhythm of language — on its ornaments — to do their affective work.

The story opens on a steamer carrying the protagonist, Ōta Toyotarō, back to Japan. He recalls that in his five years away he had written of his experiences of new sights and sounds for newspapers, but that his personal diary remains, to this moment, a blank slate, like his very spirit, which has lost its capacity to feel anything with intensity. Writing, it seems, cannot follow the heart. And writing gets stuck when it tries to narrate anguish.

The reasons for his condition, he demurs, lie "elsewhere." He knows that his self now is not the self he went with to Europe, but this too he is unable to record in words, and the reason for this, again, lies "elsewhere."

Isolated by the silence that sublimely shrouds him from his fellow passengers, "like a cloud," he eventually ends his demurrals and begins to narrate his past: his arrival in Berlin, his initial sensual openness to new stimuli — sights, sounds, and smells, his subsequent decision to cut himself off from the assaults of the outside world, to remain unmoved by beauty, and his fear of becoming a "mechanical man." Gradually, his "true self" begins to emerge from beneath his dutifully political persona, and he begins to immerse himself in literature and the arts but, even more fatefully, to fall into the arms of a poor young dancer, Elise. He becomes aware of his "true self" through the emotional pull of Elise by sensing, feeling, touching something inside him, and when he spots the poor dancing girl, he is drawn to her by the affective appeal of her sad, teary face, by her grief. Here, his narrative stops to linger on the image of this girl, a figure out of the world of art.

Perhaps we have here the makings of a sublime, still moment. He speaks his sympathy to her, and following a brief exchange she runs away, leading him on the chase until they arrive in her poor, small home. He enters her room; once again, the narrative stops, and we read: "She was an exceeding beauty."[13] He seems to have lost all will as he is drawn to her. Later she comes to his room, littered with books by Schopenhauer and Schiller. The couple becomes intimate, and he loses his job, for the intensity he feels for her draws him away from his official responsibilities. He lives as a journalist, split between his passion and his intellect, a split dramatized by Elise's pregnancy and by a letter he receives from his friend Aizawa urging him to return to Japan and his responsibilities at home.

Leaving Elise with a kiss, Ōta goes out into the snowy white cold — back toward the sublime, which he had begun to sense in his body. With a chill in his bones he goes to Aizawa, who convinces him to abandon Elise for Japan, making him feel "like a man who has lost his rudder in the seas" and as if "sighting the mountains in the distance" but unable to reach them as they remain "inside thick mists" — making him feel, that is, the fear that accompanies the sublime.[14] Before journeying there, he will first travel to Russia on official business, where, he tells us, "he was dropped above the clouds" into the court.[15] Never while he was there did he forget Elise; never was he allowed to, for she wrote him daily of her anguish.

Ōta returns to Berlin. It is a bitter cold day, the snow has frozen into the pavement and is shining brightly, glittering, sparkling as he approaches Elise's home. Everything is white and bright. He sees that she has begun preparations for their baby. Soon he leaves, called to the count in whose official charge he serves, and he is asked to return to Japan. He agrees to go, but first he must return to tell Elise. He wanders in a daze and collapses on a park bench, his mind on fire. The narrative, and his mind and body, freeze: "How long did I pass there like a corpse? When I awoke, aware of the intense cold penetrating my bones, it had become night and the snow was thickly falling, piling over my shoulders and on my cap."[16] He recalls this only vaguely: He learns later that while attending his sickbed, Elise heard of his plans to return home, and after that her mind and spirit ceased functioning, reducing her to a simple-minded child. In the last lines of the story the protagonist tells us that it is rare to have a friend like Aizawa, but that he still curses him.

The standard reading of the story is that the hero sacrifices personal love for duty to the nation. The affair with Elise was a brief fancy, a fairy tale whose quaint distance from reality was depicted in Ōgai's self-conscious use of archaic Japanese. But I think it is important to ask: If he had not collapsed, would he have changed his mind? A reader of Schopenhauer and Schiller, Ōgai certainly had on his mind questions of will and the giving over of the will to the sublime. If one pays attention to images in the story of mist-covered clouds in the distance, of frightening oceans, of whiteness, of the sensual power of feelings over the will, then the story can be read as a tale of the lures of sublimity: of being drawn to glittering white moments frozen within the linear narrative, moments associated with non-cognitive experiences of love, anguish, and physical intensity (the burning of passion, the freezing of the body in the snow). Even the "choice" to return to Japan is less a willed choice than a giving up of the will in a clouded moment to a force greater than one's self. This was perhaps a sublime moment, one not to be captured by the "transparent" prose of realism that Ōgai had mastered and rejected (a style that was coming to dominate Japanese letters and marked it as modern) but only glimpsed between the cracks of his literary language, in the patterns of rhythms of his language, which obscured access to the raw reality of the world it claimed to depict.

What happens in *The Dancing Girl* is that a young man is socialized by the sublime. The sublime resides in a visual moment sensed but not analyzed, created when language calls upon its ekphrastic, picture-making capacity.[17] This still, epiphanic moment beckons to the protagonist — and the reader — by appealing to a non-cognitive, emotional experience. The epiphany, an aesthetic experience from the Christian tradition recaptured by modernists like James Joyce, is an atemporal moment or a space of sublime beauty, disturbing the linear flow of narrative. In Edward Hirsch's words, the epiphany represents "a radical attempt to defy narrative form and dramatize an intense moment of change." While the sublime moment is aesthetically constructed, it contains existential force, for it depicts a moment when the self is broken down and infused with a higher form of consciousness. "The everlasting splendor of dramatizing epiphanies," writes Hirsch, "may well be the mystery of communicating moments when the self is both lost and reconceived."[18] Epiphanic moments thus disrupt unities, only to stitch them together aesthetically, through the "sublime turn," which occurs at the moment of disintegration and signals a creative leap, a "figurative reconstitution." These are moments when "the near-fatal stress of passion can be thought of as a turning into — as indistinguishable from — the energy that is constituting the poem."[19] With the turning away from near annihilation there is a "transfer of power . . . from the threatening forces to the poetic activity itself."[20]

Ōta loses his object of passion in a sublime interlude and awakens ready for work. This is his sublime turn, freezing his passion for the flesh-and-blood body of a woman and re-channeling it toward the abstract body of the state. Ōta has been worked on by the ideology of the aesthetic.[21] In times of political, social, and cultural rupture and crisis, the aesthetic experience can become a model for political and social wholeness fusing the individual with the whole of society and allowing him to find freedom in necessity. The aesthetic provides a sense of significance that cannot be analyzed or disputed because it is based on sensibility, which is ineffable. What we feel links us with society. And if ideology is a matter of feeling, then aesthetics can best shape it. For Japan in the 1890s, a nation requiring the thickening of ideological glue in the years of its development into a modern nation-state, the sublime may have aestheticized best of all.

The Sublime Binding of the People

By the 1930s, a native Japanese vocabulary from classical and medieval aesthetics had erased any trace of the word's original form. Sublime was no longer "*saburaimu*." In 1938, Ōnishi Yoshinori, in "Yūgen ron," attempted to connect German notions of the sublime to the classical aesthetic term "*yūgen*," which he found in the eighth-century poetry of the Manyōshū and the eighteenth-century poetry of Bashō. The same year that Ōnishi published "Yūgen ron," D. T. Suzuki published *Zen and Japanese Culture*, in which he described "*yūgen*" as the quality in art that allows one to glimpse the eternal through the world of change. An object with *yūgen* "is not subject to dialectical analysis or to a clear-cut definition." The experience of *yūgen* is a loosening of the intellect and a falling into a merging with nature.[22]

Intellectuals in the 1930s often drew their aesthetic language from classical and medieval Japanese aesthetics, in the moment when the individual merges with a larger whole through the mediation of an object.[23] As in the 1890s, this sublime was now harnessed as a cure through art for the ills of modernity — the ills born of the existential depredations of atomized life. For the Japanese state circa 1936, such a cure was to be offered through creations such as *Kokutai no hongi* (The Essence of the National Polity), the most widely diffused piece of propaganda in wartime Japan. Written by a committee of scholars and political hacks, the book aims to forge a community of all Japanese bound through eternity by the power of the sublime. This community can overcome the West, offering the possibility of cultural triumph. The book was the product of a latecomer to modernity who feels small and weak and wishes to be aligned with something large and powerful — who feels overwhelmed by political, economic, and cultural influence and wishes to establish authenticity.[24]

The Essence of the National Polity conveys sublimity in its language of excessive semantic proliferation, in the sheer variety of words evoking distances in time and space that cannot be contained by the imagination — similar to the language of superlatives and the eternal that Victor Klemperer noticed in Nazi language.[25] This multiplication of words referring to unimaginable distances bathes the declarations of imperial descent and national mission in an atmosphere of sublimity. The sublime cannot be named, but it can be riffed on in a dizzying movement of vocabulary. It is, variously, "*eikyū* (eternal), *eien fuhen* (eternal and unchanging), *eien fudō* (eternal and unmoving), *yōjō shin-en* (boundless and profound), *kodai shin-en* (vast and deep), *kodai muhen* (vast and limitless), *bandai fueki* (everlasting and eternal), *kagirinaku* (without limits), *okuchō kagirinaku* (the millions, without limits), *tenjō mukyū* (heaven and earth infinite), *mukyū* (endless), *mugen no hatten* (limitless development), and *yūdai* (sublime)."[26]

Unbounded by space or time, such words are fellow travelers in the orbit of the "sublime," its "affinity words" as described elsewhere in this volume. The "meaning" of *The Essence of the National Polity* does not exceed its six-page introduction: The Japanese people are bound together in an eternal and unbroken line through their emperors. Throughout the rest of the book the ultimate mystery of the national essence — "Our national essence is vast and unfathomable and cannot be fully captured" — is declared repeatedly. It is a performative document, what Philippe Lacoue-Labarthe and Jean-Luc Nancy call a "mimetic instrument par excellence," employing a style of "affirmative accumulation" (whose own numbing repetitions, it should be noted, threaten to undo its very power).[27]

Such accumulative mimesis, though relying on the meaning of words themselves, is deepened by an incessant repetition that hints at an inexhaustible source and an eternal future. Through repetition the words become talismanic beats in a chant, patterns of sound that fairly leave their semantic value behind. This was a style that the text itself (and other writings of the 1930s) called, following the classical tradition, the "magical power of words" (*kotodama*), performative speech acts to be felt and absorbed rather than analyzed and understood. A modern document nevertheless, the essay ostensibly relies on the authority of empirical methodology — an authority it explicitly understands to underwrite a strong Japanese nation but that it seeks to transcend. It makes the stylistic choice of reinforcing its rote repetitions with variation and amplification. The use of a variety of synonyms implying the boundlessness of eternity serves the propagandistic function of reinforcing through variation. Displaying shades of difference in the naming of boundlessness lends an air of careful philological parsing. At the same time, and at odds with this gesture toward scientific methodology, the multiple variations — the evocative repetitions — imply that that which lies beneath words cannot, or need not be fixed by language because it is beyond language's capacity to render into meaning. It is the sublime.

But the text makes the opposite move as well, fixing the meanings of words with a vengeance. It must do this because the boundlessness of the sublime here is potentially disruptive of the harnessing of citizens that is necessary for the work of nation building. The book offers the potential for personal distraction from the call of this-worldly things. In a tract whose goal is to bind people together, the sublime needs to be kept in check. The energies released by the sublime must be socialized.[28] Like Ōgai's hero, the reader must make the sublime turn away from the isolation of the individual self back toward the larger body of the nation. The turn is guided by concrete words that lash the reader to the sublime. These are words that speak directly of things; they are what Saul Kripke calls "rigid designators," whose reference to an essence cannot be shaken by any possible context.[29] The central ideological term "*kokutai*" means, literally, "national body," and the family unit at its core is described as "one body."[30] These are concrete, too: the legendary founding of the nation, the ancient emperors, the Meiji Emperor, the spirit of the Japanese, Japanese history, the movement of time in Japanese history, Japan's global mission, and the mission of each Japanese citizen to sacrifice himself to the larger body and spirit — all concrete particulars of the concrete national body.

The nation is a "national body" but not simply that. It is an "ancient and unchanging" national body. The lineage of emperors is more than that; it is a line of emperors of "tens of thousands of generations." The fundamental principle of the nation is that it is "everlasting and unchanging." The throne is no mere throne; it is "the throne coeval with heaven and earth and of tens of thousands of generations." The land never stands alone as an abstract unit but is always "our land." By repeatedly binding words to things, the text seeks to bind Japanese to the imperial state and to the emperors' unchanging lineage. Such binding signals the death of polysemy, which, the psychoanalyst Christopher Bollas reminds us, is the first death of the fascist order.[31]

Individuals are bound to the sublime by being reminded of their smallness, which is assimilated into the sublime. They are referred to as "one," "one body," or its honorific form, "one glorious body." Such words are drawn into larger wholes in phrases such as "making into one," "making the spirit of millions into one," or "effacing the self into one." The individual is extended to the polity in phrases like "the nation, one body" and "an unbroken line," and all things are synthesized, tautologically, through "all things synthesized." Finally, the process of integrating the one into the whole is "to assimilate," (*musubu*), literally, to knot, tie, fasten, and what allows the self to be assimilated is a "spirit of selflessness." The selfless self is replaced by the repeated proper names of the gods, and the abstract first-person designation is replaced by a first-person plural possessive, "our." This leads to the ultimate designation of the tract, "our national essence."

In the course of *The Essence of the National Polity*, we learn that "our nation's politics, "our nation's history," our nation's wars and colonies —

our nation's everything — are brought into being and sanctioned by the sublime will of history working through the eternal line of emperors and the Japanese citizens who are members of their family.[32]

Although the audience for the book was called into a community of "we" and "our," readers were not necessarily capable of understanding the elevated language favored by its authors. The targeted audience was the general population, including every schoolchild. As indicated by the publication and diffusion of dozens of explanatory guides to *The Essence of the National Polity*, which were often longer than the original, the audience did not necessarily have access to the language used in the book. This would suggest that it claimed its legitimacy through the prestige of its very abstruseness — through an almost sublime indifference to semantic levels — perhaps suggesting that readers could "get" the essence of words and phrases sanctioned by history without fully discerning their meanings. The circulation of glosses on the text only heightened the sense of belonging to a community of readers of a closed canon, connected through feeling rather than thought.

The Essence of the National Polity embodies the belief in the spiritual power of the unnamable. It assumes that this spiritual power, generated through a proliferation of Japanese words, creates by enunciation and naming things concretely. Japanese words are imbued with the magical power — the *kotodama* — of the ancient poets. *The Essence of the National Polity* loves language. It lavishes praise on the ancient poets, for whom Japan was "a land where words flourish," but also "a land of the gods where words are not celebrated":

> Once a word is spoken it must be put into action; and accordingly words that cannot be put into practice should not be spoken rashly. In this way, once a word is stated, it must be put into practice. Nay, if genuine words are "the spirit of words," they must be put into practice. At the roots of words that can be put into practice there exists truth. Within truth there must be no self (*ga*). Precisely in speaking and acting having completely cast oneself aside lies the truth, and the truth shines.

The truth the passage reaches through its declarations is that language can be sincere and true, and that it is so powerful it can be put into practice and turned to action. It has dispensed with the speaker, who has become one with words that shine. Throughout the book, such shining marks the sublime at the heart of the national essence: the principle of filial piety "shines shining beautifully"; the records that give evidence to the great spirit of the nation's history are the "shining records of our history."[33]

What is shining through the spirit of words that cannot be analyzed is what the book refers to as a "binding" or "fastening" (*musubi*). The "harmony" that holds the nation together is a "great harmony that keeps the body together by the existence of the parts within the whole and by acting through those parts." This harmony is no abstraction, but a "concrete harmony."[34]

The final call to the reader is made in an afterword, a lucid and logical recapping of the main points of the book. Along with the preface, which it recapitulates, the afterword frames the text, lending the entire book an air of naturalness, of being the "unwritten" place into which we sink from the clarity of logic and from which we emerge back into that clarity. By the time we read this conclusion, we have been prepared to accept it not as a novel idea or a tendentious argument but as an echo of what we already know. The "spirit of words" enacted by the book has planted its words into our memory and made them seem to be already within us, there merely to be recalled. We have been led to a conclusion through the sublimity of all things Japanese, a sublimity summed up in the last lines of the text proper, which asks us to discharge our duties to the emperor's throne, which is "infinite between heaven and earth." In the end, we are told that our duty is concrete and artistic: to do "the work of creating a new Japanese culture."[35]

And in doing that work, we would be the conduits of a lineage. We would, in other words, not be ourselves. In his remarkable book *The Language of the Third Reich*, Victor Klemperer described a Nazi language similar to that of *The Essence of the National Polity*. Such language, he said, "does not simply write and think for me, it also increasingly dictates my feelings and governs my entire spiritual being the more unquestioningly and unconsciously I abandon myself to it. And what happens if the cultivated language is made up of poisonous elements or has been made the bearer of poisons? Words can be like tiny doses of arsenic: they are swallowed unnoticed, appear to no effect, and then after a little time the toxic reactions set in after all."[36]

If the language of *The Essence of the National Polity* was toxic, it was also obscure enough to require the writing and disseminating of dozens of books explicating its meanings. Or, more to the point, it was toxic because it was obscure. If it is true, as I have suggested, that the book's message was simple and that it relied on the obscurity of its references and the opacity of its language for its ideological effect, then the effort may have been wasted. Books like *The Essence of the National Polity—A Supplement*, published in 1939, dissect the original tract paragraph by paragraph, providing summaries of chapters in contemporary Japanese, glosses on the original text, definitions and etymologies of key terms, research topics and sources, interpretations, and questions and answers regarding central points.

In writing the book, the author prays, he says, for the day when the youth he addresses become "perfect students and perfect Japanese." He prays for the day when "every word and every line of *The Essence of the National Polity* becomes your blood and becomes your body."[37]

In *The Essence of the National Polity*, the movement of words can be dizzying. Words proliferate in order to point to what cannot be named. The power of what cannot be named is then tamed by the binding of words to the Japanese people. The people are bound to the state and to its sublime mission by these proliferating words. The book depends for its appeal on the power of words as they are performed rather than explicated. In this sense, words are emptied out.

The "binding" so often mentioned in *The Essence of the National Polity*, *musubi*—the knot, tie, or bond that fastens things together—is similar to the Roman symbol of authority that Mussolini adopted for fascism: an ax bundled together by rods. All things in the book lead to this "binding" or "fastening," which is not a mechanical conjoining of independent, equal individuals though reason and logic but, rather, a great harmonic blending within the body of the state of the bodies of individuals. But what binds the Japanese cannot be rigidly equated with the term "fascism," which was one of many ideologies to enter Japan from the West as a solution to the political and cultural impasse of the time.[38] That the book does not use the word "fascism" allows it to present itself not as an ideological contention but as declaring a "natural" truth. This is a truth without a word to describe it. And this quality makes it particularly effective as ideology.

Ōe Kenzaburō's Sublime Turn to Politics

With the collapse of the Japanese state in 1945, and with the end of totalitarianism and fascism, sublimity might be supposed to have lost its binding power. But sublimity as a binding power with aesthetic and political force resurfaced after the war in the non-cognitive language of what came to be known as "the literature of the flesh" (*nikutai bungaku*), a language of mute physical suffering that stood in for an articulated language of postwar malaise at the same time that it offered a cure for that malaise through the sublime suffering of the victims of Hiroshima.

The mute language of malaise — the malaise of a disintegrating family in which human connection seems not merely impossible but also desperately suffocating — was powerfully evoked by Yasuoka Shōtarō (1920–) in the novel *Umibei no kōkei* (A View by the Sea; 1959). The family Yasuoka describes belongs to a postwar middle-class generation poised, in 1959, to leap forward into a new world of dramatic economic growth and material well-being. The novel describes a young man's tending to his ill mother in a seaside hospital. Much of the story is set in her room, whose suffocating space is only made more oppressive by the glare coming through the window and by the sense of the sea waiting invitingly just beyond the hospital walls. There is a long tradition of the sea as an image of the sublime, which the novel as a genre draws on.[39] The sea is an image of silence that contrasts with the incoherent babble that passes, among the family, for communication; the sea also offers the possibility of merging that is denied the son and his mother. Toward the end of the novel, the young man, Shintarō, increasingly experiences moments in which he senses his body opening itself to the outside world and expanding to embrace it. This is an opening to and an expanding into his mother. But intimacy with his mother is not possible, and as his senses intensify, and time seems to slow down and then stop, Shintarō comes to feel his own breath merging with the sea and the sun. Shintarō shrinks from the outside world as he comes to sense only his body, but this is a preparation for a final expansion. In the final scene, he walks along the ocean, and even his senses seem to vanish as he merges with the scene before him, with the "view by the sea." Shintarō's turn to the sublime, his aesthetic experience, leads him away from society to the numbing comfort of quiescence.

The sublime turn toward the political occurs not within the confines of the novel but a few years later, in the work of Ōe Kenzaburō (1935–), a figure as central to the moral and literary map of postwar Japan as Mori Ōgai had been to Meiji Japan. Ōe was the spokesman for the first generation of Japanese who reached maturity after the war, a novelist whose prose style effected a transformation in Japanese letters and whose ethical concerns made him the central literary spokesman of the angst of his generation and for an antinuclear politics. For Ōe, the atomic bombing of Hiroshima — in particular, its "transformation of natural human blood and cells" — represented an "eschatology" beyond our capacity to comprehend or represent in words: "The most terrifying monster lurking in the darkness in Hiroshima is precisely the possibility that man might become no longer human."[40]

The only hope of salvation from the demise of humanness lies with the physically scarred victims of the atomic bomb, who can transform their pain into an active political force: "Hiroshima as a whole must exert all its energy to articulate the essential intellectual grounds for abolishing all nuclear weapons in a way that all of the victims' dehumanizing experiences — the misery, the shame and humiliation, the meanness and degradation — may be converted into things of worth so that the human dignity of the A-bomb victims may be restored. All people with keloids and all without keloids must together affirm this effort."[41]

It is important to note that for Ōe, words like "humiliation," "shame," and "dignity" are foreign to Japanese literature: "The sentence 'That boy is full of dignity,' for example, does not flow naturally in Japanese syntax. It sounds like a sentence translated from a foreign language."[42] For Ōe, the clash of two incongruous languages seems to produce the Benjaminian "pure language" of suffering, which for Ōe was a language of silence. Ōe "discovered dignity in Hiroshima" in the silent suffering of its victims: "Indeed, words do not suffice, for the reality of human suffering transcends language."[43] His "sublime turn" hinges on that suffering: "I regain courage when I encounter the thoroughly and fundamentally human sense of morality in the Hiroshima people 'who do not kill themselves in spite of their misery.' "[44]

Ōe's dilemma, and the irony of his writing on Hiroshima, was that as a non-victim he was barred from the sublimity of suffering and its silent communication and could only ventriloquize the victims' dignified silence with words. That he was lured by their sublimity makes one somewhat uncomfortable. That he turned it into politics assuages the discomfort somewhat. This turn required a resistance to the lure of sublime totalities: "If a person is so clear-eyed as to see a crisis in its totality, he cannot avoid falling into despair. Only the person with duller vision, who sees a crisis as part of ongoing life, can possibly cope with it. It is precisely the 'dullness,' the restricted vision, that permits one to act with reckless human courage in the face of crisis, without succumbing to despair. The lesser vision is backed by patience and, in fact, is capable of penetrating insight into the nature of a crisis."[45]

Sublime Atmosphere

Following the sublime — following "*saburaimu*" — requires us to read with less attention to semantics than to the patterns and rhythms, and then the effects, of artistic forms. Following the sublime asks us to keep in mind that however inchoate and indefinite the emotions revealed in our aesthetic expressions may be, they help us understand our ethical dispositions.[46]

In each of the three historical cases I have presented, the semantic weight of the sublime yielded to the evocation of sublimity. In each a "sublime turn" was made from aesthetics to politics. In Ōgai's *The Dancing Girl*, narrative hesitations led to sublime moments that effected the shift from love to politics. In *The Essence of the National Polity*, words proliferated as they obscured meaning to forge a sublime, political bond among a linguistic and racial community. In *A View by the Sea* and in the essays of Ōe Kenzaburō, the sublimity of silence and the mute language of the body spoke for malaise and offered a cure to malaise: muteness grounded a politics of silent dignity.

In each of these three moments — shattered moments requiring the ideological stitching of aesthetics — the force of the sublime, marked by the word's very absence, created an affective experience with distinct political effects. In the 1880s and 1890s, the English word "sublime" became the Japanese word "*saburaimu*," retaining the strong mark of prestige of its foreign origin. In the 1930s, that foreign origin was considered a tainted mark, and a raft of native words moved to take its place, even as the search for native equivalents ironically confirmed the prestige of the foreign. A government-sponsored ideological tract, which like Ōgai's novella was literary in its manipulation of language, seemed to open the word up to a diversity of meanings through a dizzying proliferation and repetition of words meant to circle around and evoke the sublime. But it did so by closing off complexity of meaning and demanding silent assent to a nation — demanding not only the hearts and minds but also the lives of its citizens. What was silenced was any cognitive understanding of oneself as a political actor with choices to make. In the 1960s, the sublime, not rendered as a word but evoked as a non-cognitive force, called citizens in the opposite direction, to work against the state.

In each historical moment, the sublime released the energies of other words by not naming them. These other words represented forms of attachment. In the 1880s and 1890s, it was "national identity," which the sublime helped set into place; in the 1930s, it was "fascism," which the sublime dissolved, displaced, and energized by hiding it; and in the 1960s, it was "the antinuclear left," which the sublime silently supported.

The sublime also blocked the force of other words by occluding them. These words represented socially disruptive forces. In the 1880s and 1890s, it was "individualism" that the sublime redirected; in the 1930s, it was "erotic, grotesque nonsense" (*ero guro nansensu*), whose antisocial pleasures the sublime worked to repress; and in the 1960s, it was "militarism" that the sublime silently but vehemently rejected.

"Sublime," a word of foreign origin and complex, elusive, even slippery meaning, could not be expected to move easily. When it erased itself and became the atmosphere of sublimity evoked in narratives, it moved assuredly if imperceptibly, as atmospheres do. Indeed, the atmosphere of sublimity was the vernacular form of the word. And as atmosphere, it was capacious, hard both to discern and argue against.[47] It moved from being a mere word in high literary and intellectual circles in the 1880s and 1890s to being an amorphous atmospheric force breathed in by an entire citizenry in the 1930s. After 1945, the sublime suffused the atmosphere with a humanist antifascism that sought to work as a filter to keep the citizenry from breathing that foul air again.

Notes

1. Before arriving in Japan, "sublime" had moved from third-century Greece (Longinus) through a revival in seventeenth-century France (Longinus entered European thought when his work was translated in 1647) and then, for modernity, to its most important resurfacing in the eighteenth century, particularly in the work of Edmund Burke and Immanuel Kant. See Thomas Huhn, "The Kantian Sublime and the Nostalgia for Violence," *Journal of Aesthetics and Art Criticism* 53, no. 3 (Summer 1995): 268–75.

2. Edmund Burke, *A Philosophical Enquiry into the Origin of our Ideas of the Sublime and Beautiful*, ed. Adam Philips (Oxford: Oxford University Press: 1998), 59.

3. For a description and critique of this tradition, see Barbara Claire Freeman, "The Awakening: Waking Up at the End of the Line," in *Sticky Sublime*, ed. Bill Beckley (New York: Allworth Press, 2001), 3–5.

4. Gary Shapiro, "From the Sublime to the Political," *New Literary History* 16, no. 2 (1985): 214–21.

5. In 1934, Henri Focillon argued that the ornament was the best example of a style that leaves content behind as it moves but maintains its forms: see Henri Focillon, *The Life of Forms in Art* (New York: Zone Books, 1992), 69.

6. Walter Benjamin, "The Task of the Translator," in *Illuminations*, ed. Hannah Arendt, trans. Harry Zohn (New York: Schocken Books, 1968), 77. Also see Shapiro, "From the Sublime to the Political," 230.

7. Richard Moran has argued that "it would appear to be the very features of the [fictional] work that do indeed detract from the realistic presentation of the fictional world that actually enhance, and don't inhibit, the intensity and richness of one's emotional involvement with it": see Richard Moran, "Expression of Feeling in Imagination," *Philosophical Review* 103, no 1 (1994): 81, 84. The narrative arts, according to Philip Fisher, are particularly ill-suited to evoking the sublime moment because they are structured through time and memory, forces that pull one away from the instantaneous moment of vision: Philip Fisher, *Wonder, the Rainbow, and the Aesthetics of Rare Experiences* (Cambridge, Mass.: Harvard University Press, 1998), 22.

8. I thank Craig Reynolds for this formulation.

9. *Wayaku-ei jisho* (1869), University of California, Berkeley Library, East, 5840.9.0404.

10. *Kitamura* Tōkoku, "Jinsei ni aiwataru to wa nan no wake zo," in *Nihon kindai bungaku taikei* 9 (Tokyo: Kadokawa shoten, 1973), 196. Tōkoku described the sublime in a famous poem about a jailed man discovering his interior self in an epiphanic moment bathed in the whiteness of the moon: "*Sōshu no shi*," in *Nihon kindai bungaku taikei* 9 (Tokyo: Kadokawa shoten, 1973), 44–67.

11. Ōgai was a serious translator of European philosophy and aesthetics and certainly knew of the sublime, if not directly from Kant and Burke, or even from Longinus (though my hunch is that he did know it from them), then from Schilling, whose book lies stacked in the Berlin apartment of the hero of *The Dancing Girl*, or even from Schopenhauer, Hartman, or Emerson: *Mori Ōgai, Maihime*, in *Nihon kindai bungaku taikei* 60 (Tokyo: Kadokawa Shoten, 1974), 57.

12. I thank Carol Gluck for this formulation.

13. *Mori Ōgai, Maihime*, 47.

14. Ibid., 54.

15. Ibid., 155.

16. Ibid., 58–59.

17. Murray Krieger, *Ekphrasis: The Illusion of the Natural Sign* (Baltimore, Md.: Johns Hopkins University Press, 1992), 1–3.

18. Edward Hirsch, "A Shadowy Exultation," *Sewanee Review* 57, no 2 (1999): 227.

19. Neil Hertz, *The End of the Line: Essays on Psychoanalysis and the Sublime* (New York: Columbia University Press, 1985), 14, 5.

20. Ibid., 6.

21. Terry Eagleton, *The Ideology of the Aesthetic* (Oxford: Blackwell, 1990), 17–28, 89.

22. See Makoto *Ueda*, "Yūgen and Erhabene: Ōnishi Yoshinori's Attempt to Synthesize Japanese and Western Aesthetics," in *Culture and Identity: Japanese Intellectuals during the Interwar Period*, ed. J. Thomas Rimer (Princeton, N.J.: Princeton University Press, 1990); and Daisetz T. Suzuki, *Zen and Japanese Culture* (Princeton, N.J.: Princeton University Press, 1970), 220–21.

23. For example, *Zeami* Motokiyo's (1363–1443) poetics of the Nō theater: see

Makoto Ueda, *Literary and Art Theories in Japan* (Ann Arbor: University of Michigan Press, 1992), 63–66, 291–95.

24. Michael Fried calls this a "counter offensive of identification or mimesis": see Michael Fried, *Realism, Writing, Disfiguration* (Chicago: University of Chicago Press, 1987), 69.

25. Victor Klemperer, *The Language of the Third Reich: LTI, Lingua Tertii Imperii: A Philologist's Notebook*, trans. Martin Brady (London: Athlone Press, 2000), 110.

26. Drawn from *Kokutai no hongi* (Tokyo: Naimushō, 1941).

27. Philippe Lacoue-Labarthe and Jean-Luc Nancy, "The Nazi Myth," trans. Brian Holmes, *Critical Inquiry* 16, no. 2 (1990): 278, 304.

28. Huhn, "The Kantian Sublime and the Nostalgia for Violence," 268–75.

29. Saul Kripke, *Naming and Necessity* (Cambridge, Mass.: Harvard University Press, 1980), 69.

30. *Kokutai no hongi*, 43.

31. Christopher Bollas, "The Fascist State of Mind," in *Being a Character* (New York: Hill and Wang, 1992), 202.

32. The family is what Kaja Silverman calls, in a different context, the "dominant fiction" of the social formation and its "fundamental image of unity": Kaja Silverman, *Male Subjectivity at the Margins* (New York: Routledge, 1992), 42.

33. *Kokutai no hongi*, 62, 47, 84.

34. Ibid., 51.

35. Ibid., 142–43.

36. Klemperer, *The Language of the Third Reich*, 16.

37. *Hosaka* Hiroshi, *Kokutai no hongi seikō* (Tokyo: Ōbunsha, 1939), 3.

38. Ibid., 14.

39. Freeman, "The Awakening," 15–20; Steven Z. Levine, "Seascapes of the Sublime: Vernet, Monet, and the Oceanic Feeling," *New Literary History* 16, no. 2 (1985): 377–400.

40. "The bomb embodied the absolute evil of war, transcending lesser distinctions such as Japanese or Allies, attacker or attacked": Ōe Kenzaburō, *Hiroshima Notes*, trans. David L. Swain and Toshi Yonezawa (New York: Marion Boyars, 1995), 114, 182.

41. Ibid., 106.

42. Ibid., 104.

43. Ibid., 84.

44. Ibid., 85.

45. Ibid., 125.

46. Charles Altieri, *The Particulars of Rapture: An Aesthetics of the Affects* (Ithaca, N.Y.: Cornell University Press, 2003), 69.

47. Like the word "security" discussed in the chapter by Itty Abraham in this volume.

WORDS THAT COVER

'Aqalliyya/**Minority**

in Modern Egyptian Discourse

The Arabic word " *'aqalliyya*" (minority) is an unstable presence in public
and intellectual discourse in modern Egypt. It appears and disappears in
discussions of national identity, difference, and religion, and its applicability to the Egyptian Christians known as Copts has generated particularly
contentious debate. The domestic and global circulation of words, the
transnational character of Arabic and Arab public discourse, and the role
of Coptic diasporas have combined over time to produce the meanings
and uses of the word "minority" in Egypt today.

The translation of " *'aqalliyya*" for "minority" is straightforward enough.
Difficulties arise when it comes to deciding whether the word applies to
Egyptian, Arab, and Muslim societies — and if so, which groups should be
designated as such — and whether acknowledging the word "minority" necessarily implies a political and social "problem." Many criticize the term as a
translation of Western concepts and preoccupations, even though the word
itself is neither borrowed nor linguistically problematic. Some suggest replacing it with terms historically associated with Islamic history and political
experience; others concentrate on which groups qualify to occupy this contested semantic space.

I explore these questions as they evolved during the long period of
transition from empire to nation in Egypt, which saw a discursive move
from the "protection of minorities" in the late-nineteenth-century imperial context to the notion of "minority rights" in early-twentieth-century
nationalism. After the formation of the independent republic in 1952, the
word " *'aqalliyya*" was used to debate the place of Copts in the broader
political communities of Egyptians, Arabs, and Muslims. And now, in the
contemporary global context, the status of the Copts in Egypt is discussed

in terms of international human rights (rather than minority rights) and is influenced by the role of the Coptic diaspora in the United States.

Political institutions, intellectuals, and representatives of ethnic and religious communities all play their part in mediating these local–global intersections. But when the national and international come face to face — as in recent "fact-finding" missions from the United States to Egypt — the dissonance and disparate genealogies of the two discourses become quite clear. To highlight the motion of the word in its absence as well as its presence, I conclude with a look at the implications of the fact that neither Nubians nor Sudanese in Egypt are generally identified as "minorities" — only the Copts. Examining these "null cases" shows the limits of the circulation of the word " *'aqalliyya*" in Egyptian discourse and the ways in which it conceals and obscures as much as it reveals.

The Lexicon

The word "minority" as a reference to ethnic, linguistic, or religious groups is part of the idiom of nation-states. The empires that preceded them were multiethnic and multiconfessional and had developed legal categories and policies for managing and constructing social difference. These legacies continue to be important; however, the politics of the modern word "minority" is a corollary of the process of constructing a "majority" that is alleged to represent the nation. Although the term may sometimes seem to be used neutrally in a statistical or demographic sense, the political nature of the nation-making process means that "minority" nearly always marks a category of exclusion — or, at least, of exception. Even if the debate focuses on positive aspects such as minority rights, tolerance or diversity, or the privileging of a certain social group, the minority–majority pairing is a dichotomy that asserts the (often unwelcome) interruption of the allegedly homogeneous or harmonious national community by a group that is "out of place."

For this reason, contestations in Arab intellectual discourse over who is and is not a "minority" should not be read as denial, repression, or ethnic cleansing, though there are instances of these practices. Instead, these debates are better seen as attempts to reconcile the fact of social difference, not simply though ensuring legal rights but also through developing ideologies that foster a sense of belonging across social groups, and to do so in ways that resonate with historical and cultural contexts.

The issue of minorities in Arab countries is fraught with a history of certain groups' being used to provide a pretext for foreign intervention, so that contemporary debates on minority rights are quickly tarred as complicit with Western aspirations to exert power over the region. In addition, in Egypt, as in other Arab countries, domestic contestations are often overshadowed by the "larger" geopolitical issues of the region. The Arab–Israeli conflict, the struggle for Palestinian statehood, the politics of oil, the Iraq war — all deflect energy and focus away from "smaller" issues of difference within the nation. In a hostile international environment, national solidarity retains discursive priority, even when divisive social issues force themselves on the attention of the public through violence. The Sudanese writer Haydar Ibrahim 'Ali points out that, despite the manifest ethnic and confessional strife in Lebanon and Sudan (and latent conflict in other countries), Arab intellectual and political energies have not been invested in this issue.[1] In Egypt, arguments over the political and legal status of Copts are perennially linked to colonialism and contemporary international power struggles. Yet, as Haydar rightly stresses, it is a misapprehension to conclude that because the issue of minorities arises within these contexts, it is therefore *not* a problem.

The word " *'aqalliyya*" seems to appear first in Egyptian public discourse in the early 1920s in debates over whether the new constitution should include specific language concerning "the protection of minorities" and whether representative bodies should have a system, such as quotas, to ensure the representation of minorities. Twentieth-century Arabic dictionaries and lexicons often either omit the word completely or link it directly to issues of "protection," "minority problems," "representation," and "rights." The word that " *'aqalliyya*" displaces (though only partially) is "*ta'ifa*," a much older word for social difference, which translates as "sect," with its attendant religious connotations. "*Ta'ifa*," for example, is used in Lebanon in its sectarian meaning, just as it is in Iraq to refer to the Sunni–Shi'i conflict. On the brink of modern nationhood, Egyptians oscillated between defining Copts through the earlier word, "*ta'ifa*" (sect), and a new word, " *'aqalliyya*" (minority).

The two words remain intertwined in their meanings and usage, or it may be more accurate to say that "*ta'ifa*" continues to inflect the understanding of " *'aqalliyya*." A recent dictionary defines " *'aqalliyya*" as "a small segment that follows a religion or sect," further explaining that it refers to ethnic or racial minorities, the representation of minorities, or the rights of minorities.[2] In this way, religion stands above race or ethnicity as the main differentiation among peoples. This is not an unexpected legacy of a succession of Islamic empires, whose legal systems dealt with difference mainly in terms of the rights of religious groups to organize their worship and regulate affairs of marriage, death, and inheritance.

"*Dhimma*," is another word associated with religious difference — as in "*'ahl al-dhimma*," for the "protected peoples," which refers to Christians and Jews living in Islamic states. *'Ahl al-dhimma* is in opposition to *'ahl al-milla*, the followers of Islam.[3] Under the Ottomans, the word "*milla*" turned into "*millet*," used to refer to religious groups that had negotiated some measure of autonomy over their internal community affairs. Later it took on the "secular" meaning of "nation." The same "secularization" of a word away from its religious connotations also occurred with "*'umma*" in Arabic, which changed from a reference to the global community of Muslims to the contemporary meaning of "nation." Recently "*dhimma*" has re-emerged in contemporary Islamist discourse on the Coptic issue in Egypt, indicating the "Islamization" of the discussion and a deliberate turn away from "*'aqalliyya*," the secular, nationalist word for minority.

"*Jaliya*" is another affinity word in the cluster within which "*'aqalliyya*" struggles to find its meanings. Often translated as community, it is, however, community with a difference in that it refers to an in-migrating group fleeing persecution and seeking protection. (The modern Arabic word for refugee, "*laji'*," comes from the same root.) While Copts in Egypt are never referred to as a *jaliya*, in the United States and Canada they are called the Coptic *jaliya*, as indeed are Arab Americans or any other Arab group living in "exile." In contrast to the Copts, the Sudanese in Egypt remain a *jaliya*, forever, at least linguistically, in exile.

Nationalist Discourses: Coptness, Arabness, and Egyptianness

The Copts of Egypt are one of the oldest Christian communities in the region and are generally considered to constitute 10–20 percent of the current population, spread across all social classes and all of Egypt's provinces, though with a concentration in the south, or Upper Egypt. Coptic Christians were the majority of the population until the Islamic invasion in the seventh century and the gradual Arabization of Egypt, which transformed Copts into a *dhimmi* group (non-Muslims living under Islamic rule) and Coptic into a liturgical language. The opening sentences of Abu Sayf Yusuf's *The Copts and Arab Nationalism* provides a good summary of the conventional discourse on Copts and on the notions of "majority" and "minority" in contemporary Egypt: "There lives on the land of Egypt one people formed out of a majority that follows Islam and a minority (*'aqalliyya*), represented by the Copts who follow Christianity. The terms majority and minority here refer to numerical percentages. For the Copts as a religious minority do not constitute a racial or ethnic or linguistic minority. . . . [H]istorically social integration has primarily been linked to the Arabization of the Egyptian people, both Muslims and Christians, that is, their adoption of the Arabic language as a tool of communication and cultural terminology."[4]

According to Yusuf's formulation, the only significant difference among Egyptians is that of religion, and there are glosses and elisions even there. Copts are the only Christian group recognized, in spite of the existence of (albeit smaller) numbers of non-Coptic Christians as well as the various sects within the Copts themselves. The Jews, who represented a sizable group as late as the 1950s, are erased in this sweeping view of homogeneous continuity. This conflation derives largely from the assimilation of all other Christian and Jewish groups into the category of "foreigner" and "non-Egyptian," which took place in the colonial period. Having stated that the only minority were the Copts, the formula forecloses the possibility of other groups to be distinguished by race or ethnicity, including, for example, the Nubians. Arabness is presented as a linguistic patina that brings national ethnic unity and continuity. In this reckoning, differences within Islam are also effaced. The long (pseudo) historical view taken here also precludes any future emergence of groups that might disrupt Egyptian cohesion and integration.

Such were the views of a nationalist author who was not a Copt. While focused on the specificity of Egypt, it echoed many Arab nationalist texts in other places. Since the Arab "nation" remains an incomplete project and, ideologically, current Arab states are seen as provisional solutions to the realization of the pan-national project, problems of managing difference can be indefinitely postponed.

For the Islamists, the framework is different, although many of their interpretations of foreign intervention echo that of the nationalists. For them, Islamic history and legal practice defines the status of non-Islamic groups, while other kinds of difference besides religion did not exist in the

Islamic community (*'umma*). Fahmi Huwaydi presents a mainstream Islamist view, arguing that discriminatory practices concerning non-Muslims living in Arab society (*dhimmis*) were misinterpretations of the Qur'an since Islam has always insisted on equality. The issue is simply the assurance of the right to worship; in every other aspect, there should be no distinction on the basis of religion. Huwaydi reviews the long history of Islam as well as that of colonial intervention in the region and the ways in which minorities and *millets* offered a basis for Western "penetration," including a substantial section on how French and British colonialism in Egypt created and exacerbated conflicts between Copts and Muslims. Huwaydi also insists that the problem of minorities is a result of internal weakness as much as it is due to French and British colonialism, for "penetration only succeeds in the case of a body that is penetrable."[5] Here the word " *'aqalliyya*" is replaced by the Islamic word "*dhimma*," and non-religious forms of difference are erased.

Coptic "official history" closely follows the nationalist formulation and, indeed, partakes in it. In this history, Copts are depicted as the original Egyptians and have always been an integral part of Egyptian society. The fact that the Coptic church early on sought independence from Rome and resisted its domination is cited as a sign — indeed, proof — of the Copts' Egyptianness, characterized by the rejection of foreign domination. Ethnic unity is asserted, and the role of prominent Copts in all fields of life, politics, and nation building is emphasized. The word "minority" is overtly rejected as not applicable to Copts, and the word "citizen" is highlighted, with the discussion focusing on the meanings and practices of citizenship.

How do these variations — secular, Islamist, Coptic — on the nationalist theme relate to the discussion in the colonial period, when the word " *'aqalliyya*" was coined and first debated? How and when were Copts constituted as a category in the instruments of power wielded by colonial rulers? I now turn to the census and the press as two arenas where the concepts of "Copt" and "minority" were produced.

From Empire to Nation-State: Changing Categories

In their nineteenth-century struggles with the Ottomans, European imperialist powers deployed the argument of a purported need of religious groups for "protection." One of the many "capitulations" demanded of the weakened Ottoman state, this claim had everything to do with European economic interests and their dependence on groups acting as middlemen for their commercial activities in the Ottoman Empire. Various religious denominations were thus divided among the British, French, and Russians, whose consuls increasingly interceded with Ottoman authorities on behalf of these communities. The situation was further complicated by missionaries, especially British and American, who mainly succeeded in converting Christians from Eastern churches to various Western denominations, thus creating new religious groups who were also said to be in need of "protection."

The Egyptian case was complicated by the overlapping imperial jurisdictions of Ottoman, Egyptian (khedival), and British rule. In addition, Egypt's growing economy attracted a large influx of immigrants in the early and mid-nineteenth century from other parts of the Ottoman Empire, as well as from Europe. Syrian and Lebanese Christian communities formed in Cairo and Alexandria. Jewish migrants from Syria, Lebanon, Turkey, and Europe coexisted in complex relations with the indigenous Jewish community, and the same was true for incoming Greeks and Cypriots. Adding to the colonial presence of the British and the French, numbers of Hungarians, Austrians, Poles, and Germans arrived from Europe.

The presence of these immigrants led to a new word in the social lexicon: "foreigner" (*frangi* or *khawaga*), defined now in contrast to the "Egyptian." Although this label came to be applied to the Jews, Armenians, and Greeks who had lived in Egypt before the new influx, it was never used for the Copts because of their indisputable indigenous status. This framing of large, long-standing communities as outside the ethnic identity of "Egypt" meant that the exodus of these groups after the establishment of the republic in 1952 required no reimagining of the nation, even in the face of the vast disruptions in economic, social, and cultural networks caused by their departure.[6]

The break-up of the Ottoman Empire brought the redrawing of the map and the creation of twenty-two Arab states, all of which passed under colonial rule, predominantly French and British. In Egypt, the transition from Ottoman to colonial rule differed from that of most other Arab states in that the khedival regime remained in power and because British colonial rule had already begun during the Ottoman period. The instruments of power and ways of marking populations, such as laws and censuses, thus showed some continuity, even as constitutions were written and new representative bodies were defined during the 1920s. It was during this transition from empire to nation that the word "*'aqalliyya*" emerged, producing a new concept of a "minority."

Censuses and Their Categories

The censuses taken in Egypt between 1848 and 1986 mark the route from multiethnic empire to allegedly homogeneous nation-state in the context of changing national and global politics. The modernization of population categories and census schedules began with the census of 1882, "often called the first 'modern' census of Egypt, because it made use of European methods."[7] Important here was the transition from the household to the individual as the basic census unit, as well as the aggregation of individuals according to ever more complex categorizations of race, nationality, and religion rather than residence and location. The 1882 census was the last one undertaken before the British occupation of Egypt and reflects the multiple imperial powers involved: The preface of the report was signed by a French census director working under a British "Financial Counsel" to the Ministry of Finance headed by an Egyptian. The first British census of 1907 appeared under the direction of C. C. Lewis "of the India Civil Service." In contrast, the first post-independence census in 1959 was issued by the Department of Statistics and Census of the United Arab Republic.[8] The 1962 census, titled "Ten Years of Revolution," included graphics of workers, students, and soldiers to signify the brave new world of the rational, socialist nation-state, prefaced by a quotation from President Gamal Abdel Nasser.[9]

The reports also address a changing international administrative community. Thus, the 1917 census report explained that the wealth of information supplied in the report was meant "to give to foreign statisticians a full description of the adaptation of modern census methods to eastern countries of a cosmopolitan character."[10] By 1986, the census was produced by the Central Agency for Public Mobilization and Statistics of the Arab Republic of Egypt and acknowledged "the foreign assistance from international agencies such as the United States Agency for International Development (USAID), U.S. Bureau of the Census, [and] United Nations Fund for Population Activities (UNFPA)."[11]

The word "minority" did not appear in any of these censuses, in any of the languages used, whether French, English, or Arabic. Yet the censuses taken under colonial rule focused significantly, almost obsessively, on "nationality" and "race' and over time developed ever finer categorizations of the population. In contrast, the post-republic censuses abandoned race, simplified the definition of nationality, and maintained only a minimal categorization by religion.

The 1882 census divided the population into three major categories: "Sedentary Egyptians" (divided into indigenous Egyptians, Egyptians originating elsewhere in the Ottoman Empire, and Sudanese), "Egyptian Bedouins" (divided into nomadic and semi-sedentary), and "Foreigners" (*étrangères*, listed in order of size of community, from Greeks at the top to Danes, then "Persians and other Asiatics" at the bottom). According to the report, "foreigners" constituted 1.34 percent of the population but had an importance beyond their numbers: "The foreigners form the least important numerical fraction of the general population; working mainly in commerce, they exercise a great influence in the country. Constituted in colonies under the jurisdiction of their consuls, the inhabitants of foreign nationality established on Egyptian territory enjoy diverse privileges conceded by the Ottoman capitulations."[12]

In the 1897 census, the Copts appear as a category of their own in a new section on "religions and cults," which is divided into Muslims, Christians (Orthodox, Catholics, and Protestants), and Israelites. Each of the Christian dominations was further subdivided into various churches, including Coptic Orthodox and Coptic Catholic. The report was replete with indications of the importance of noting the Coptic presence in the population. For example, a note on regional representation stated that Christians were found in relatively large numbers in Upper Egypt, a region particularly inhabited by Christians "of the Coptic race."[13]

The 1907 census continued presenting tables on Copts, as well as a map showing the distribution of Copts over the country. It also added a new section for "Nationality," which the 1917 census expanded into "Nationality and Race." Jurisdictional boundaries were crucial at that time, since "foreigners" and even "Egyptians" came under the jurisdiction of different states, consular sections and courts, and, importantly, churches. But the distinctions made the category of "Egyptian" both increasingly exclusionary and also fragmented. Thus, in the 1907 census "foreigners" included "not only Europeans, but Turks, Armenians, Syrians, and all other non-Egyptian nationalities, except Sudanese, who in 1897 were treated as part of the indigenous population and were not returned separately."[14]

Significantly, all tables (on distribution by age, sex, civil condition, education, etc.) were now segregated by religious group: Musulmans, Copts, Jews, and "other religions."[15] In this way, religion became the main indicator of difference, as opposed to the settled–nomad distinction.

The 1917 census drops the section on "Religion" and subsumes such data into the section on "Nationalities." Nationalities are now divided by religion as well as by "race." There is a separate table for "Distribution of Copts by District," and in the table for "non-Moslems of Egyptian race by sect" (*ta'ifa* in the Arabic headings) where the term "Egyptian" appears under race, there is a footnote stating "presumed Copts." The instructions for collecting data on religion read, "The terms Christian, Copt or Greek, should not appear alone in this column."[16] However they also read that, "In the case of Copts, notwithstanding the theoretical objection that the word 'copt' does not designate a special race or religion, it should be entered in the race column because it embraces a definite community."[17] Thus, the Copts are a race but not a nationality and are not a separate religion but categorized according to their denominations. The report states, "Nationality must not be confused with race or religion. There is no such nationality as Jewish or Coptic."[18]

Continuing the trend in increasingly exclusionary categories, in the 1917 census the Sudanese were separated from Egyptians. Also, for the first time Egyptians appeared not only under the heading "Local Subject" but also as British, French, and Italian subjects. With regard to "foreigners," in a note on fertility and growth rates, distinctions were drawn between "foreigners" who looked on Egypt as their home (such as Greeks and Italians) and those (such as the British and the French) who saw their presence as temporary.

Thus, Copts first become more visible as a religious community (1897 and 1907 censuses) and then less distinguished by religion than as a racial category (1917 census). In the subsequent censuses, the categories of religion, sect, and nationality continued to be elaborated. While Muslims remained undifferentiated, non-Muslims were now divided into Orthodox, Catholic, Protestant, and Jews, with further subdivisions within these categories. In the first post-republican census in 1959, "nationality" simply meant citizen of a particular country; the race categories disappeared; and religion was reduced to "Musulmans; Christians (divided into Copts and Other Christians), and Israelites."[19] The 1962 census celebrating "Ten Years of Revolution" listed only Muslims, Christians, and Jews. In contrast to the colonial censuses, this "nation-state" report introduced sections on the "national economy" and the different economic sectors, services, health, and education, while the homogenization of the population was symbolized by the graphics of soldiers, students, and workers, without any further identity markers, even those of gender. Indeed, the temporary constitution of 1964 did not mention religious difference at all, except to declare the freedom of belief and worship. And representative quotas in the parliament were assigned not to ethnic or religious groups but to workers and peasants.[20]

From the French colonial vision of a population divided between nomadic and sedentary to a British imperial obsession with nationality and race to an Egyptian national denial of all identity differences, the Copts of Egypt became increasingly visible during colonial rule, only to be erased as a census category under national rule.

The Press: The Copts between "Sect" and "Minority"

A reading of the press during this period of transition to the nation-state provides another perspective on the position of the Copts in the emergent nation and the corollary appearance of the word " *'aqalliyya.*" In *Al-Ahram*, the prominent Egyptian daily established in 1875 (and still the most influential national newspaper today), the word " *'aqalliyya*" began to appear in the 1920s in heated discussions over the terms of Egyptian independence from Britain and whether the new constitution should specifically allocate quotas for minority groups in representative bodies. Ten years earlier, the discussion in the paper concerning the Coptic "Assiut conference" of 1911 had consistently used the word "*ta'ifa*" to refer to the Copts, although the discussions foreshadowed the need for a new word that would emerge ten years later.

The Assiut Conference of 1911: Copts as Sects (*Ta'ifa*)

At a time when Muslim–Coptic relations were being worked out in the context of newly established political parties and representative bodies, some Coptic political leaders called for a "conference" on 6 March 1911 to discuss "Coptic demands." The conference was supported or opposed by segments of the political elite and strongly opposed by the British. Despite repeated attempts by the government to block the conference, the organizers prevailed, and the conference was held in Assiut at a Coptic school and attended by more than one thousand Copts.

Al-Ahram covered the conference in great detail for almost two weeks in March 1911, presenting the opinions of the editors and of prominent public figures who wrote letters to the paper or whose public statements were reprinted. The coverage gives a flavor of the language of Egyptian and Arab nationalism in this formative period.

Al-Ahram supported the conference insofar as it represented a right of assembly, freedom of discussion, and opposition to British policies. Still, it expressed ambivalence about the nature and the details of the event and the demands it presented. It consistently refused to acknowledge the specificity of the Coptic situation. In response to the demand for more high-level government positions, the paper both denied that Copts and Christians had been discriminated against by Egyptian rulers and also asserted that Copts were not the only ones denied political office by the British. A more confrontational tone crept into the discussion of the issue of Sunday as a holiday for government employees. One editorial stated, "The government of Egypt is Islamic. It will not change this attribute, and the holiday of its offices is Friday. Christian employees are allowed to be late to work in order to perform their religious duties as well as absenting themselves on major holidays. Isn't this enough?"[21] In addition, "The Sunday holiday is not restricted to the Copts but affects all sects (*tawa'if*), from the English employees in the service of the Egyptian government or in control of it and even the least important Christian from the smallest Christian sect who is a member of this service."[22]

The first of the two main (and interrelated) critiques of the conference was that Copts were separating themselves from the rest of the national polity: "The biggest problem would be if those who convened the Coptic conference would appear to be a sect (*ta'ifa*) separated from the total of the nation (*'umma*) with its Muslims and Christians and Jews."[23] The second criticism was that the conference blurred the distinction between what is religious and of concern only to a particular sect and what is political and "are issues that do not pertain to the Coptic sect alone but to the whole nation."[24]

A letter from the head of the Ahrar (Freedom) Party summarized the position this way: "The slogan of the party is that 'the religion of an individual is personal belief and the religion of the nation is patriotism'." The letter continued, "We ask your association in the name of the one patria (*watan*) and the one nation (*'umma*) to alter the religious nature of its stance in the discussion of matters that are purely national, because working with a religious tone in this society leads to general division and competition among the totality of the nation."[25]

Everyone in the paper, including the conference conveners, asserted that the conference was, or should be, for the good of the Egyptian nation. In response to the Coptic patriarch, who had been enlisted by the government to censure the conference, the bishop of Assiut asserted that "the purpose is to strengthen the bonds of love between all Egyptian elements by protecting the rights of the Coptic sect (*ta'ifa*). . . . [I]t only aims at the benefit of the whole Egyptian nation (*'umma*)."[26] Reports of the conference proceedings focused on the participants singing the khedival anthem and chanting slogans such as, "Long live Egypt for the Egyptians."[27]

The sentiment that Egypt was one body and one nation was repeated again and again, along with the conviction that Egypt was a *modern* nation. The paper listed the demands of the Copts as "religious freedom, justice, and equality" which, it continued, "already exist in the Egyptian state, [alone] among all other Eastern states." The editorial expanded on this theme:

> The spirit of Mohammad 'Ali that created Egypt as a state and took in its service all good men without regard to their sect or nationality or religion is still flowing in the body of Egypt. If the English have divided and dispersed and discriminated, this action of theirs affects all Egyptian sects (*tawa'if*) equally for there is no internal strife between those sects, because the issue is not in the hands of one sect and not another, but rather it is in the hands of a foreign stranger who rules with absolutism.[28]

As many of the commentators feared, one of the repercussions of the "Coptic conference" was indeed an expression of religious confrontation. Thus, "With discreet government sponsorship, a counter-congress was held to refute the sectarian bias of the Assiut conference."[29] The opposing conference was initially called the "Muslim conference" but then changed to the "Egyptian conference," because "Muslims constitute the absolute majority in the country."[30]

Here, the word "majority" was used for the first time in the discussion. Could the word "minority" be far behind?

Hostility to the Coptic conference appeared after the Egyptian conference was announced. The newspaper saw the competing conferences as proof that the Coptic conference had created religious friction and also weakened the Egyptian polity vis-à-vis the colonizer. An editorial titled "The Two Conferences" commented that the way Egypt handled this matter would "cross the seas to Europe; it will be recorded in the dossiers of London as a [judgment] on our people . . . and it will be the biggest proof as to whether Egypt deserves self rule or not."[31] Another editorial put it this way: "The clearly sad and dangerous issue in all this is that we should be in the twentieth century and see Egypt dividing into sects and factions, instead of being one body. This is due to the policies of the occupiers and the negligence or lack of experience of Egyptian politicians. So let those among the English who would laugh, laugh today, for they have in Egypt a second India."[32]

Decolonization: Copts as 'Aqalliyya

In 1922, the British issued a declaration announcing the end of the British Protectorate and giving Egypt independence but stipulating that the British government reserved the absolute right to control, among other things, the "defense of the interests of foreigners in Egypt and the protection of minorities." *Al-Ahram* waxed indignant, stating that the British government was wrongly dealing with the independence of Egypt as an internal affair of the empire rather than as an international matter. The paper's editorial also pointed out that the notion of the protection of minorities was emerging in the context of the new international system and establishment of the League of Nations in 1920. And further, "It appears that England felt that acknowledging the independence of Egypt means that the League of Nations would be able to extend its protection on minorities and thus some countries will interfere in the affairs of Egypt."[33]

The press reported a division between Egyptian political leaders on this issue, with some arguing that minority rights should be included in the constitution. Under the headline "The Representation of Minorities According to a Noble Lawyer and a Dangerous Sociologist," *Al-Ahram* summarized the arguments for and against, according to two members of the committee drafting the constitution. For Tawfiq Duss (the "noble lawyer"), the protection of minorities should be included in the constitution so as not to give the British and other Europeans any legal pretext for future interference in Egypt's affairs. He argued that all sorts of reasonable legislative action could be construed by Europeans as an attack on the rights of minorities. Furthermore, he said, ignorant people could be swayed by false promises and might themselves request the protection of foreign powers. He addressed his letter "to the thinkers of the Egyptian nation" and insisted that he was putting forth the case not as a Christian but as an Egyptian. He mentioned that Belgium and Spain protected minority rights and continued, "I am the first who would wish for the disappearance of religious quarrels and the first to hope that one day we reach a unified system even in our purely personal affairs."[34]

The response by Abdel 'Abd al-Hamid Badawi (the "dangerous sociologist") argued that, although Europe had religious minorities, only political differences were represented in political councils, which had no room for religion. His own statement was replete with religious terms. In reference to Copts and to religious difference, he used the word "sect" (ta'ifa) and other phrases meaning religious communities. He expanded the use of the word "ta'ifa" (in fact returning it to its older meaning) when he said that the majority was also divided into "sects" and divisions, each with its own interests, such as merchants, landowners, and the different professions. His sociological analysis described a patriarchal system in which the power of the father had been based on compassion and kindness. However, he said, the new era was determined by law, which made matters contentious and caused families to split apart. He looked forward to a time when unified interests rather than religious doctrine would bind people together: "I hope to keep national unity, and I hope that we do not create with our own hands a system that distinguishes between elements of the nation and divides it into minorities and majorities. For life after that would only be strife between them. Or do you hope after that that the foreigner will refrain from entering into our affairs under the pretense of protecting the minorities?"[35]

Under the headline "No Minority and No Majority," *Al-Ahram* reported on a meeting of Coptic lawyers, engineers, doctors, notables, and employees who rejected British demands: "Then Mr. Wisa Wasef spoke and said the word 'minorities' that the Versailles conference approved does not apply to the Copts of Egypt but refers to those like the Jews in Romania and the Germans in Transylvania—for they are groups that have been deprived of many of their national rights as opposed to the Copts who participate with their brothers in patriotism and nationality and social and legislative rights."[36] Another editorial rejected the doctrine of "the protection of minorities," saying:

I do not deny that in Egypt there are minorities of Copts and Arabs and Jews and sects of eastern Christians and that many of these minorities enjoy special laws and different privileges of representation in representative bodies. . . . The reasons for the existence of minorities . . . is that nationalism in the past was based on religion rather than the unity of blood and history and the patria. . . . The West has progressed over the East in the idea of building national unity on the basis of the unity of blood and history and patria. This is a result of the fanaticism of the Westerners for their religions. They fought for their religions for centuries and many sects became extinct and others emigrated and enmity took root in the hearts of the rest until human thinking became enlightened and religion was restricted to doctrine and the basis for general social issues became a civil one. But in the East, the tolerance of the Islamic religion and its compassion did not prevent the non-Islamic sects from living with it. . . . Each sect had its own rules and semi-autonomy. . . . I assure my brother Egyptians that the majority and the minorities present now in Egypt are historical products and will fade ere long as their counterparts disappeared in the lands of the West. . . . Political parties will be based on interests and ideas rather than religion and doctrine.[37]

Through these public debates, the politics of the word " '*aqalliyya*," and the ways in which the Copts were, or were not, described by it, were set in a context of foreign interventionist designs and nationalist resistance and sovereignty. Now, almost a century later, there is a remarkable consistency with these earlier usages.

The Contemporary Politics of Intervention

Although there has been no shortage of commentary concerning the place of Copts in Egyptian society, the issue took on an added urgency in the late 1990s when violent clashes occurred between Copts and Muslims in Egyptian provincial towns and villages. This occurred in the context of a rise in Islamist militancy and severe government repression of organized Islamist movements. Two events illustrate how the issue was once again linked to "foreign intervention" and how the word " '*aqalliyya*" again became the site of contestation, although now couched in new terms such as "democratization," "human rights," and "freedom of expression."

The attempt of the sociologist Saad Eddine Ibrahim's Ibn Khaldun

Center to include a discussion of the Copts in a conference on minorities in the Arab world in 1994 raised such a furor that the conference was relocated from Cairo to Cyprus. Ibrahim himself was later taken to court by the government for his research activities and alleged that his attention to Coptic concerns was the primary reason for his being targeted by the government. The conference was criticized by no less a personage than Muhammad Hasanayn Haykal, the leading Egyptian journalist and public thinker. Under the headline "Citizens or Protected Minority?" *Al-Ahram* summarized Haykal's view: "Copt and Muslim in Egypt are two parts of a single civilizational bloc, he argues, and to divide them would set the country back hundreds of years."[38] An article in the Arabic newspaper *Al-Hayat* (published in Paris) commented that "a number of our Coptic brethren think, and they are right, that discussion of their affairs through a conference that deals with the rights of minorities in the Middle East means downgrading them from full citizenship in their country Egypt, to the level of isolated minorities in other countries of the region."[39] *Al-Hayat* later reported that "Coptic, Islamist, and Egyptian nationalist personages expressed their relief at the moving of the conference to outside the Arab world."[40]

The second event that highlighted both continuities and changes in the ways in which Copts are construed involved a delegation of the U.S. Commission on International Religious Freedom,[41] which visited Egypt in March 2001 as part of a regional tour. The commission was to meet with government and religious officials to consult on issues of religious freedom as defined in the Universal Declaration of Human Rights and the International Covenant on Civil and Political Rights. The International Religious Freedom Act of the United States, under which the commission was established, mandates the imposition of economic sanctions on countries found by the United States to persecute religious minorities. The delegation met with Shaykh Tantawi, grand imam of Al-Azhar, as well as with the Coptic Pope Shenouda III and other clergy. But many Egyptians, including human-rights and Coptic activists, boycotted the commission and refused to meet with it.[42]

Prior to its visit, the commission had written to U.S. President Bill Clinton asking him to raise with Egyptian President Husni Mubarak "his government's on-going violations of certain religious freedom rights of the Coptic Christian community," who were described in the letter as "the largest religious minority in Egypt" and as experiencing "serious and pervasive religious discrimination."[43]

The role of the Coptic diaspora was highlighted in this event. Emigration of Copts to North America had begun mainly in the 1950s, with the present population estimated at more than five hundred thousand. A member of the Al-Majlis Al-Milli (Coptic Community Council) in Egypt "blamed extremist elements in the Coptic community in the U.S. and Canada for this intervention."[44] Soon after the commission's visit, Pope Shenouda II addressed expatriate Copts and urged them "not to act in a way that dishonors Egypt's reputation and hurts the interests of the church."[45] During a meeting with the commission, Shenouda stressed that Egypt's Copts do not face "systematic persecution," and the Coptic church issued a press release titled "Take Your Hands Off Us." Reports stated that only a small segment of the Coptic community abroad had orchestrated "this anti-Egypt campaign," quoting a high Coptic official as saying that these people have a "vested interest in portraying Egypt as a minority-persecuting country."

The word "minority" was used in these texts only in reference to the perspective of the outsiders, with the Coptic diaspora also cast in an external role. The nationalist response denied that the Copts were underrepresented or marginalized. Echoing a parallel sentiment of almost a century before, *Al-Ahram* accused the United States of usurping the role of the United Nations and arrogating to itself the right to be solely responsible for monitoring the status of religious minorities around the globe.

Null Cases: Nubians and Sudanese

Discussions concerning Copts might give the impression that the word " *'aqalliyya*" is widely used in contemporary Egypt. Yet in the cases of the Sudanese and the Nubians, who would seem on most counts to qualify as "minorities," the word is entirely absent. Although both groups appeared in the colonial censuses and were gradually distinguished from the emerging category of "Egyptians," neither is part of the current debate about whether the term "minority" is applicable to Egyptian society.

The Sudanese presence in Egypt, clustered in sections and suburbs of Cairo, has a long and complex history. Historical interaction and domination along the Nile valley goes back to Pharoanic times, the latest manifestation of which was British rule of the "Egyptian–Sudanese condominium." Constant migration and interaction gave rise to the phrase "sons of the Nile," through which Egyptians and Sudanese asserted their fraternal relations, even if this relation did not eliminate national and ethnic differences. The groups resident in Egypt today include the descendants of Sudanese who came in the early twentieth century and mainly served in the British armed forces, where they were favored over Egyptian peasant recruits. These northern Sudanese are Muslim and Arab-speaking, as are later migrants, who opposed the Sudanese regime in the 1980s and moved their base of opposition to Cairo. These groups had access to Egyptian citizenship and, in the absence of citizenship, had de facto access to education, public services, and jobs. The situation is different for southern Sudanese who fled the war zone in the 1990s: They live in Cairo as refugees, seeking asylum or repatriation through the United Nations. In recent years, partly due to the economic downturn, Sudanese of all three groups are finding that they are deprived of public goods and subjected to increasing discrimination. And yet the Sudanese in Egypt are not an *'aqalliyya* but a *jaliya*, a group in exile, however long they stay.

Another, perhaps more perplexing silence surrounds the Nubians, a people indigenous to southern Egypt and northern Sudan. Nubians in Egypt strongly affirm Egyptian citizenship. Yet despite historical ties to Arab migrants and rulers in old Nubia, they do not clearly identify as "Arab"; nor are the Nubian languages linguistically related to Arabic. Arab Egyptians have long referred to Nubians with the derogatory term "*barabra*," a term of unknown origin though popularly understood as a variant of "barbarian."[46] Many Nubians occupy the lowest echelons of Egyptian society, their original agricultural base having been gradually eroded, first by the building of the Aswan Dam in 1902 and then by the building of the Aswan High Dam in 1964, which flooded their entire ancestral homeland and submerged the forty-four villages in Egyptian Nubia. The relocation of most of the inhabitants to new government-constructed villages north of Aswan was recognized at the time as a "great sacrifice" of the Nubian people for the sake of the nation. The large-scale migration to the cities, common since at least the seventeenth century, escalated sharply, as Nubians moved to Cairo, where they typically work as doormen, waiters, and cleaners.

Recognition of Nubian culture and antiquity appears in official discourse on the Aswan High Dam and in the construction of the Nubia Museum of Aswan in 1997, which was the latest in a series of UNESCO projects to save the ancient monuments of Nubia. But debates about the appropriateness of the term "Nubian literature" in the 1990s suggest the difficulties attending contemporary assertions of Nubian identity. According to Haggag Oddoul, critics accused Nubians who favored the term, as he did, of working to harm Egypt by taking racist, even secessionist, positions.[47] For Oddoul, the term compares to designations like feminist literature," "war literature," "Amazigh (Berber) literature," "Russian literature," and so on. He bases his claim on genre, ethnicity, and historical experience and sees Nubian literature as a natural and naturalized reflection of the difference of the Nubians themselves.

In this discussion, the word " '*aqalliyya*" is carefully avoided in favor of locutions that describe the Nubians as "a segment of Egyptian society" who were Islamicized and Arabized like the rest of Egypt. Oddoul responds to accusations of secession by listing prominent Nubian politicians who promoted Egyptian nationalism, the participation of Nubians in Arab–Israeli wars, and, finally, the great national sacrifice of the Nubians in giving up their homeland for the Aswan High Dam. The dispute centers on a definition of Egyptianness that recognizes and makes place for Nubianness rather than for mutually exclusive categorization. Like the Copts, the Nubians argue that they are the original Egyptians. Unlike them, however, they are differentiated not by religion but, rather, by marginality and an "invisible" existence in the lower sectors of society.

Circulation and Vernacularization

The word " '*aqalliyya*" has circulated in Egypt for nearly a century now, and yet its motion has been frequently halted by the refusal to countenance the existence of "minorities" in Egyptian society. While public uses of the word " '*aqalliyya*" may have faltered in controversy, the word nonetheless moved into the vernacular, where it is used to mean a group that is powerless. Thus, people might say that they are in a "minority" because of lack of access to resources or jobs or if they feel cheated in a market transaction.

In sum, the word remains a negative one, denoting exclusion, denial of rights, lack of access to resources. The word also evokes the specter of foreign intervention and the importance of national solidarity. As illustrated in censuses, legislation, and public discourse over the course of a century, the Copts became the only group labeled a minority — that is, recognized as Egyptian yet not fitting comfortably in the body of the nation. Other groups who might fit that bill and who were indeed sometimes discussed in those terms in the colonial period gradually became cast as "non-Egyptian" or simply ignored. The Copts, however, are too large a community, too integrated in all segments of society, and have too strong a historical claim to indigenous as well as nationalist credentials to be marginalized in this way. Yet the fact remains that they are not Muslims. And so the words "minority" and "Copt" remain an inseparable pair. In the Egyptian context, one cannot be thought or said without implicating the other. The parallels between the present and the turn of the twentieth century in this regard show that, despite the continuous circulation of the word, it really cannot be said to have moved very much at all.

Notes

I am grateful for research assistance by Elizabeth Smith, especially for the section on the Nubians. Thanks also to Mohammad Sawaie and Walid Hamarneh for linguistic and literary guidance; to Magdi Guirguis for Coptic sources; and to the participants at the Arabic Words in Motion workshop (Montecatini, March 2004) for their comments on an earlier draft.

1. Haydar Ibrahim 'Ali and Milad Hanna, *'Azmat al-'Aqalliyyat fi al-Watan al-'Arabi* [The crisis of minorities in the Arab world] (Damascus: Dar al-Fikr, 2002).

2. *Al-Munjid* (Beirut: Dar al-Mashriq, 2000).

3. Frants Buhl and Clifford Edmund Bosworth, *"Milla" Encyclopaedia of Islam*, CD-ROM ed., version 1.1 (Leiden: E. J. Brill, 2001).

4. Abu Sayf Yusuf, "Al-'Aqbat wal-Qawmiyya al-'Arabiyya," in *The Copts and Arab Nationalism* (Beirut: Center for Arab Unity Studies, 1987), 7.

5. Fahmi Huwaydi, *Muwatinun la Dhimmiyun* [Citizens, not *dhimmis*] (Beirut: Dar al Shuruk, 1985), 56.

6. There is much to be done on this topic, and this assertion will probably not stand the test of time, given recent research that shows the engagement of several of these "foreign" communities in anticolonial struggles.

7. Kenneth M. Cuno and Michael J. Reimer, "The Census Registers of Nineteenth-Century Egypt: A New Source for Social Historians," *British Journal of Middle Eastern Studies* 24, no. 2 (November 1997): 194.

8. The United Arab Republic (UAR) was supposed to be the first step toward Pan-Arab unity. It was formed by the union of Egypt and Syria in 1958 and existed until Syria's secession in 1961, although Egypt continued to be known as the UAR until 1971.

9. UAR, Department of Statistics and Census, *Ten Years of Revolution, Statistical Atlas* (Cairo: Department of Statistics and Census, 1962).

10. Egyptian Government, Ministry of Finance, Statistical Department, "Introduction," in *The Census of Egypt Taken in 1917*, vol. 1 (Cairo: Government Press, 1920).

11. Central Agency for Public Mobilization and Statistics, "Census of Population, Housing and Establishments 1986," ref. no 871/89.CAC, Cairo, 1989, B.

12. Ministère de l'intérieur, *Direction du recensement, recensement général de l'Égypte*,

3 mai 1882 (Le Caire: Imprimerie nationale de Boulaq, 1884), 2. The translation is mine.

13. Gouvernement Egyptien, *Recensement général de l'Égypte — 1er Juin 1897* (Cairo: Imprimerie nationale, 1898), xviii.

14. Idem, Ministry of Finance, *The Census of Egypt Taken in 1907* (Cairo: National Printing Department, 1909), 28.

15. Ibid., 93.

16. Instructions on the census schedule sheet in Egyptian Government, Ministry of Finance, Statistical Department, *The Census of Egypt Taken in 1927*, vol. 2 (Cairo: Government Press, 1921).

17. *The Census of Egypt Taken in 1917*, xv.

18. "Instructions," in *The Census of Egypt*.

19. Republique Arabe Unie (Region d'Egypte), Departement de la statistique et du recensement, *Annuaire Statistique 1959* (Cairo: Al-Hay'a al-'Amma li-Shu'un al-Matabi' al-'Amiriyya, 1961), 13.

20. UAR, *Nahwa dustur al-sha'b* (Toward the People's Constitution) (Cairo: Ministry of National Guidance, 1967).

21. *Al-Ahram*, 7 March 1911, 2.

22. *Tawa'if* is the plural form of *ta'ifa*. *Al-Ahram*, 10 March 1911, 1.

23. Ibid.

24. Ibid.

25. Letter from Mohamed Wahid, in ibid., 6 March 1911, 2.

26. Ibid., 6 March 1911, 2.

27. Ibid., 7 March 1911.

28. Ibid., 1 March 1911, 1.

29. Barbara L. Carter, *The Copts in Egyptian Politics, 1918–1952* (Cairo: American University in Cairo Press, 1986), 14. The name "Assiut" is Romanized in the original as "Asyut." Here I follow the conventional English spelling of the city's name.

30. *Al-Ahram*, 13 March 1911, 2.

31. Ibid., 10 March 1911, 1.

32. Ibid., 7 March 1911, 2.

33. Ibid., 3 March 1922, 1.

34. Ibid., 15 May 1922, 1.

35. Ibid., 16 May 1922, 1.

36. Ibid., 20 May 1922, 2.

37. Ibid., 8 March 1922, 1.

38. *Al-Ahram Weekly*, 21 April 1994. This is the English weekly edition of *Al-Ahram*. Interestingly, in the Arabic edition the report on Haykal's critique was titled "The Copts Are Not a Minority."

39. Mustafa al-Fiqqi, "The Issue of Minorities in the World: The Heritage of Egypt Is One Group with No Discrimination" *Al-Hayat*, 2 May 1994.

40. *Al-Hayat*, 4 May 1994, 7.

41. The U.S. Commission on International Religious Freedom is described on its website as "an independent, bipartisan body that advises the government of the United

States on issues related to religious freedom around the world. . . . As part of its mandate to recommend policies to promote religious freedom, the Commission prepares its own annual report, the first of which was issued in May 2000": "Delegation from the U.S. Commission on International Religious Freedom Visits Egypt," press release, 16 March 2001, available online at http://www.uscirf.gov/ (accessed 4 February 2008).

42. Vickie Langohr, "Frosty Reception for U.S. Religious Freedom Commission in Egypt," *Middle East Report Online*, 29 March 2001, available online at http://www.merip.org/mero/mero032901.html (accessed 4 February 2008).

43. "Commission Asks Clinton to Address Religious Freedom with Egyptian President Mubarak," press release, 27 March 2000, available online at http://www.uscirf.gov/ (accessed 4 February 2008).

44. "U.S. Commission Faces Closed Doors," *Al-Ahram Weekly Online*, no. 526, 22–28 March 2001, available online at http://weekly.ahram.org.eg/2001/526/eg1.htm (accessed 4 February 2008).

45. "Addressing the Prodigals," *Al-Ahram Weekly Online*, no. 527 29 March–4 April 2001, available online at http://weekly.ahram.org.eg/2001/527/eg12.htm (accessed 4 February 2008).

46. The 1917 census is the only one that uses the term "Berberi" as one of the possible "races" to which "Local Subjects" may belong. The other colonial censuses use the term "Sudanese" in ways that often encompass Nubians.

47. Haggag Oddoul, "Hawla Mustalah al-Adab al-Nubi" [On the term 'Nubian literature'], lecture, American University of Cairo, 3 October 1994.

Hijāb/Headscarf

A Political Journey

May the small differences between the clothes that cover our weak bodies, between all our inadequate languages, all our petty customs, . . . all our foolish opinions . . . may all these small nuances that distinguish the atoms we call men not serve as a basis for hatred and persecution. . . . May those who show their love for thee by wearing white cloth not detest those who express their love for thee by wearing black wool.

— Voltaire, *Treatise on Toleration*

When merchants, missionaries, and soldiers subjugated colonial lands, their languages traveled with them, and over time many of their words settled in new linguistic neighborhoods. A few words from Muslim colonies made the reverse voyage from conquered territories to imperial homelands. Some of these newcomer words carried overtones of strident masculinity, as did *"jihad," "fatwa,"* and *"mujahideen."* Others, such as *"harem"* and *"chador,"* suggested the allure of an exotic feminine. When these Arabic words circulated in postcolonial Europe, they became vectors for passionate disagreements about national identity and civil society. During the 1990s in France, an unassuming feminine word, *"hijāb* (or *hidjāb*),"* the generic Arabic term for Islamic headscarf, sparked a fractious national controversy that was less about Islam than about French identity.

It was not a foregone conclusion that *"hijāb"* would find a niche in French or any European language because several other words were already available. Since Muslim women's garments vary across cultures, each vernacular language has its own word for "woman's covering." But most of these nouns, such as *"chador"* (Persian), *"abaya"* (Saudi Arabian), *"khimar"* (classical Arabic), *"niqāb"* (worn throughout the Muslim world), and "*burqa*" (Afghan), refer to robes that cover their wearers' bodies and thus do not describe the simple headscarves most commonly worn in Europe. The Christian connotations of "*voile*" (veil) and the secular usage of "*foulard*" (scarf) disqualified these words as adequate translations for the Muslim head covering. And so in the late 1980s and 1990s, the word "*hijāb*" immigrated to France and became the term of choice for the headscarves that cover their wearer's hair, ears, neck, and sometimes shoulders.[1]

The travelogue of "*hijāb*" through post-Cold War French society also tracks key elements in the political disarray that resulted when Muslim immigrants challenged officially secular but de facto Judeo-Christian civil society. The appearance of an Other marked by veiled women in the midst of European society provoked intense disagreements about private and public spaces and the nature of civil society in between.[2] The representational force of the *hijāb* was at once so amorphous and so forceful that its meanings shifted according to observers' image of the "France" they lived in. To alarmists, a *chador* symbolized the invasion of an intolerant religion into a France that had clearly demarcated private and public spheres with a neutral space between. To multiculturalists, a *voile* or *foulard islamique* suggested a custom with no European equivalent that would enrich a cosmopolitan France within which citizens could negotiate identity and civic obligation. Because the ethnic politics implicit in these two worldviews did not coincide with conventional political parties or ideological affinities, the *hijāb* "wars," as one writer put it, were "tearing France apart."[3]

"*Hijāb*" did not settle gracefully into French discourse but instead vied with French translations and other words derived from Arabic. Observing the deployment of "*hijāb*" and its near synonyms during eighteen years of the "headscarf wars" in France reveals the evolving meanings of the word in the context of French secularism, or *laïcité*. A chronicle of two particularly intense debates about the meanings of "*hijāb*," "*chador*," "*voile*," and "*foulard*" helps to identify the two competing understandings of French universalism that emerged in a France challenged internationally by an expanding European Union and domestically by a growing, and largely unassimilated, Muslim population.

Unlike other religious items of apparel, such as a yarmulke, turban, or cross, a veil cordons off its wearer within public space, becoming a visual synecdoche of a ghettoized, "inscrutable" subculture. Whether worn by a Muslim woman or a Catholic nun, a veil declares its wearer off limits. In one of its earlier Arabic usages, "*hijāb*" meant simply "curtain," and "to veil," of course, means "to conceal." Since colonial times Western painters and writers have viewed the Muslim veil as a barrier to be overcome in order to savor the delights of a hidden world of sensual richness.[4] Fawzia Zouari, a Tunisian-born writer living in Paris, described its spatial symbolism: "Just as the high, sun-baked walls conceal the shade and privacy of lush courtyards and patios, scarves set up a game of hide and seek between an austere outward demeanor and the hedonism within."[5] A *hijāb* separated women from men and simultaneously set Muslims apart from the European mainstream.

Before the expansion of Islamism (often called "fundamentalism") in the 1980s, few Europeans had seen veiled women outside Muslim countries. During the post-Second World War decades, several hundred thousand Maghrebian men left their families behind when they immigrated to France to seek employment. From the late 1960s, when North African women began to join their husbands and sons in France, mothers typically wore headscarves, but their daughters did not. During the 1980s, however, some Muslim girls whose mothers did not cover their heads decided to wear headscarves. The sight of young Muslim French women wearing headscarves signaled the intention of many immigrants to reside permanently in France without relinquishing their Muslim traditions. French and European policymakers were caught unprepared. When political leaders negotiated the terms of the European Union (EU), the possibility of large non-Christian subcultures attracted little attention. No one had considered, for example, how much toleration a democratic political system should extend to an intolerant subculture or thought about the role of sub-state ethnic enclaves. With an iron curtain sealing off Eastern Europe, anticommunism solidified the idea of Europe as a white, Judeo-Christian Western Europe in which Muslims were transients. And when, thanks to liberal naturalization laws, former colonial subjects became French citizens, they became "strangers" in this Europe. In Georg Simmel's classic definition, strangers are "not just wanderers, who come today and go tomorrow." They are, rather, "people who come today and stay tomorrow."[6] In contentious debates about immigration, a woman wearing a headscarf became a compressed symbol of the guest who does not go home. In 1985, when the conservative newspaper *Le Figaro* published the cover story "Will France Still be French in 2015?" it was illustrated by an image of Marianne, the symbol of France, wearing a Muslim veil. Right-wing populist movements like the French National Front (NF), the Belgian

Vlaams Blok, the Swiss People's Party, the Dutch Freedom Party, and the Austrian Freedom Party openly demeaned non-European immigrants, but in post-Holocaust Europe, most mainstream politicians avoided overt racism. National constitutions and the 1947 Declaration of Human Rights had banished race from the language of citizenship. Celebrities praised cultural diversity; politicians espoused toleration; and EU laws punished hate speech. In a public culture where overt racism was taboo, cultural essentialism provided a language of prejudice that remained within the bounds of acceptable speech. The uneven path of "*hijāb*" within French political discourse suggests the volatility and extent of Islamophobia beneath the surface of public discourse.

Anxiety about Muslim immigrants spread on fertile ground in France, which had the largest non-white population in Europe (10–12 percent) and a sluggish economy. Unlike other European nations in which Muslims were divided by sectarian rivalries and language, most of the four to five million Muslims in France shared a relatively homogeneous Maghrebian culture. Living in dilapidated housing projects on the peripheries of urban areas, Muslims formed a geographically bounded subculture. Second- and third-generation Muslims (called *Beurs*) discovered that legal equality and fluency in French did not necessarily mean access to good education, better pay, or decent housing. Turning their backs on a society that rejected them, some Muslims turned to Islamism in the 1980s, while others turned to gangs as an alternative to a hostile French society.[7]

In this tense atmosphere, teenagers wearing headscarves collided with two pillars of French national identity: *laïcité* and education, both of which had taken their modern shape during the 1880s. Unlike other European nations, where organized religion has a recognized place in the state, church and state have been rigorously separated in France since the passage of a law in 1905. Where other governments adjudicate among religions, French laws exclude religion from state institutions. No public oath can refer to God, for example, and no public school can teach religion. The 1958 constitution guaranteed: "France is a republic, indivisible and secular." But in practice, French education has not been not so secular. Twenty percent of all students attend religious schools (95 percent of which are Catholic) that receive state subsidies. The academic calendar (and paid national holidays) mark Christian holy days. Religious buildings built before 1905 are maintained at state expense, and until 2004 students could wear crosses or yarmulkes to public schools. Another exception that rankled secularists was the anomaly created by religious education in public schools in Alsace-Lorraine, which had been part of Germany in 1905 and thus escaped the constraints of *laïcité*, even after it became French again in 1945.

The centralized French educational system that was specifically designed to prepare children to live in a secular nation evolved simultaneously with the colonial "civilizing mission." In theory, secular schools molded French citizens and colonial subjects according to universal standards of reason and civic obligation. In 1884, Minister of Education Jules Ferry, an avid imperialist and author of the education laws, explained, "The superior races have a duty to civilize the inferior races."[8] For female colonial subjects, removing the *hijb* (or *haïk*) was the precondition for gaining access to French civilization. A century later, in 1989, lavish festivities commemorated the two-hundredth anniversary of the revolution that had given birth to the values enshrined in French schools. Yet the collapse of communism and the spread of Islamism unsettled the triumphalism that suffused this national moment. Ayatollah Khomeini's *fatwa* against Salman Rushdie, Algerian fundamentalists' declaration of war against the secular government in Algiers, and the first *intifada* in Palestine aroused fears of an international conspiracy.

Against this backdrop, the first headscarf controversy began in Creil, a working-class suburb north of Paris. In October 1989, Ernest Chenière, the principal of a secondary school that had eight hundred students from twenty-five different ethnic backgrounds, expelled three students whose parents had been born in North Africa because they refused to remove their headscarves. Principals in four other urban areas followed his example. Television and print news media dramatized this local dispute as a major confrontation between secular France and fundamentalist Islam. Chenière, a devout Catholic whose family had emigrated from Guadeloupe, insisted that only by asserting his authority could he bring order to a chaotic school. "What kind of democracy is it," he asked, "that backs down in the face of fanaticism?"[9] Meanwhile, the irate father of one of the girls talked to reporters in front of a portrait of Ayatollah Khomeini and defended the girls' right to an education. The three students, Fatima, Leila, and Samira, achieved instant name recognition, even though they fled photographers and declined to be interviewed. Journalists groped for the right word for the headscarf. "We don't know whether this is a cloth or a symbol, a *fichu* (bandana) or a religious garment. No one knows any more what to call the object of this scandal."[10] French people who were anxious about Islamism tended to speak about the Arabophone *chador* as an alien element in French public life. Defenders of girls' rights usually spoke of the Francophone *voile* or *foulard islamique* as a legitimate personal choice in a pluralist society. Whatever they were called, the headscarves designed to protect Muslim women from public view catapulted the young women who wore them into the full glare of the media spotlight.

Predictably, the National Front demonstrated under such banners as "Wearing a *tchador* is not the expression of a French tradition! It is a declaration of war" and "No to the *tchador* in schools! No to mosques!" But people who were otherwise politically moderate also denounced the *tchador* in immoderate terms. Angry parents of non-Muslim students chanted, "Away with the *tchador*."[11] Academics and intellectuals mounted campaigns against the headscarf in France's two major news magazines, the leftist *Nouvel Observateur* and the conservative *L'Express*. During the weeks when the Soviet withdrawal from Eastern Europe captured head-lines, both periodicals featured cover stories headlined "Resistance to Is-lamism" and "The *Foulard* Plot: How the Islamists Infiltrate France." Five respected intellectuals wrote an open letter to the government defending the expulsion of girls with headscarves. The *Nouvel Observateur* featured the letter under the cover headline, "Teachers! We Must Not Give In!"[12] In the midst of this turmoil, experts on Islam explained that "*chador*" or "*tchador*" actually referred to a full covering commonly seen in colonial representations of North African women, but "*hijāb*" or "*hidjeb*" was the appropriate word for the modern headscarf worn by Muslim women. Gradually, *hijāb* found a place in mainstream French discourse.

Supporters of the girls' right to wear headscarves to school domesti-cated the headscarf by calling it a "*foulard islamique*," as in the banners carried by the parents of the five hundred Muslim students in Creil who demonstrated against Chenière's decision. Mme. Mitterand, the presi-dent's wife, assured Kurdish refugee students at a school she visited that two hundred years after the French Revolution it would be unthinkable to ban the *foulard*. Headlines like "*Foulard*: The Code of Tolerance" inserted the headscarf into the language of civil rights. In conversations with the press, some Muslim girls from Creil emphasized the religious significance of the *voile*. Others saw it as a fashion choice. As one put it, "I paid ten francs for my *foulard* at the same discount store where other girls buy their *foulards*." Muslim parents objected to state interference with their authority to allow (or forbid) their daughters to wear *voiles*. In Avignon, non-Muslim girls wore *foulards* to class in support of their expelled classmates. The humble headscarf, worn by about a dozen schoolgirls in France, became a *foulard politique*, which made it the target of irreverent humor, as when two male delegates to the National Assembly appeared on prime-time news wearing headscarves and a television comic took out his handkerchief and mimicked a girl wearing a *hijāb*.[13]

Confronted by what appeared to be an intractable dilemma, President François Mitterand asked the Supreme Court (Conseil d'État) for a ruling. A month after the *affaire* erupted, the court declared, "Every person has the right to liberty of thought, conscience, and religion." Wearing a veil (*voile*) did not contradict *laïcité* or republican values; moreover, EU and French law guaranteed the right to free expression and education. Although the justices defended wearing "religious signs," they made it clear that freedom of religion was not absolute. The court stipulated that "ostentatious" attire should be banned if it interfered with education. This left school administrators and parents to negotiate on a case-by-case basis.[14] The headscarf controversy vanished from the media as suddenly as it had appeared. Most disputes were resolved quietly by negotiation. A girl might agree, for example, to wear only a bandana, or a principal could excuse a girl from swimming lessons because she was allergic to chlorine. Because of flexibility on both sides, only thirty of roughly twelve hundred *hijāb* disputes during the 1990s had to be settled in court, and of those only four resulted in suspensions.[15] It is worth noting, however, that "compromise" in about eight hundred of those cases resulted in the girls' finishing their secondary education by correspondence.

As the furor subsided in the winter of 1989–90, politicians took stock of what the *hijāb* had wrought. Public opinion split, with 48 percent supporting assimilation of immigrants and 46 percent in favor of sending them back to their countries of origin. Jean-Marie Le Pen of the National Front triumphantly observed that "the *chador* wars" had moved immigration from the margins to the respectable mainstream of political opinion. At the next National Front convention, he described the *chador* as a sign that France was being "colonized" by its former subjects. The passions aroused by the *hijāb* revealed the depth of anti-foreign, or anti-Muslim, sentiment across the political spectrum. As one journalist commented, liberals could no longer dismiss the National Front as a "wart on the French body politic."[16] The hysteria created by the *hijāb* made immigration a central question for all parties.

In the mid-1990s, controversies about the *hijāb* broke out briefly when terrorist attacks in Tunisia, Morocco, Algeria, and France fed anti-immigrant backlash. Two judicial decisions outside France also kept the headscarf in the news. In 1997, the Turkish government under the secularist Necmettin Erbakan outlawed wearing headscarves in public buildings. One year later, a German teacher of Afghan descent challenged the school board's right to dismiss her because she wore a headscarf to work. Over the course of the 1990s, "*hijāb*" settled uneasily into common parlance via television, newspapers, and documentaries.

Unlike the sensationalist coverage in 1989, reports of skirmishes about the *hijāb* during the following decade were brief and relatively balanced. A popular television series about teenagers' lives included one ninety-minute episode titled "A Life of Her Own" that featured opposing views of the *hijāb* issue.[17] Documentaries explained the distinctions between Islam and Islamism. With about 124,000 Muslim girls in secondary schools, a few teenagers wearing *hijābs* attracted little attention. In a poll taken ten years after the original headscarf controversy, 95 percent of teachers reported that no student had ever worn a headscarf to his or her classes, and 65 percent had never seen a student with a *hijāb*. Academics wrote confidently about the controversy in the past tense.[18] In 2000, the recently created High Commission on Integration declared, "Today the question of the veil [*voile*] is finished [*dépassé*]." A popular television drama filmed in the summer of 2001 impartially explored the dilemma created by a Muslim student's religious freedom and a principal's commitment to *laïcité*.[19] As negotiations replaced confrontation, the words "*hijāb*" and "*voile*" or "*foulard islamique*" displaced the more negatively loaded word "*tchador*" in all but the most bigoted circles.

The destruction of the World Trade Center in 2001 shattered the fragile status quo. In the immediate aftermath of 9/11, Europeans mourned with Americans. Headlines pledged solidarity. "Nous sommes tous des Americains" (We are all Americans). "Nous sommes tous New-Yorkais" (We are all New Yorkers). Soon another theme emerged: "Nous sommes tous vulnérables." We could be next. Hate crimes against Jews and Muslims increased. Not surprisingly, fewer French citizens defined themselves as Muslims in opinion polls. Polls registered a dramatic rise in anti-Muslim sentiment throughout Europe. In the autumn of 2001, opposition to the *hijāb* in French public schools grew from 38.8 percent to 41.2 percent. Amid scattered reports of opposition to the *hijāb* in the civil service, schools, and business, one observer quipped, "A French woman with a scarf is chic, but a Muslim woman with a scarf is a threat to civilization."[20] "*Hijāb*" entered the next phase of its discursive journey. After 1989, "*hijāb*" had displaced "*chador*" as a more distinctively Muslim term than "*foulard*" or "*voile*." Proponents of ethnic diversity usually spoke of the *hijāb*, which avoided the religious overtones of *voile* and the secular connotations of *foulard*. But during the first years of the new century, *hijāb* absorbed some of the negative qualities that *chador* represented.

Even as Chirac and other leaders called for toleration after September 11, 2001, journalists and news anchors often conflated Islam, Islamism, and terrorism. The right-wing Le Pen capitalized on his rivals' reticence to take a stand on "the Muslim question" and won second place in the presidential elections of April 2002 — a victory that set off shockwaves across the political spectrum. Crimes committed in Muslim slums captured tabloid headlines. In 2002, when a young man doused his seventeen-year-old ex-girlfriend with gasoline and burned her to death in the presence of his comrades, the case aroused passionate anti-Muslim denunciations. Muslims reported that the taunt "dirty Arab" became as common as "gypsy."

The *hijāb* became the trigger for a new "outbreak of collective hysteria," which revived debates not just about Islam or Islamism, but about France itself. As one Muslim French commentator remarked, "The Republic seems about ready to disappear under the veil [*voile*]."[21] In April 2003, Interior Minister Nicolas Sarkozy created a new "veil question" when he addressed the largest ever national convention of French Muslims. First, he promised Muslims that they, like Catholics, Protestants, and Jews, would have an official organization to represent them. His audience cheered. Then he declared that Muslims must obey French laws, including the requirement that identity photos show a woman's hair. The audience booed. The issue was not resolved.

The *hijāb* incited new and more divisive national debates during the following autumn when the schools reopened. Although the extent of the so-called *hijāb* problem was statistically miniscule (of 1,256 girls wearing a *hijāb* to class, only six were expelled in 2003), its torque was immense. As in 1989, this "crisis" began with a confrontation. In Aubervilliers, a poor northern suburb of Paris, Lila and Alma Lévy refused to remove their headscarves in school. Lila, eighteen, and Alma, sixteen, eloquently defended their choice. With divorced parents (a secular mother raised by Muslim parents and an atheist father of Jewish parentage who was a civil-rights lawyer), the girls attributed their values to their devout Muslim grandmother and to Laura Ingalls Wilder's *Little House on the Prairie*, which had been featured on French television a year earlier. Talk-show hosts and reporters asked the girls to tell their story, which they did with panache. Their best-selling book resulted in more talk-show appearances.[22] Pictures of the two Muslim girls being encouraged in their faith by their Jewish atheist father became a staple of news coverage of the affair.

With all sides clamoring for clarity, President Jacques Chirac temporized. In a similar situation, Mitterrand had set the headscarf in the context of constitutional rights. Chirac framed the *hijāb* within the context of endangered French identity. This shift in emphasis was consistent with Chirac's views on immigrants from North Africa—which he had made explicit in the early 1990s in disparaging comments about immigrants. "How do you think a French worker feels when he sees on the landing a family with a man who has maybe three or four wives, about twenty kids, who receives around 50,000 francs in social services, of course without working . . . and if you add the noise and smell . . . no wonder the French worker across the landing goes mad."[23] As president of an officially tolerant nation, however, Chirac spoke more discreetly.

In July 2003, Chirac appointed a blue-ribbon committee of nineteen educators, scholars, and religious leaders chaired by Ombudsman Bernard Stasi to examine the principle of secularism, or *laïcité*. Stasi's comments suggested that he was not neutral on the topic: "There are without any doubt forces in France which are seeking to destabilize the republic, and the time has come for the republic to act." For four months, the French equivalent of C-SPAN televised large portions of the testimony of 140 specialists before the Stasi Commission. A television documentary, *Behind the Veil*, brought viewers the "inside story" that featured specialists pontificating amid the splendor of an eighteenth-century palace.[24] Stasi Commission witnesses and members defended their opinions on editorial pages and talk shows. Almost without exception, the witnesses confirmed negative stereotypes about Islam. Teachers described girls tormented by teenage boys and controlled by parents. Health-care professionals complained that Muslim husbands refused to allow male physicians to treat female family members. Academics pictured an endangered republic eroded from within by fanatical Islamists.

Among the three members of the commission who came from a "migration background" was Hanif Cherifi, the Education Ministry official in charge of mediating headscarf disputes, who agreed with the ban. To survey students' opinion, the commission sent delegates to interview students in French schools in foreign capitals like Rome and Istanbul but overlooked students in nearby Muslim ghettos. Autobiographical narratives enlivened lengthy academic disquisitions. Iranian-born Chahdortt Djavann, author of *Bas les voiles* (Down with the Veil), declared, "When I see those girls covered with the *chador* I feel like I am witnessing an abuse of power. I cannot endure feeling like an accomplice to such injustice." She caused an uproar when she charged parents of girls wearing headscarves with being child abusers.[25] The sister of the teenager who had been murdered by her jealous boyfriend told the commission on the first anniversary of her death, "I am tired of hearing that if my sister had worn a *voile* she would not have been murdered. . . . The Republic, not God, protects girls. I'm sorry, but the Republic did not protect my sister."[26] At least some of the commission members must have realized that their witness-selection process had been skewed, because on the final day they invited two hundred students from the Paris region. They also heard from the only witness who wore a headscarf, Saïda Kada, author of the film *One Veils, the Other Doesn't*. Kada appealed for patience. "We struggle against our families who want to trap us in the kitchen and also against a prejudiced society. . . . Islam is young in France. Give us time."[27] She had barely finished when the champagne corks began to pop.

Considering the length of the hearings, the Stasi Commission was surprisingly unconcerned about such topics as ascertaining the extent of problems originating with the *hijāb*, the implications of a possible *hijāb* ban in the workplace, girls' rights to public education, and parents' rights over their children. The commission endorsed twenty-five proposals to protect *laïcité* and integrate minorities — such as allowing students to substitute non-Christian for Christian holidays and to be served special meals in school cafeterias. Although the commission had not discussed crosses, turbans, yarmulkes, and partisan political apparel, it unanimously recommended a ban on "all *ostensible* religious and political attire" in public schools.[28]

With midterm elections approaching in March 2004, and Le Pen's popularity holding strong, legislators drafted a prohibition against all partisan clothing in high schools. In the National Assembly the bill carried by 494 to 36 (with 31 abstentions), and the Senate followed by a vote of 276 to 20.[29] Clarity, however, remained as remote as ever. Because lawmakers wanted to avoid the impression that the law was anti-Muslim, it prohibited all *"signes religieux ostensibles"* (as opposed to *"visible"* or *"ostentatoire,"* which legislators rejected). Whether the adjective *"ostensible"* meant "conspicuous" or "supposedly" depended on the eye of the beholder. The ten thousand members of a Christian sect, the Assyro-Chaldeans, insisted that their very large crosses were not *"ostensible."* What about monks' robes and nuns' habits? Could Hindu girls come to classes wearing traditional makeup, *vibhuti* or *kumkum*? When six thousand Sikhs declared that appearing in public without turbans was like being naked, Luc Ferry, the education minister, told them to be contented with "invisible turbans."

Demonstrations for and against the *hijāb* ban in France were followed by protests against the ban in London, Delhi, Cairo, Beirut, and Berlin. In a nationally televised debate, Marine Le Pen (daughter of Jean-Marie Le Pen) called the *hijāb* "a small atomic bomb" that destroyed conventional political alliances. Orthodox Jews, Islamist imams, and the Green Party lined up against the ban. Feminists divided between "new" and "historical" camps. The former found themselves in the company of Chirac and the National Front in support of the ban; the latter agreed with clerics and proponents of multiculturalism. Former Minister of Culture Jack Lang explained the intensity of these debates: "This is not about schools, but about politics and civilization. We talk about a secular republic, but we're really talking about French identity."[30]

Over the next year, the *hijāb* remained in the eye of a media storm. Everyone wanted to contain Muslim extremists, but people arrived at opposite strategies for achieving that goal. The word choices, metaphors, and narratives deployed by each side revealed a deep gulf between two imagined Frances. Proponents of a ban on headscarves lived in a public sphere purged of particularism and protected by strong walls. Defenders of the girls' right to wear the *hijāb* inhabited a nation that welcomed ethnic diversity within porous borders. In the rhetoric of the ban's proponents, walls, blocs, and cells revived Cold War images of "Fortress Europe." To Chirac, *laïcité* represented the very "cornerstone" (*pierre angulaire*) of the republic. France would not tolerate internal barriers or anything that divides, excludes, or diminishes the nation.[31]

Advocates for a ban eulogized a "pure," universal, "emancipatory" academic space open to all students—provided that they shed all signs of sectarian allegiance. Regis Debray, a former supporter of Castro's Cuba, praised the school as a "sanctuary" and "inviolable refuge"—the "lynchpin of the republic." The *hijāb* and *chador* focused anxiety, so that enclaves of Islamists became "cells" of an international conspiracy. A ban on headscarves would teach Muslims that "any sign of allegiance to an Islamist and partisan community contradicts equality." The widely read conservative essayist Bernard-Henri Lévy perceived France as caught up in a "power struggle between the values of democracy and of fundamentalism." From Casablanca to Kabul, he wrote, Islam does not divide public from private and cannot be reconciled with *laïcité*: "It cannot be repeated often enough. The *hijāb* is not a religious but a political signal. It is not a sign of piety but of hate." A square piece of cloth became "a clever means of dissimulation." Despite some Muslim women's insistence on their right to religious freedom, mainstream pundits insisted, "The veil is not a religious sign like the others. It is a powerful symbol . . . that says a woman is not considered an equal to men." A prominent feminist from a Muslim background who in 2002 had defended girls' right to wear the *hijāb* changed her mind and described veiled girls as the "soldiers of green fascism." Respected scholars, whom the sociologist Vincent Geisser called the "geopoliticians of fear," established the discursive conventions that identified the *hijāb* as a marker of Islamism. "It is important to show that the republic will not let itself be eaten from within." The intellectuals Jean Pierre Molina, Liliane Kandel, and Elizabeth Altschull likened the *hijāb* to a cloud from Chernobyl that "will not stop at the borders of the Hexagon." Journalists quoted the sociologist Nilüfer Göle's description of veiled women in Turkey as "the flag of politicized Islamism," implying that the headscarf had the same meaning in France. The Islamic scholar Gilles Kepel described the headscarf controversy as a battle within a larger war: "The future of Islam is in Europe. It has a huge Muslim population. Either we train our Muslims to become modern global citizens, who live in a democratic, pluralistic society, or, on the contrary, the Islamists win, and take over those Muslim European constituencies. Then we're in serious trouble."[32]

Feminists who demanded a ban on the *hijāb* modernized the emancipatory themes of colonialism in the journal *Pro-Choix* (Pro-Choice). Cleverly named to imply that it supported Muslim girls' freedom to decide for themselves, its logic in fact ran in the opposite direction. Because Islamism commands utter obedience, Muslim girls must be rescued from its grasp before they can make any free choice at all. During the late nineteenth century, the French feminist Hubertine Auclert and other activists had made the same argument in campaigns to unveil North African women. Five decades later, during the war against Algerian independence, French officers' wives tried to persuade Algerian women to unveil in the name of emancipation.[33] Early in the twenty-first century, when women wearing headscarves lived in France, proponents of a headscarf ban merged their defense of a republic menaced by Muslim immigrants with a crusade to defend Muslim women against Muslim patriarchy.

Defenders of the girls' right to education regardless of their clothing lived in a France that bore little resemblance to the nation of thick walls and pure spaces evoked by the supporters of the ban. According to advocates of Muslim girls' rights, French universalism meant welcoming students from all religions (and atheists, too, they added). By integrating students from diverse backgrounds, teachers would inspire toleration of individual differences. In making these arguments, they placed the *hijāb* on a par with the yarmulke and cross and rarely referred to the *foulard* or *voile*. As "*chador*" disappeared from mainstream usage, "*hijāb*" came to signify a distinctively ethnic garment, while "*foulard*" carried a secular valence and "*voile*" signaled a religious meaning. Some opponents of the ban emphasized their demand for parity by using "*hijāb*," as in the slogan of one demonstrator against the ban: "The *hijāb* on my head; the star of David on my back; and a cross around my neck." *Hijāb* could also underscore a citizen's complementary loyalties to nation and religion, as one slogan declared: "France you are my country. *Hijāb* you are my life." Another proclaimed, "Down with *laïcité* terrorists!" During one demonstration, hecklers jeered that in many Muslim countries a woman could be killed for not wearing a *hijāb*. Smiling, the twenty-year-old, veiled Nabila retorted, "But in France, we wear a *foulard* as an act of freedom."[34]

Opponents of a headscarf ban envisioned *laïcité* as an open secular society within which every religious and ethnic minority enjoyed full respect. Universalism, to them, meant a culture founded on the right to be different. Secular human-rights organizations joined rabbis and imams in criticizing the unacknowledged Christianity that permeated supposedly neutral French public culture. Having classmates who wore *foulards*, they noted, would enrich the narrow "Catholic secularism" of public education. Joseph Sitruk, the grand rabbi of France, joined imams in criticizing the stigmatization of any religious garment. For entirely different reasons, the secular Green Party agreed. The *hijāb*, it said, offered a healthy alternative to crass popular culture.

Proponents of diversity in the classroom used "*hijāb*" to underscore their demand for parity among all faiths, choosing the Arabic word to make the Muslim connection clear. But when they based their logic on individual rights, they often spoke instead of the *foulard* and *voile islamique* —making the headscarf a French garment worn freely by French citizens. In her documentary film *When Girls Put on the Veil*, Leila Ditlji took viewers into the homes and gathering places of the mainly Muslim suburb in which she had grown up. Whatever their individual choices, women and girls eloquently supported the right to wear a *foulard*. In a televised discussion, international feminists debated the *foulard*—not the *hijāb*—as if the word could move the question beyond the confines of a specific religion to the realm of universal women's rights.[35] In these and other venues, young women defended their decisions to wear the *foulard*, but when pressed to divulge their reasons, they usually demurred, implying that their right to wear a headscarf did not require justification.

Samira Bellil, who described growing up in a Muslim ghetto in *Dans l'enfer des tournantes* (Gang Rape Hell), explained the dilemma Muslim girls faced: If they wore veils, Islamophobes would insult them, and if they did not, Muslim men would harass them.[36] Thus, a Muslim woman could decide to wear a *hijāb* for tactical reasons. If a young woman wished to find employment outside her neighborhood, wearing a veil would ward off taunts from neighborhood thugs. A devout Muslim might believe she had no choice. Regardless of motive, expelling students who wore headscarves would push the most vulnerable members of a ghettoized community still farther away from the education they so badly needed. The sociologists Farhad Khosrokhavar and Françoise Gaspard observed that it was precisely these young women who needed the teachers' support. If headscarves were outlawed, then Islamists would establish schools and make Muslim separatism a self-fulfilling prophecy.[37]

When non-Muslim opponents of the ban spoke about the "*hijāb*," they expressed respect for difference. Grassroots Muslim women's organizations, however, used "*voile*" and "*foulard*," terms that evoked continuity with ethnic French traditions. Despite differences among them, these new associations displayed a remarkable talent for public relations. In Lyon, the Femmes Françaises Musulmanes Engagées (FFME) organized demonstrations and public forums to transform the symbolism of the veil from a sign of oppression to a *"means of liberation."* In January 2002, about three hundred women from urban housing projects convened an Estates General of Women at the Sorbonne. Safia Lebdi, one of the organizers, explained that girls needed encouragement to rebel against Muslim traditions that cast women as either submissive (respectable) or assertive (loose). From this discussion emerged the slogan "Ni Putes, Ni Soumises!" (Neither whores nor doormats!), which became the rallying cry for dozens of activists from Muslim backgrounds who traveled across France, from Paris and Lille to Strasburg, Lyon, Marseille, and Narbonne, holding press conferences and meeting with women from the projects.[38] On International Women's Day in March, these women marched separately from traditional feminists in Paris. In April, the leaders trademarked "NPNS" as the name of their organization. The NPNS captured media attention with pungent blogs, witty slogans, and in-your-face images on its website. NPNS spokeswomen called for a two-front struggle against oppressive Muslim patriarchy and mainstream French prejudices.

While proponents of a headscarf ban saw the *hijāb* as a danger to monolithic France, opponents of the ban embedded their cause in patriotic culture by redesigning Marianne to include ethnic variety. On Bastille Day (14 July 2003), women activists hung fourteen immense photographs of multiethnic women wearing the Phrygian caps of the French Revolution high on the austere columns of the National Assembly. "Who is Marianne?" asked Fadela Amara, president of the NPNS. "She's the ordinary working-class woman facing all sorts of pressures and struggling for freedom from the tyranny of the housing projects. And she is saying, 'No matter what my origin, I am a citizen of the French Republic.'"[39] The NPNS joined a broad coalition of civil-rights activists, leftists, some Green Party members, and the Collectif des Musulmans de France (CMF) to lobby for "one school for everyone!" Accompanied by rap music in the 2004 International Women's Day march, defenders of the right to wear a headscarf wore red, white, and blue *foulards* and chanted "The veil is my choice" and "My veil, my voice!" Displaying placards with a pink hand in a "Stop" position and the slogans "Touche pas à mon voile (Don't touch my veil)" and "Ne touche pas à ma pudeur" (Hands off my modesty), they joined ranks with the antiracist movement SOS-Racisme. Recalling France in the Age of the Enlightenment, one group marched behind a banner asking, "Oh France, what has become of tolerance?" During the summer of 2004, an avalanche of books, colloquia, conferences, and documentaries on Islam and *laïcité* kept the *hijāb* in the media spotlight. The latest edition of the definitive dictionary *Le petit Robert* included "*hijāb*" (along with "*Wi-Fi*" and "*islamo-phobie*") in the French language. As the school year approached, no one knew whether Muslim students would comply with the new law.

Only days before the beginning of the new semester, terrorists in Iraq kidnapped two French journalists and vowed to kill them unless Chirac suspended the ban. The journalists pleaded with Chirac to comply. After months of internecine wrangling about how to react to the headscarf ban, the Muslim community declared its solidarity with the government and asked girls to comply with the law. When students returned to school, 639 girls wore headscarves, compared with 1,256 a year earlier. Within a few days, the Ministry of Education announced that 550 of these girls had agreed to compromise, and the others would either transfer to private schools in France and Belgium or continue their studies via distance learning.[40] Once again, headscarves became newsworthy but this time because their number seemed so insignificant.

During the hostage crisis, the itinerary of "*hijāb*" changed abruptly. Reporters wrote about the "*foulard*" or "*voile islamique*." "*Hijāb*" all but vanished from news about France. Images of patriotic Muslim girls with bare heads replaced the ubiquitous veiled teenagers of previous years. Proponents of the *hijāb* ban conceded that these students "have demonstrated their true patriotism [*fibre patriotique*]!" A reporter for the conservative *Le Figaro* "unequivocally" praised Muslims' "impeccable patriotism." *Le Monde* editorialized, "Far from dividing the French Muslim community," the kidnapping "aroused a feeling of national communion." French Muslims stood at the "front line in defending the republic." Muslim leaders offered to intercede with the terrorists because, as the president of the Union of Islamic Organizations in France declared, "We are all hostages in this affair."[41]

Just before Christmas, the kidnappers freed the two hostages. As the *affaire* of the headscarves disappeared from headline news, "*hijāb*" yielded to its Francophone near-equivalents, "*foulard*" and "*voile*." Whereas *foulard* is a fairly accurate translation for *hijāb*, a scarf that covers only the hair, the *voile* is a veil that obscures the face. Yet *voile* has gradually displaced *foulard* in popular parlance, as if to domesticate the issue by bringing the word back into the fold of French ideologies of secular citizenship, which have long treated diversity by insisting on assimilation.

When the word "*hijāb*" crossed the Mediterranean from North Africa to Europe, its polysemy and high visibility provided a catalyst for passionate and long-deferred discussions about citizenship, ethnic diversity, and the clash of civilizations in a postcolonial world. The chronology of these controversies suggests a correlation between *hijāb* anxiety and an unstable geopolitical environment. In a time of national self-doubt, the *hijāb* provided an emotionally charged symbol that enabled a conversation about what it meant to be French. Caught between a growing Muslim population in France and an expanding EU in which the position of France remained uncertain, politicians and intellectuals directed their attention to the *hijāb*, an object that exerted such symbolic torque that it diverted attention away from xenophobia and the deteriorating conditions in the vast urban housing developments where most Muslims live. At the same time, the proponents of a headscarf ban, in the name of protecting a few girls from Muslim patriarchy, were in fact seeking to protect their idea of France against what they perceived as an Islamic enemy within.

Initially, "*hijāb*" had distinguished Muslim headscarves from the *chador* and other more restrictive forms of covering in the Middle East. The word jostled with "*voile*" and "*foulard*" during the 1990s, when its multiplicity of meanings enabled it to represent either an invasive alien force (in the language of xenophobic populism) or a symbol of religious toleration (in the vocabulary of pluralism). But after the hostage crisis in 2004, "*hijāb*" seemed to return to the Islamic world, appearing primarily in news reports about head coverings worn in North Africa and the Middle East. Paradoxically, by quietly disappearing from classrooms and from France, the word "*hijāb*" facilitated Muslims' desires for acceptance into mainstream French society.

Notes

1. While conservative theologians trace the origins of veiling to Qur'anic texts, liberals insist that not even the *hadith* requires any form of veil, and historians note that the custom predates Islam by three millennia: see Jacqueline Geno-Bismith and Chiheb Dghim, *Du voile, de l'antiquité à Islam* (Paris: Éditions de Paris, 2003); Saba Mahmood, *The Politics of Piety* (Princeton, N.J.: Princeton University Press, 2005), 160–61; Anne Sofie Roald, *Women in Islam: The Western Experience* (London: Routledge, 2001), 255–62. After de-colonialization, the practice of "new veiling" offered an alternative to modernization on Western models and a way of retaining the authenticity of pre-colonial times. In North Africa, the colored *hijāb* displaced both the white *haik* im-

posed by Ottoman rule and the scarf loosely wrapped around the head that bad been common in colonial times: Leila Ahmed, *Women and Gender in Islam: Historical Roots of a Modern Debate* (New Haven, Conn.: Yale University Press, 1992), 144–69; Fatima Mernissi, *The Veil and the Male Elite: A Feminist Interpretation of Women's Rights in Islam*, trans. Mary Jo Lakeland (Reading, Mass.: Addison-Wesley, 1991), 86–88, 96–99.

2. Talal Asad, "Reflections on *Laïcité* and the Public Sphere," *Items and Issues* 5, no. 3 (2005): 1–5.

3. Cited in Christopher Caldwell, "Veiled Threat," *Weekly Standard*, 19 January 2004.

4. Frantz Fanon, "Algeria Unveiled," reprinted in *Veil: Veiling, Representation and Contemporary Art*, ed. David A. Bailey and Gilane Tawardos (Cambridge, Mass.: MIT Press, 2003), 75–80.

5. Fawzia Zouari, *Ce voile qui déchire la France* (Paris: Ramsay, 2004).

6. Georg Simmel, *On Individuality and Social Forms*, ed. Donald Levine (Chicago: University of Chicago Press, 1971), 143–49.

7. Joel S. Fetzer and J. Christopher Soper, *Muslims and the State in Britain, France, and Germany*, ed. David C. Leege and Kenneth D. Wald, (Cambridge: Cambridge University Press, 2005), 62–69. Because French census forms do not note respondents' religion or ethnic background and because tracking undocumented residents is difficult, estimates vary widely.

8. Dounia Bouzar, *"Monsieur Islam" n'existe pas: Pour une désislamisation des débats*, ed. Institut National des Hautes Études en Sécurité, Littératures (Paris: Hachette, 2004), 118–19; Jules Ferry, "Speech before the French Chamber of Deputies, March 28, 1884," *Discours et opinions de Jules Ferry*, ed. Paul Robiquet (Paris: Armand Colin, 1897), 1–5.

9. Jean-François Guyot, "Ernest Chenieres: 'C'est atroce . . . '" *Le Figaro*, 27 October 1989; A. Barbot et al., "Creil: Foulards," television broadcast, France, TF 1, 1989. Institut National de l'Audiovisuel (INA) VH T VIS 19891202.

10. Robert Solé, "Islam et laïcité," *Le Monde*, 21 October 1989.

11. François Bonnet, "À Dreux, les partis ont fait profession de voile," *Libération*, 28 November 1989; Patrick Poiver d'Arvor, "Rentrée Creil," *Vingt Heures*, television broadcast, France, TF1, 1989, INA VH T VIS 19891106; Michel Fromentoux, "L'Islam à l'école," *Aspects de la France*, 19 October 1989.

12. Elizabeth Badinter et al., " 'Profs, ne capitulons pas!' " *Le nouvel observateur*, 2 November 1989; André Glucksman and Jean-Claude Casanova, " 'Le voil est taché de sang,' " *L'Express*, 24 November 1989.

13. Philippe Lançon, "Rencontre avec les adolescentes de Creil," *L'evenement du jeudi*, 26 October–1 November 1989; Christine Ockrent, "École de Beaucaire," television broadcast, France, Antenne 2, 1989, INA VH T VIS 19891023, 20:02:53; Barbot et al., "Creil"; Guyard Roland and Jean Rocas, *Le Bebette Show*, television broadcast, France, TF1, 1989; Maya Khelifi, "L'affaire des foulards Islamiques et la télévision [l'automne 1989]," Université Paris VIII, 1996, 5–27, 55–68.

14. Elisa T. Beller, "The Headscarf Affair: The Conseil D'etat on the Role of Religion and Culture in French Society," *Texas International Law Journal* 39, no. 4

(Summer 2004): 581–624; Sebastian Poulter, "Muslim Headscarves in School: Contrasting Legal Approaches in England and France," *Oxford Journal of Legal Studies* 17, no. 1 (1997):43–74; Jean Quatremer, "Foulard: Le code de la tolérance," *Libération*, 28 November 1989.

15. Xavier Ternisien, "Pourquoi la polémique sur le foulard à l'école?" *Le Monde*, 17 June 2003; Chrisophe Lucet, "Marianne et le foulard," *Sud Ouest Dimanche*, 23 November 2004; Sophie Rouquelle, "Quelque 220 cas de port du foulard," *Le Figaro*, 9 December 2003.

16. Pascale Krief, "Le Pen: 'La colonisation de la France s'accentue,'" *Le Quotidien de Paris*, 27 October 1989; Alain Touraine, "Identité: La question nationale et la politique Française," *Le Monde*, 13 March 1990.

17. Romain Goupil, "Sa vie à elle," in *Les années lycée*, television broadcast, France, ARTE, Canal +, 1996, INA VHT VIS 19960419 ART 001 FR 2; Sylvie Kerviel, "Les mystères d'une jeune fille voilée," *Le Monde*, 15 April 1995; John Bowen, *Why the French Don't Like Headscarves: Islam, the State, and Public Space* (Princeton, N.J.: Princeton University Press, 2006), 87–92.

18. Elizabeth Altschull, *Le voile contre l'école* (Paris: Seuil, 1995); Beatrice Gurrey, "Quels devoirs pour l'école?" *Le Monde*, 29 September 1999; Solenn de Royer and Florence Couret, "L'intégration des Musulmans peut s'améliorer," *La Croix*, 15 December 2000.

19. Jerome Cornuau, Miguel Courtois, and Gilles de Maistre, "Un voile pudique," in *Dans un instant, Le lycee*, television broadcast, France, M6, 2001.

20. Jean Marie Colombani, "Nous sommes tous Américains," *Le Monde*, 13 September 2001; Dominique Trezeguet et al., "Attentats terroristes aux États-Unis. Nous sommes tous vulnérables," *La Croix*, 13 September 2001; Ziahuddin Sardar, "Racism, Identity, and Muslims in the West," in *Muslim Minorities in the West*, ed. Syed Z. Abedin and Ziauddin Sardar (London: Grey Seal, 1995); Joel S. Fetzer and J. Christopher Soper, "The Roots of Public Attitudes toward State Accommodation of European Muslims' Religious Practices before and after September 11," *Journal for the Scientific Study of Religion* 42, no. 2 (2003); C. Allen and J. S. Nielsen, *Summary Report on Islamophobia in the E.U. after 11 September 2001* (Vienna: European Monitoring Center on Racism and Xenophobia, 2002).

21. Sara Millot, "La République disparait-elle sous le voile?" *Regards*, May 2003; Joan Wallach Scott, *The Politics of the Veil* (Princeton, N.J.: Princeton University Press, 2007), 90–123; Henry Maitles, "Scarves Aren't Scary," *Times Educational Supplement*, 4 June 2004.

22. Daniel Schneidermann, "Alma, Lila, Tariq, demandez le scandale," *Libération*, 24 October 2003; Pierre-Yves Le Priol, "Lila et Alma ou le retour du refoulé," *La Croix*, 4 November 2003; Ariane Chemin, "Le retour à la religion de Lila et Alma," *Le Monde*, 14 October 2003.

23. Naima Bouteldja, "The Reality of L'affaire du Foulard," *Guardian Leader*, 25 February 2005.

24. Bernard Stasi, "Rapport au President de la République" (Paris: La documentation Française, 2003); Scott, *The Politics of the Veil*, 115–123; Bowen, *Why the French*

Don't Like Headscarves, 112–27. Bernard Gorce, "Le reportage montre comment les 20 sages ont été tattrapés par la polémique sur le voile à l'école," *La Croix*, 5 March 2004; Dorothée Thénot, "Derrière le voile: Dans les coulisses de la Commission Stasi," *Le Journal*, Public Senat satellite transmission, 2005, INA CLT VIS 20040305 LCP 16h. "What no one wants to say out loud is that the seeding of France with Arabs has brought with it crime in the streets and disturbances in the schools": Andree Seu, "France's Veil," *World Magazine*, 7 February 2004. Historical tradition became an inviolable law, as in this statement from the report, "History created this ideal. It is not unstable, disconnected from changing society. Constructed in a permanent dialogue, *laïcité* has allowed us to progressively establish, without a hint of dogmatism, an equilibrium that corresponds to the needs of society": preamble to "Le rapport de la Commission Stasi sur la laïcité," quoted in *Le Monde*, 12 December 2003.

25. Catherine Coroller, "'Le port du voile doit être considéré comme un acte de maltraitance,' L'écrivaine Chahdortt Djavann à la Commission Stasi," *Libération*, 22 September 2003; Chahdortt Djavann, *Bas les voiles!* (Paris: Gallimard, 2003); Béatrice Gurrey, "Entre laïcité et diplomatie, Jacques Chirac en quête de cohérence," *Le Monde*, 1 January 2004. "The encouragement of the silly young yuppies who defend the veil supports the repression of all the women in Muslim countries who risk their lives trying to avoid the compulsion of wearing the chador": quoted in Antonella Tarquini, "Iranian Writer in France Denounces Chador," ANSA English Media Service, 15 September 2003.

26. Annie Sugier, "Le voile n'est pas un signe religieux comme les autres," in *Le livre noir de la condition des femmes*, ed. Christine Ockrent (Paris: Editions XO, 2006), 376–87.

27. Philippe Bernard, "Nadia, Saïda et Fatiha, avec ou sans voile devant la Commission Stasi," *Le Monde*, 8 December 2003.

28. Charlotte Nordmann and Jérome Vidal, eds., *Le foulard Islamique en question* (Paris: Démocratique, 2004).

29. The law of 15 March 2004 stated, "Dans les écoles, les colleges et les lycées publics, le port de signes ou tenues par lesquels les élèves manifestent ostensiblement une appurtenance religieuse est interdit."

30. Elaine Ganley, "Muslims March around the World in Protests against French Head Scarf Ban," *Aljazeerah*, Associated Press, 17 January 2004; "Les petites phrases et dérapages de Jean-Marie Le Pen," Agence France-Presse, 12 January 2005; Christophe Barbier and Romain Rosso, "Pourquoi Le Pen peut gagner," *L'Express*, 8 January 2004.

31. Jacques Chirac, "Le discours de Jacques Chirac sur la laïcité: Extraits du discours 'Relatif au respect du principe de laïcité dans la République,' Prononcé par Le Président de la République, le 17 Décembre 2003, à l' Elysée," *Le Monde*, 19 December 2003.

32. Kepel, interview, cited in Lawrence Wright, "The Terror Web," *New Yorker*, 2 August 2004; Nilüfer Göle, *Musulmanes et modernes: Voile et civilisation en Turquie*, trans. Jeanine Riegel (Paris: La Découverte, 2003), 148.

33. Hal Lehrman, "Battle of the Veil in Algeria," *New York Times*, 13 July 1958;

Todd Shepard, *The Invention of Decolonization: The Algerian War and the Remaking of France* (Ithaca, N.Y.: Cornell University Press, 2006).

34. Sibylle Rizik, "Le voile unit les Arabes contre Chirac," *Le Figaro*, 24 December 2003; Jean-Pierre Tuquoi, "Comment une Grande Nation peut-elle oser interdire le voile à l'école? S'interrogent des Algériennes. Laïcité la loi sur les signes religieux," *Le Monde*, 4 February 2004; Delphine Saubaber, "À Paris, les féministes, divisées sur la question du voile, défileront en ordre dispersé," *Le Monde*, 6 March 2004.

35. Leila Djitli, "Quand les filles mettent les voiles," *Journée de Programme*, television broadcast, France, ARTE, Doc en Stock, 2003, INA, CLT VIS 20031209 ARTE: Leïla Djitli and Sophie Troubac, *Lettre à ma fille qui veut porte le voile* (Paris: Éditions de la Martinuère, 2004); Bowen, *Why the French Don't Like Headscarves*, 223–26; Madeleine Avramoussis and Caroline Mutz, "La laïcité en France et en Allemagne," *Merci pour l'Info*, television program, France, ARTE/GEIE, 2004, INA CLT VIS 20040203Art16h.

36. Samira Bellil, *Dans l'enfer des tournantes* (Paris: Denoël, 2002); Xavier Ternisien, "La religion, l'orthodoxie, la femme et le sexe," *Le Monde*, 1 March 2004.

37. Cécile Daumas, "Khosrokhavar, Farhad, une façon ambiguë de s'affirmer," *Libération* 2003; Ismahne Chouder, Christine Delphy, and Pierre Tévanian, "Une loi contre les femmes," in Ockrent, *Le livre noir de la condition des femmes*, 383–87.

38. Chahala Chafiq-Beski and Fatima Lalem-Hachilif, "Voile: la crise des valeurs," *Libération*, 16 December 2003.

39. Amara's skill at crafting sound bites is evident in statements such as, "Everyone is talking about us, but no one is listening to us" and "The feminist movement has deserted our neighborhoods": Fadela Amara and Sylvia Zappi, *Breaking the Silence: French Women's Voices from the Ghetto* (Berkeley: University of California Press, 2006), 111–13, 126–28. Elaine Sciolino, "Back to Barricades: Liberty, Equality, Sisterhood," *New York Times*, 1 August 2003.

40. Jane Marshall, "Wave of Muslim Pupils Excluded under Headscarf Law," *Times Educational Supplement*, 29 October 2004; Sophie Rouquelle, "Quelque 220 cas de port du foulard," *Le Figaro*, 9 December 2003, 8. Since fall 2004, the legal system has been confronted with dozens of minor issues, such as whether a T-shirt showing Che Guevarra should be considered political or historical and whether headscarf-wearing mothers would be allowed to serve as chaperones on school trips.

41. Lucet, "Marianne et le foulard"; "Muslims Pray for Two French Journalists, Urge Their Release," Agence France-Presse, 31 August 2004.

FEAR WORDS

LYDIA H. LIU

Injury

Incriminating Words and Imperial Power

> Might a letter on which the sender retains certain rights then not quite belong to the person to whom it is addressed? Or might it be that the latter was never the real receiver?
> —Jacques Lacan, "Seminar on the 'Purloined Letter'"

Had it been a matter of tracing the semantics and trajectory of a word such as "injury," writing this essay would have been more or less straightforward. But my task was complicated by the double bind of language itself, especially when the usual etymological and philological approaches are part of the very historical processes I propose to examine. So I ask myself: Are there other ways to approach words in motion? Linguists and philosophers of language have long stressed the importance of networks of words, signs, and meanings in which verbal enunciations exist in structured and grammatical relationship to one another and are also in constant flux, making the meaning of a word notoriously difficult to capture.

In examining "words in motion," it might be instructive to recall some earlier attempts to resolve the quandaries posed by language. John Locke, for one, analyzed words and their signification in his theory of language in book 4 of *An Essay Concerning Human Understanding*. The word "motion," Locke wrote, names one of those "simple ideas" that do not lend themselves to definition. The atomists, who define "motion" to be a "passage from one place to another," merely substitute one synonymous word for another, but what is "passage" other than "motion"?

> For is it not at least as proper and significant to say, Passage is a motion from one place to another, as to say, Motion is a passage, &c.? This is to translate, and not to define, when we change two words of the same signi-

fication one for another; which, when one is better understood than the other, may serve to discover what idea the unknown stands for; but is very far from a definition, unless we will say every English word in the dictionary is the definition of the Latin word it answers, and that motion is a definition of MOTUS.[1]

And ad infinitum. With the hindsight gained from semiotics and deconstruction, Locke's observations may strike contemporary readers as archaic, yet his mode of analysis highlights the perennial problem inherent in etymological approaches to language: circular reasoning whether within one language or through translation. As Paul de Man observed, Locke's own "passage" in the philosophy of language continued a perpetual motion that never quite moved beyond tautology.[2]

If scholarly recourse to the roots of a word tends to turn into the repetitive stutter of tautology (such as the motion of motion), what does one stand to gain by repeating this exercise? De Man suggests that "it is indeed not a question of ontology, of things as they are, but of authority, of things as they are decreed to be. And this authority cannot be vested in any authoritative body, for the free usage of ordinary language is carried, like the child, by wild figuration which will make a mockery of the most authoritarian academy."[3] Almost in spite of himself, Locke appears to engage in wild figurations himself as he draws on seemingly random examples of motion, manslaughter, incest, parricide, and adultery to illustrate his philosophical propositions. De Man playfully mimics Locke's selection of tropes by spinning some of his own: "We have no way of defining, of policing, the boundaries that separate the name of one entity from the name of another; tropes are not just travelers, they tend to be smugglers and probably smugglers of stolen goods at that. What makes matters even worse is that there is no way of finding out whether they do so with criminal intent or not."[4] The seemingly free flow of metonymical figures from Locke's manslaughter, incest, parricide, and adultery to de Man's illicit "smugglers" raises some interesting questions of authority, transgression, injury, and punishment, all of which are articulated as words in motion that cross linguistic and legal borders and which point to the slippage of meaning in speech acts. In other words, can words incriminate? Do words make history?

I hope to show that the discourse of injury, which has figured so importantly in Western liberal and legal theories of the past few centuries, literally set words and minds in motion across the globe and helped to shape modern theories of subjectivity as we know them today. I will trace how the discourse of injury produced and *smuggled* words, meanings, and psychic energies across languages in the service of imperial objectives. I will also examine how alternative claims of injury can be silenced, foiled, or otherwise prevented from reaching their destination because they stood on the wrong side of that imperially impelled discourse. I conclude by offering some reflections on the postcolonial situation and about how we might deal with a discourse of injury that continues to mobilize the public in times of crisis today.

1836: How the British Were Injured in India and China

In the early years of the British colonial campaign against the thugs in India, its architect, William Sleeman, published a curious thug lexicon entitled *Ramaseeana*. In this first attempt to identify who the thugs were and how they communicated with one another, Sleeman's lexicon appeared to provide hard linguistic evidence for a newly discovered threat to the British presence in India. *Ramaseeana* cobbled together a group of mostly Hindi words and phrases and built them into a coherent image of the thug, thus producing the authenticity of Hindu thuggism. The details of the thugs' cold-blooded strangling of innocent travelers, for example, were graphically suggested by numerous verb and noun entries such as "*dhurdalna*" or "*dhurohurkurna*."[5] And what could be more telling than the fact that the word "thug" was of Hindi origin ("*thag*," "*theg*," or "*thak*")? Yet, as several studies have shown, thuggism was a myth invented by the British as they sought to extend their control over a mobile population and to seize criminal jurisdiction in areas that had been in the hands of the Mughal rulers. Martine Van Woerkens, for example, views the construction of thug monstrosity as "the foundation of a ritual of conjuration" in the play of mirrors between the British and the colonized.[6] The British conjuration and suppression of *thuggee* appeared to be the source of a colonial view of criminality that also fed into the discourse of sedition and terrorism in India discussed by Partha Chatterjee in this volume.

The Hindi words and their mirror images — notably, the English loan-word "thug" — were both set in motion by Sleeman's lexicon, and both were produced by one of those imperial conjurations that rendered a certain class of indigenous words and, by extension, those who spoke them potential or actual threats. Words in motion with respect to the official language of the British empire often meant that certain non-English words were made into fetish objects that inspired fear and had therefore to be exorcised. This conjuration of fear brings to mind Jacques Derrida's insight that "those who inspire fear frighten themselves; they conjure the very specter they represent. The conjuration is in mourning for *itself* and turns its own force against itself."[7] But there is another question we need to consider here: Can we ground the mirror of fear and fearfulness in more substantial arguments than psychoanalytical speculations? Can we identify systematic patterns of thought and behavior in the history of colonial conquest that can better explain the seemingly neurotic evocation of fright? Does the conjuration of fear and fearfulness resonate with a coherent view of rights and privilege in the realm of moral reasoning? If so, how might an analysis of such reasoning lead to a new understanding of modern theories of subjectivity and sovereignty? I will explore these questions by reframing Sleeman's lexicon and his thug extermination campaign in light of simultaneous and not unconnected developments in China.

In 1836, the same year that Sleeman's book *Ramaseeana* appeared in print, an equally influential work—with similar implications for British imperial policy—was published by the leading British opium dealer James Matheson. His book, *The Present Position and Prospect of Our Trade with China*, was written to persuade the British government and the public to go to war against China. In both works, the authors were preoccupied with the foreign Hindi or Chinese words and the dangers they posed or implied. One of the chief complaints brought by Matheson against the Qing government was the ubiquitous presence of the written character *yi* in official Chinese documents. He charged that the word "*yi*"—for "stranger" or "foreigner"—meant "barbarian" and that its usage insulted the British by naming them "barbarians" (*yi*) or "English barbarians" (*ying yi*). Matheson, together with the belligerent party in Parliament, pointed to the word "*yi*" as the evidence of the xenophobia of the Chinese, their universal contempt for foreigners, and their rejection of free trade and Western civilization.[8] This philological argument advanced an effective claim of injury and pressed British demands for reparations. Queen Victoria reiterated the point in her address to Parliament on 26 January 1841 at the close of the first Opium War when she stated that her government had dispatched the naval and military forces to the coast of China to "demand reparation and redress for the injuries inflicted upon some of my subjects by the officers of the Emperor of China."[9]

The queen was referring not only to the destruction of British opium by Imperial Commissioner Lin Zexu in 1839 but also to the alleged insulting of British subjects by the Chinese government after Lord Napier's arrival in Guangzhou in 1834. Napier's official title, chief superintendent of British trade in China, had been rendered as *yimu* in classical Chinese, and the literal sense of *"yimu"* was explained by Napier's interpreter as meaning "the barbarian eye." (George Staunton, a noted Sinologist in Napier's time, disputed that translation, pointing out that *"yimu"* should be translated as "foreign principal.") Thus the unfortunate catachresis of "the barbarian eye" helped to fuel one of the early military confrontations between the British and the Qing five years before the opium fiasco. After the defeat of the Qing troops in the Opium Wars, the British introduced a specific provision into the Anglo-Chinese Treaty of Tianjin in 1858 banning the Chinese use of the character *yi* when referring to the British (and by way of the most-favored-nation clause, the French inserted a similar prohibition in the treaties they signed with the Qing government). And so Article 51 of the Treaty of Tianjin became the first international legal instrument to outlaw a word from the lexicon of its own language.

By virtue of their involvement in British imperial warfare, the Hindi word *"thag"* and the Chinese character *"yi"* appear to embody a different mode of signification from our concept of the normative aspects of language as a social institution. We assume that the meanings of words may be unstable and change with time and usage, and we believe that etymology bears witness to such semantic evolution. But this commonplace notion does not carry us very far toward explaining precisely how meanings emerge as a conceptual process. Instead of taking words as conventional bearers of meaning, the Swiss linguist Ferdinand de Saussure would have us focus on a shift in the relationship between the signified and the signifier that takes place in language. With respect to observed linguistic metamorphoses, he argues: "Let there be no mistake about the meaning that we attach to the word 'change,' one might think that it deals especially with phonetic changes undergone by the signifier, or perhaps, changes in meaning which affect the signified concept. That view would be inadequate. Regardless of what the forces of change are, whether in isolation or in combination, they always result in a *shift in the relationship between the signified and the signifier.*"[10] The idea of a shifting relationship between the signified and the signifier raises some basic questions in the study of language and semiotic processes: What do we mean by words? Do they constitute a distinct class of reified material signs in contrast to syntax? How do they relate to other material signs such as numerals and electronic signals across languages and diverse media? Can the signifying processes we commonly attribute to words be grasped on other grounds than reified meanings on the printed page and their scholastic etymologies?

Inasmuch as the words "*thug*" and "*yi*" were articulated in a generalized enunciation of "injury" in the imperial warfare of the past centuries, our task can hardly be limited to establishing the semantics of a word through history, etymology, and related institutions. We must open up the reified *wordness* by focusing on situated acts of enunciation in concrete discursive situations. Words in motion, in such a non-reifying moment, can thus be conceived as a movement of verbal elements as mobile signs through a shift in the relationship between the signifier and the signified or, as I have put it elsewhere, between heterolinguistic signs that move across the boundaries of languages. I call this translingual process the invention of "super-signs."[11]

The distinction between words and super-signs is fundamental to an analysis of heterocultural processes of meaning making. "*Thag*/thug," "*yi*/barbarian," and "injury/*injuria*" are super-sign units that traversed two or more languages through repeated acts of translation and enunciation. This translingual motion was generally occulted, so that the English words "thug," "barbarian," and "injury" appeared free of the traces of the super-signs that animated them. Treating "*thag*/thug," "*yi*/barbarian," and "injury/*injuria*" as a network of interconnected super-signs rather than merely as "words" derived from Hindi, Greek, Chinese, or Latin helps to redirect our attention away from the etymologist's preoccupation with reified words. This analytical approach can take us into the realm of enchanted meanings, camouflaged traces of foreignness, and potent but disavowed forms of translingual speech and meaning making across languages.

In that sense, the words "thug" and "barbarian" belong to a realm of enchanted meanings haunted by their super-signs — "*thag*/thug" and "*yi*/barbarian/*barbarus*/*barbaros*." They are likely to withhold their mode of signification from the sovereign gaze of national language(s) that reduce them to isolated cases of words and expressions with fixed etymological attributions. We have to find ways to de-word "thug," "*thag*," "*yi*," and "barbarian" in order to see them as interrelated super-signs and analyze them in mutually intelligible terms under the rubric of what I call the "enunciation of injury." The enunciation of injury provides the interpretive grid through which to discern and analyze the conjuration of fear and fearfulness—which routinely evokes these "foreign" words as marks of authenticity and identity. If the verbal fetishism surrounding the Hindi word "*thag*" and the Chinese character "*yi*" were capable of releasing extraordinary energy, putting into motion numerous acts of *ressentiment*, punishments, and legal and military campaigns to redress the alleged "injury," it behooves us to ask why.

When William Sleeman launched his anti-Thug campaign in India in 1831, he was by no means behaving like a paranoid eccentric but was fully convinced of the justice of his action. The same may be said of Queen Victoria's allegation that the Qing government's use of the word "barbarian" had injured British subjects before the Opium War. Yet the British authorities could not possibly have been blind to the fact that the large quantities of opium their traders were importing into China had caused massive injury to the Chinese population. To press this argument, Imperial Commissioner Lin Zexu addressed a letter to Queen Victoria in 1839 on the eve of the Opium War with the objective of putting a stop to drug trafficking. But this later legendary letter was never delivered into the hands of the British sovereign. That failure, I argue, must be understood in relation to James Matheson's open "letter" to the British government and the general public in the form of his *The Present Position and Prospect of Our Trade with China*, which did successfully reach its destination. In reassessing Lin's attempted enunciation of injury due to the damaging effects of opium, therefore, we must not lose sight of that other letter by the opium dealer Matheson, whose discourse of injury turned out to be much more effective and powerful than the claims of damage made by Lin Zexu.

The Purloined Letter of the Opium War

Following his forceful seizure of the contraband opium from the British in 1839, Imperial Commissioner Lin Zexu (1785–1850) addressed a formal appeal to Queen Victoria to inform the British crown of the new regulations and deadlines for stopping future opium shipments and to ask the queen to cooperate with the Qing government in this effort. Lin opened his letter thus:

Over the many years in which foreign countries have enjoyed trade relations [with us], there has been a mixture of law-abiding merchants and misbehaving merchants arriving here. The latter have been smuggling opium to seduce the *Hua* people and to cause every province of our land to overflow with that poison. These merchants seek only to profit themselves and do so by hurting others. Their selfish behavior cannot be tolerated by the principle of universal justice [*tianli*] and is repugnant to all with a human sensibility. Upon hearing of this situation, our great emperor was greatly indignant and dispatched me, the Commissioner, to investigate and work with the Viceroy and Lieu. Governor of the province in Zhuangzhou, to resolve the matter.[12]

With the approval of the Daoguang emperor on 3 August 1839, Lin had multiple copies made of the letter and entrusted them to captains of a few British and European ships, for he was wary of the British traders' attempt to intercept his attempt to communicate with their sovereign.[13] Lin's suspicion proved prescient. To take one example, Captain Warner of the *Thomas Coutts* had promised to take a copy to the queen on 18 January 1840, but after he arrived in England and requested an interview with Lord Palmerston on 7 June 1840, the Foreign Office refused to see him or accept the letter.[14]

Would a successful delivery of Lin's letter to Queen Victoria in the winter of 1839–40 have helped to avert the Opium War and alter the course of history? It is impossible to speculate. But in the eyes of those who had caused the original letter to disappear, the timing of the interception was critical because the queen was just then being asked to authorize the war in the face of strong opposition from members of the Parliament (the majority vote was too close to call), and she did in fact give such an order on 4 April 1840. As far as Lin himself was concerned, the ill-fated letter never reached its intended destination in spite of his precautions. When the letter was diverted from its course, the document did not disappear, however, but went on to reach for a new audience through a public channel of circulation: the printed periodical. For when Lin's letter was printed in the February 1840 issue of *Chinese Repository*—a missionary journal published in Guangzhou, whose readership consisted largely of the foreign community and the opium traders—the present and future readers of the periodical became the unintended recipients of the letter.[15]

This situation reminds us of what Jacques Lacan discovered in Edgar

Allan Poe's short story "The Purloined Letter." In Lacan's reading, an interesting question arises concerning the delivery and non-delivery of meanings through Poe's clever maneuvering of a storyline that hinges on the loss and recovery of a letter purloined from the queen. Lacan asks: "Might a letter on which the sender retains certain rights then not quite belong to the person to whom it is addressed? Or might it be that the latter was never the real receiver?"[16] Perhaps, we can ask these tantalizing questions of the letter under discussion: Might the letter on which Lin retained certain rights not quite have belonged to the person to whom it was addressed? Might it be that Queen Victoria was never the real receiver? Indeed, among the unintended audience of the missionary periodical *Chinese Repository*, those who were responsible for intercepting the letter had the satisfaction of knowing that Lin's argument of *hai* (harm, damage, or injury) would not reach beyond China, much less gain the ear of their sovereign. This turn of events was no trivial matter when we consider how hard the opium traders had been lobbying the British public to gain moral support and build momentum for war. Many of them had been busily testifying in Parliament to the injuries that the British subjects had suffered at the hands of Chinese officials.[17] This brings us back to Matheson's competing letter, which circulated widely through the medium of print.

In his book, Matheson had asserted that the "Emperor of China, by ratifying the act of the local authorities in their outrageous treatment of Lord Napier, has rendered himself responsible for such treatment; it has 'become a public concern, and the injured party is to consider *the nation* as the real author of the injury, of which the citizen was only the instrument.' "[18] To press the legal point about the British claim to injury, Matheson drew on the principles of justice in the law of nations and, in particular, Vattel's authoritative text, which, according to Matheson, conferred an essential right on the British trader. Citing Vattel's position on trade in book two of *The Law of Nations*—while carefully suppressing the word "opium"—he argued: "Men are, therefore, under an obligation to carry on that commerce with each other, if they wish not to depart from the views of nature. And this obligation extends also to whole nations, or states."[19] China had violated the law of nations by refusing to trade with the British and shutting out the rest of the world from participation in "the benefits of so prodigious a portion of the most desirable parts of the earth."[20] To bear witness to such violation, Matheson included copies of the British merchants' petitions to the queen outlining their grievances, statistics of trade revenue from the archives of the East India Company, and a sampling of the edicts of the Qing emperor in English translation — all these to marshal evidence in support of the pro-war position he promoted in *The Present Position and Prospects*.

Matheson's book was conceived as an open letter addressed to the British government and the general public as part of an elaborate lobbying effort on behalf of the largest drug-smuggling cartel in Asia, the famous Jardine–Matheson partnership. Not only had his "letter" arrived three years earlier at its intended destination, but it also proved to be more powerful and effective than what Lin could possibly have said in his letter to Queen Victoria. Indeed, Matheson's letter had pre-empted Lin's attempt by his careful avoidance of the word "opium" while emphasizing equal trade and the charge of injury by China on the discursive ground of international law. Lin's letter focused exclusively on opium smuggling, its injurious effects on people, and the ways in which drug trafficking might be stopped:

> We have heard that opium is strictly forbidden in your own country, which indicates that you are thoroughly aware of its harmful effects. If opium is not allowed to injure your own country, it ought not to be allowed to injure other countries either, much less the Central States because, of all the goods we export to foreign countries, there is not a single item that is not beneficial to people: they are beneficial when eaten, beneficial when used, beneficial when resold. They are beneficial on all accounts. Is there a single article from the Central States that has done any harm to foreign countries?[21]

As if contradicting Matheson's rhetoric about China's opposition to free trade as the main source of conflict, Lin's letter pinpointed the opium trade as the real point of contention between Britain and China. His argument of moral reciprocity would certainly have struck a chord among some of the Christian groups who were opposed to the opium trade at this time. However, what Lin had to say about the *moral* value of export–import goods would have sounded strange both to the political economists of his time and to the critics of British imperialism and liberal political economy such as Karl Marx.

Writing for the *New York Daily Tribune*, Marx caught the grotesque mismatch between the terms of debate between China and Britain during the Opium Wars. He called it "a deadly duel, in which the representative of the antiquated world appears prompted by ethical motives, while the representative of overwhelming modern society fights for the privilege of buying in the cheapest and selling in the dearest markets — this, indeed, is a sort of tragic couplet stranger than any poet would ever have dared to fancy."[22] A deadly duel, to be sure. But those who fought to preserve the privilege of buying in the cheapest and selling in the dearest markets also deemed themselves morally superior to the antiquated world and resented being called a nation of shopkeepers. They preferred to be the ones, in ethical terms, to lay the groundwork of moral reasoning and win the war on that ground as well as on the military front. Thus, the name of the drug trade had to be suppressed, abstracted, rendered invisible, and banished from moral argument so that the discourse of injury could be safely grounded in the de-territorialized capitalist economy and be legitimated by it.

And we should not be surprised when John Quincy Adams, the sixth president of the United States, told the Massachusetts Historical Society in 1841 that opium was a mere incident to the dispute between the British and the Qing. It was "no more the cause of the war than the throwing overboard of tea in Boston harbor was the cause of the North American revolution." The cause of the war, he said, was "the arrogant and insupportable pretensions of China that she will hold commercial intercourse with the rest of mankind not upon terms of equal reciprocity, but upon the insulting and degrading forms of the relation between lord and vassal."[23] Was it really so? Adams's judgment fully corroborates the propaganda of the opium dealer Matheson who had circumvented the word "opium" as he tried to tell a different story about the British–Chinese conflict. The reciprocity to which Adams referred was not the same argument of reciprocity as Lin made in his letter with respect to the kinds of merchandise being traded. Adams reiterated Matheson's accusation that China had injured the British honor and deserved punishment. In his open letter to the British government, for instance, Matheson had adumbrated the "principal sources of our grievances" and urged, "We must resolve upon vindicating our insulted honour as a nation, and protecting the injured interests of our commerce.[24] With the help of Lord Palmerston and other pro-war ministers, this belligerent message finally reached the ear of the queen, who responded with the order to authorize war at Buckingham Palace on 4 April 1840:

Whereas we have taken into consideration the late injurious proceedings of certain officers of the Emperor of China towards certain of Our officers and subjects; and whereas We have given orders that satisfaction and reparation for the same shall be demanded from the Chinese Government; and whereas it is expedient, with the view to obtain such satisfaction and reparation, that ships and vessels and cargoes belonging to the Emperor of China and to his subjects, shall be detained and held in custody; and if such reparation and satisfaction be refused by the Chinese Government, the ships, vessels, and cargoes so detained, and others to be thereafter detained, shall be confiscated and sold, and that the proceeds thereof shall be applied.[25]

Once again, the word "opium" was carefully suppressed in the queen's address, although the control of the drug trade had been the true cause of tension between the two countries as well as the rationale of Lin Zexu's letter protesting it. Instead, the discourse that emerged from the British side was a thoroughly abstract legal discourse having to do with rights, grievances, injuries, and reparations but very little to do with opium or opium traders such as James Matheson and William Jardin.

In short, injury claims were meaningful in this context only insofar as trade rights and related grievances were concerned. Matheson invoked the natural rights granted by the law of nations and urged the British government to take action against the Qing prohibition of the (opium) trade. Freedom of trade, in his view, conferred on the British an inalienable right to conduct commerce with China by imposing a reciprocal obligation on the Chinese to open their doors to the British (opium) merchants. Cynicism might lead us to treat all this talk about rights and injury as a mere pretext for war, but then we would miss an important opportunity to examine how this manner of reasoning prevailed when it did and how it has endured to this day. In my view, the British enunciation of injury raises fundamental questions about the moral and legal grounding of violence in colonial history.

The modern Western discourse of injury can be traced to the early colonial conception of natural rights in the so-called encounter between civilization and barbarity. The reciprocity of natural rights in the theory of *jus gentium* implied that, if the Europeans' rights to trade with the natives were violated by the natives, the natives could be said to have injured the natural rights of the Europeans. "The vindication of injuries constitutes a just war, and ultimately it was only by means of such a war that the Spaniards could legitimate their presence in America."[26] This sixteenth-century colonial fashioning of the *jus gentium*, sovereignty, and rights of war in the so-called New World provided the legal and moral ground for the subsequent development of the law of nations in European conquests of other parts of the globe.[27] In due time, freedom of travel, trade, and proselytizing evolved into the standard of "civilization" as we know it today.[28]

Steeped as he was in Chinese humanistic traditions, Lin evoked a different discourse of legality, reciprocity, and injury to argue his case, and he insisted on drawing Queen Victoria's attention to the opium problem in his official letter:

> Your honorable nation buys and ships the goods from our inner land not only for your own use and consumption but also for the purpose of making threefold profits by re-selling them to other countries. Even if you did not trade opium, this threefold profit would still have been guaranteed. How can you bear to sell a drug that is so injurious to your fellow men just to satisfy your unbridled craving after gain? Suppose foreigners from another country carried opium into England and tried to seduce your people into buying it and smoking it, would your honorable sovereign not feel indignant and do everything in your power to uproot the sources of evil? Since Your Highness enjoys the reputation as a benevolent and magnanimous ruler, you would naturally not wish to do unto another that which you do not wish another to do unto you. We are gratified to learn that the ships coming to Canton [Guangzhou] have been provided with the regulations in which it is specifically stated that they are not permitted to carry contraband goods. This shows that the administrative orders of your honorable rule were originally strict and clear. It must have been because the trading ships have become so numerous lately that inspections and supervision have lagged behind. For this reason, we address this communication to you with the prohibitory orders of our dynasty so you will have a clear understanding and require your subjects not to violate them again.[29]

Had Lin's letter not been physically removed from the diplomatic channels of communication, would Queen Victoria and her cabinet have been persuaded by this argument and understood that it was the British who had injured the Chinese with their drug operations rather than the converse, as alleged by Matheson?

Montgomery Martin, who wrote a postwar report to the queen and her government describing the situation of China in 1847, had the opportunity to read an earlier and shorter version of Lin's letter in English and was moved by "this beautiful and convincing letter" to comment: "Why, the 'slave trade' was merciful compared to the 'opium trade.' We did not destroy the bodies of the Africans, for it was our immediate interest to keep them alive; — we did not *debase their natures, corrupt their minds, — nor destroy their souls.* But the opium seller slays the body after he has corrupted, degraded and annihilated the moral being of unhappy sinners — while, every hour is bringing new victims to a Moloch which knows no satiety — and where the English murderer and Chinese suicide vie with each other in offerings at his shrine."[30] If Lin seemed willing to extricate the British crown and its government from the behavior of opium traders, Martin is unforgiving in his scathing criticism: "The blame ought not to be cast solely on the individuals engaged in this dreadful traffic; it rests chiefly on the government of our Gracious Sovereign, and on that of the East India Company."[31] Martin's condemnation of the "opium trade" as worse than the "slave trade" brought the long-standing legacy of colonial violence into the picture and can be taken as representative of the position of many Christian missionaries in China. It also anticipated the anti-opium Quaker movements in England that arose in the 1870s. But what Martin did not grasp any more than Lin had at the time was that the colonial violence he deplored was thoroughly intermeshed with the theory of natural rights and sovereignty to which Matheson repeatedly appealed in his testimonies.

That is to say, Matheson spoke the language of international law when he cited Vattel systematically to argue that the injured party was to consider *the nation* the real author of the injury, of which the citizen was only the instrument. Of course, the architects of international law could never predict how the law would be used on every single occasion, but the governing principles of rights and freedoms, as well as the discourse of injury and reparations, did provide a consistent and coherent rhetoric of moral reasoning that proved extremely effective in authorizing colonial warfare.

In this sense, Lin's letter to Queen Victoria had been stolen not just once but twice, because all were not equally entitled to the claims of injury.[32] In the colonial world order, the power to injure was structurally related to the ability to claim injury and adjudicate the matters of revenge and reparation. The Opium Wars and the history of modern colonialism provide overwhelming evidence that the imperial powers regarded injury as their own prerogative and tried to suppress other injury claims until the legal and moral conditions of aggressive warfare were met. It seems to me that acknowledging the *work of injury* as a powerful force is the first step toward a better understanding of the political structure of suffering in the modern world. It leads to interrogating the colonial legacy of the past centuries with a view to bringing the legal and ethical grounding of colonial violence to light. We must also ask in what ways this legacy has evolved to energize today's imperial war on terror so that a generalized "enunciation of injury" continues to prevail. In discussing the evolution of the discourse of "terrorism" from the colonial era through militant nationalism in contemporary India, Partha Chatterjee argues in this volume that "the return of 'terrorism' as a category makes sense within a new global discourse of security in liberal-democratic societies." The structural relationship between the discourse on "terrorism" and the norms of the liberal state that Chatterjee emphasizes should help us see the centrality of the discourse of injury in the liberal theory of rights and sovereignty.

The Work of Injury

As a theoretical problem, injury has dominated the liberal considerations of political rule and civic liberty. In the realm of public health, injury claims have been central to the processes of public policymaking and changing industrial behavior as, for example, in the government's regulation of hazardous technologies involving automobile manufacturers.[33] In her study of injury as a focus of political rule and civic liberty in the modern state, Elaine Scarry suggested a set of structural attributes that constitute the core of what appear to be unstable and incoherent invocations of consent across the thresholds of medicine, law, and political philosophy. That core is what she terms "the material anchoring of consent in the body."[34] It is often in the injured, sleepy, anesthetized, dying body, Scarry argues, that "we have the sudden grounding of rights, sovereignty, dignity."[35] Consent carries active powers by holding the notions of sovereignty and authorization within it; yet the issue of consent has tended to arise whenever there is an extreme condition of passivity. The intervention of political philosophy in medicine — in the determination of patients' rights and the distribution of activity and passivity — is the inevitable outcome of the centering of the body in citizenship understood in liberal terms. Scarry's insights notwithstanding, her argument is framed by the legal terms of the liberal state, in which the protection of a person's body, property, and rights and the prevention of injury to them are an established point of reference for both criminal law and politics.[36]

In her book *States of Injury*, Wendy Brown seeks to understand how the social agenda of politicized identity in North America has allowed disenfranchised groups to press injury claims against the state. She argues that those who have been excluded or subjugated — women, people of color, Jews, homosexuals, and so on — by the dominant power have tried to install pain and injury at the heart of their demand for political recognition and reparations. Drawing on Nietzsche's speculations about the unhappy vindictiveness of the oppressed, Brown identifies a political structure of *ressentiment* in North American feminism and elsewhere: "In locating a site of blame for its powerlessness over its past — a past of injury, a past as a hurt will — and locating a 'reason' for the 'unendurable pain' of social powerlessness in the present, [politicized identity] converts this reasoning into an ethicizing politics, a politics of recrimination that seeks to avenge the hurt even while it reaffirms it, discursively codifies it. Politicized identity thus enunciates itself, makes claims for itself, only by entrenching, restating, dramatizing, and inscribing its pain in politics."[37] Brown's analysis suggests how injury can articulate and be articulated by identity politics whenever the socially oppressed attempt to appeal to law and the state for social justice. She sees the politics of recrimination as an ironic act of revenge based on a fundamental misrecognition of the identity and role of the state. This critique draws our attention to the typical impasse in liberal conceptions of freedom and justice, where law and the state are placed in a position of "neutral arbiter" of injury rather than themselves vested with the power to injure. While the thrust of Brown's argument seems convincing as far as it goes, the missing figure is the state, which is busily engaged in the productive work of injury and in what she calls the politics of recrimination.

What I wish to emphasize is that the state (or empire) is given the power not only to injure but also of being injured and making claims to that effect. There is no place for this seemingly perverse figure in mainstream discussions of liberal politics precisely because that figure has continually been occulted by the dialectic of "state" and "individual," which effectively camouflages the work of injury and its power in global politics. Consequently, one rules out a priori the scenario in which the strong and the powerful can be the first to lay legal and moral claims to injury against the disfranchised and retain an enormous stake in maintaining the political structure of *ressentiment* in the larger imperial order.

The idea of a "pre-emptive strike" in the United States today is proof that the discourse of injury continues to perform the legal and rhetorical work of empire as it did in the old colonial days. For too long we have allowed the liberal understanding of injury and its limited critique within the discursive space of the modern state to dominate political thinking to the exclusion of other interpretive possibilities. Inasmuch as the liberal state emerged in the wake of colonial expansion and is indebted to it in so many ways, some of the tenets that liberal thinkers and their critics have enshrined in modern political theory — "rights," "justice," "freedom," "sovereignty," and so on — are better understood in relation to the centuries of European colonial exploration that generated these ideas long before they became incorporated into the theories and practices of the modern state.

That suggests why liberal notions of rights, property, body, and liberty ought no longer serve as the sole lens through which we examine the question of suffering in the colonial past or in the present, since these ideas have evolved through the privileged enunciations of "injury" in colonial history. We would do well to re-ground the work of injury in a postcolonial critique of liberal amnesia and ask how the inhibited or uninhibited physical movement (the literal meaning of "freedom") of the imperial subject have provided the occasion for thinking, imagining, legislating, and removing any perceived threats and injuries posed to such freedom of movement. Unpacking the colonial legacy of "injury" is crucial to understanding how moral reasoning operates and is seen to operate in imperial warfare, past and present.

Understanding the *work of injury* entails recognizing it as a dangerous and productive force in the making of the modern world. To the degree that the project of world taking cannot be accomplished on the basis of military technology alone, legal justification and moral reasoning were employed to bring about a consensus, a worldview, or, if neither could be achieved, at least the authorization of a course of action by those in power. Whereas narratives of trauma have tended to dwell on memories of the past as a means to sanction present or future action, the work of injury in imperial warfare was primarily future-oriented: a premeditation and prefiguration of violence in a future mode, much like the "pre-emptive strike" on Iraq by the United States. Similarly, the September 11 attack on the

Twin Towers in New York aroused familiar outpourings of *ressentiment* and precipitated claims of injury. And just as the originary wrong vanished in the warfare of the past, so the claims of injury continued to elaborate grounds for revenge and punishment of "terrorism" on behalf of a new imperial order. The imperial state continues to present its suffering as the rationale for its exercise of power.

Two observations may be made on the discursive front. One is that the state's injury claim might be viewed as moral posturing that should be exposed by analyzing its true intent and those of the oil interests that drove the war machine. This does not, however, explain why the discourse of "injury" remains so central to the legal and affective determination of human rights in the West and why both liberal thinkers and their critics have so much to say about the state of injury in civil society and the international community.

The other possibility would be to acknowledge a political structure of suffering in global politics that can be traced to its earlier enunciations in colonial history and explained in light of that history. This seems to me a more promising way to show that the accepted moral consensus is itself the product of a political structure of suffering that underlies the claims of injury on the part of a state or empire and provides the moral vindication for further acts of retaliation. Terrorism, not unlike thuggery or the threat posed by the mirror image of the barbarian, provides the name that fuels this cycle of retaliation and violence. Is there a way out of this vicious cycle of recrimination? As we saw in Lin's reasoning to Queen Victoria, alternative articulations of injury existed in the past and continue to exist in the present, even if they are often silenced or expressed in the form of political fantasy. If the imperial discourse of injury remains in motion, it makes all the more sense for us to take historical narratives and philosophical reasoning beyond the circularity of rights, injury, and retaliation and reach toward a more complex and dignified understanding of the history of one's own suffering and also that of others.

Notes

1. John Locke, *An Essay Concerning Human Understanding*, ed. Peter H. Nidditch (Oxford: Clarendon Press, 1975), 423.

2. Paul de Man, *Aesthetic Ideology* (Minneapolis: University of Minnesota Press, 1996), 38.

3. Ibid., 39.

4. Ibid.

5. William H. Sleeman, *Ramaseeana, or a Vocabulary of the Peculiar Language Used by the Thugs with an Introduction and an Appendix Descriptive of the System Pursued by That Fraternity and of the Measures Which Have Been Adopted by the Supreme Government for Its Suppression* (Calcutta: Military Orphan Press, 1836). *"Dhurdalna"* and *"dhurohurkurna"* in the example here derive from *"dhur,"* or "dust," and *"dharna,"* or "to hold" (the fact of strangling: *dharohur*), according to Sleeman's lexicon.

6. See Martine Van Woerkens, *The Strangled Traveler: Colonial Imaginings and the Thugs of India*, trans. Catherine Tihanyi (Chicago: University of Chicago Press, 2002), 292.

7. Jacques Derrida, *Specters of Marx: The State of the Debt, the Work of Mourning, and the New International*, trans. Peggy Kamuf (New York: Routledge, 1994), 116.

8. For a detailed analysis of the dispute over the meaning of the word *"yi,"* see Lydia H. Liu, *The Clash of Empires: The Invention of China in Modern World Making* (Cambridge, Mass.: Harvard University Press, 2004), 31–69.

9. F. Sidney Ensor, ed., *The Queen's Speeches in Parliament from Her Accession to the Present Time* (London: W. H. Allen, 1882), 22.

10. See Ferdinand de Saussure, *Course in General Linguistics*, trans. Wade Baskin (New York: McGraw-Hill, 1966), 74–75.

11. Liu, *The Clash of Empires*, 11–15.

12. Lin Zexu et al., "Ni yu yingjili guowang xi" [A draft declaration to the sovereign of England], in Lai Xinxia, *Lin Zexu nianpu xinbian* [Revised chronicles of Lin Zexu's life], (Tianjin: Nankai daxue chubanshe, 1997), 341. The translation is mine.

13. See Lai, *Lin Zexu nianpu xinbian*, 311–13.

14. See Hsin-pao Chang, *Commissioner Lin and the Opium War* (Cambridge, Mass.: Harvard University Press, 1964), 138.

15. Through an effective network of prewar intelligence, the British got hold of an earlier draft of Lin's letter and printed it in *Chinese Repository* as early as May 1839.

16. Jacques Lacan, "Seminar on the 'Purloined Letter,'" in *The Purloined Poe: Lacan, Derrida, and Psychoanalytic Reading*, ed. John P. Muller and William J. Richardson (Baltimore, Md.: Johns Hopkins University Press, 1988), 41.

17. For their testimonials and related documents, see *British Parliamentary Papers, China 30* and *31* (Shannon: Irish University Press, 1971).

18. James Matheson, *The Present Position and Prospect of Our Trade with China* (London: Smith, Elder, 1836), 67.

19. Ibid., 34. Emmerich de Vattel, *The Law of Nations* (1758), ed. Joseph Chitty (Philadelphia, Penn.: T. and J. W. Johnson, 1883) book 2, chap.18, 74.

20. Ibid., 35.

21. Lin Zexu et al., *Lin Zexu nianpu xinbian*, 342. The translation is mine.

22. Karl Marx, "Trade or Opium," *New York Daily Tribune*, 20 September 1858.

23. *Chinese Repository*, vol. 11 (1842), 274–89; see also Edgar Holt, *The Opium Wars in China* (London: Putnam, 1964), 101–2.

24. Matheson, *The Present Position and Prospect of Our Trade with China*, 79.

25. "Order in Council," *British Parliamentary Papers, China*, vol. 30, presented to Parliament by command of Her Majesty, April 1840, 196.

26. Anthony Pagden, "Dispossessing the Barbarian: The Language of Spanish Thomism and the Debate over the Property Rights of the American Indians," in *The Language of Political Theory in Early-Modern Europe*, ed. Anthony Pagden (Cambridge: Cambridge University Press, 1987), 87.

27. For further discussion, see Anthony Anghie, "Finding the Peripheries: Sovereignty and Colonialism in Nineteenth-Century International Law," *Harvard International Law Journal* 40 (Winter 1999): 1–80.

28. See Gerrit W. Gong, *The Standard of "Civilization" in International Society* (Oxford: Clarendon Press, 1984), 37.

29. Lin Zexu, et al., *Lin Zexu nianpu xinbian*, 343.

30. Robert Montgomery Martin, *China: Political, Commercial, and Social in an Official Report to Her Majesty's Government* (London: James Madden, 1847), 2:261.

31. Ibid., 2:260.

32. In their 1954 translation of Lin's letter, the American Sinologists Ssu-yü Teng and John King Fairbank methodically replaced all instances of the character *yi* from the original English translation's "foreigner," which had appeared in the *Chinese Repository*, with the incriminating word "barbarian." The new translation reiterates Matheson's injury claims against the Qing government.

33. For an analysis of state power and automobile manufacturers in their continual redefinition of automobile injuries, see Carol A. MacLennan, "From Accident to Crash: The Auto Industry and the Politics of Injury," *Medical Anthropology Quarterly* 2, no. 3 (September 1988): 233–50.

34. Elaine Scarry, "Consent and the Body: Injury, Departure, and Desire," *New Literary History* 21, no. 4 (Autumn 1990): 868.

35. Ibid., 873.

36. For a contemporary discussion of the liberal stand on this issue, see Joel Feinberg, *Harm to Others: The Moral Limits of the Criminal Law* (Oxford: Oxford University Press, 1984).

37. Wendy Brown, *States of Injury: Power and Freedom in Late Modernity* (Princeton, N.J.: Princeton University Press, 1995), 74.

VICENTE L. RAFAEL

Conjuración/Conspiracy

in the Philippine Revolution of 1896

In the years since September 11, 2001, many travelers, including this writer, have been detained by the authorities, often without knowing the reason why. Taken, or more likely mistaken, as part of some far-flung conspiracy, they have suffered violations that range from public humiliation to secret torture in the name of the "war on terror." And it is likely that their detention began with a name, a name on a list with other named persons putatively engaged in plotting acts of terror. In this context, names had the capacity to conjure up conspiracies and set in motion forces to unearth, contain, and eliminate such plots — or, depending on who compiles the list, to join and expand them. The power that names have to menace and remake the world is read into them by those who are convinced of their secret references and the strength, or danger, of their motivations.

To read a name in terms of such secret relations with other names is to begin to trace the outlines of a conspiracy. The word "conspiracy" comes from the Latin "*conspirare*," literally "to breathe together," hence, "to accord, harmonize, agree, combine or unite in a purpose, plot mischief together secretly." It thus asserts linkages, both with collective action and with mischief, or terror. How can we think of this relay that runs from conspiracy to community, secrecy to terror?

Here I follow the word "conspiracy" in the specific sociohistorical context of the Spanish Philippines in the second half of the nineteenth century. I ask how the word was used by the Spanish colonial state and its clerical allies to describe the emanations of nationalist sentiment in the circulation of the names of secret organizations. Rendered in Castilian as "*conjuracion*," "conspiracy" meant "conjuring," the calling forth of beings by way of ritual speech, performative utterances, and the exchange of vows. "*Conjuración*" also evoked the act of swearing as well as cursing: the sending forth of magical speech with which to affect someone against his or her will. Indeed, the notion of "conspiracy" as "conjuring" framed colonial officials' understanding of Filipino nationalist discourse. Initially asking for reform, and then eventually for separation and independence, Filipinos gathered to meet in secret societies where they took blood oaths to form new associations and assume new identities distinct from the racialized ascriptions of colonial society. Learning of these societies and oaths from rumors, captured documents, and forced confessions extracted by means of torture, Spaniards imagined a web of conspiracies to wage a campaign of terror and a race war that threatened to end colonial rule. Seen as a series of *conjuras* that infected the colonized populace, Spaniards heard in Filipino nationalism only a kind of death sentence. Just as names on a terror watch list convey the sense of hidden identities and uncertain motives, so "conspiracy" in this context served as a medium for communicating conflicted but no less powerful messages about death, freedom, and justice between Spanish rulers and Filipino nationalists.

I

To understand the motion of the word "conspiracy" (which serves, as we shall see, as a trope for tracing the motion of a political movement) on the eve of the Philippine Revolution of 1896, some preliminary remarks about the latter are in order. As with all revolutions, the anticolonial struggle against Spain precipitated a massive socioeconomic crisis that also had a distinctive linguistic aspect. The revolution was both generated and generative of profound challenges to colonial social relations to the extent that it also defied the existing linguistic regime. Such a regime mandated a linguistic hierarchy that originally arose out of the exigencies of Christian conversion, yoked, however unevenly, to the demands of the Spanish colonial state from the mid-sixteenth century on. It was characterized by the systematic privileging of Castilian as the language for mediating the relationship between Latin—God's word—and the vernacular languages of the people. It also insisted on the notion that in the end all messages were knowable and receivable by a single source and addressee, God the Father, through the ineluctable mediation of the clergy, the state, and the Spanish Crown.[1] Revolutionary nationalism raised the possibility of language occurring outside these linguistic constraints, escaping the linguistic hierarchy and working through obscure and secret signs undecipherable from above. By positing an alternative source for speech, revolutionary nationalism indicated a power working separately from colonial society yet claiming its attention.

By the same token, revolutionary nationalism radicalized the question of agency and address. "Who speaks?" and "Who is spoken to?" were seen to come from elsewhere — from a future yet to be foreclosed. It was an "I" or a "we" that was so new that it appeared then to have no recognizable place in colonial society. Escaping the protocols of recognition and representation, it seemed like a foreign presence but of a decisively different sort from that of the colonial rulers. It brought with it a welter of messages about separation and revenge, response and responsibility, freedom and death — messages whose meanings remained unclear and for this reason continue to resonate with us, whoever "we" are, today.[2]

How do we approach this "I" or "we" in its newness? Where and how do we understand the crisis of address it brought about? How was that crisis thought of as the consequence of conspiracy?

II

One place to begin is with José Rizal, the acknowledged "father" of Filipino nationalism. Let us look briefly at his second novel, *El Filibusterismo* (1891), usually translated as *Subversion*. In a chapter titled "Pasquinades," Rizal tells the story of anonymously authored posters appearing on the university's walls a day after the denial of a petition of a student association to establish an academy for the teaching of Castilian.[3] We are never told about the contents of the posters, which are judged by the authorities to be subversive by virtue of their presumably satirical nature and their unknown origins. Rumors quickly spread that they are the signs of a secret conspiracy. Perhaps they are the work of students in league with the bandits hiding out in the mountains, some say. Or perhaps not. In any case, their appearance unleashes rampant speculation, as one character says, that "other hands are at work, but no less terrible" (*andan otros manos, pero no menos terrible*).[4]

The colonial police soon arrest students and other *ilustrados* (elite nationalists) who were known to have been critical of the influence of the Spanish friars. But rather than put fear to rest, the spectacle of their arrest incites more talk, adding to anxieties up and down colonial society. Rumors abound of an impending attack on Manila and of German boats anchored off the coast waiting to lend assistance to such an attack. Mysterious disturbances and noises trigger panic as they are taken to mean "that the revolution had begun–it was only a matter of seconds."[5] The appearance of the posters thus raise the specter of language beyond colonial control. The posters suggest an origin outside of what can be accounted for. Wild speculations seek to trace the path of this mysterious origin but only serve further to obscure it. Arresting the usual suspects, authorities hope to find the source of the posters but discover that there is always something yet to be uncovered.

The posters, then, are significant less for their content than for what they reveal: the existence of "other hands at work . . . no less terrible." They give rise to the sense of unseen forces working in secret to bring about what cannot be fully known, much less anticipated. Occurring outside the established hierarchy, the posters reveal something that defies revelation. It is this defiant power that draws intense interest from everyone in colonial society. That no one can resist hearing, passing on, and amplifying rumors suggests something of the power of the secret as it holds everyone in thrall, endowing them with a commonality they did not previously possess.

Rizal's story about the posters is most likely an allusion to the appearance of anonymous leaflets at the Dominican university in Manila in October 1869. The leaflets were critical of the friars and called for "academic freedom." Referring to themselves as "we indios" (native Filipinos), the authors protested the disrespectful practice of friars in addressing them condescendingly with the informal second person singular pronoun "*tú*" instead of the more formal "*usted*." And they demanded an end to racial insults. Spanish authorities construed the leaflets as signs of a growing conspiracy among liberal elements in the colony intent on launching a revolt. They proceeded to arrest a number of students, while professors and secular clergy thought to be sympathetic allies were removed from their posts. Many others who even remotely advocated reform in the colony were placed under surveillance, and their mail was periodically intercepted and opened.[6]

Three years later, in January 1872, a local mutiny erupted at the Spanish arsenal in Cavite led by a disgruntled creole officer and two Spanish peninsular soldiers. The uprising was rapidly put down, but it further stoked the currents of fear among the Spanish residents convinced of the existence of imminent plots to terrorize Spaniards and overthrow the state. Believing that the Cavite Mutiny was a prelude to a much larger revolt, Spanish authorities ordered the arrest and exile of a number of prominent Filipinos and indios who had been vocal in their calls for economic and political reforms and were critical of the reactionary and racist views of the friars. These events culminated in the public execution of three secular priests — Jose Burgos, Mariano Gomez, and Jacinto Zamora — who had been prominent figures in the secularization controversy when they called on Spanish friars to devolve more control over parishes to Filipino priests. Their execution is widely acknowledged as a milestone in the history of Filipino nationalism. Rizal himself (whose brother Paciano had been a student of Father Burgos) was moved to dedicate the *El Filibusterismo* to the memory of the three priests and vowed vengeance on their behalf.[7]

The Spanish governor-general, Rafael de Izquierdo, had presided over the hunt for suspected subversives, relying mostly on "rumor and anonymous communication." It seems he never doubted the veracity of such rumors, which merely confirmed what he was already certain about: that a plot was afoot to overthrow the regime by killing all Spaniards and declaring independence for the colony. So it did not matter how many were arrested, exiled, and executed. The Spaniards imagined subversives — or, in Spanish, "*filibusteros*" (from the Dutch "*vrijbuiter*," the root of "freebooter," or pirate) — meeting continuously in secret in both the colony and the metropole. Capturing and killing one suspect led to the discovery of yet other subversives and other plots. Like most other friars and Spanish officials, Izquierdo thus believed in the existence of conspiracies in advance of any evidence, "public rumors and confidential reports."[8] It did not matter, then, that *ilustrados* sought to counteract this belief by claiming their innocence and loyalty to Spain. Spanish conviction in the subterranean spread of *filibusterismo* across different groups in the colony yielded neither to debate nor to demonstration. For the Spaniards, then, there was a constitutive relationship between conspiracy and the existence of subversives, or *filibusteros*, by virtue of which one gave rise to the other.

What was the nature of the Spanish belief in conspiracies? The word for conspiracy that commonly appears in Spanish accounts is "*conjuración*," which the dictionary of the Real Academia defines as unlawful gatherings with the presumed aim of overthrowing the state or the prince. Aside from "conspiracy," "*conjuración*" also translates as "conjuring": "the act of summoning another in a sacred name." It comes from the verb "*conjurar*," to "conjure up": "to implore, entreat, to ask anything in a solemn manner." It also means "to bind oneself to another through the means of an oath for some end," thereby recalling its Latin origin in "*conjuro*," or "to swear together, to unite by oath."[9]

To understand conspiracy in the sense of *conjuración* is to imagine previously unrelated individuals coming together in secret to take oaths. It is to think of the remarkable — indeed, magical — ability of a linguistic act, the exchange of promises, to establish new forms of being in the world.[10] In taking an oath, one binds oneself to others, thus forming a group that in turn gives to each of its members an identity different from what the individual previously had. Oaths are speech acts that bring about the very thing they refer to — in this case, a "conspiracy" — which from the point of view of the state is a new or alternative association. It is new to the extent that it is composed of members who, thanks to having taken an oath, become other than who they previously were. They take on the capacity to move about covertly, armed with double identities, individual passwords, and encrypted gestures with which to recognize one another and gain access to meeting spaces hidden from official view. Eluding the purview of state authorities, such groups were suspected to be in touch with other sources of power. In their calculated duplicity, they operated at a tangent from colonial society.

Masonic lodges were the prototypical example of these secret associations in the late nineteenth century. Though lodges of Europeans had existed in the colony since the late eighteenth century, lodges for Filipinos did not emerge until 1891, only after *ilustrado* nationalists had been accepted into membership of those in Barcelona and Madrid. Given their liberal politics and anti-friar sentiments, members not surprisingly incurred the suspicion of colonial officials. Forbidden from meeting openly, they were forced to convene at different houses, often disguising their gatherings as innocuous social events. Women pretended to host dinner parties and dances while men met in backrooms away from public view. In these moveable lodges, members took on fanciful ranks, performed initiation rituals, held elections, discussed political matters, and referred to themselves with pseudonyms — usually in Tagalog — while pledging themselves to the aid and welfare of every member in need. Private spaces were thus transformed into a different sort of public space, one that fell away from official supervision.[11] Constituting a covert public sphere, lodges in the late-nineteenth-century Philippines were in constant contact with lodges in the metropole, effectively bypassing the mediation of the colonial state. Like the telegraph celebrated in *ilustrado* writings, lodges were a form of communicative technology, allowing for discreet transmissions and connections among members across state borders.

Regardless of their aims, such societies compelled the attention of the state not so much for what they did and said as for what they held back from view. By the late nineteenth century, Spanish officials had become increasingly concerned with the signs of this holding back. Yet every attempt to read those signs and assign their origin to particular figures and meanings seemed to draw officials and friars farther away from the secret locus of imagined conspiracies. In 1896, a royal decree banned secret societies, targeting in particular Masonic lodges. These were widely believed by Spaniards to be the "womb" (*seno*) from which separatist plots were born.[12] Indeed, nearly every *ilustrado* nationalist had belonged at one point or another to a Masonic lodge. While many members were not even remotely involved in revolutionary activities, it was the form of the lodge that was important. At the very least, it furnished the ritual vocabulary and symbols used by other secret societies such as the Liga Filipina, founded by Rizal in 1892, and its more radical successor, the revolutionary organization called the Kagalanggalangan Kataastaasan Katipunan ng mga Anak ng Bayan (Most noble and highest gathering of the sons and daughters of the nation), or Katipunan for short (literally, the gathering), which was led by Andres Bonifacio. "These societies," the royal decree stated, "by the mere fact of being secret, are illicit and illegal, harmful in every state and the source of insidious evil in a territory like the Philippines. . . . It is absolutely necessary to prosecute them with diligence and constancy . . . until this evil is rooted out or at least until those who still persist in the wicked enterprise are made powerless and harmless."[13]

From the perspective of state authorities, the mere fact of secrecy constituted a crime. Members were thought to evade recognition from above rather than seek to solicit it. Out of reach, they were able to tap into other circuits of communication beyond the hierarchy of languages. Indeed, lodges, by operating under cover, served as networks for the circulation of news, money, and banned books between the colony and the metropole as well as within the country itself. Placed under surveillance, members became even more secretive. For this reason, they were endowed by the state with the foreignness, and thus the criminal status, of *filibusteros*. They were deemed to be carriers of "evil"—because unknown—intentions. Like witches, they had to be repressed, periodically hunted down, and exorcized from the body politic.

III

In responding as they did, Spaniards ascribed to the secrecy of these secret societies catastrophic possibilities: revolution, the destruction of the regime, and the murder of Spanish residents. In short, they were forced to think the unthinkable and entertain the possibility of the impossible arriving suddenly and without warning.

A month prior to the eruption of the revolution, for example, Manuel Sityar, a creole lieutenant in the Civil Guard, wrote about the growing sense of "a formidable conspiracy against Spain" (*una formidable conjuración contra España*). He noted a change in the faces of the indios. "Insignificant details perhaps for those who were born in another country . . . had made me suspicious that something abnormal had occurred, something which could not be defined, making me redouble my vigilance." He also noted the existence of "an atmosphere of distrust and suspicion among the locals whose characteristics had always been those of apathy, indifference, and stoic tranquility in all other circumstances."[14] In a similar vein, the Spanish journalist Manuel Sastron noted the transformation he saw among different classes of natives once news of the revolution began to spread. An "atmosphere of pure hatred against Spanish domination" was palpable. Once accommodating to a fault, natives increasingly refused to step aside in the road to let a Spaniard pass. In certain Tagalog towns in Laguna and Batangas, natives began openly to insult Spaniards, at times greeting them "in the most cruel and injurious tone: *the Spaniards are pigs* [*castila ang babui*]."[15] University students fell under the spell of the Katipunan, and thus "catipunized" (*catipunado*), they were writing "grossly injurious" things about Spain. Suddenly, servants began to talk back to their masters, complaining about their wages while *cocheros* (coach drivers) felt entitled, in "harsh tones, sometimes punctuated with a few well placed blows [on their horses]" to haggle with their Spanish passengers about the fare. Even well-off Filipinos and mestizos thought nothing of cutting off the carriages carrying Spaniards, further evidence of the erosion of deference and the loosening of hierarchy.[16] Meanwhile, rumors circulated of Katipunan plots to poison the Spaniards in Manila by placing toxic chemicals in their drinking water and in the food they were served at home. "What other proofs," Sastron wailed, "were needed that thousands of conjured Filipinos (*conjurados filipinos*) were frantically seeking to gain their separation from the Mother Country, and that they were thinking of accomplishing this by beheading (*degollando*) all of the peninsular Spaniards?"[17]

The equation of Filipino independence with Spanish death had existed in official circles since the aftermath of the Cavite Mutiny of 1872. It took even firmer hold in Spanish accounts after the discovery of the Katipunan by the Spanish Friar Mariano Gil, along with various documents relating to uprising in August 1896. The Spanish journalist and bibliophile W. E. Retana, for example, reproduced a Spanish translation of a Katipunan document from 1896 stating that "our principal objective is to leave no Spaniard alive in the future Filipino Republic" and that, to carry out this goal, it would be most expedient to "procure the friendship of these barbarians with the purpose of dispatching them with greater security and promptness once the moment of the cry of independence comes."[18] In another captured document, Retana called attention to the "monstrous" nature of a plan to kill all friars and burn them rather than bury their bodies. It would be an act of vengeance, according to the Katipunan document, for all of the "felonies that in life they committed against the noble Filipinos during three centuries of their nefarious domination."[19] Destined for a double desecration, friars were to be killed, then burned and left unburied.

In his account of the early months of the revolution, another Spanish journalist, Jose M. Castillo y Jimenez, reproduced a similar document from the Supreme Council of the Katipunan, which commanded fighters to attack Manila and "assassinate all of the Spaniards, their women and children, without any consideration of generation, or parentage, friendship, gratitude, etc."[20] It also ordered the sacking of convents and the "decapitation of their infamous inhabitants" (*degollaron a sus infames habitantes*). Once killed, Spaniards were to be buried (except friars, who were to be burned) in graves at Bagumbayan field, the site of public executions. On the graves of dead Spaniards, Filipino independence would then be declared.[21]

It did not seem to matter that these atrocities did not occur — neither the beheading of Spaniards nor their mass murder. Only a handful of friars were actually killed, and none were burned. Still, Spaniards like Castillo believed that these horrible crimes were about to take place. To clinch his point about the fate that awaited Spaniards, Castillo reproduced a photo-graph in the middle of the book that illustrates the link between Filipino independence and the death of Spaniards. It is a photograph of an apron, the sort used in Masonic rituals, found buried along with other Katipunan documents in the barrio of Trozo just outside the walls of Manila. The apron depicts two upraised arms, presumably belonging to a Filipino. The right hand clutches a knife while the left holds aloft the severed head of a bearded Spaniard, blood dripping from its neck.[22] One recalls the line from Rizal's novel: "Other hands are at work, but no less terrible." The terror arises precisely from sensing the otherness of these hands detached from an identifiable body. Working as if of its own accord, its origin remains hidden from view.

Drawn by the workings of a secret power, Spaniards searched after signs of conspiracies and conjurings. They found themselves living among a population "bewitched" or "catipunized" by the workings of *filibusteros*. Lurid figures continued to appear, predicting the imminent loss of their colony, while calls for their death and dismemberment turned up with greater frequency. The crime of revolution would begin with subtle acts of disrespect, turning into gross insults and ingratitude for the "debts owed to Spain,"[23] then finally erupt into a frenzy of killing and the decapitation of Spaniards. In seeking revenge and passing judgment on the putative crimes of the colonizers, the colonized would commit even greater crimes. "These are the laws of the Katipunan, their sole and criminal intention," wrote Castillo, summing up Spanish sentiment.[24] For the Spaniards then, revolutionary nationalism on the part of Filipinos perverted the order of things, making crime the foundation of law. In doing so, it brought forth the unimaginable — death followed by dismemberment rather than re-membrance, or death by burning rather than mourning — as the basis for what could be imagined.

How do we understand this notion — the unimaginable as that which insists on shaping the imagination? How can formlessness be the basis for giving form to experience, or the unspeakable be the basis of expression? Let us look once again at this persistent motif in Spanish accounts of the revolution: the equation of Spanish death and Filipino independence. Manuel Sastron cited what he imagined to be a typical Katipunan slogan: "Death to the Spaniard and long live independence!" (*muere al castila y viva la independencia*). "This and no other was the slogan that was embla-zoned in the banner of the *insurrectos* . . . the cry of the natives led by

Andres Bonifacio and his slippery Katipunan gang, all of whom have entered into a pact (*pactaron*) to exterminate all the Spaniards, conquerors of this land not by brutal force but through the sweet (*dulce*) preaching of the Gospel."[25]

In response to the "gentle" word of conquest, Filipinos can only cry, "Death to the Spaniard." Led by Bonifacio's Katipunan, they become who they are because of an oath (*pacto*) they have taken to "exterminate" all the Spaniards in the colony. It is as though Filipino independence — or, better yet, "*kalayaan,*" the Tagalog term for "freedom" used in Katipunan documents — can only come through the "medium" of Spanish death. "That which the people wished to obtain was their independence," Sastron wrote, "and the means (*medio*) for doing so was the slaughter of Spaniards."[26] Betraying Spain's generosity, Filipinos had shown a criminal lack of hospitality. And this inhospitality was the product of a prior promise. As members of a secret society, Katipuneros came into being by virtue, first of all, of the linguistic act of entering into a pact. Spanish writers repeatedly remarked on the peculiar nature of this pact and the rituals surrounding it. Called "*pacto de sangre,*" or "blood compact," it was thought to be the decisive event in the conversion, as it were, of passive indios and docile mestizos into fierce fighters eager to take Spanish lives.

The putative desire to spill (*derramar*) Spanish blood begins, in the *pacto de sangre,* with the shedding of one's own. By the 1880s, *ilustrado* nationalists had developed a fascination with the history of the *pacto de sangre* as mentioned in sixteenth-century Spanish accounts. The Portuguese explorer Ferdinand de Magellan, who had landed in the Philippines in 1521 and claimed it for the Spanish crown, as well as Miguel Lopez de Legazpi, the first governor-general of the colony in 1565, both entered into blood compacts with local chiefs as a way to establish alliances with them. Nineteenth-century *ilustrados* idealized these events. They saw in them nothing less than a contractual agreement entered into by equals pledging to come to each other's aid. The renowned Filipino artist Juan Luna, brother of Antonio, depicted the scene in the painting *El Pacto de Sangre* in 1885 to suggest that colonization began with an oath of friendship sealed by the "mixing of blood taken from an incision in the arms" of the Spanish and native leaders.[27]

For Filipinos, then, the ritual mixing of blood signified a promise of mutual recognition and the exchange of obligations. In return for pledging allegiance to the Spanish king, Filipinos were entitled to be treated as

"Spaniards in the full sense of the word."[28] This story of the blood compact thus became an allegory about the promise of mutual assimilation of the descendants of one group into that of the other. The mixing of blood signified a shared genealogy. As the privileged medium for connecting colonizer with colonized, the blood compact established a relation of filiation between them and a history of male-ordered miscegenation meant to mitigate existing inequalities. Though attributed to precolonial practices, the blood compact undoubtedly echoed for nineteenth-century *ilustrados* the miracle of Christian transubstantiation, whereby Christ's body and blood are believed literally to reside in the consecrated bread and wine shared by communicants during mass. By eating His body and drinking His blood, believers acknowledge their indebtedness to Christ and enter into a sacred contract with God. The *pacto de sangre* was a secularized version of this Catholic belief. Native and Spanish men (for no women were known to have engaged in such practices) shed their blood for each other. In doing so, they took on a new identity: no longer strangers but friends and even, perhaps, fellow citizens. Hence did the blood compact, like other vows, bring about the very condition that it signified.

But *ilustrado* nationalists argued that centuries of Spanish abuse amounted to a betrayal of this ancient agreement. By refusing to recognize Filipinos as fraternal equals, Spaniards had broken their part of the deal. In the face of this injustice, Filipinos felt justified in reneging on their promise as well. They would continue to perform what they construed to be an indigenous custom but this time in secret and only with one another, to the exclusion of Spaniards. In this way, the *pacto de sangre* became an integral part of the initiation rituals of the secret society, the Liga Filipina, founded by Rizal, and its revolutionary successor, the Katipunan.[29]

In Filipino nationalist historiography, the *pacto de sangre* tends to be regarded as a relatively minor part of the rites of passage that allowed one to join the Katipunan. Other aspects of the initiation rituals have attracted more attention, such as the formulaic interrogation of candidates about the past and present conditions of the country: that it was once highly civilized and prosperous, then fell into poverty and backwardness with the coming of Spain, but would rise up again with the revolution. Trials by ordeal, the ceremonial concealment and revelation of the symbols of the Katipunan, and the sermons preached by the presiding brother are other aspects that have been described by scholars.[30] The *pacto de sangre* occurs at the end of the initiation ritual. An incision is made with a knife on the left forearm of the initiate. With his own blood he signs an oath pledging to defend the country to the death, to "keep all secrets and follow the leaders blindly, [and to] help all the brothers in all dangers and needs."[31] Variations of these rites existed in different places, but the basic structure remained the same through the revolution against Spain and later against the United States in the early twentieth century. In Filipino nationalist historiography, the blood compact came across as a relatively benign oath that had little to do with addressing the Spaniards.

For Spaniards, however, the *pacto de sangre* took on enormous significance. It was no less than the "anchor of the revolution" (*ancora de la revolución*), the very means for "fanaticizing" (*fanatizando*) the masses. By taking the oath, they were driven to hate the "white race." Thanks to this "horrible pact," the native populace had become mad (*enloquecido*), taking up arms against "la Patria."[32] Where Filipinos saw the blood compact as a means of pledging oneself to a common cause, Spaniards like Castillo imagined the moment of incision to be a kind of "hypodermic injection" (*inyección hypodermica*) that corrupted the blood and poisoned the heart. Once "fanaticized," he wrote, Filipinos "live in eternal convulsion, in permanent delirium; they sleep soundly in the execution of their crimes and awake in the fire of their victim's blood; they are afraid neither of death, nor punishment, nor the law, nor conscience, nor the human, nor the divine, because they swear (*juramento*) by the following: to conquer or to die (*vencer o morir*)."[33]

By entering into a blood compact, Filipinos become possessed. The oath turns them into monstrous figures. Unable to control their own bodies, they live in a state of "permanent delirium." They thus exceed the boundaries of nature and culture. And because they fear neither death nor the law, they exist outside the human and the divine. They are therefore beyond social recognition. It is as if the blood compact converted its pledges into agents of a power that outstripped social conventions and political control. Judging from the breathless prose of Castillo — the hyperbolic piling up of images, the string of negations that he is unable to consolidate into a single figure of speech — it is a power that also eludes linguistic description. Its negative force, afraid of neither death nor punishment nor law, neither human nor divine, and so on, keeps coming, with no end in sight. Lurid images conjured up by the writer fail to bring this power under control, narrative or otherwise. By eluding representation and disclosure, this power brings the writer to reiterate the very vow that carries its force: "*vencer o morir.*"

Beyond articulation, this covert power nevertheless demanded to be heard. It compelled the attention of Spaniards and Filipinos alike, though for different reasons. For just as the Spaniards dreaded what they saw in the "terrible curse" (*terrible juramento*) of the *pacto de sangre*, Filipinos who joined the revolution enthusiastically took to it. In this sense, the blood compact worked as it had in the past, bringing together the colonizers and the colonized. They found themselves sharing something through their enmity: a fascination with the ability of language to bring forth a power that escaped full articulation in a total disclosure of its origin and meaning. But by defying such attempts, it was also a power that made articulation itself possible — articulation in the sense of connection and transmission. The oath linked Filipino fighters together in the expectation of a future they could barely begin to imagine. This current of expectation in turn created an experience of fraternal solidarity among men (and the small number of women) from different classes and regions. But as far as the Spaniards were concerned, the oath transmitted a message whose meaning they could neither absorb nor accommodate.

We can see another moment of this secret power at work if we return to the photograph in Castillo's book. Recall that the "horrible apron" (*horrible mandil*) found among Katipunan documents depicts a pair of arms holding the severed head of a Spaniard in one hand and a knife in the other. On the same page is a picture of another knife whose handle bears the Katipunan symbol and the Tagalog word "*taliba*," or guard. The caption below the picture says that the knife was used to make incisions on the arm of prospective Katipuneros during the blood compact. By force of association, the writer and reader are led to think of the two knives as if they belonged together. That which decapitates the Spaniard in one photograph becomes the one that cuts the Filipino's arm in the course of the ritual. Following this logic, it would be possible to assume that the left arm that appears on the apron is the arm cut by the knife that appears below.

Of course, the two knives are not the same instrument. They remain objectively distinct. But by way of juxtaposition, which we can think of as a method of articulation, one thing is connected to another, leading the reader to imagine an equivalence between the two. It is like the cinema technique of montage that brings previously unrelated and distinct objects and scenes together to form a narrative whole. When we see two things within a common frame, we think they must somehow belong together, where "must" implies the workings of faith: we *believe* they belong together in advance of any explanation or knowledge of the actual facts. What actually connects the two images, however, remains invisible and nowhere explicit in either the photograph or the text. Yet it is a force that is undeniably at work, shaping not only what Castillo saw and wrote but our own reading of his book as well. Such a force makes possible the thought, for example, that the knife is a ritual object that connects not only Filipinos with one another by virtue of the *pacto de sangre*, leading them to form new identities by joining secret societies. The knife is also a kind of transmitter that allows "catipunized" Filipinos to communicate with Spaniards no longer as subordinate subjects but as agents of the latter's death.

The knife can be thought of, then, as an instrument for realizing the oath in that it is itself, like all ritual tools, a kind of "congealed language."[34] As an integral part of the *pacto de sangre*, it, too, is a kind of speech that links men together in common cause. For the Spaniards, however, the knife as part of the oath is a medium for communicating Spanish death. It speaks of destruction, not solidarity. The knife appears in these contexts as a powerful instrument for articulating messages, however conflictual and unsettling. It also acts to connect men both as friends *and* as enemies. Yet as with every communicative medium, the source of its power, that which endows it with the capacity to make possible such articulations, remains unseen. It is a power that persists and insists in the world but as a secret, withdrawing at the very moment that its agents appear and its effects are felt.

IV

Spaniards learned about Katipunan plots and the *pacto de sangre* from captured documents and confessions (*declaraciones*) coerced from imprisoned Filipinos. In the available sources, these documents and confessions all appear in Castilian, even if they might have been given originally in other vernacular languages.[35] In addition, the text of the confessions is paraphrased in such a way that the captive's speech never appears in the first person singular but always in the third person, as in, "He said that he. . . ." As in the Catholic ritual of confession, the language of the Katipunero is translated and made to appear in the linguistic and juridical terms of colonial authority. The voice we hear in these *declaraciones* brims with the language of the law, ordered to reflect not so much the singularity of the speaker—his accent, intentions, and interpretations of events—as the capacity of colonial authority to capture and contain that singularity. Whatever the speaker revealed was thus contextualized and domesticated in ways readily accessible to official interlocutors. Similarly, the Katipunan documents translated into Castilian were meant to decode the vernacular in terms readily understood by the Spaniards. Or so it was hoped.

Complications developed almost immediately. Whether they quoted captured revolutionary documents or wrote about the confessions of captured Filipinos, Spaniards invariably heard themselves addressed. Yet they could barely account for what came through. Although the confessions and documents were translated into Castilian, they communicated a message that surpassed what the Spaniards could understand. The most significant example was the phrase "*pacto de sangre.*" For what the Spanish heard in this phrase was a kind of death sentence. In effect, it said, "Your death is our freedom." If we rephrase this in the simplest of formulas, "Filipino freedom = Spanish death," the "=" that connects one term to the other also establishes a relation of substitution between the two—to wit, freedom for death.

The sign "=" is neither Castilian nor Tagalog. As with other diacritical marks, it is not a word itself but a sign that makes words intelligible, placing them in some sort of syntactical and discursive order. Such marks are indispensable supplements of language, even if they are themselves non-discursive. They work to connect and articulate even if they themselves escape articulation. Similarly with the word "for" in "freedom for death": by connecting words and phrases, it allows for predication and the transmission of meaning while remaining itself free of reference. We can think of the workings of these marks as analogous to the copulative action of the *pacto de sangre.* The oath, as we have seen, consists of a set of linguistic acts that join together disparate peoples and thoughts and so allows for the utterance of, among other things, such unlikely possibilities as "freedom for death." The tool that enacts this joining is the knife used to make incisions on the forearm. By leaving a permanent mark on the body—"branding" it, as one historian shrewdly observed[36]—it alters the person's identity. He becomes and belongs to someone else: no longer a dockworker, peasant, student, or local bureaucrat but a revolutionary fighter dedicated to the movement. It is a sign that one has taken a vow. As a sort of signature or brand, the incision is like a piece of writing that marks one as the carrier of a promise: to kill or be killed for the sake of the nation's freedom. From a docile indio or a reformist *ilustrado*, one becomes through the pact and the mark it leaves behind a new and therefore foreign presence in colonial society. Being new, one has yet to be assimilated and remains unassimilable as long as one is seen as a medium for transmitting the message "Filipino freedom for Spanish death."

Hearing the news of their coming death, the Spaniards panicked. They hunted down suspected fighters only to realize that, thanks to early successes of the movement, people were eager to take the *pacto de sangre* as more and more fighters emerged. "Looking for a clever medium to facilitate the conspiracy (*conjura*)," wrote a Spanish official in a letter to the Overseas Ministry, "they foment it by means of the *pacto de sangre*, making them swear to a war to kill Spaniards, and placing on them an incision on their left arm, and with their blood, they were made to sign and they signed the frightful oath (*espantoso juramento*)."[37]

What was frightening (*espantoso*) about this promise, of course, was that it brought with it a contract to murder Spaniards—or so the Spaniards thought. Like the ancient practice of mixing blood to seal an agreement, blood was drawn and used as ink to sign an oath. One's body was marked and, in turn, left behind its own mark. Some of the signatures or their copies survive, preserved in the Philippine National Archives.[38] Long after their original signers disappeared and were barely remembered, their traces persist. They are there to be read as part of a larger historical moment whose effects continue to be felt today. As with many marks, the signatures survived the moment as well as the context of their production. Signatures connected their signers to a future beyond their own death, a future that they could not control or even anticipate. But by signing an oath, they evinced a trust in this coming, if unknown, future. This is perhaps what was meant by one side of the equation implied by the *pacto de sangre*. "Freedom" for Filipinos connoted a future, an afterlife, if you will, where one's traces would survive and be inherited by those yet to come, although there could never be a guarantee as to the form this survival or this coming might take.

The other side of the equation meant precisely the opposite to the Spaniards. "Death" implied no future: no life and no afterlife, for even their corpses, they believed, would be dismembered and left unmourned. This was how they heard the substance of the terrifying oath, the terms of the contract to which they could not affix their signatures or even affect the wording of the agreement. For unlike the history of Christian conversion predicated on the control of translation, the revolution expropriated the colonial legacies — Christian rituals and Castilian words, for example — and converted them into a message that Spaniards could translate but could not understand. They were faced with a term in their own language, *pacto de sangre*, which when uttered by the revolutionary fighter exceeded what the Spaniards could recognize and recuperate. The revolution coursing through secret locations radicalized the very terms of translation in ways that terrorized those at the top of the colonial regime.

We can begin to understand the Spanish obsession with the blood compact and its link to conspiracy as distinct from, yet clearly related to, the interest of Filipino nationalists. Both were drawn to a secret power that possessed the power of that which cannot be wholly known — death, freedom, the future. It was a power that defied disclosure and representation even as it solicited belief. Various attempts to localize and contain this power by associating it with such loaded figures as the "*filibustero*," "friar," "Rizal", "Balagtas," and so forth tended to fail, although their failure produced important long-lasting effects. To call this power "translation," or the "untranslatable" — or even, at its most extreme, the power of death — merely hints at its workings; it does not define its nature, trace its source, or fix its meaning once and for all.

As one of the envoys of this secret power, the *pacto de sangre* had magical effects, conjuring up secret societies and new identities while delivering a message of conspiracy and terror to Spaniards. For the performative capacities of the oath, as the Spaniards realized, could not be fully represented and appropriated, not even by the Filipinos themselves, who could only act as its agents. The Spanish saw the promise as a diabolical curse that prophesied the end of their rule and the obliteration of their lives. The discourses of conspiracy, and its shadowy agents — secrecy, evil, blood compact — traversed historical periods to evoke a sense of justice yet to be served. For the Filipinos, the prospect of *kalayaan*, or freedom, would sweep away the colonial regime and bring a future open to new possibilities, including the prospect of a social revolution that would demolish not only Spanish privileges but other forms of social inequities, including those on which elite influence rested.

The possibility of a social revolution and the coming of justice promised by the oaths and conspiratorial conjurings of the *pacto de sangre* frightened Spaniards even as it mobilized the revolution of 1896. The future of

that revolution was foreclosed not by Spanish actions, which proved inef-
fective, but by the re-colonization of the nation, first by the *ilustrado*-
dominated First Republic in Malolos, and subsequently by the United
States and its *ilustrado* successors: Quezon's Commonwealth and Republic
of the Philippines. They, too, sought to tap into this powerful evocation of
a different future, calling it at various times "democracy," "progress," "the
modern," "independence," "nationalism," and "development." But like
the Spaniards, the new dominating regimes were unable to exhaust its
possibilities, with the result that, while the postcolonial Philippines expe-
rienced a series of political revolutions, it has yet to realize a social revolution or entirely to overcome the colonial legacy of linguistic hierarchy.
Nonetheless, the workings of the secret power that once conjured "freedom" and "death" into impossible juxtaposition continues to make the
unthinkable — for instance, the revolutionary transformation of social
life — the ground on which historical thinking can take place. For this
reason, it continues to call, periodically issuing from sources that we can
never fully locate, in languages just beyond our capacity to translate, and
often at the fringes of what is socially recognizable. It is a call that remains
to be heard.[39]

Notes

1. For a detailed discussion of the linguistic regime set forth by the history of
conversion and colonization, see Vicente L. Rafael, *Contracting Colonialism: Translation
and Christian Conversion in Tagalog Society under Early Spanish Rule* (Durham: Duke
University Press, 1993).

2. On the language of revolutionary nationalism in the Philippines, see idem, *The
Promise of the Foreign: Nationalism and the Technics of Translation in the Spanish Philip-
pines* (Durham: Duke University Press, 2005), on which this essay is based. See also
Reynaldo Ileto, *Pasyon and Revolution: Popular Movements in the Philippines, 1840–1910*
(Quezon City: Ateneo de Manila University Press, 1979).

3. José Rizal, *El Filibusterismo* (Manila: Asian Foundation for Cultural Advance-
ment, 1957), 201–206.

4. Ibid., 221.

5. Ibid., 219.

6. For details, see John Schumacher, *Revolutionary Clergy: The Filipino Clergy and the
Nationalist Movement, 1850–1903* (Quezon City: Ateneo de Manila University Press,
1981), 16–17. According to Schumacher, Felipe Buencamino was believed to have
been the student leader responsible for these leaflets.

7. For an account of the Cavite Mutiny and the secularization controversy, see John

Schumacher, ed., *Father Jose Burgos: A Documentary History* (Quezon City: Ateneo de Manila University Press, 1999); and idem, *Revolutionary Clergy*, chaps. 1–2. See also Nick Joaquin, *A Question of Heroes: Essays on the Key Figures of Philippine History* (Makati: Ayala Museum, 1977).

8. Schumacher, *Revolutionary Clergy*, 26–27.

9. *Diccionario de la lengua española* (Madrid: Real Academia, 1984); *Velázquez Spanish–English Dictionary* (Chicago: Follett Publishing, 1974).

10. I am thinking of promises as an example of performative speech acts, and much of what follows in my discussion of conspiracies and oaths as performative utterances productive of magical effects is indebted to the work of Jacques Derrida: see, e.g., Jacques Derrida, "Signature Event Context," in *Margins of Philosophy*, trans. Alan Bass (Chicago: University of Chicago Press, 1982); idem, "Faith and Knowledge: The Two Sources of 'Religion' at the Limits of Reason Alone," in *Acts of Religion*, ed. Gil Anidjar, trans. Samuel Weber (New York: Routledge, 2002); and many of his other writings.

The most astute reader of Derrida in a Southeast Asian context is James Siegel: see esp. James T. Siegel, *Fetish Recognition Revolution* (Princeton, N.J.: Princeton University Press, 1997), 183–230; idem, "The Truth of Sorcery," *Cultural Anthropology* 18, no. 2 (May 2003): 135–55, which has been of crucial importance in my reading of Spanish accounts of the revolution.

11. The standard account of Philippine Masonry is Teodoro Kalaw, *Philippine Masonry: Its Origins, Development and Vicissitudes up to the Present Time* (1921), trans. Frederic Stevens and Antonio Amechazura, repr. ed. (Manila: McCullough Printing, 1955). See also John Schumacher, "Philippine Masonry to 1890" and "Philippine Masonry in Madrid, 1889–1896," in *The Making of a Nation: Essays on Nineteenth-Century Filipino Nationalism* (Quezon City: Ateneo de Manila University Press, 1989), 156–67, 168–77, respectively. A more recent and insightful discussion of "Masonic power" is Filomeno Aguilar Jr., *The Clash of Spirits: The History of Sugar Planter Hegemony on a Visayan Island* (Quezon City: Ateneo de Manila University Press, 1998).

Of great utility for situating Masonry within the context of Enlightenment notions of civil society and the shaping of a bourgeois public sphere is Margaret Jacobs, *Living the Enlightenment: Freemasonry and Politics in Eighteenth-Century Europe* (New York: Oxford University Press, 1991). See also Georg Simmel, "The Secret and Secret Societies," in *Sociology of Georg Simmel*, trans. and ed. Kurt H. Wolff (New York: Free Press, 1964), 306–95.

12. See José M. del Castillo y Jiménez, *El Katipunan, o el Filibusterismo en Filipinas* (Madrid: Imprenta del Asilo de Huérfanos del S. C. de Jesus, 1897), 52.

13. Quoted in Kalaw, *Philippine Masonry*, 126–36.

14. See W. E. Retana, *Archivo del bibliófilo Filipino* (Madrid: Viuda de M. Minuesa de los Rios, 1897), vol. 3, 159–64. A creole, Sityar fought on the Spanish side against the revolution until 1898. During the second phase of the revolution, however, he switched sides and joined the Filipino forces.

15. Manuel Sastron, *La insurrección en Filipinas y Guerra Hispano-Americana en el archipielago* (Madrid: Imprenta de la Sucesora de M. Minuesa de los Rios, 1901), 56–57. The Tagalog as given is grammatically incorrect, mangled by the Spanish author.

16. Ibid., 57–58.

17. Ibid., 59. For similar sentiments, see Castillo, *El Katipunan*, 14–16.

18. Retana, *Archivo del bibliófilo Filipino* vol. 3, no. 17, 150–51.

19. Ibid., vol. 3, no. 54, 156–58.

20. Castillo, *El Katipunan*, 115.

21. Ibid., 113–17.

22. Ibid., 212–13.

23. See Sastron, *La insurrección*, 5–16, 158–59; Castillo, *El Katipunan*, 7–10; Juan Caro y Mora, *La situación del pais* (Manila: Imprenta del Pais, 1897), 11.

24. Castillo, *El Katipunan*, 125.

25. Sastron, *La insurrección*, 82.

26. Ibid., 124.

27. See John Schumacher, *The Propaganda Movement: 1880–1895*, 2d ed. (Quezon City: Ateneo de Manila University Press, 1998), 228–30.

28. Ibid., 228.

29. Ibid.

30. See, e.g., Gregorio F. Zaide, *History of the Katipunan* (Manila: Loyal Press, 1939), 5–10; Teodoro Agoncillo, *Revolt of the Masses* (Quezon City: University of the Philippines Press, 1956), 49–50; Ileto, *Pasyon and Revolution*, 116–20.

31. Agoncillo, *Revolt of the Masses*, 49–50. See also William Henry Scott, *Ilocano Resistance to American Rule* (Quezon City: New Day Press, 1986), 118–19.

32. Castillo, *El Katipunan*, 37; 15–16.

33. Ibid., 35–36.

34. The term is from Marcel Mauss, *A General Theory of Magic*, trans. Robert Brain (London: Kegan Paul, 1972). See also Siegel, "The Truth of Sorcery."

35. See Retana, *Archivo del bibliófilo Filipino*, vol. 3.

36. Scott, *Ilocano Resistance to American Rule*, 119.

37. Martin Luengo, "Algo sobre los sucesos en Filipinas," in Retana, *Archivo del bibliófilo Filipino*, vol. 3, 331.

38. See Scott, *Ilocano Resistance to American Rule*, 119. Copies of signed oaths from 1900, some in Tagalog, and others in Spanish and English translation, can be found among the records collected in the Philippine Insurgent Records. See especially reels 8, 31, and 38 in the Philippine National Archives.

39. For a recent example of this calling and the unexpected hearings it spawned, see Vicente L. Rafael, "The Cell Phone and the Crowd: Messianic Politics in the Contemporary Philippines," *Public Culture* 15, no. 3 (Fall 2003): 399–425.

Terrorism

State Sovereignty and Militant Politics in India

It is often said that one person's terrorist is another's freedom fighter. Words like "terrorism" that emerge out of discourses fraught with antagonistic power relations carry with them a dual structure of meaning — one radically opposed to the other. Such words are also discursively related to others in a family, together describing a set of political activities or ideologies that are often seen to have something in common. A word like "terrorism" could then be used in different historical periods to suggest connections to movements or ideologies that earlier went by other names — or, indeed, to distinguish as novel something that might otherwise have been regarded as a continuation of older phenomena. By following the movement of the word in India from the beginning to the end of the twentieth century, I will point out some curious features of such "fear words."

Origins

The idea of "terror" associated with modern forms of political violence is usually traced to the French Revolution. Robespierre explicitly described the means used to impose a new revolutionary order as a "reign of terror." Edmund Burke, in his condemnation of the French Revolution, used the term "terrorism," possibly its first use in the English language. In its early use, then, "terrorism" was associated with state violence of a revolutionary kind, claiming to create a new political order different from the traditional regime. In its travel to British India, the word initially carried its association with revolutionary violence.

The received history of "terrorism" in colonial India usually begins with the killing in Poona, a city in western India, in 1897 of two British officials by the Maharashtrian brothers Damodar and Balkrishna Chapekar. It is said that they had an intense hatred for the British rulers of the country and scorn for the useless chatter of nationalist politicians. They promoted the formation of clubs of young Indian men to pursue gymnastics, wrestling, and other kinds of physical exercise. When the plague outbreak in Poona led to an aggressive search by the police of native neighborhoods and private residences, there was much resentment in the city. The Chapekar brothers managed to procure revolvers and shoot Dr. Rand, the plague commissioner, on a Poona street, along with Lieutenant Ayerst who had witnessed the act. Both Damodar and Balkrishna were later arrested, tried, and hanged.

At the time, this incident did not suggest a broader political movement or pattern of violence to deserve a specific name in the official or journalistic literature. Its later canonization into a sort of foundational act of the "terrorist movement" in India was, as we will see, the result of a retrospective act of history writing. Within a decade of this incident, however, a new movement appeared in Bengal in the east of India that would command greater attention. As the Swadeshi movement, the first major mass movement of Indian nationalism, opened in Bengal in 1905–1906, secret groups committed to assassinations and armed insurrection also began to be organized there. For the next three decades, this constituted a distinct movement that came to be known in British Indian colonial history as "terrorism in Bengal." But this, once more, was a name acquired over time. There were other terms and associations by which the movement was known. To identify these other names, and clarify their relative significance, we need to understand the discursive formation within which "terrorism" came to be located in British India and the dual structure of meaning it produced.

Discursive Context

Within the Swadeshi movement, it was the so-called extremist wing of the Indian National Congress, led in Bengal by Aurobindo Ghose and Bepin Chandra Pal, which attracted a lot of attention for its call to militant action instead of sterile speeches. The extremist leaders of the Indian National Congress were distinguished from their rival moderates, who were liberal constitutionalists favoring gradual admission of Indians into the representative institutions of colonial government. "Extremist" and "moderate" were the names for two relatively distinct and stable political formations within the Indian nationalist movement of the early twentieth century. The names emerged from debates within the movement and are still used in standard textbook histories of Indian nationalism. Like Bal Gangadhar Tilak in Maharashtra and Lajpat Rai in Punjab, the extremist leaders of Bengal declared that the goal of their struggle was not some form of limited self-government within the British empire but complete independence. This could only be done by engaging the foreign rulers in a just war. The *Bande Mataram*, edited by Aurobindo Ghose, declared in 1907:

> The old gospel of salvation by prayer was based on the belief in the spiritual superiority of the British people — an illusion which future generations will look back upon with an amazed incredulity. . . . We do not acknowledge that a nation of slaves who acquiesce in their subjection can become morally fit for freedom. . . . Politics is the work of the Kshatriya [the warrior caste] and it is the virtues of the Kshatriya we must develop if we are to be morally fit for freedom. But the first virtue of the Kshatriya is not to bow his neck to an unjust yoke but to protect his weak and suffering countrymen against the oppressor and welcome death in a just and righteous battle.[1]

Hence the claim that colonial rule was not to be judged by the quality of its governance; it was illegitimate because of what it was — rule by a foreign power.

> The new movement is not primarily a protest against bad Government — it is a protest against the continuance of British control; whether that control is used well or ill, justly or injustly, is a minor and inessential consideration. It is not born of a disappointed expectation of admission to British citizenship[;] it is born of a conviction that the time has come when India can, should and will become a great, free and united nation. It is not a negative current of destruction, but a positive, constructive impulse towards the making of modern India. . . . Its true description is not Extremism, but Democratic Nationalism.[2]

It is important to note that these discursive conditions created by the so-called extremist section of anticolonial nationalism provided the frontier of possibilities for the more militant and violent actions of the revolutionary groups. The extremist leaders, who were not necessarily supporters of the secret revolutionary groups, nevertheless provided a critique of the currently prevailing conditions and the imagining of alternative political futures that the revolutionaries shared. Actual and active links between the armed groups and the broader Congress movement, in the form of direct coordination of activities or shared leadership, were not necessarily very frequent, even though colonial state agencies were always keen to allege such links. But Congress leaders and armed revolutionaries participated in the same anti-imperialist and nationalist discourse, drew from the same stock of historical memory, often used the same arguments, and ultimately contributed to one another's successes and failures. It is particularly significant that even in its avowal of the political aims of the extremist section of the movement, the *Bande Mataram* editorial was keen to disavow the negative connotations of the label "extremism." Asserting a more radical version of nationalism, it described the movement as "democratic nationalism" rather than "extremism."

First Acts of "Terrorism"

The first serious "terrorist" act occurred in Bengal in December 1907 when an attempt was made in Midnapore to blow up a train carrying Governor Andrew Fraser. A mine had been laid which exploded when the train passed, producing twisted rails and a huge crater, but miraculously the train was not derailed, and Fraser escaped unhurt. Some laborers employed by the railways were charged and convicted for having assisted in the attempt, but the real authors of the plot were not discovered at this time.

In April 1908, a bomb was thrown at a carriage in Muzaffarpur town in Bihar, killing two European women. The real target was District Judge Douglas Kingsford, who, in his earlier posting as a magistrate in Calcutta, had become a hated figure in nationalist circles because he had ordered the flogging of political agitators for defying the police. Khudiram Bose, aged eighteen, was arrested the next day as he was on the run, while Prafulla Chaki, only a year older, when cornered in a gun battle with the police shot himself to death. It transpired that the two had mistaken the carriage for one that belonged to Kingsford. Khudiram was tried, sentenced, and hanged in Calcutta in August 1908. Khudiram Bose and Prafulla Chaki became the first martyrs of the new movement.

The bombing in Muzaffarpur immediately led to searches in a house in Maniktala in Calcutta that had been under watch for some time. The police found a stock of arms, ammunition, and chemicals for making bombs and soon arrested the key figures of the Jugantar group that had planned the bombing, as well as the train wreck. The Alipore conspiracy case, the first major trial of a revolutionary group in Bengal, ended with ten of the accused being transported for life to the infamous cellular jail in the Andaman Islands.[3]

For the next few years, even though there were not many significant attacks on British targets in Bengal, the revolutionary organizations spread quickly, especially in the districts of eastern Bengal. A list, compiled in 1912 by the intelligence branch of the police, of those suspected of being members of secret groups in the different districts of Bengal had more than eight hundred names, along with information about the activities and associations of each person.[4] The list of persons connected with revolutionary groups in Bengal who were actually convicted in court on various charges added up to 651 at the end of 1920.[5] There was no doubt that the call to take up arms to rid the country of its foreign rulers held a great attraction for young men from educated upper-caste Hindu families.

The networks also extended outside Bengal. Hemchandra Kanungo, closely associated with the Jugantar group, went to Paris in 1906–1907 to make contacts with socialist and anarchist revolutionaries and returned with instructions for making bombs and maintaining underground organizations.[6] In northern India, Rashbehari Bose was a key organizer, setting up branches in different cities, attempting to incite a mutiny within the army, and planning the spectacular bomb attack in 1912 on the viceroy's ceremonial procession in Delhi. Lord Hardinge, the viceroy, though badly injured, survived the attack. Rashbehari Bose escaped and spent the rest of his life in exile in Japan. With the outbreak of the First World War, some Bengal revolutionaries set up a plan to import a shipload of German arms by sea. Narendra Bhattacharya was sent for this purpose to Batavia; he would later become famous in the international communist movement under his assumed name of M. N. Roy. Jatin Mukherjee, better known as Bagha, and four others made their way to the Orissa coast to receive the arms. The plot was discovered by British intelligence. Bagha Jatin's group was intercepted by armed police and, after a gun battle, surrendered. Bagha Jatin died from his wounds to become one of the most celebrated martyrs of the movement.

In Bengal itself, a couple of attempts were made in this early phase to assassinate senior British officials, including Governor Fraser; both attempts were attributed to the Anushilan Samiti, and both failed. Otherwise, the list of "terrorist outrages" compiled by the police in the period up to 1917 is dominated by robberies of private homes of wealthy and not-so-wealthy Indians (in a bid to collect funds to procure arms); the killing of dozens of Indian policemen, mostly of low rank; and a few murders of activists suspected of betraying the cause.[7] Not surprisingly, these incidents, far more numerous than the few spectacular strikes against the alien rulers, are largely forgotten in the memorialized history of the revolutionary movement in Bengal.

"Anarchist and Revolutionary Movements"

In this early phase of the movement, British official sources did not use the term "terrorism" at all. The terms "anarchist" and "revolutionary" were thought to be more appropriate to describe the violent activities of the secret armed groups, whereas the broader term "sedition" was widely used to apply to all activities and speech deemed to "spread disaffection against the lawfully constituted government."

The terms "anarchist" and "revolutionary" became relevant as soon as it was realized that these new "crimes and outrages" were being committed not by rebel warlords or insurgent peasants or habitual criminals but by young men from educated, propertied, and socially respected families — in fact, by young men who were precisely the products of modern Western education. The point was made most strikingly in the report of the Rowlatt committee set up in 1918 to look into the phenomenon of "sedition" in India: "The circumstance that robberies and murders are being committed by young men of respectable extraction, students at schools and colleges, is indeed an amazing phenomenon the occurrence of which in most countries would be hardly credible."[8] The similarity in tactics with revolutionary groups in Europe led to the Bengal revolutionaries' initially being called "anarchists" and "nihilists." A revolutionary of the time mentions in his memoirs that after the failed attempt on the Bengal governor's train in 1907, a government official told him very knowledgably that some Russian nihilists had arrived in India with the intention of spreading anarchy.[9] It was also suggested in official circles that the reason these educated young men were throwing bombs at British officials was because they were against all forms of government — an idea planted in their minds by the perverse doctrine of anarchism.

The suspected association with European revolutionary movements was strengthened by the official discovery that a small group of Indian students in Britain, including Lala Hardayal and V. D. Savarkar, had been trying to establish links with revolutionary groups in Europe and Ireland. Hardayal subsequently moved to the United States and was a key figure in mobilizing, in 1916–18, a group of Sikh migrant workers in California, Washington, and British Columbia to join up with demobilized Punjabi soldiers of the British Indian army to launch, with German assistance, an armed uprising in India. The movement took the name Ghadar, a Persian Hindustani word meaning "revolt," vividly invoking the memory of the Great Revolt of 1857 known in British colonial history as the Sepoy Mutiny. But the international associations of Indian revolutionaries in this period strengthened the sense that ideas, organizations, and tactics were traveling across the seas along with arms and activists. And the common term that described this association in the years of the First World War was "anarchist revolutionary."

But not everyone in the colonial establishment was persuaded that Indian revolutionaries could be motivated by the same ideas as European revolutionaries. After all, detestable as they were, European anarchists were inspired by thoroughly modern and European ideologies. How could Indians act in the same way? British officials in Bengal were fascinated by the presence of religious literature, especially the *Bhagavad Gita*, in the libraries maintained by the revolutionary groups, the use of religious invocations in the initiation ceremonies for fresh recruits, and most of all by the seemingly ubiquitous appeal of what was described as the cult of the goddess Kâlî. The portrayal of the Bengal "anarchist" as a religious fanatic produced by some of the darkest and most mysterious strands in his culture was one way in which the official mind sought to resolve the paradox of Western education giving birth to terrorism. The educated Bengali, despite his knowledge of English, was still susceptible to the secret attractions of a savage religion:

> Anarchism has a particularly objectionable religious accompaniment. While the initiate kneels at the feet of Mother Kali, represented in her wildest aspect, with matted hair pulled about her head, her bloodshot eyes glaring mercilessly down, her hands squeezing the last life blood out of a dummy man. Two bombs lie at her feet. . . . The exotic atmosphere bemuses the worshippers, leads them into a trance. Perhaps Mother Kali's

hellish eyes have hypnotized them. . . . The doped struggling worshippers work themselves into a paroxysm of fanatical fervour. . . . The climax of the ceremony is reached; the anarchists claim another follower . . . .

We have them there, struggling against another depressing aftermath of primitive savagery, working once more from the bestiality that is the cornerstone of anarchism, until they again meet in another orgy.[10]

The same colonial stereotype that had appeared in the mindlessly violent figure of the "thug," described by Lydia Liu in this volume, enters here once more. More than half a century after "*thuggee*" had been officially suppressed in India, it still announced its spectral presence within what was seen to be a radically alien, fundamentally inscrutable, and dangerous culture.

Once the "anarchist" had been identified as at core a religious fanatic, the moderating influence of Western education could only be of limited effectiveness. The Rowlatt committee was not very hopeful of achieving results merely by punishing the offenders: "We may say at once that we do not expect very much from punitive measures. The conviction of offenders will never check such a movement as that which grew up in Bengal unless all the leaders can be convicted at the outset. Further, the real difficulties have been the scarcity of evidence. . . . The last difficulty is fundamental and cannot be remedied. No law can direct a court to be convinced when it is not."[11]

The most promising option was preventive detention of potential offenders for which special powers were needed. The Defense of India rules enforced during the First World War had given the government such powers, but they would lapse with the end of the war. The Rowlatt committee recommended new "emergency" powers to deal with sedition, involving speedy trials, no right of appeal, and detention without trial of suspects. "By those means alone [the Defense of India rules] has the conspiracy been paralysed for the present, and we are unable to devise any expedient operative according to strict judicial forms which can be relied upon to prevent its reviving, to check it if it does survive, or, in the last resort, to suppress it anew. This will involve some infringement of the rules normally safeguarding the liberty of the subject."[12]

But the committee was careful to add that the "interference with liberty" must not be penal in character: If suspects were to be detained, they should be kept in a special asylum and not in jail, and no one was to be convicted without a proper judicial trial. Detentions should be supervised by a periodic judicial review of each case. The emergency powers should also be for a limited period only, to be renewed by a fresh notification by the government.[13]

Armed with these recommendations, the Imperial Legislative Council passed new laws in March 1919 to give the government of India special powers to curb seditious activities. The laws were condemned by virtually all sections of Indian opinion, from constitutional liberals to fire-eating revolutionaries. They were condemned for being arbitrary and excessive; indeed, they were condemned for being in violation of the law. Within a few days, Gandhi launched his first nationwide mass campaign against the so-called Rowlatt Act. Despite his fervent calls for nonviolent resistance to the government, the protest was marked by considerable violence and bloodshed in most cities of northern India.[14] The Rowlatt Act was never put into operation, and following the constitutional reforms in late 1919, it was repealed.

That left the government with the conventional legal tool of punishing the offender. But how was revolutionary anarchism to be identified and proved as a crime and the accused punished in a court of law? Some of the armed actions were merely plans that were never executed; others had been botched. Most of the leaders, strategists, and ideologues were not directly associated with the actions: How could they be charged with the crime? Most crucially, how could an individual motive be established for each single act committed by each individual offender? The fact was that the crimes in question were not ordinary criminal acts. The crimes of the revolutionaries added up to a political offense — that of challenging the sovereign powers of the state. How was such a crime to be proved in court?

This is where an older idea that belonged to British colonial perceptions regarding threatening Orientals acquired the solid form of a powerful legal doctrine. Lydia Liu shows how the idea of "conspiracy" arose as part of the image of the secretive but vicious "thug" in India and traveled to China to become a key element in the British understanding of Chinese secret societies during the Opium Wars. There was, as Vicente Rafael explains in this volume, a similar idea of "conspiracy" in the Spanish imperial understanding of the revolution in the Philippines in 1896. With the rise of militant nationalist politics in India in the twentieth century, "conspiracy" became the key legal concept in the construction of revolutionary politics as a crime. Leaders might not be present at the scene of an assassination, or a bomb could miss its target; plans for an insurrection might never fructify, or a revolutionary cell could restrict itself only to secret propaganda and recruitment. But all of these would come under the umbrella of the most serious political crime of all if a conspiracy could be proved. The proof of a conspiracy consisted in evidence of the existence of a party or group or cell, of leadership and propaganda, of recruitment of cadres, of secret meetings and communications, of the acquisition and storage of arms, of secret training and indoctrination, and so on. Each of these activities could be proved in court by the production of material evidence and the testimony of witnesses. The doctrine of "conspiracy" allowed for the pooling together of these distinct and diverse activities by a large number of often unconnected individuals to constitute a single criminal offense with a single motive shared by all of the accused. Beginning with the Alipore conspiracy case of 1908, the history of political trials in British India is marked by a series of famous conspiracy cases each involving dozens — in some cases, hundreds — of accused. Leaders of the "conspiracy" were usually given the harshest sentences — death, life imprisonment, or transportation for life.

Revolutionary Nationalism

Ideologues of the revolutionary groups in India quickly rejected the suggestion that they were anarchists. They also refused to accept that their activities were seditious. The *Jugantar*, regarded as a mouthpiece of the early phase of the movement in Bengal, declared in 1907:

> When foreign rulers such as the English accuse all Indians of sedition, it is a meaningless charge. . . . When Russia and Japan in their recent war tried their utmost to destroy each other, neither accused the other of sedition. . . . England has occupied India by deception. . . . Hence there is no legality in her occupation of India; indeed, at every step one finds the grossest injustice and immorality. . . . So if the entire nation desires to end its subjection and become free no matter what, then whose demand is right in the eyes of justice — that of the English or of the Indians? We must say that no ruler has the right to shackle the desire for freedom — there is simply nothing else to say. The struggle for freedom will of necessity move on towards its objective. It will overcome a thousand impediments and take every step to reach its goal.[15]

In fact, in the literature of these groups, the most frequent historical examples cited were the American Revolution and the unification of Italy as successful cases of nationalist armed struggle against imperial rule, the continuing struggles in Ireland as an example of armed anticolonial resistance, and the military successes of Japan as a demonstration of what can be achieved with sovereign nationhood. In each case, the lesson drawn was the moral legitimacy and historical viability of nationalist armed resistance. Their preferred self-description was that of "*biplabi*" (revolutionary), not anarchist or seditious troublemaker, as the official statements would have it. This is the description that has persisted in the nationalist historiography of India. To be a revolutionary freedom fighter was, in this view, a political virtue of the highest order. The official colonial attribution had been turned on its head.

"Terrorism as Distinct from Other Revolutionary Methods"

The inauguration of constitutional reforms in 1919 led to the release of many revolutionary leaders held in detention. In a significant shift in tactic, revolutionary groups in Bengal, especially the so-called Jugantar Party, decided to join the Swarajya Party of C. R. Das, Bengal's preeminent Congress leader, and engage in open constitutional politics. It is said that there was a pact between the Jugantar leaders and C. R. Das by which, in return for political protection, the revolutionaries supplied the cadres with whose help Das managed to win support in the district committees of the Congress for his plan to contest elections and enter the newly formed provincial council.[16] In fact, from this time onwards, the Congress organization in the districts, especially in eastern Bengal, as well as the provincial committee, continued to be dominated by leaders with "revolutionary" links right up to independence.

The 1920s, then, was a period of relative lull in armed nationalist activities in Bengal, although several Bengal revolutionaries played important roles in the spread of secret organizations in the United Provinces and Punjab that carried out several daring acts in this period. But there was an explosion of armed actions in Bengal as soon as Gandhi's civil disobedience movement was launched in April 1930. The most spectacular were the raids in Chittagong on the police and military armories and the gutting of the telegraph office. The actions were planned on Easter weekend in deliberate emulation of the Easter rising in Ireland in 1916. After the attacks, the raiders retreated to the hills and were hunted down four days later.[17] The Chittagong revolutionaries — their leader, Surya Sen, who was arrested three years later and hanged; Ambika Chakrabarti, Ganesh Ghosh, Ananta Singh, and Loknath Bal, who were transported to the Andamans; and two women, Pritilata Wahdedar, who chose to swallow cyanide rather than surrender, and Kalpana Dutt, who spent nine years in prison — became stellar figures in the growing pantheon of revolutionary martyrs and heroes in Bengal. The Chittagong raids had an electrifying effect. "The younger members of all parties," an official report says,

> clamored for a chance to emulate the Chittagong terrorists. Their leaders could no longer hope, nor did they wish, to keep them back, for the lesson of Chittagong had impressed itself on their minds no less than on those of their more youthful followers, and there seemed to be no reason why their over-cautious policy should be maintained. Recruits poured into the various groups in a steady stream, and the romantic appeal of the raid attracted into the fold of the terrorist party women and young girls, who from this time onwards are found assisting the terrorists as housekeepers, messengers, custodians of arms and sometimes as comrades.[18]

Assassination attempts against senior British officials came thick and fast. Lowman, the inspector-general of police, was shot dead in Dacca; Simpson, the inspector-general of prisons, was shot dead in his office inside the Writers' Buildings in Calcutta; and Tegart, the most famous (or infamous, depending on one's point of view) anti-terrorist policeman, narrowly escaped death when his car was bombed on a Calcutta street. Garlick, a district judge, was shot through the head in his courtroom at Alipore. Between 1931 and 1933, Peddie, Douglas, and Burge, three successive district magistrates of Midnapore, were assassinated. In December 1931, Stevens, district magistrate of Tippera, was shot dead in his bungalow by two young women, Suniti Chaudhuri and Shanti Ghosh. Two months later, Governor Stanley Jackson was delivering his address at the convocation of the University of Calcutta when Bina Das, a fresh graduate, pulled out a pistol from under her academic robes and shot at him; she missed and was overpowered and arrested. The next governor, John Anderson, introduced a tough regime of emergency laws with wide powers of search and detention. He was shot at in Darjeeling in 1934 and miraculously escaped unhurt.

It is from the 1920s that the term "terrorist" became the standard official label for what was earlier called "revolutionary" or "anarchist" politics. The shift highlights some important discursive changes. First, in the course of debates within Indian nationalism, especially with the launching of the mass movements associated with the Indian National Congress under Gandhi's leadership, and the elaboration by parties, groups, and ideologues of the political goals of their struggles, it became obvious that the term "anarchist" was a complete misnomer for the revolutionary nationalist groups. By the mid-1920s, the term had largely disappeared from official colonial discourse. Second, with the self-identification of militant nationalism with revolutionary politics, the debate over political strategy shifted to the question of the use of armed violence. Gandhi insisted, on both moral and strategic grounds, that *himsa*, or violence, should have no place in Indian nationalist politics and that *ahimsa*, or nonviolence, should be its creed. Those who disagreed with Gandhi, especially members of the revolutionary groups, argued that alongside the peaceful mass movements there was a legitimate political space for organized armed action. In this debate, the term "revolutionary" was no longer a meaningful marker of distinction, because even Gandhians laid claim to the appellation, although, they said, they were "nonviolent revolutionaries." The earlier divide between moderates and extremists had been superseded, because Gandhians were no moderates in their politics, repeatedly breaking the law, inviting punishment, and filling up the jails. Hence, instead of "revolution," it was the specific strategy of nationalist revolutionary politics — armed or nonviolent — that became a key issue of political debate. Revolutionary leaders such as Bhagat Singh, hanged in 1931 for the assassination of a British police officer, called the Gandhian method "utopian nonviolence": "Force when aggressively applied is 'violence' and is, therefore, morally unjustifiable, but when it is used in the furtherance of a legitimate cause, it has a moral justification. The elimination of force at all costs is Utopian, and the new movement which has arisen in the country . . . is inspired by the ideals which guided Guru Gobind Singh and Shivaji, Kamal Pasha and Reza Khan, Washington and Garibaldi, Lafayette and Lenin."[19]

Yet the revolutionary groups were themselves at pains to argue that merely a "cult of the bomb" would not bring national freedom. Assassinations and spectacular acts of violence must be followed by propaganda and mobilizations among the people. Acts of heroic violence would break the stranglehold of fear among the people; the sacrifice of a few martyrs would give courage to millions.

Curiously, while rejecting all forms of violent resistance, Gandhian nonviolence also spoke the same language of sacrifice and martyrdom. Gandhian activists (*satyagrahi*) voluntarily offered their bodies to the violence of the colonial state, inviting bodily harm and injury. When Jairamdas Daulatram was wounded in a police shooting in Karachi during the civil disobedience movement in 1930, Gandhi sent a telegram to the Congress office saying, "Consider Jairamdas most fortunate. Bullet wound thigh better than prison. Wound heart better still."[20]

With the systematic arrest and detention of their leaders, the armed revolutionaries appeared to lose steam by the mid-1930s. The intelligence branch reported in 1937 that "the parties in most districts lack competent leadership and are disorganized, but recruitment is going on."[21] It was also in this period that the colonial government appeared to settle on a clearer definition of terrorism: "Terrorism, as distinct from other revolutionary methods such as Communism or the Ghadr Movement, may be said to denote the commission of outrages of a comparatively 'individual' nature. That is to say, the terrorist holds the belief that Indian independence can best be brought about by a series of revolutionary outrages calculated to instil fear into the British official classes and to drive them out of India."[22]

Interestingly, it was in the mid-1930s that the Bengal revolutionaries, too, appeared to make serious choices between "individual terrorism" and other forms of organized revolutionary action. Mass nationalist mobilizations were now a familiar feature of Indian politics. However, new questions about the economic and social future of the nation were being raised within the national movement. Confined to prisons and detention camps, the leaders of the armed revolutionary groups became acquainted with the new ideas of Marxism and the possible role of the Communist Party in the anti-imperialist struggle. Many of them now renounced the politics of terrorism and assassination and embraced the idea of sustained mass organization among workers and peasants, regarded as the proper political work of revolution — *inqilab* or *kranti* (in Urdu/Hindi) or *biplab* (in Bengali). A considerable part of the leadership of the leftist parties in Bengal at the time of independence, including the Communist Party, the Revolutionary Socialist Party, and the Forward Bloc, came from the ranks of the former nationalist revolutionary groups. Needless to say, the Congress Party that came to power in West Bengal after independence contained many leaders with "terrorist" pasts. Now ranged on opposite sides of a new political divide, the former revolutionaries joined in giving birth to the new postcolonial orthodoxy — condemnation of the politics of individual terrorism while memorializing the sacrifice of the martyrs.

Militant Opposition to the Postcolonial State

The most militant and sustained armed opposition to the newly independent state in India came from the communists in the Telengana region in 1947–49. But "terrorism" had been rejected as a method of revolutionary politics by the communists, even though several of their leaders had cut their political teeth in the armed revolutionary groups of the 1920s and 1930s. The Telengana revolt was an armed peasant uprising using guerrilla tactics; individual assassinations of state officials were not a part of its methods. Interestingly, since terrorism was now also associated in official discourse with acts such as individual assassination, the communist insurgency was never described in official sources as terrorism. The uprisings were put down by force; the Communist Party was banned for a time and its leaders were put in prison. By 1951, the Communist Party itself had decided to abandon the path of armed insurrection and adopted the role of a parliamentary opposition.[23]

The key issue posed by movements of armed opposition to the Indian state concerned the forms of state violence to be used against them and the degree to which normal civil liberties and democratic rights might be curtailed for reasons of security. The postcolonial state retained special legal powers to keep people in prison on suspicion and without trial, but these were carefully designated as "preventive" rather than "punitive" detention, and no reference was made to the now discredited colonial notions of sedition or terrorism.

Indeed, with national sovereignty now vested in "the people" and individual liberties and democratic rights guaranteed by the constitution, there was a deep problem in acknowledging that armed opposition to the state might emerge from within the domain of the nation. Insurgents therefore were said to be motivated by a perverse ideology that preached the destruction of the state itself. Or else they might belong to ethnic groups or regions that had not yet been fully "integrated" into the nation.

The 1950s and 1960s were marked by an armed insurgency in Nagaland, spearheaded by the Naga National Council led by the exiled A. Z. Phizo, demanding separation from India. In the 1960s and 1970s, there was a similar insurgency in Mizoram organized by the Mizo National

Front under the leadership of the exiled Laldenga. These ethnic separatist movements provoked a prolonged and full-scale war with the Indian security forces and were finally put down by a combination of state violence and co-optation of rebel leaders. But despite much bloodshed, the insurgencies were kept localized in the hill regions of the Northeast, with little media attention, and did not seriously affect political debates in the rest of India.[24]

In the period 1969–71, a breakaway group of Maoist communists, retreating to the towns and cities of West Bengal after a failed attempt at a peasant uprising in a region called Naxalbari, took up the tactic of killing policemen and minor government officials. The tactic was reminiscent of the nationalist revolutionaries in the early decades of the century. But the Maoists, often called Naxalites, were described as "extremists" in the official and journalistic sources, in implicit contrast with the more "moderate" methods of the parliamentary communists. The Naxalite tactics were condemned as "terrorist" in the debates among different sections of communists. No one was ready to own up to the label of being a "terrorist." However, the scale of insurgency and unrest, this time affecting industrial cities and densely populated agrarian regions, pushed the state into claiming in 1971 much wider powers for the "maintenance of internal security."[25] As it happened, the suppression of the Naxalite movement was followed by a much more widespread mass agitation in northern and western India against the government of Indira Gandhi, culminating in the declaration of a state of emergency in June 1975.

The period of the Emergency from 1975 to 1977 marks a watershed in the political history of postcolonial India. The emergency regime of Indira Gandhi was widely criticized as authoritarian, and the suspension of civil liberties and constitutional rights was seen as a fundamental violation of the liberal-democratic principles of the Indian state. The end of the emergency regime and the electoral defeat of Gandhi saw the forging of a broad consensus from the right to the left of the political spectrum on the value of constitutional propriety as a necessary limit on arbitrary governmental power, as well as a protection for the opposition. This consensus provided the framework for the subsequent debates over armed resistance to the state and the return of "terrorism."

Terrorism in Contemporary India

Terrorism re-emerged as a category of political discourse in India in the 1980s. This was in the context of the new religious and ethnic movements of separatism in Punjab and Kashmir.

The demand for an independent Khalistan—a sovereign homeland for Sikhs—gathered strength in the early 1980s under the leadership of the fiery preacher Jarnail Singh Bhindranwale. His followers carried out assassinations of prominent Sikh political leaders, senior police officers, and members of deviant Sikh sects. By 1983–84, Bhindranwale had established his influence over the major Sikh religious organizations. Faced with an insurgency, the government of Indira Gandhi ordered the armed forces to storm the Golden Temple in Amritsar, the holiest Sikh shrine, where Bhindranwale and his armed supporters were hiding out. In June 1984, after a bloody battle in which eighty-three soldiers and about five hundred militants, including Bhindranwale, were killed, the temple was captured. The storming of the Golden Temple, and subsequent security operations in Punjab, deeply disturbed Sikh sentiments. In October 1984, Prime Minister Indira Gandhi was assassinated by two of her own Sikh security guards. This was followed by the retaliatory killing of thousands of Sikhs in Delhi and other places in northern India. For the next three or four years, Khalistan militants carried out numerous attacks on civilian targets, including passenger aircraft in flight, railway trains, bus stations, and crowded markets. The actions were now officially described as "terrorism." The allegation was that the militants were being given arms and training from across the border in Pakistan. From 1988, Punjab saw drastic security operations, with the shooting down of people on suspicion, draconian laws, and the suspension of normal political activities. By 1993, the militant insurgency had been put down.[26]

An insurgency began in Kashmir in 1989, following, it is said, the end of the Soviet occupation of Afghanistan and the dismantling of the *mujahideen* camps in Pakistan. The Indian government alleged that trained fighters were sent into the Indian side of Kashmir by Pakistan's security agency to attack government targets and create civil disturbance. For the next decade or more, the confrontation between the militants and the Indian security forces led to some fifty thousand to eighty thousand deaths. Kashmir was effectively under army occupation. There were numerous acts of terrorism by the militants, as well as atrocities by the Indian forces.[27]

The term "*atankvad*" emerged in the 1980s as a widely circulated Hindi neologism for "terrorism." Postcolonial statist discourse now used "terrorism" and "terrorist" as terms of unqualified condemnation, reserved for those acting violently against the nation-state, with the implication that they were either foreigners or acting in league with anti-national foreign interests. The assassinations of two prime ministers — Indira Gandhi and Rajiv Gandhi — by individuals connected with the Sikh and Sri Lankan Tamil militant groups strengthened the designation. The Terrorist and Disruptive Activities (Prevention) Act was passed in 1987 to give the state special powers of surveillance, seizure, and arrest, and an average of four thousand persons were held under the act at any given time in the early 1990s.[28] Following widespread complaints about the misuse of the act, it was replaced in 2001 by a new law on Prevention of Terrorism. After a gap of four decades, the word was definitely back in circulation in India.

The return of "terrorism" as a category makes sense within a new global discourse of security in liberal-democratic societies. In contemporary Indian debates, the term is used in the context of civil liberties, on the one hand, and the state's responsibility in providing security, on the other.

The assumption of special powers of surveillance and detention without trial at home during times of war with foreign countries has a long tradition in Western democracies. Both Britain and the United States promulgated and used such powers as recently as the Second World War. These included special powers of search and seizure, control over information circulated in the media, and detention on suspicion of links with the enemy. This also included internment in camps of ordinary people having the same ethnicity as the enemy — Germans in Britain and Japanese in the United States, even when they were British or U.S. citizens. Clearly, these powers involved curtailments of ordinary civil liberties. But the justification was provided by the exceptional nature of a time of war. The curtailment of liberties was meant to be temporary — normal liberties were to be restored at the end of the war.

Curtailing normal freedoms in times of peace to deal with threats to security required other justifications. But the key was to trace the source of the threat to an external Other. One tendency has been to link internal political opposition with foreign enemies. During the Cold War, communists, anarchists, and even leaders of the Civil Rights Movement in the United States were alleged to be acting as agents of the Soviet Union and were subjected to surveillance not sanctioned by the ordinary law. During the war in Algeria in the 1960s, Algerians in France were subjected to detention and torture for alleged support to the cause of Algerian liberation.

Indeed, as noted earlier, there is a fundamental difficulty in admitting that terrorism, in the sense of an extraordinary threat to the internal peace of national society, may have its source within the body of the nation. The admission would imply that normal civic institutions and political processes have broken down and are incapable of resolving internal disputes and that extraordinary police powers have become necessary to maintain domestic peace. To suggest that there is a state of war with those whom the terrorists claim to represent would create the further difficulty of having to admit that a section of the nation has turned against it. That is the description of a "civil" war. Further, there is also a difficulty in determining the temporal duration of an internal emergency in the absence of a model of war: When, and by what criteria, can it be determined that the threat has been overcome and the normal conditions of civic freedoms resumed? What is the guarantee that the state of emergency will not pass into a permanent state of authoritarianism?

The conditions for these arguments have been laid by the history of the normalization of state practices on a global scale. All state practices are now considered to be comparable; states can be classified and ranked in relation to the norm. Some states claim to represent the norm in the sense of the right and the good; they see themselves as belonging to a superior rank in relation to others. Even if it is true, as some recent commentators have pointed out by referring to Carl Schmitt, that sovereignty still lies in the power to declare the state of exception,[29] the gradation among modern states puts a premium on concealing that power by not having to use it. The level of superiority of contemporary state institutions in their domestic aspect is globally measured by the maximum and efficient use of disciplinary and governmental power and the minimization of the use of force. A state of internal emergency is a sign of the failure of the modern regime of power. Clearly, the history of the modern state in the twentieth century has supplied numerous examples of the slide of liberal-constitutional governments into authoritarian regimes. Europe in the 1920s and 1930s provided the classic examples, but there have been many others in the second half of the twentieth century in Central and South America and among the postcolonial countries of Asia and Africa. Retaining the "superior" rank among modern states requires liberal democracies today not to become vulnerable to the charge of curtailing civil liberties to meet the threat of internal political violence.

The recourse, then, is to the argument that the source of the terrorist threat lies in an external Other. Both in the case of the Khalistan movement in Punjab (which had vocal and active support among the Sikh diaspora in Britain, Canada, and the United States) and the insurgency in Kashmir, the Indian government claimed that the terrorist acts were the result of arms, money, and training provided by official agencies in Pakistan. The allegations became stronger with the consolidation of a Hindu right-wing politics in India from the early 1990s under the leadership of the Bharatiya Janata Party (BJP). In December 1992, the Babri Mosque in Ayodhya was destroyed by Hindu agitators who claimed that it had been built in the sixteenth century by Mughal conquerors on the holy site of the birthplace of the legendary warrior god Rama. In January 1993, rioters organized by the Hindu right-wing parties carried out attacks in Mumbai on Muslim lives and property, killing several hundred Muslims. In March 1993, in retaliation, there were coordinated explosions in Mumbai at the stock exchange, banks, hotels, shopping malls, and airline offices, causing nearly three hundred deaths. The government alleged that the attacks had been masterminded by the exiled underworld dons, Dawood Ibrahim and Tiger Memon, operating from Pakistan and Dubai. Since then, there have been several spectacular terrorist attacks on prominent civilian targets in many cities of India, including crowded trains, temples, markets, and airports. The government has alleged that they were all carried out by Islamic terrorist groups such as Jaish-e-Muhammed and the Lashkar-e-Taiba in the news following the massacre in Mumbai in 2008 and supposedly connected to the Al-Qaeda network, operating from foreign bases.

The resultant security measures and special legal powers have been justified mainly by the argument of threats from an external enemy. Once again, this is in conformity with the contemporary global discourse on terrorism. This is the line that has been systematically adopted by the U.S. administration since its declaration in 2001 of the "war on terrorism." The terrorist threat has been identified in cultural-political terms as coming from militant Islam whose sources lie outside the United States. Sometimes, the threat is identified more specifically with Al-Qaeda and similar Islamic organizations, or with the Taliban in Afghanistan, or, most improbably, with the Ba'athist regime in Iraq. Action to deal with the threat prominently features the use of force on the model of war against a foreign enemy. It has been claimed, therefore, that there is no question of having to respect the civil liberties of those associated with the enemy. And since enemy combatants are not organized in a formal army of any recognized state, even the obligations of the laws of war need not be observed. Suspects are being held without trial outside the territory of the United States or moved from one country to another for interrogation. Since all of this is part of war with a foreign enemy, the considerations are entirely a matter of expediency, not of principle. When specific powers have been used to infringe on normal conditions of civil liberties at home, the strongest argument used is that of war. Thus, the illegal surveillance of telephone and e-mail communications of U.S. residents is being justified by claiming that the powers of the president as commander-in-chief in a time of war entitles him to authorize such actions. It has also been asserted that only those with "suspicious foreign connections" are wiretapped.

The recent "war on terrorism" has produced a new global arena where the curtailment of normal civil liberties to combat terrorism in one country can justify similar curtailments in other countries. It is as though the norm of civic freedoms in the superior rank of liberal-democratic states has been lowered. Other states can now curtail civil liberties in their domestic spaces by citing the examples of the United States or Britain. These arguments stemming from the global discourse on terrorism have become available to political leaders and commentators in India.

Needless to say, the discourse of Khalistani or Kashmiri nationalism uses the mirror image by which the officially designated "terrorist" can be turned into the nationalist freedom fighter — the same mirror image used by revolutionary nationalists against the colonial state. The same mythography of sacrifice and martyrdom is mobilized to de-legitimize the power of the Indian state. "The idea is to break the stranglehold of fear," the new freedom fighters can be heard to say. "The blood of the martyrs will mobilize thousands." The tables have been turned. But the new defenders of the "lawfully constituted state" scarcely recognize the irony.

Notes

I am grateful to the editors of this volume and the participants in the Fez conference for their valuable comments on an earlier draft. I am also grateful to Malika Ghosh for her research assistance.

1. "Many Delusions" (5 April 1907), in Sri Aurobindo, *Bande Mataram: Early Political Writings* (Pondicherry: Sri Aurobindo Ashram, 1973), 234–37.

2. "Nationalism, Not Extremism," *Bande Mataram*, 26 April 1907, in Aurobindo, *Bande Mataram*, 296–99.

3. The most recent and careful account of the Alipore conspiracy case is in Peter Heehs, *The Bomb in Bengal: The Rise of Revolutionary Terrorism in India 1900–1910* (Delhi: Oxford University Press, 1993).

4. "List of Political Suspects, Corrected up to the End of August 1912," repr. in *Terrorism in Bengal: A Collection of Documents on Terrorist Activities from 1905 to 1939*, vol. 5, ed. Amiya Kumar Samanta (Calcutta: Government of West Bengal, 1995), 457–666.

5. Intelligence Branch, Criminal Investigative Division, Bengal, "List of Persons Connected with the Revolutionary and Anarchical Movement in Bengal, Part 2: Conviction Register," repr. in Samanta, *Terrorism in Bengal*, 667–773.

6. Hemchandra himself narrates the story in Hemchandra Kanungo, *Banglay biplab prachesta* (1928), repr. ed. (Calcutta: Chirayata, 1997).

7. *Notes on Outrages* (1917), comp. J. C. Nixon, repr. in Samanta, *Terrorism in Bengal*, 1–635.

8. Sedition Committee 1918, *Report* (Calcutta: Superintendent, Government Printing, India, 1918), 26–27.

9. Upendranath Bandyopadhyay, *Nirbasiter atmakatha* (1921), repr. ed. (Calcutta: National Publishers, 1999), 18.

10. Moki Singh (pseudonym), *Mysterious India* (London: Stanley Paul, 1938), 44–45.

11. Sedition Committee 1918, *Report*, 197.

12. Ibid., 205.

13. Ibid., 206.

14. See Ravinder Kumar, ed., *Essays on Gandhian Politics: The Rowlatt Satyagraha of 1919* (Oxford: Clarendon Press, 1971).

15. "Sidishan o bideshi raja," *Jugantar*, vol. 2, no. 20, 30 July 1907, in *Agniyuger agnikatha: Jugantar 1906–1908*, ed. Angshuman Bandyopadhyay (Pondicherry: Sri Aurobindo Ashram, 2001), 615–16. The translation is mine.

16. R. E. A. Ray, "Brief Note on the Alliance of Congress with Terrorism in Bengal" (1932), in Samanta, *Terrorism in Bengal*, 933–57.

17. For a recent account, see Manini Chatterjee, *Do and Die: The Chittagong Uprising 1930–34* (New Delhi: Penguin Books India, 1999).

18. H. W. Hale, *Terrorism in India 1917–1936* (Simla: Government of India Press, 1937), 34.

19. Statement by Bhagat Singh and other accused in the court of F. B. Pool, May 1929, in Manmathnath Gupta, *Bhagat Singh and His Times* (Delhi: Lipi Prakashan, 1977), 165.

20. Telegram to N. R. Malkani, 17 March 1930, in M. K. Gandhi, *Collected Works of Mahatma Gandhi*, vol. 43 (New Delhi: Publications Division, 1958–2006), 282.

21. Hale, *Terrorism in India 1917–1936*, 60.

22. Ibid., 1.

23. For a history, see Barry Pavier, *The Telengana Movement 1944–51* (New Delhi: Vikas, 1981).

24. For an account of these movements, see S. K. Chaube, *Hill Politics in North-East India* (Bombay: Orient Longman, 1973).

25. For a history of the movement, see Sumanta Banerjee, *In the Wake of Naxalbari: A History of the Naxalite Movement in India* (Calcutta: Subarnarekha, 1980).

26. For a history of the Khalistan movement, see Mark Juergensmeyer, *Religious Nationalism Confronts the Secular State* (Delhi: Oxford University Press, 1994).

27. For the historical background and analysis of the insurgency, see Sumantra Bose, *Kashmir: Roots of Insurgency, Paths to Peace* (Cambridge, Mass.: Harvard University Press, 2002).

28. National Crime Records Bureau, *Crimes in India, 1994* (New Delhi: Government of India, 1995).

29. The reference is to Carl Schmitt, *Political Theology*, trans. George Schwab (Cambridge, Mass.: MIT Press, 1985). For a recent elaboration of the argument, see Giorgio Agamben, *State of Exception*, trans. Kevin Attell (Chicago: University of Chicago Press, 2005).

WORDS THAT SET STANDARDS

Komisyon/Commission and *Kurul*/Board

Words That Rule

In their travels across space and through time, words linked to governance carry with them practices of power and cloaks of legitimacy. Following their movement, it is therefore possible to track changing patterns of rule and note the moments in which a term seems to move from the foreign and unacceptable to the home-grown and necessary. This is not to suggest that words are ever fixed in their relationship to the prevailing arrangements of power in any given historical context. On the contrary: The very nature of words in motion is that words suddenly find themselves embedded in power relations different from those with which they were initially associated. In this sense, words are not merely signifiers but also agents that help to create new environments of power and as such are implicated in the contradictions that attend such processes of transformation. So while the provenance of words certainly matters, their motion cannot be described as a simple translation from here to there or from one time to another. By focusing attention on the systems and ideologies of rule inaugurated by these transplanted words of governance, as well as the unexpected shifts in the course of their motion, we can trace the lineaments of political change sometimes into unexpected territory.

Here I follow the word "*komisyon*," or "commission," in the nineteenth-century Ottoman Empire, as well as the word "*kurul*," or "board," in contemporary Turkey, to show how the two concepts were mobilized to signal new patterns of governance. These words were linked both to processes that established the political domination of one group and to the ways in which that domination could be challenged and negotiated. The multinational character of the Ottoman Empire made it difficult to establish representative parliamentary government of the sort developing elsewhere in Europe in the nineteenth century. Conflicting national allegiances hindered the formation of a common ground from which to conduct meaningful parliamentary debate, as was demonstrated in the Ottoman constitutional experiment of 1876. In this context, "*komisyon*," borrowed from the French revolutionary "*commission*," emerged as a new institution capable of representing different positions in formulating and implementing the rulings of a central bureaucratic state in the midst of change, as well as resolving disputes associated with these processes. By making it possible for contending social and economic interests to participate in the administrative process, "*komisyon*" provided an arena where social and state actors met to negotiate and, in so doing, forge the terms of modern bureaucratic rule. Thus, the word "*komisyon*" attested to a transformation of social reality, a transformation that is too often reduced to "Europeanization" in conventional Ottoman historiography. In this view the modern transformation appears as a continuous struggle by elites to adopt European institutions, often in the face of resistance by large segments of society.

Follow the word "*komisyon*" and the institutions that carried its name, however, and a different trajectory becomes visible: one that was enmeshed in local politics and carried the imprint of social struggles. Rather than the adoption of European forms by a modernizing elite, we glimpse a process through which — regardless of the alien origins of the innovation — different groups actively engaged to make the institution their own. The use of the foreign word "*komisyon*" did not signal an aspiration so much as it underlined the novelty of the process and the different way in which the new bureaucracy conducted business.

Earlier views of modernity as resting on the politics of the central bureaucratic state have changed radically over the past several decades, signaled in part by the emergence of a new term of governance. "*Kurul*," the Turkish word for "board," borrowed from the corporate world of the late-twentieth-century transnational economy, has increasingly accompanied, or even replaced, the older "*komisyon*." "*Kurul*" refers to an administrative body of experts characterized precisely by its independence from the central bureaucracy. Whereas the *komisyon* had been associated with the political form of the nineteenth-century state, the *kurul* arose from a latter-day vision of transformation — that of global market development. These "boards" highlight the contemporary prominence of transnational actors as against the domination of the older bureaucracies represented by the continued presence of the *komisyon*. "*Kurul*," a concocted Turkish word not in common usage, distinguished the new world of governance from the old, underlining both its novelty and its distance from earlier practices.

Here I first follow the movement of "*komisyon*" from France to the Ottoman Empire as the word metamorphosized to foster new venues for political participation in bureaucratic administration. Then I trace the predicament of contemporary *kuruls* in their entanglements with entrenched bureaucracies and sectors of the local business elite in contemporary Turkey. These entanglements were disapproved of, for different reasons, by both the International Monetary Fund (IMF) and the Turkish government, suggesting that yet another word — and administrative form — might be needed to serve the transnational market order in the context of proposed integration with the European Union (EU). My point is that in some ways the *komisyon* and the *kurul*, both of which emanated from the international geopolitical order of their respective times, have been more common and also arguably more effective than parliaments in managing the tensions between state and society in modern political life. Their story has a great deal to tell us about how societies are positioned to carry the project of building a new Europe into the twenty-first century.

Commissions and Bureaucratic Rule

The French words "*commission*" and "*comité*" evoke different forms of governance that have evolved since the nineteenth century. The terms go back to the French Revolution, which originated the idea of commissions or committees as governing bodies responsible for formulating the institutional framework for a new central administration. Since that time, the relationship between commissions and democracy has never quite been settled, since either the representative character or the "expert" dimension of the commissions could be emphasized, depending on the goal of the moment. During the revolutionary decade of the 1790s, committees in France were largely responsible for the actual tasks of administration; some were endowed with significant powers, as was the case with the Committee of Public Safety.[1] With the consolidation of the power of the central bureaucracy and the army under Napoleon, committees were no longer charged with direct administration and security, but committee formation remained a bureaucratic prerogative invoked when a task needed to be done. Committees and commissions were seen as essential to the new French Republic because they brought together representative individuals as well as those with expertise to perform a specified task, thus providing for deliberation among different interests as well as for the production and dissemination of knowledge.

Nineteenth-century polities in continental Europe were receptive to the French model of administrative rationalization, in part because they had been engaged in state-to-state competition since the fifteenth century and also because they now faced similar needs to centralize fiscal and military power in order to finance and deploy the new infantry armies. In addition, earlier forms of government premised on accommodation of interests through an elaborate system of privileges and exemptions relating to taxation and military service had become increasingly cumbersome. Beginning in the eighteenth century, Eastern European empires, among them the Ottoman, had embraced administrative reforms, which signaled a radical transformation of the state, one that saw a shift in hegemonic power from a ruling coalition of claimants to taxes or economic surpluses to central bureaucracies with a monopoly over those surpluses. As in France, commissions contributed to the hegemony of state bureaucracy, not only because of their central role in rule and decision making, but also because they so often set the terms under which bureaucratic rules and decisions could, or could not, be challenged. If, through their rulings and regulations, commissions established the all-important categories of taxation and conscription, they were also seen as providing spaces for the deliberation and contestation of these categories.

In the French case, a distinction was increasingly made between "committees," which referred to organs of the central government and, "commissions," the word used for local bodies of deliberation.[2] The Ottomans generally used the word "commission" (in Ottoman spelling, "*komisyon*") rather than "committee (*komite*)" to designate both central and local bodies. Whatever the reason for this choice, it more or less avoided the overtones of revolution associated with the French committees of the 1790s. Indeed, in Ottoman usage, "*komite*" came to refer to coup-d'étatist revolutionary bodies, such as the Committee of the Union and Progress (İttihat veTerakki Komitesi), which seized power in 1908; and its derivative, "*komitaci*," signified a political agitator. This association continued under the Turkish Republic. The military junta that seized power on 27 May 1960 called itself Millli Birlik Komitesi, or Committee of National

Unity. Today the association of the word "committee" with revolutionary practice has weakened to the point that *"komite"* and *"komisyon"* are used interchangeably to refer to specialized parliamentary bodies.

*Komisyon*s in the nineteenth-century Ottoman Empire can be said to have facilitated the emergence of the modern administrative order. This order brought the rise to power of a centralized bureaucracy that replaced the palace and its reliance on localities in the governing of the empire. Of the many commissions established by the Ottoman bureaucracy, one of the most important — and most visible — was the Land Commission (Arazi Komisyonu), which drafted the Land Code of 1858 introducing individual ownership and creating a new administrative regime of property. The commission remained in force after the code was promulgated, assuming responsibility for resolving disputes arising from its implementation, which meant, in effect, taking on a role as the site for the mediation of divergent interests.[3] The Land Commission was composed of leading Ottoman jurists who also occupied top positions in the central bureaucracy, among them Cevdet Paşa, the head of the Land Commission as well as the initiator of the drafting of an Ottoman Civil Code and the Ottoman governor in the Balkans on various subsequent occasions. The text of the Land Code and the introductory statement by its drafters revealed an understanding of governing that was mediational and reconciliatory. *Komisyon*s — including the Land Commission, the Commission to Draft the Civil Code, and others — fostered such mediation inasmuch as they presupposed the participation of actors with divergent interests that had to be reconciled. In fact, the work of the Land Commission — as well as of local commissions established throughout the empire to settle land disputes and to register land, property, and population — became the grounds for discursive constitution of the Ottoman central bureaucracy in the second half of the nineteenth century. This meant that the legitimacy of the state and its ability to govern would now rest in part on the extent to which its representatives could mediate among multiple claims to land use and revenues.

The Land Code defined individual ownership rights and, following its issuance in 1858, provided the vocabulary through which all land disputes were to be articulated. In this vocabulary, individual ownership overrode competing claims to land use and tax revenues. To accomplish this, the code abandoned earlier classifications of landed property according to revenue grants given to charitable or religious endowments, military commanders, members of the Ottoman court, and various groups of tax farmers. Instead, the Land Commission introduced a classification of landed property on the basis of conditions of access or use—for example, common lands or uncultivated lands. In practice, this classification led to a separation of revenue claims from property claims and established the central bureaucracy as the sole claimant to taxes by excluding the claims of other groups. It also established the individual titleholder as the sole claimant to access to land. Yet both claims—of individual ownership and of the central bureaucracy's monopoly over taxes—were qualified in the text of the code. First, its precepts applied only to state lands or lands over which the central bureaucracy had established control. They did not apply to the properties of *vakif* (charitable or religious endowments) and *mulk* (freehold property). By separating state lands from the properties of charitable endowments and those of freeholders, the land *komisyon* required the central government to concede its revenue claims on holders of these properties.[4] The reconciliatory tone of the *komisyon*'s work was also apparent in the contradictions in descriptions of land transactions. For instance, while provisions were made for the irrevocable transfer of land, restrictions were imposed on such transfers in the event of indebtedness, in effect an attempt to prevent large-scale dispossessions of land.

Again consistent with this reconciliatory tone, the *komisyon* painstakingly emphasized in its introductory remarks that the code represented continuity rather than a rupture with past practices. The *komisyon* insisted that its task had been simply to compile regulations relating to landed property dating back to the time of Suleiman the Law Giver and gather together what was already contained in the edicts of past Ottoman rulers. Yet it was subtly noted that the reason for this new compilation was the change in entitlement to land revenues, which had been brought about by revoking the land-grant system.[5] A similar understatement of the consequence of these changes characterized an earlier document issued by the Council of Reform (Meclis-i Tanzimat), which helped to pave the way for the new Ottoman code to be issued at the relatively early date of 1858. In France, by contrast, the intensity of the struggle in the countryside and the intransigence of the propertied classes—especially in relation to rules of tenancy—did not permit the issuing of a rural code until well into the 1880s.[6]

Despite the moderate and reconciliatory nature of its wording, the *komisyon*'s work in fact facilitated radical changes in who had access to land use, who held title, and under what conditions. As a result, the code was debated and negotiated further as the central government attempted to implement its provisions in different parts of the empire. In the process, numerous *komisyon*s were established on the local level to mediate land claims as they began to be formulated under the new code.

Cevdet Paşa, the principal architect of the Land Code, provided a vivid account of a local *komisyon* working to settle a dispute between former estate holders and sharecropping cultivators on the Parga estate in Yanya, in present-day Greece.[7] Under the new code, estate holders who had previously farmed the estate's taxes were now seeking to acquire title to the land. The cultivators objected and demanded a redefinition of their own rights of use, which amounted to individual ownership under the terms of the new code. To deal with the issue, Cevdet Paşa, then the governor of Yanya, established a *komisyon* in 1875 that included himself, members of local councils, administrators of the estate, one representative from each of the five quarters of the town where the estate was located, as well as the representatives of the parties to the dispute. Estate holders were represented by the venerable Rauf Beyefendi, the son of a deceased high-ranking central government official, whose presence appears to have inspired awe even in the eyes of Cevdet Paşa, himself no stranger to power circles in Istanbul. Rauf Beyefendi succeeded in getting the cultivators to recognize the ownership rights of the estate holders, effectively ensuring that the cultivators accepted their status as tenants.

Despite this outcome, the ownership rights of the estate holders were significantly restricted through the deliberations of the *komisyon*. For example, the cultivators successfully resisted both the specification of time limits in lease contracts and any increase in the amount of rent. They couched their resistance as a call for adherence to local customary practices, most of which had been incorporated in earlier sultanic edicts. Use rights, such as those established on state lands, had previously lasted for long periods, often spanning the lifetimes of individual tenants and their descendants. When estate holders laid claim to title under the new code, the cultivators expected them to abide by these older practices, which essentially meant that the titleholders could not revoke a tenancy, evict a tenant, or raise the rent. Nor could the titleholders, upon the death of one tenant, lease the land to another. The family of the deceased tenant was expected to continue to cultivate the land as before and pay the rent. The only condition under which a lease contract could be revoked and the tenant could be evicted was when the tenant ceased to cultivate and stopped paying rent. The process and result of the *komisyon*'s deliberations thus managed to combine the new administrative principles with the interests of both the estate holders and the cultivators.

As in France, local commissions in the Ottoman Empire were capable of provoking the reformulation of government rulings, as in the case of the Property Commissions. On the basis of the settlement reached by the *komisyon* at the Parga estate, Cevdet Paşa recommended to the Council of State (the highest decision-making organ of the central government) that a special regulation be formulated for Yanya Province. This proposal for a special regulation recognizing the demands of cultivators for heritable tenancy rights, however, in effect compromised the universality of the code with respect to the absoluteness of individual ownership rights of title-holders. From the perspective of the central government, achieving universal applicability for individual ownership rights would eliminate multiple claims to land use and revenues. This would simplify the administration of taxation and property and give the administration direct access to taxes based on the income of the individual property owner. Coupled with this fiscal advantage was the nineteenth-century perception that individual property meant increased productivity and therefore larger tax revenues. Despite the advantages to the state of a universal principle of individual ownership, different groups sought to limit the principle by asserting such claims as heritable tenancy rights. These contestations often took place in local commissions, whose conclusions could result in modifications of the general administrative law in response to local circumstances. At the same time, while these modifications represented negotiations of certain provisions of the law, they did not seek to reject the general regime of property that it introduced. The code remained the ultimate reference point of all negotiation. And yet the new order of property was produced not only by proclamations of general laws by the central bureaucracy, but also by the social and political processes of debating and negotiating the provisions of those laws.

In this way, the commissions provided a venue for political participation and deliberation at the same time that they helped to establish the domination of the reformed central bureaucracy, which was inseparable from the new order of property and society. Bureaucratic domination carried with it a concern for legitimacy that would make its actions acceptable to different social groups. Not surprisingly, this concern often came into conflict with the government's fiscal imperatives. In earlier Ottoman statecraft, an accommodative political language had managed conflicting interests through particularistic settlements negotiated between the ruler and different groups, including diverse and multiple rulings on rural land use and revenues.[8] But in the nineteenth century, with the ascendancy of the central bureaucracy to power, rulings assumed a general character representing the universal claims of the bureaucracy to land revenues and manpower. Commission-formation became a means for the negotiation of diverse interests that also rendered the new general rulings politically viable and legitimate. Such legitimacy derived in part from the participation of different social groups in the realization of the new administrative order. A striking example of such participation was the village commissions appointed for groups of six villages, with each village providing one member. Expected to meet weekly in the summer and biweekly the rest of the year, village commissions, which reported to provincial councils, decided on the distribution of taxes among households according to their ability to pay and were also responsible for reporting on changes in population and the status of property in their region.[9]

Because the order that emerged out of the participatory and deliberative environments provided by *komisyon*s was politically negotiated, its effects were mixed. Particularistic interests frequently prevailed even as the principle of generality was upheld. By taking the bureaucracy's general rulings or codes as the reference point for all deliberations and employing the vocabulary and categories of these rulings, *komisyon* thus represented both the limits and the possibilities of challenging the order of property that centralized bureaucratic rule had introduced.

The new nineteenth-century order of centralized bureaucratic states in the Ottoman Empire and elsewhere was inseparable from the development of national market societies. Individual ownership was central to these market societies, as was the contention of utilitarian political economists like Jeremy Bentham that such societies had to be administratively constituted if they were not to disintegrate into an arena of self-interest and destructive divisiveness.[10] Bentham regarded property as an expectation on the part of individuals formed in the context of commercial development. This expectation could be realized in law, which for Bentham was synonymous with administration. In practice, achieving his desired "greatest happiness of greatest numbers" through law or administration required mediation among the diverse interests always at play in such a regime of property. Commissions provided spaces where mediation could occur, where different interests could hold the central bureaucracy accountable for its actions and participate in making its rulings. Since the second half of the nineteenth century — most intensely after the Great Depression of the 1930s and under the emerging welfare states — regulatory commissions in national market societies served both to reconcile conflicting interests and to reinforce the dominance of centralized bureaucratic administration.[11] Regulatory commissions relating to finance, labor, commodity markets, and welfare services provided different social groups with political access to the process of administrative decision making while strengthening the authority of the state.

The various Ottoman commissions established in the second half of the nineteenth century could not ultimately bring about a national market society because they functioned in the context of a dispersed multinational empire. Yet even after the Ottoman state collapsed at the end of the First World War, commissions remained a central institution of political participation and accountability in the Ottoman successor states in the Balkans and the Middle East. In this sense, commissions, which were less visible and often unrecognized institutions of participation that helped to make government politically accountable to society, can be counted a prominent feature of modernity. Commissions represented an aspect of modern political processes that were widely shared by European and non-European regions alike — more widely shared, certainly, than parliaments.

Boards: From Participatory Legitimation to Expert-based Efficiency

With the sharp ascendancy of transnational capital since the 1980s, there was a shift in the administration of market societies from the domain of hierarchically organized central bureaucracies to autonomous bodies of experts. In the Turkish Republic, one of the successor states of the Ottoman Empire, I mark this process as a shift from commissions (*komisyon*) to boards (*kurul*). Initially, the new boards of experts posed a challenge to the political character of commissions and, more generally, to the political entanglements with interest groups that characterized the bureaucratic form of administration. Boards promised to assign priority to market efficiency, which was increasingly interpreted to give transnational capital interests precedence over the interests of national market and non-market sectors. Yet for boards to be effective in the transnational market environment, they had to operate as corporate bodies subject to their own rules. These rules of corporate governance rendered the boards accountable within themselves, marking a shift from the public political accountability that characterized *komisyons*. Their governing processes were not open to the participation of diverse interests, so that accountability was in a sense privatized. Here I trace the contradictory character of these attempts to de-politicize government and in the shift of governing activity from *komisyon* to *kurul*. The shift in governance words signified a complicated process of change in power relations as groups within the bureaucracy and interests rooted in national markets each tried to maintain a foothold in the new governing bodies, as they rushed head-long into confrontation with global organizations like the International Monetary Fund (IMF) and transnational capital interests.

As a new type of governing body in market societies, autonomous boards are generally depicted as groups of "professionals with recognized expertise and competence in a particular domain and an authoritative claim to policy-relevant knowledge within that domain or issue area."[12] Their technical character is held up as a contrast to bureaucratic agencies, which are said to be vulnerable to "capture" by the interests they deal with. Such "capture" refers to the "political responsiveness" of bureaucracies, so that the recent critique of bureaucratic administration goes to the heart of the system of political accountability that made bureaucratic agencies organized under elected cabinet ministries responsible to elected parliaments. The "autonomy" of the new boards exempted them from such accountability, placing them "above politics" and allegedly improving their performance by removing the political mediation among multiple interests that were thought responsible for the inefficiencies of bureaucratic governance. Autonomy would enable the boards to pursue the objective of promoting the interests of the business community, especially that part with transnational linkages. In this way, boards became the locus of another politics which did not call itself "politics" and which limited those included in the purview of their mediation. In the interests of performance efficiency within their "limited" objective, boards were expected to develop internal rules of self-governance and accountability, in effect becoming corporate entities and employing techniques of corporate management and governance culture.[13] It is thus no accident that the new terminology of governance was largely appropriated from the business world. Governing bodies are boards, and citizens are called stakeholders, shareholders, consumers, or customers—as if to align the social universe with the corporate world.

Despite their depiction as non-political and technical bodies, the *kurul*s in fact became a venue for the politics of reform, bearing witness to the contentious process of evolving new institutions of governance in transnationalizing societies. Since the 1980s, Turkey has been a major importer of reform packages from the IMF, the World Bank, and the EU. In compliance with the dictates of these packages, Turkey has sought to decrease the bureaucratic presence in the economy through privatization, reduction of agricultural subsidies, and liberalization of the financial sector. Progress, however, has been uneven. Despite repeated claims that economic growth results from efficient techniques of governing the economy and on the elimination of the old, cumbersome "political" modes of government, the labored nature of the reform process is in fact rooted in the politics of reform itself. The debate about *kurul*s has been entangled in the checkered history of the Banking Regulation and Supervision Board (BRSB). As a result of this saga, even the IMF retracted its insistence on the autonomy of the *kurul*, expressing a revised preference for "semi-autonomous" governing bodies to carry out reform of the financial sector. In 2004, the attempts to establish the Gelirler Idaresi (Incomes Administration)—which, significantly, is not called a *kurul*—seemed partly a response of the Turkish government to the IMF's dissatisfaction with the BRSB. Moreover, in the heat of the clashes with the BSRB, the IMF representative went so far as to propose the formation of a transnational board to supervise financial services in Turkey.

The tumultuous history of the BRSB began when the *kurul* was established under the Banking Law of 1999 and commenced operations in 2000. It was charged with regulating the banking sector, ensuring that the Banking Law was implemented in compliance with the principles of the global financial system, most notably with the Basel Accords of 1988 and 2004. The BRSB was also given responsibility for supervising the activities of financial institutions, a task that had formerly rested with the Finance Ministry. To carry out its supervisory tasks, BRSB relied on the Yeminli Murakıplar Kurulu (Board of Sworn Bank Auditors), an important entity within the finance bureaucracy which was relocated to the BRSB.

In concrete terms, the Banking Law empowered the BRSB to close failing banks and issue permits to open new banks. Turkey's major financial crisis in late 2000 and early 2001 provided the context for exercising these new powers, placing the *kurul* at center stage of the process to rationalize the banking system. This was the price demanded by the IMF from the Turkish government in exchange for bailing it out of the crisis. In the rash of bank closings and opening of foreign banks, the BRSB found itself open to all manner of allegations of partiality to certain banks over others. The *kurul* initially had the responsibility of collecting the debts owed by private banks to the government, which some private banks had incurred when they were accused of channeling deposits to various companies that belonged to the owners of these banks. Under the law, the government had to make up the losses to the depositors, and the BRSB was saddled with the task of collecting the billions of dollars from the bank owners through confiscation and sale of their properties. As this legal process continued, dramatic takeovers of the bank owners' property as well as warrants for their arrest became the bread and butter of the Turkish media. Yet after 2003, the majority government that replaced the previous coalition government was critical of the "excessive" autonomy of the BRSB and sought to limit its powers by removing its powers of collection. It established instead the Tasarruf Mevduatı Sigorta Fonu Satış Komisyonu (Commission of Sales for the Insurance Fund for Bank Deposits Fund). Not surprisingly, this new *komisyon* followed the older pattern, being placed under the jurisdiction of a cabinet ministry. In the process of these trials and tribulations, the autonomy of the BRSB was continuously redefined as it found itself embroiled in local and national power relations and developed a certain distance from transnational actors. And so the *kurul*, a word that carried a definition imposed by transnational market society, was re-cast in the context of a new configuration of local or national power actors. The *kurul* itself helped to cause this power shift when it became entangled in the cases of particular bank owners. In this respect, the *kurul* behaved more like the old bureaucracy — displaying partiality to local business interests and remaining suspicious of IMF intervention — at the same time that it espoused the IMF's demands for its autonomy in the name of efficiency.

From its inception, the debate over the BRSB was dominated by the question: To whom or what the *kurul* is accountable?[14] While both the Banking Law and the establishment of the BRSB were part of the reform agenda introduced by the IMF, it seemed that in the Turkish context — unlike the practice in more advanced market societies — the IMF preferred not to subject these autonomous entities to the scrutiny of parliamentary commissions. Instead, the BRSB's activities were overseen by the Sayıştay, or specialized court, a supervisory agency of the prime minister's office. Only when the BRSB was found to be clearly at fault was a parliamentary commission formed to investigate its activities. The Imar Bank affair in 2003 was one such occasion, and parliamentary investigation led to the police moving in to confiscate the *kurul*'s documents. Imar Bank, a private bank, had evaded BRSB supervision through corrupt bookkeeping practices that enabled it to channel its depositors' funds to its own affiliated companies. The evasion occurred during the period when BRSB representatives were sitting on the bank's board, precisely with the objective of keeping its activities under close scrutiny.[15]

By not subjecting the BRSB to parliamentary scrutiny, the IMF perhaps hoped to shield the *kurul* from the exigencies of local politics and make it accountable to transnational networks of governance, including its own. In practice, however, loopholes in non-parliamentary mechanisms of control over the BRSB's activities frustrated such hopes. The IMF kept a critical eye on the BRSB, objecting, for example, to its reluctance to provide the IMF with all of its information regarding local banks, a condition the Turkish government had agreed to in the standby agreement of 1999. The IMF also criticized the Banking Law drafted by the BRSB in 2004.[16] It objected to provisions giving the Board some control over the activities in Turkey of transnational financial institutions, and it questioned the wording of the objectives of the law, which initially read: "also taking into account the exigencies of the economy, [the] BRSB will seek to ensure stability and security in financial markets and ensure the effective working of the credit system."[17]

The IMF took the phrase "exigencies of the economy" to mean that the BRSB could use the pretext of special circumstances in the Turkish economy to obstruct the entry of transnational banks and encourage the opening of new local banks instead. In response, the BRSB accused the IMF of promoting the interests of transnational banks at the expense of local banks. When the Association of Turkish Banks supported the BRSB on this issue, the IMF countered by suggesting that a transnational body replace the BRSB.[18] Although the phrase "exigencies of the economy" was removed from the final draft law submitted to the government by the BRSB,[19] there was little doubt that the autonomy of the *kurul* had taken a turn different from what was originally intended, thus prompting new attempts to limit the autonomy the BRSB had appropriated for itself. The autonomy of the *kurul* was reinforced, however, by a decision of the Constitutional Court in November 2006, which blocked the government's claim to dismiss *kurul* members before they had completed their term.[20] In the crisis over the Banking Law draft in 2004, the Turkish government and the treasury notably did not side with the BRSB in the controversy with the IMF. The minister in charge of the economy declared that the ultimate responsibility for passing a law redefining the status of the BRSB lay in Parliament, thus calling the autonomy of the *kurul* into question.[21] At issue was the meaning of the word "*kurul*," which since 2000 had become identified with ways to socially negotiate political power that remained rooted in the local or national environment and were increasingly incompatible with transnational norms. In fact, the word had migrated from its corporate origins to the domain of societal governance, where its connotation of expert neutrality did not guarantee that such "boards" would give priority to transnational concerns over local ones or that expert neutrality would readily blend with external transnational vocabularies.

In the case of the BRSB, the *kurul* did remain true to its corporate premise even as it displayed a markedly nationalist flair by turning its face toward the local rather than the transnational corporate environment. Indeed, in its composition as well as its modus operandi the *kurul* revealed the incestuous relationship between the local business community and the remaining strongholds of the financial bureaucracy. Seven members of the *kurul* were appointed from candidates proposed by the treasury, the Finance Ministry, the State Planning Organization, the Association of Turkish Banks, and the Capital Securities Board. Board members were required to have served in an executive capacity at leading financial institutions for at least three years prior to their appointment. Moreover, the supervisory staff of the BRSB consisted of auditors organized in the Board of Sworn Public Auditors, which had relocated from the Finance Ministry bureaucracy.[22] This important group of experts, together with the historical Maliye Teftiş Kurulu (Finance Auditing Board), represented a powerful group within the bureaucracy. Bureaucratic *kurul*s like those of the auditors operated as training grounds for experts in government agencies as well as in the private sector. Solidarity among the members of these bureaucratic *kurul*s was rooted in a male culture embellished with images of gun-slinging upholders of bureaucratic integrity over corrupt business practices.[23] In the BRSB controversy, these bureaucratic *kurul*s supported the interests of the national economy and national business classes over transnational interests.[24] This made them a prime target for the IMF, which blamed the auditors for the failings of the BRSB, as in the Imar Bank scandal, and for its nationalistic tendencies. The IMF accordingly demanded that the system of auditors be omitted from the new Banking Law. The chair of the BRSB countered forcefully that elimination of the auditors would weaken the supervisory process and that the auditing system belonged to the internal affairs of the BRSB in its status as an autonomous body. The Association of Auditors joined him in condemning the IMF's accusations.

The Turkish government also criticized the performance of the *kurul* and took the occasion of the Imar Bank affair to order an inquiry by an international commission. The commission submitted its report in August 2004, which called for radical reform of the *kurul* and, specifically, a curb on the power of auditors within the *kurul*. The report suggested that the autonomy of the *kurul* had empowered the auditors by emphasizing the practice of periodic bureaucratic inspection limited largely to procedural matters. The report concluded that this limited approach to inspection allowed the national banking sector to get away with corrupt practices at the expense of public depositors. Instead, the report recommended that the BRSB be made responsible for regular supervision, assigning a single auditor to each bank, and that the autonomy of the BRSB be re-cast in terms of corporate self-regulation, whereby the *kurul* would assume a corporate identity and take responsibility for its work.

Despite the recommendations of the international commission, it did not seem likely the government would be able to curb the power of auditors within the BRSB. On the one hand, government ministers insisted that the ultimate responsibility for financial policy lay with Parliament.[25] And the Commission of Sales for the Insurance Fund for Bank Deposits Fund continued its dramatic operations, arresting former bank owners and confiscating their property. On the other hand, the government refused to hire new inspectors in the Finance Ministry so as not to add to existing numbers.[26] The leverage of auditors — which was also the leverage of the bureaucracy — was conceded, and the discussion moved in the direction of reform of the institution of auditors.[27] The IMF, too, toned down its stance against the BRSB, possibly reassured by the fact that the government, which commanded a majority in Parliament, might be able to promote transnational interests more effectively through certain concessions to the bureaucracy and to the BRSB. By 2008, nearly 30 percent of the Turkish banking sector was in the hands of transnational concerns, and the BRSB could not be expected to turn the tide. Yet the *kurul* had approved sales of national banks to foreign concerns, often following a prolonged and arduous process of investigation during which the *kurul* had placed every possible bureaucratic obstacle in the way of the sales.[28] The result was the continued displeasure of the government with the BRSB "bureaucracy," while groups critical of transnationalization regarded the *kurul*, representing "public authority" in the banking sector, as responsible for ensuring that national priorities be considered in the process.[29]

Conclusion

Initially, *"komisyon"* and *"kurul"* were words that came from afar: one associated with the centralized bureaucratic administration of the European nation-state of the nineteenth century; the other, with the technical expertise and corporate governance of the transnational economy of the late twentieth and early twenty-first century. Once they arrived, the words continued to move as they became entangled in the negotiations of political power by different social actors and thus helped to constitute new patterns of governance and domination. And as they moved internally, they ceased to signify what they had when they arrived from the world outside.

*Komisyon*s in the Ottoman context were implicated in the evolution of participatory politics at a time when the dominance of the central bureaucracy was established, ending earlier patterns of accommodating diverse interests in the empire. As an integral part of the politics of bureaucracy, *komisyons* assumed functions of representation and mediation of multiple interests. As a common and widely shared governmental form, commissions were both sign and practice of a modern transformation that, in the Ottoman case, became associated with "Europe." In its long struggle for the survival of the empire, the Ottoman government turned to adopt the institutions of the rival European powers. The visible success of post-revolutionary French techniques of government—which the Ottomans observed firsthand during Napoleon's invasion of Egypt—made French institutions like the *"commissions"* extremely attractive. No doubt that its origins endowed the *komisyon* with its initial legitimacy. Yet like other imported institutions, the *komisyons* were soon involved in the struggle of the new Ottoman bureaucracy to establish its own legitimacy within the empire. In the process, different groups in society negotiated the conditions of their existence in the new bureaucratic order. The word "*komisyon*" thus epitomizes the complexity of the modern transformation, in which "foreign borrowings" (or Europeanization) and local power relations interacted in such a way that different groups participated in creating the new order and making it their own. The "opening to modernity" embodied by the *komisyon* is a far more accurate rendering of this conflicted and negotiated process than the term "Europeanization" or non-European "imitation" of European forms of governance.

Boards, for their part, provided an opening for a different sort of modernity, one that was premised on establishing the domination of transnational actors, often at the expense of local or national interest. *Kuruls*, which derived their legitimacy from ideologies of efficiency associated with corporate governance, were part of market reform packages imposed by transnational institutions and designed to integrate local practices with the global market. Yet in the Turkish context, *kuruls* responded to the painful process of transnationalization with a bureaucratic panache for preserving national sovereignty and a practiced partiality to actors in local and national markets. These *kuruls* became arenas where different groups negotiated the conditions of their social, economic, and political existence in a globalizing world. Despite the sometimes dramatic interventions by transnational actors like the IMF, these political struggles did not turn the *kuruls* into the streamlined entities said to be essential to participation in the European Union. Thus, on the one hand, the word *kurul* no longer signifies autonomous governing bodies acting in concert with corporate norms and transnational actors. This divergence may explain the disenchantment with *kuruls* on the part both of these transnational actors and of the Turkish government, even as the government increasingly staked its future on European integration. On the other hand, because the *kuruls* became embroiled in, and thus constitutive of, changing power relations, they continued to shape governance practices in the transnationalizing market environment, imparting to these practices twists and turns specific to the Turkish context.

Both "*komisyon*" and "*kurul*" moved from "foreign" origins to local political arenas in which social actors staked their claims in the processes of modern transformation, one national, and the other transnational. Out of the struggles they embodied and enabled emerged the specific modernity of a given society—a modernity that is part of the lived and living experience of the people in the region and that is not imposed from outside.

Notes

1. Isser Woloch, *The New Regime: Transformations of the French Civic Order, 1789–1820's* (New York: W. W. Norton, 1994). Establishment of commissions as expert bodies especially addressing economic issues heralded the process of bureaucratic reform, or "administrative revolution," in Britain beginning in 1780: John Torrance, "Social Class and Bureaucratic Innovation: The Commissioners for Examining the Public Accounts 1780–1787," *Past and Present*, no. 78 (February 1978): 56–81.

2. For a discussion of regional property commissions, see Sergei Aberdam, *Aux origines du code rural, 1789–1900: Un siècle de debat* (Paris: Institut national de la recherche agronomique, 1982), 23.

3. Ahmet Cevdet Paşa, *Ma'ruzat*, ed. Yusuf Halaçoglu (Istanbul: Çagri, 1980), 65–66.

4. For a discussion of this issue and definitions of freehold in the Ottoman context, see Huri Islamoglu, "Property as a Contested Domain: A Re-evaluation of the Land Code of 1858," in *New Perspectives on Property and Land in the Middle East*, ed. Roger Owen (Cambridge, Mass.: Harvard University Press, 2000), 3–61.

5. Ahmet Akgündüz, *Mukayeseli Islam ve Osmanlı Hukuku Külliyat* (Diyarbakır: Dicle Universitesi, 1986), 679–81.

6. Aberdam, *Aux origines du code rural.*

7. Ahmet Cevdet Paşa, *Tezakir*, ed. Cavit Baysun, vol. 4 (Ankara: Turk Tarih Kurumu Basimevi, 1986), 140–41.

8. For a discussion of the notion of justice in the early modern Ottoman state in terms of the ability of the ruler to ensure social peace, see Huri Islamoglu, *State and Peasant in the Ottoman Empire* (Leiden: E. J. Brill, 1994).

9. "'Tahrir-I Emlak ve Nufus Nizamnamesi,' 14 Cumade'l-ula 1277 (28 November 1860)," *I. Tertip Düstûr*, 2d ed., vol. 1 (Istanbul: Matbaa-I Amire, c. 1866), 889–902.

10. Jeremy Bentham, *The Theory of Legislation*, ed. C. K. Ogden, (London: Harcourt, Brace, 1931).

11. For an excellent discussion of such regulatory commissions in the 1930s, see John R. Commons, *Legal Foundations of Capitalism* (New York: Macmillan, 1939).

12. Anne-Marie Slaughter, *A New World Order* (Princeton, N.J.: Princeton University Press, 2004), 42–43.

13. A report by a commission set in train by the government of the Turkish Republic and presented in August 2004, which emphasized the corporate governance aspect of the BRSB, (Bank Regulatory and Supervisory Board), pointed to the need to ensure top-down accountability within the Board and to introduce measures whereby the Board could evaluate its own performance: Jean-Louis Fort and Peter Hayward, *Report of the Commission of Inquiry into the Supervisory Implications of the Failure of Imar*

Bank, mimeograph (Ankara: Government of Turkey, Treasury Department, August 2004).

14. When autonomous *kuruls* were first established in the aftermath of the financial crisis in 2001, Bülent Ecevit, then the prime minister, who was known for his nationalist–statist positions, lamented the stealing of the state by these bodies that lacked political accountability.

15. For a detailed description of the Imar Bank incident, see Fort and Hayward, *Report of the Commission of Inquiry into the Supervisory Implications of the Failure of Imar Bank.*

16. Ahmet Erhan Celik in *Milliyet*, 24 November 2004, 7.

17. 19 August 2004 version of "Draft Law for Credit Institutions," *Milliyet*, 5 December 2004.

18. For a detailed discussion, see the column by Yaman Toruner, a former president of the Central Bank, in *Milliyet*, 15 November 2004, 6.

19. *Draft Law of Financial Services*, 24 November 2004.

20. This decision reversed an amendment to the Banking Law initiated by the government in 2001 to end the membership of five members of the *kurul* before their term expired: see the website at http://www.nethaber.com, 29 November 2006.

21. For instance, Ali Babacan, minister in charge of the economy, has taken this position: *Milliyet*, 12 November 2004.

22. For a recent discussion of its significance in the power struggles in the reorganization of the Turkish Finance Ministry involving the *murakıp* (auditors): see *Milliyet*, 23 November 2004, 7, ibid., 29 November 2004, 8; ibid., 30 November 2004, 7.

23. An article in the leading daily *Milliyet* pointed to the all-male character of the Board of Financial Inspectors, claiming that women could not pass the oral part of the examination required of inspectors for admission to the Board. It also stated that the job of inspector has been deemed to involve serious dangers that might make it inappropriate for women: ibid., 12 December 2004, 10.

24. A recent conference on the European Union and the Turkish economy, representing a cautious position on European accession and pointing to the priorities of the national economy and classes, was attended by the top brass of the bureaucracy, leftist economists, and the leadership of the Social Democratic Party. The board traces its origin to the nineteenth-century Heyet-I Teftişiye-I Maliye, established in 1879, and speaks for national interests in the Turkish economy: ibid., 5 December 2004, 9.

25. This tendency on the part of the government to challenge the autonomy of governing bodies is not entirely disapproved of by the IMF, which showed some apprehension about *kuruls* turning into autonomous domains for the bureaucracy and its nationalist claims: ibid., 12 November 2004, 7. Faik Oztrak, a former secretary of the treasury and a former vice-chair of the BRSB, was critical of government intervention in the affairs of the BRSB and the challenge to its autonomy: ibid., 22 November 2004, 8. He also criticized the operations of the Board and the emphasis on control at the expense of supervision: ibid., 29 November 2004, 8.

26. In 2004, there appeared to be about 111 financial inspectors on duty. Although there were more than four hundred more bureaucratic slots for new appointments, the government refrained from making these appointments: ibid., 12 December 2004, 10.

27. For a discussion of the power of auditors in the financial bureaucracy, including the tax auditors, accountants, and bureaucrats in income-tax bureaucracies in different regions, see the column by Gungor Uras in ibid., 23 November 2004, 7.

28. For a description of the prolonged process of approval of the sale of Sekerbank, a public bank, to the Kazak Turan Alem Group, which included among its shareholders the European Bank for Reconstruction and Development, the Raiffeisen Bank, the International Finance Corporation, and the Netherlands Development Finance Company, see *Vatan*, 11 May 2006. The approval came in December 2006.

29. For a call for balanced transnationalization of the banking sector, see *Dunya*, 20 October 2006.

Chumchon/**Community**

in Thailand

"Community" is now everywhere in the vocabulary of modernization and development. International financial institutions such as the World Bank and the Asian Development Bank try to exert influence on how the term is to be used because, for them, community is a target of aid and financial assistance. In movements that espouse "community" as a moral ideal, the word has cachet for the right and the center, to say nothing of the strong leftist and anarchist associations of such words as "commune" and "communist" that one might think would discredit the moral ideal for some people. In an effort to challenge the logics of development, "community economy" has lately been championed as a post-development concept because of its emphasis on relationships and its potential as an ethical and politically progressive space.

The term "community" is notoriously slippery to define, partly because of the heavy investment that international financial institutions as well as NGOs have in the efficacy of its meanings. The term has almost too much significance. "Trying to study community," says one social scientist, "is like trying to scoop up jello with your fingers. You can get hold of some, but there's always more slipping away from you."[1] Yet for all of its amorphous, illusory, and elusive qualities, "community" continues to be valorized for its moral, spiritual, holistic, and utopian characteristics. Its powers to bind are reflected in its use in English to translate the Arabic *'umma*, the community of all those who profess Islam.[2] By the time the Prophet died in 632, the *'umma*/community was already seen as a new "super-tribe" that could transcend differences and unite Muslims, pagans, and Jews.[3] "Community" is an empowering word, even as it is exploited or manipulated by its natural enemies.

I was first drawn to "*chumchon*," the Thai word for community, while working on the historical antecedents of the Thai response to the Asian financial crisis of 1997. I was intrigued by the cluster of affinity words that traveled with "community" — words for self-sufficiency, subsistence economy, and local knowledge, or "native wisdom," as Thai public intellectuals prefer to translate it.[4] Although these words were already well known and actively deployed long before 1997 to debate the politics of the environment and resource management, they were given new currency at the height of the financial crisis. Thailand's most famous public intellectual, the king, gave a speech on 5 December 1997 in which he warned that people were living beyond their means. They should practice an "economics of enough-ness" (*setthakit phor phiang*).[5] The king's message was that people should be satisfied with what they needed and not consume unnecessarily, a stern admonition from the greatest moral authority in the land, which further boosted the fortunes of "community."

Here I trace some of the pathways by which "community/*chumchon*" acquired almost charismatic status in Thai public discourse — both the official discourse of the development bureaucracy as well as in the campaigns of critical urban intellectuals and NGO workers acting in concert with villagers and their elected representatives. One path by which community arrived in Thailand was in the late 1950s and 1960s via the language of development in which American aid programs were couched. But at least a decade before that time, Thai socialists, struggling to adapt Marxian thought in Thai, had used "*chumchon*" to translate Marx's "primitive commune." In the 1980s and early 1990s, NGOs and academics working in development began to champion community culture as a defense against the deleterious effects of development and state interference in village life. Foremost among those promoting community culture was Professor Chatthip Nartsupha, an economic historian whose research had long espoused the sanctity, autonomy, and self-sufficiency of village life. In addition to the anarchists and socialists who inspired Chatthip throughout his long career, he turned in the post-1997 period to the writings of Mahatma Gandhi, particularly Gandhi's notion of the Indian village as an independent republic, the *swaraj*. The genealogies of "community/*chumchon*" are thus multiple: Russian and Thai socialist thought; Western social science; American aid and development rhetoric; and the Gandhian village utopia.

Genealogies

"Community" as it appears in hallowed tenets of Marxian thought — the commune and the communist utopia — later encountered the structural and systemic tendencies of postwar American social science. Marxism and American social science, particularly as it became a servant of development theory, were both influential in propelling "community" into plans for the developing world, and Thailand was a strategic target for these studies after the Second World War.

In *Origin of the Family, Private Property, and the State* (1891), Friedrich Engels delved into a comparative study of early European family life and found communal or shared property and agricultural labor at the basis of early social life and village community as rooted in family community.[6] Engels doubtless drew on Marx's extended discussion in the *Grundrisse* about the relationship between human settlement, the commune, labor, and property in the age of primitive accumulation.[7] But the commune or community in the Marxian narrative is merely an early stage of human social life to be transformed by the economic forces of later modes of production. It is not an ideal form to which human beings can aspire, in the Marxian perspective, because it is an archaic form of social life. Still, communes exist in many societies. The Russian thinker N. G. Chernyshevskii (1828–89) imagined village communes as the basis of a socialism that would emerge following a peasants' revolution in the nineteenth century.[8] Communal living had a distinguished history in nineteenth-century America and returned with a flourish in the counter-culture movements of the 1960s and early 1970s, by which time it was estimated that there were between two and three thousand communes in the United States.[9]

The concept of community grew in the 1970s from a number of directions, most notably from the rediscovery of the 1887 work of Ferdinand Tönnies, who associated community with "intrinsic and non-logical values." Tönnies's distinction between *Gemeinschaft*, referring to "social situations of intimate relationships in which social status is ascribed, roles are diffuse, and styles of doing things are traditional," and its opposite, *Gesellschaft*, "social situations of large-scale impersonal relationships," cast a long shadow over sociology.[10] *Gemeinschaft* evoked "solidary, total, natural," whereas *Gesellschaft* pointed to "solitary, partial, contrived."[11] The same distinction holds in Russian, where "community" (*obshchina*) contains the root "*obshch*," meaning "common property" or "to hold in common." In both Soviet and post-Soviet dictionaries, community is said to be chiefly characteristic of primitive social structures, as in Marx's originating social formation, "the primitive commune."

The notion of community encapsulating "a total system of inter-connected and complementary relationships" can also be traced through the anthropological work of Robert Redfield published between 1947 and 1960. Jeremy Kemp, an anthropologist who has written several critical studies of social-scientific approaches to the study of Thailand, neatly summarizes the tendencies of this literature. Community study, he says, was in keeping with functionalist fashions of the day in that it "presented a rather static, corporatist image. Furthermore there was a trend towards an undue emphasis on order and, if not on actual cohesion, on the absence of divisions and conflict."[12] A lot of this social-scientific literature was bent on trying to single out the distinctive features of community as against other social units. But often what emerged was a primordial, timeless, traditional unit of rural organization whose basic assumptions went un-questioned.[13]

Typical of this literature is a work by the sociologist Dennis Poplin in which he contrasts "moral community" with "mass society," a distinction that derives from *Gemeinschaft* versus *Gesellschaft*. Individuals in commu-nities feel a sense of identity and unity with their group; they feel a sense of involvement and wholeness; they feel enmeshed in a tightly knit web of meaningful relationships.[14] Elsewhere, Poplin singles out what he calls the psycho-cultural dimension of the term while recognizing that many soci-ologists would prefer to keep the term squarely within a territorial defi-nition.[15] Here Poplin recognizes an Othering aspect to community, an inclusive–exclusive fencing off of outsiders by community members and the feeling of "we-ness" as opposed to "they." This is certainly one of the penumbra of meanings that has traveled with "community" as it entered the Thai language, a meaning sharpened by the response to the financial crisis of 1997 and the perceived assaults on Thai sovereignty, both national and local.

The history of "community/*chumchon*" in Thai might be described both as discontinuous and very recent. Although it is definitely a word with a past, it does not appear in the Thai–Thai dictionary of the Ameri-can missionary D. B. Bradley of the early 1870s; nor is there an entry for "*chumchon*" in the comprehensive if overly erudite McFarland Thai–English dictionary of 1944.[16] A Thai–Thai dictionary published as recently as 1950 also has no entry for "*chumchon*." Certainly, "*chumchon*" gained currency only in the postwar period.

The first term, "*chum*," literally means "to swarm"; the second, "*chon*," means "living beings, creatures," according to MacFarland, but derives ultimately from the Pali-Sanskrit term "*jana*" of similar meaning. Not all the Pali-Sanskrit forms sprinkled throughout the Thai language belong to the vocabulary of government, administration, or religion; some common words that have been in the language for centuries have Pali-Sanskrit pedigrees, despite their ordinariness. Separately, the terms "*chum*" and "*chon*" are very old. Both, for example, appear in the lexicon drawn from the Three Seals Law Code of the late eighteenth and early nineteenth centuries compiled by Japanese and Thai scholars, but they appear separately. The two apparently became fused for the first time only after the Second World War. Literally, then, the Thai word means something like "the coming together of people." "*Chumchon*" does not have the resonances of shared property or mutual assistance that the English word with its Latin pedigree possesses. Moreover, while "community/*chumchon*" can apply to both urban and rural communities, it is to the countryside, villages, and villagers that the term became attached. Sometimes the word "village" is combined with "community" to reinforce the rural dimension (*chumchon muban*).

Was this neologism the work of the royal wordsmith Prince Wan, who lists "*chumchon*" in a revised list of 1967 as one of the words he coined himself, possibly as early as 1934?[17] As an aristocrat, Prince Wan believed by birthright in the power of the elite to influence the language. For him, the very act of translation was "to put [the word] into circulation with a stamp of authority."[18] At the same time, he was a natural linguist, for he also knew that the word would not catch on if the language did not adopt it. "Criticism is inevitable and coiners of words must be prepared to face critics," he declared with his customary courtliness. He credited the speakers of the language with the power to decide whether or not the word would stick and called that power "the sanction of the genius of the language." In the case of "*chumchon*," the alliteration of palatals and nasals was agreeable to the Thai ear and helped ease the word into the language, as did its doubled form, also a Thai favorite. In his various papers and memoirs, Prince Wan cheerfully admits his failure with some of his coinages. They simply did not catch on. This is quite a Saussurean perspective for a diplomat trained in the law who had not been exposed to the structural turn in modern linguistics.

Of special interest for the history of community in the Thai language is the usage of "*chumchon*" by Thai socialists in the mid-1950s. Kulap Saipradit, a prolific political author, used "*chumchon*" to translate "primitive commune" in his *The Origins of the Family* and *The Human Social System*, of 1954, which borrowed heavily from Engels and Henry Morgan.[19] A few years later Jit Poumisak, arguably Thailand's most famous "political poet," followed Kulap's use of "*chumchon*" for "primitive commune" in his pathbreaking *The Real Face of Thai Feudalism Today*.[20] Yet "*chumchon*" was not firmly established as a translation for "commune" even by 1957. Other socialist authors used "*chomrom*" or "*chumnum*." The word was still in motion. At the same time that "community" was breaking into the Thai language via Marxian sociology, Japanese scholars began to debate "community" via a similar route. Hisao Ōtsuka published *Basic Theory of Community* in Japanese in 1955, which exploited an eclectic Weberian–Marxian sociology. Ōtsuka interpreted Marxian communities (Asiatic, Ancient, Germanic) as unilinear stages of development, a position that came under heavy criticism, with Japanese scholars through the early 1980s debating whether "commune/community" was a product of Western colonialism.[21] This serious Japanese interest in the meaning of "community" was to have repercussions in Thai studies in the late 1990s, as Thai economic historians and sociologists forged networks with Japanese scholars of a similar intellectual bent.

"*Chumchon*" entered the Thai bureaucratic lexicon just after midcentury as American aid flooded into the country for development projects. In a sense, "community" thus belongs to the history of the structuring of village society by the state.[22] In the detailed if mind-numbing histories of Thai ministries that make it possible to track the word "community/*chumchon*," we can see that at this stage it meant a distinct administrative level with fixed boundaries, perhaps close to "the village" (*ban* or *muban*) that lay beneath the district level and historically eluded the attentions of government.[23] As American aid increased in amount and strategic value, the Thai bureaucracy evolved to accommodate the aid, particularly in two ministries. For a decade after 1950 in the gargantuan Ministry of Interior, which from ancient times to the present day has been the fief of the most powerful officials and politicians in the country, plans were put forward for rural development, although they were rejected each time because of budgetary constraints.[24] Only when Field Marshal Sarit Thaanart came to power in 1958—"He was interested in development rather than democracy," says the ministry's history in an unguarded moment—did the money begin to flow for rural and community development. In 1962, a reform of the bureaucracy saw the creation of a Department of Community Development. This measure was seen, at least by the American aid authorities, as a means of training village workers to serve "as information conduits downward for advice from technical ministry officials, and channels upward for village ideas."[25]

"Community development" was important enough to inspire the launch in 1962 of the *Warasan phatthana chumchon* (Community Development Bulletin), an in-house publication of the Ministry of Interior. The bulletin carried news of meetings, some chaired by Field Marshal Sarit himself, and of projects concerning rural infrastructure, rural economy, education, and health. By the end of the decade, however, the bulletin had deteriorated into a soft, eclectic publication filled with cooking recipes and miscellaneous essays about tourism and democracy. Here, too, in May 1962 was evidence of a shift to "*chumchon*" as opposed to other words for community, such as "*thongthin*" (locale, the local), in play at the time. The links with American aid policy and its preoccupation with counterinsurgency were also evident. In a report published in the May 1962 issue of the bulletin, an American speaker, J. Sheldon Turner, identified as head of the Department of Community Development in the U.S. Operations Mission (USOM), the local office for the U.S. Agency for International Development, began his remarks by thanking his hosts, the Thai Psychological Warfare School, thus making plain the link between community development and counterinsurgency.[26]

The Ministry of Interior's history relates this particular version of the story with little mention of American aid. American planners probably found it awkward and time-consuming to deal with this ancient ministry, through which everything from policing to education has sometimes been administered, and the ministry itself was probably not as flexible or as responsive as the American aid agency might have wanted. In any case, the swiftly emerging regime of development programs and projects and concerns about rural insurgency led to the creation of an entirely new Ministry of National Development in June 1963, about six months before Sarit died. It was his creation, and he spoke at the opening ceremony of its establishment. One of the ministry's precursors was a committee that had been established in 1950 as a conduit for American aid and that eventually evolved into the Department of Technical and Economic Cooperation within the new Ministry of National Development. The Ministry of National Development's history acknowledges that the United States, through USOM, had assisted in 1957 with the establishment of a Community Development Project that later evolved into a Department of Community Development with responsibilities for agriculture, health, and education when the new ministry was established.[27] Community development was then becoming part of the global discourse of development. In Gunnar Myrdal's massive study of 1968, community development represented an effort "to spark a cumulative process of rural uplift in village societies encrusted by centuries of stagnation."[28]

Community development in midcentury Thailand — CD in the aid argot — as well as accelerated rural development, had demonstrable counterinsurgency functions. Especially in the Northeast where rural poverty was seen to breed insurgency, community development was a strategy for drawing villages and villagers closer to the sovereign government in order to keep them out of the hands of insurgents or communists. In the Thai bureaucracy's effort to grapple with the sub-sub-district level of the village community it tried to create another level of government activity. Something very similar happened in the history of British colonialism in Burma, where the hereditary circle headmen, the *myo-thu-gyis*, were turned into government officials to allow government infrastructure to penetrate further into the countryside.[29] The conversion of these hereditary officials into colonial officials weakened bonds of community beyond the village.[30]

Thus, "community/*chumchon*" acquired an identifiable history in the Thai bureaucracy in the name of administrative units charged with managing rural development programs; training officials and youth; improving the well-being of the community (*chumchon*); and improving rural productivity, family income and village industry, health facilities, and education.[31] The aims of these programs were strategic as much as human betterment. In the bureaucratic upheaval during the Sarit period, which began in 1957–58, the precise moment of the infusion of American aid, "*chumchon*" came to replace "*thongthin*" as if something new had come into being. "*Thongthin*" migrated into another semantic box and came to mean "local." The meanings of "community/*chumchon*" began to change again during the open politics of the 1973–76 period, when the government's rural development policy shifted away from the construction of infrastructure for farming and toward infrastructure for the community.[32] The village community was no longer merely poor, backward, and in desperate need of development. It was now to be esteemed for values and norms that were being eroded by modernity. In this sense, "community" was also an alternative to "modernity."

To close this discussion of the genealogies of the word, it is worth citing a provocative statement by Anan Ganjanaphan, a Thai anthropologist based in Chiang Mai who expresses more curiosity than most about the career of "community/*chumchon*" in Thai. He wonders whether *chumchon* is a figment of the academic imagination or a real thing that exists (or existed) and needs to be studied. "Is *chumchon* something real that previously existed in Thai society and is now being destroyed? Or is it an academic theoretical concept constructed for the purpose of analyzing society? Or is it an ideological and romantic thing? And if community (*chumchon*) really exists can we not ask to have its distinctive features described? Do these distinctive features still have consequences and the potential to influence social movements today?"[33] Anan is a hard-headed social scientist in sympathy with the NGO movement and with the attempts of academics to forge cooperative links with development workers, but as his searching questions about community suggest, he is skeptical of the discursive powers of "community" to forge or reify the relationships, participation, and autonomy the word is presumed to embody. He goes on to trace the career of the term "community" in the anthropological literature on Thailand, noting that the views of academic and government development workers in the 1960s were little different from the official attitudes in developing rural societies everywhere — namely, the view that "community life was terrible" and had to be corrected or improved.[34] This is not the view today — or, perhaps, it would be better to say it is only partly the view today.

Community Culture

In the boom times of the late 1980s and early 1990s, public intellectuals, academics working in development, and NGOs began to embrace something called "community culture" (*watthanatham chumchon*). The term "community culture" was not the creation of the bureaucracy or of government policy, and its history is fragmentary and difficult to document precisely. Although intellectuals had a hand in its creation, the idea grew out of seminars, workshops, and collective efforts to factor culture into development projects. One social scientist, Kanchana Kaewthep, who left academia for NGO work, points to the influence between conditions in Thailand in the late 1980s and the resolution of the United Nations General Assembly to make 1988–97 the "World Decade of Cultural Development." The economic boom in Thailand spurred the export of "Made in Thailand" brands in world markets, and a public fuss in 1988 about a purloined Khmer lintel discovered in the Art Institute in Chicago pricked the national consciousness about Thai culture slipping away overseas.[35] Actually, in this case it was not Thai culture but Cambodian heritage being appropriated as Thai. In Kanchana's telling of the story, culture was ignored in development policies of the late 1950s and 1960s, but now, in the second half of the 1980s, development theorists were disenchanted with economic development "from outside," which did not take local culture into account. UNESCO and other global organizations were also taking cognizance of culture and fostering "indigenous theories of development."[36]

Typical of this shift in alternative development strategies in Thailand was interest in Mahatma Gandhi; some of Gandhi's work on the village was translated, published, and disseminated in Thailand in 1985.[37] What NGO workers in Thailand found appealing is epitomized in the classic Gandhian statement on the village that dates from 1942: "My idea of village *swaraj* is that it is a complete republic, independent of its neighbors for its own vital wants, and yet interdependent for many others in which dependence is a necessity. Thus every village's first concern will be to grow its own food crops and cotton for its cloth.... Any village can become such a republic today without much interference even from the present Government whose sole effective connection with the village is the exaction of the village revenue."[38] For Gandhi, self-sufficiency, one of the affinity words of "community/*chumchon*," does not connote "narrowness" or isolation, since villagers may venture outside the village for some of the things they need.[39]

Gandhi's thinking about the village resurfaced again in the late 1990s in the work of Chatthip Nartsupha, who drew together different strands of the "community culture" movement in his advocacy for it. In an intensively researched volume funded by the Thailand Research Fund in 1998, Chatthip paid homage to all of his heroes: the nineteenth- and twentieth-century Russian socialist thinkers; Gandhiji and Village *Swaraj*; Latin American economic historians; and the more recent community cultural-ists.[40] Chatthip is an economic historian known for his Marxist interventions in the tumultuous 1970s and for founding a Chatthip "school" of economic history through his supervision of numerous graduate students. For two decades, his approach to economic history had repercussions in Thai debates about development and the impact of the global economy on small producers. Even before the 1997 crisis he had embraced "community culture" as an alternative response to the unintended consequences of rampant growth. Having been introduced early in his education to the work of Kropotkin (*Mutual Aid: A Factor of Evolution*) and to Alexander Herzen's vision of a peasant revolution that would bring forth small village communes, he sees himself — and has been described as — a "communitarian anarchist."[41] Reading Chatthip's work gives the distinct impression that he has already found these communes in the Thai countryside. He is an "intellectual" Buddhist and not a very pious one. He hates what he calls "superstition" in the animistic practices of ordinary Thai people but always respectfully acknowledges the importance of Buddhism at all levels of Thai life.

English readers now have access to Chatthip's *The Thai Village Economy in the Past* in which he argued that subsistence economies in rural Thailand continued through the late twentieth century in some regions.[42] Indeed, peasant economies tend to be defined as subsistence agriculturalist.[43] Many times Chatthip has stated the argument that the village community is one of the most ancient institutions of Thai society; that the economic base of the village community was subsistence production and craft for its own use; that the kinship structure supported the communal nature of village life; and that the village community was a self-sustaining and relatively autonomous unit.[44] He cites a 1978 World Bank report on Thailand that documented a subsistence economy in most rural areas at the start of the first six-year development plan of 1961.[45] This picture of autonomous village communities sounds very much like a modified version of Marx's Asiatic Mode of Production (AMP), and indeed, such an analysis can be seen to be an outgrowth of Chatthip's endorsement of the AMP view during the 1970s. In *The Thai Village Economy in the Past*, however, Chatthip turned away slightly from the AMP and rejected some of his earlier work that failed to recognize the extent to which the subsistence economy continued well into the middle of the twentieth century. In his revised thinking, the subsistence economy stalled, as it were, and failed to develop. Partly this happened because capitalism was fostered by — or was in cahoots with — the state as it sought to perpetuate some areas of the country in subsistence economies as sources of cheap labor. Chatthip's ongoing adherence to the AMP as a social formation appropriate to Thailand's economic history is difficult to understand without reading Gandhi on Village *Swaraj*. Chatthip is really what one might call a Gandhian Marxist and "thought" Gandhi before he had actually read him.

For Chatthip, the state and capitalism are "outside" institutions, "foreign" and "unnatural" to village life, and villagers resent them both. In his earlier work on the ideology of millennial movements Chatthip wrote about "primitive communal consciousness" sustaining the village community in its resistance to outside influence.[46] More recently, he advocated community culture for its spirit, "heart" (*nam jai*), and great inner strength; perhaps he would also say solidarity. Because Thailand was never directly colonized, the state did not intervene directly in production and culture. There was no plantation economy. The premodern state merely collected taxes and levied corvée demands, leaving the village basically to its own devices. Although the village economy lacks dynamism and its sturdiness and durability can be obstacles to its development, Chatthip believes it can be a force in the contemporary world. At times he seems to be saying that "this is not poverty" but a praiseworthy way of life that we should try to preserve. He argues that because the village community was spared interference by the state and retained its integrity, it can be a leader in economic development in a way that bourgeois culture cannot.[47]

One interesting aspect of Chatthip's thinking is his interaction with Japanese anthropologists and sociologists — which derives from Japanese interests in community and the village that date from the 1950s — and even the occasional European social scientist. Many of these scholars contributed to a recent felicitation volume on village communities in honor of Chathip.[48] A brief, undocumented essay by the Hungarian scholar Ferenc Tokei returned to many of Chatthip's favorite themes: the commune (or the land community, as Tokei calls it in the Hungarian case) in world history; property relations and redistribution of land in the commune; and the dissolution of communities under certain historical circumstances. One Japanese contributor revisited the village commune in the eyes of A. S. Khomiakov, D. N. Strukov, and N. G. Chernyshevskii, and another Japanese scholar discussed cooperative ventures in rural development through the work of Thai Buddhist monks. A Thai political economist studied "the buds of community business under capitalist domination." The scholarly networks Chatthip cultivated over three decades and his catholic reading—not many Thai academics have looked into the history of socialism in tsarist Russia—help account for the way in which the qualities of the commune have been inserted into the Thai *chumchon*. Some of these qualities, such as mutual cooperation and generosity, that are attributed to community in this literature go beyond the evidence. According to one astute assessment of how this scholarship has been applied to the Shan people in northern Thailand, "communal" is "hyped" to the extent that Thai interpretations of their largely rural siblings, the Shan, demonstrate an elite Thai yearning for simplicity and tradition. At the same time, an impulse for authenticity and unity in these interpretations muddies differences between Shan in Burma and Shan in Thailand in the name of Thai community, or Thai-ness, though this objective is almost never made explicit.[49]

Chatthip, a keen advocate of the "community culture" movement, has produced one of its most complete histories in Thai, linking it to the work of four intellectuals.[50] One is Bamrung Bunpanya, from a wealthy peasant family in Surin Province and a graduate of Kasetsart University. Another is Apichart Thongyu, a middle-class graduate in geography and lecturer (in 1991) in the Central Region Public Health College. Apichart has worked in development for the Norwegian Save the Children Fund, and once upon a time he was a freelance musician and painter. He is also a poet. The third public intellectual, Prawet Wasi, is perhaps best known in the development field. He is a hematologist, a graduate in medicine from Mahidol University and the University of Colorado, and a longtime critic of government who manages to retain the confidence and respect of the elite and those in power. Finally, there is Father Niphot Thianwihan, director (in 1991) of the Center for Social Development of the Catholic Council of Thailand for Development (CCTD), who has worked with the Karen. According to Chatthip's account, Father Niphot began to develop the "community culture line of thinking" in 1977, following a meeting of the Federation of Asian Bishops in Taipei in 1974 and a meeting of the Bishops' Institute for Social Action held in the Philippines.[51] What these people have in common, with the exception of Bamrung Bunpanya, is they did not grow up in community culture.

While "community culture" has currency in the region and across religions, according to Chatthip's account, it is not altogether clear what inspired Father Niphot to develop his community culture idea. What can be said is that the conference of bishops wanted to contextualize evangelical work in Asian societies where Catholicism had to compete with religions such as Hinduism and Buddhism. The centralized, institutional church encountered the limits of its authority as it came up against local community.[52] Interestingly, considering that Thailand has a majority Theravada Buddhist population, the Catholic church played a major role in funding projects and disseminating the idea of community culture. Through the CCTD, established in 1960, it published a number of books by these public intellectuals and development workers, including Kanchana Kaewthep. In her own writing she acknowledges the work of a Catholic priest, Father Philippe Fanchette, in arguing for the importance of recognizing local culture in development projects.[53]

A final example of how community has been launched into the realm of social movements may be seen in the work of Phitthaya Wongkun, a social scientist and public intellectual who worked on a series of publications called the Vision series, under the overall editorial guidance of Thianchai Wongchaisuwan, who studied with James Petras and Immanuel Wallerstein at the State University of New York, Binghamton.[54] These volumes, funded originally by the government's Thailand Research Fund, appeared at the astonishing rate of about one per month since the 1997 financial crisis. There were two separate series: one on globalization, and the other on local knowledge. Phitthaya contributed to many of the volumes and in 1999 produced a book of his own, *Building a New Society: Communitocracy — Dhammocracy*.[55] Here community is both a governance word — rule by the community and by *Dhamma*, the teachings of the Buddha — and a word that implies certain social practices and politics.

Whereas Chatthip combined ethnography and economic history with a sense of the movement of "commune/community" across cultures, languages, and the East–West divide, Phitthaya was more interested in community as a political movement. He discussed strategies, maneuvers, and methods for achieving his goals. He wanted to reform the economy — eliminate the income gaps, halt the severe damage to the environment that was taking place; create a just society and more humane politics. Genuine reform would bring a kind of Buddhist Utopia — and, indeed, the penname of his Phittaya's collaborator, Thienchai, is "Age of the Maitreya Buddha." Phitthaya's approach to the problems reminds us that just as there are families of affinity words of which community is a part, so there is a dialectics of words — and word play — that sharpens their meanings. Community is pitted against state "above" and outside, and against, family below and "inside." According to Phitthaya, community is superior to family, as family is too nuclear and individualistic. Community also contrasts with village, especially in contexts where the state has imposed the village order or set out bossy plans for its development.

It is difficult to say whether the advocacy of "community culture" should be identified as a new social movement, as some academic observers, such as the Thammasat University political scientist Chairat Charoensinolan suggest.[56] Without wanting to join Chairat in seeing community culture as a discursive invention of academics and public intellectuals, I think its use as a polemic against inappropriate models of development and undue interference from the outside is undeniable. The lingering lure of community culture has to do with its ineffable qualities of shared labor, reciprocity, and resistance to the outside menace of bureaucracy and meddling development workers. When some of these ideas are translated into English, they sound irredeemably romantic and anachronistic, or just plain messy and hard to handle — the jello metaphor comes to mind — but the people who use these ideas sincerely seem to be able to overlook and even to embrace such shortcomings.

On the Defensive

Reading through the voluminous and sometimes repetitive literature about community and community culture I was reminded of the Vietnamese folk saying that the power of the emperor comes to a halt at the bamboo fence of the village. There are a host of statements in Thai about the ability of the community — or the village community — to withstand or resist threats from the outside. Here we are talking about the bounded territorial community, to use the old sociological terminology, rather than about networks or virtual communities of scholars and NGO workers or about community/village as a discursive category.[57] We can recall the late 1950s when the Thai government captured "*chumchon*" to designate a bounded administrative unit that could serve policy interests, delimiting community and reorienting those who live there. This deployment of community has been a long-standing interest of the Thai state. While the authenticity of Apichart Thongyu, a middle-class lecturer in geography and advocate of community culture, as a village voice may be suspect since he is not of the village even if he has lived in one, his poems often refer to the village-under-development as if it were bounded by that proverbial bamboo fence.

The sentiments in his verses extol village labor, particularly the agricultural labor that produces the food that feeds the rest of the country.[58] The poems use the language of the city, of bureaucracy, and of the specialized sciences that apply their expertise to development "problems" in order to illustrate the irrelevance of these outside worlds for daily village life. Whether or not this is an unrealistic approach to village development, I suggest that the autonomy, self-sufficiency, and self-containedness described here echo the hoary caricature that features in Marx's oversimplified and out-of-date primitive, Asiatic commune.

The prehistory of the word "community/*chumchon*" in a language spoken by millions of peasant agriculturalists over ten centuries lies in the village, although as I have tried to show, the career of the word is discontinuous at best. Communal land was made available to these peasants, and they enjoyed help from fellow villagers, which they reciprocated, when they worked their paddy fields. Their labor and its fruits were taxed by the premodern feudal state. The term for village in Thai languages — and it is an old term — is "*ban*," which can be paired with the term for city or state, "*muang*," to mean homeland or native land (*ban muang*). *Ban* also refers to domestication and cultivation and is opposed to jungle or wild (*pa*).[59] "Community/*chumchon*" only has the force it has in modern parlance as a word traveling into and out of the language and into and out of international conversations about development because its discontinuous history is anchored in older if idealized notions of village, villager, and village life. As "community" has been advocated through the community culture movement and fortified by contact with Japanese social scientists and their own encounter with "community," it has shaken off its postwar history in the bureaucracy of development to acquire decidedly Gandhian meanings. Conferences of Roman Catholic theologians also played their part in reinvesting "community" with moral force. The hybrid version of "community/*chumchon*," which now prevails, contains elements of development, identity, and political empowerment, but it also bears traces of an earlier social formation in the primitive commune. Many village leaders, NGOs, and engaged anthropologists are able to overlook the static character of the earlier social formation and champion "community/*chumchon*" as a worthy opponent against the state and globalized capitalism. When one looks closely at the word "community," valorized for empowering its proprietors to withstand the disruptive effects of progress and development, it would seem that both Uncle Karl and Uncle Sam have a lot to answer for.

Notes

1. Marcia Pelly Effrat, ed., *The Community: Approaches and Applications* (New York: Free Press, 1974), 1.

2. Virginia Hooker, "Islamic Perspectives on the New Millennium," in *Islamic Perspectives on the New Millennium*, ed. Virginia Hooker and Amin Saikal (Singapore: Institute of Southeast Asian Studies, 2004), 3.

3. Karen Armstrong, *Islam: A Short History* (London: Phoenix Press, 2001), 5–12.

4. Craig J. Reynolds, "Thai Identity in the Age of Globalization," in *National Identity and Its Defenders: Thailand Today*, ed. Craig J. Reynolds (Chiang Mai: Silkworm Books, 2002).

5. "*Setthakit phor phiang*" is usually translated as a "sufficiency economy" or "economic self-sufficiency," but I prefer "the economics of enough-ness," an imaginative translation for which I am indebted to my colleague, the economist Peter Warr, Research School of Pacific Studies, Australian National University.

6. Friedrich Engels, *The Origin of the Family, Private Property, and the State* (New York: Pathfinder Press, 1972).

7. Karl Marx, *Grundrisse, Foundations of the Critique of Political Economy*, trans. Martin Nicolaus (Harmondsworth: Penguin Books, 1973), 472–501.

8. Takeo *Suzuki*, "Modernization and the Village Commune in Russia: Intellectuals' Discussion on the Eve of the Emancipation of the Serfs in 1861," in *Village Communities, States, and Traders*, ed. Nozaki Akira and Chris Baker (Bangkok: Thai–Japanese Seminar and Sangsan Press, 2003), 88–90.

9. Dennis E. Poplin, *Communities: A Survey of Theories and Methods of Research* (New York: Macmillan, 1979), 60.

10. Effrat, *The Community*, 28.

11. Charles Tilly, "Do Communities Act?" in Effrat, *The Community*, 209–40.

12. Jeremy Kemp, *Seductive Image: The Search for the Village Community in Southeast Asia* (Amsterdam: Center for Asian Studies, 1987), 5–6.

13. Jeremy H. Kemp, "The Dialectics of Village and State in Modern Thailand," in *The Village Concept in the Transformation of Rural Southeast Asia*, ed. Mason C. Hoadley and Christer Gunnarsson (Richmond: Curzon Press, 1996), 45.

14. Poplin, *Communities*, 5.

15. Ibid., 18–19.

16. George Bradley McFarland, *Thai–English Dictionary* (Stanford, Calif.: Stanford University Press, 1944).

17. Prince Narathipphongpraphan, Krommamun, *Witthayathat phra-ong wan*

[Learned views of Prince Wan] (Bangkok: Prince Narathippraphanphong Foundation, 2001). Prince Wan, who served as a chair of the Thai Parliament's select committee on the charge of communism being leveled at Pridi Phanomyong, one of the leaders of the 1932 revolution, was most likely responsible for the coinage in the mid-1930s: Kasian Tejapira, personal communication, 8 June 2004. I am very grateful to Kasian for comments on my account of the longer history of the word "*chumchon.*"

18. Prince Narathipphongpraphan, *Learned Views of Prince Wan,* 107.

19. Kulap Saipradit, *Kamnoet khong khropkhrua* [The origins of the family] and *Rabiap sangkhom khong manut* [The human social system] (Bangkok: Phiphi Press, 1954).

20. Translated in Craig J. Reynolds, *Thai Radical Discourse: The Real Face of Thai Feudalism Today* (Ithaca, N.Y.: Cornell University, Southeast Asia Program, 1994).

21. Atsushi *Kitahara, The Thai Rural Community Reconsidered: Historical Community Formation and Contemporary Development Movements* (Bangkok: Chulalongkorn University, Faculty of Economics, Political Economy Centre, 1996), Section 2, 74–75.

22. The process is described in Craig Johnson, "State and Community in Rural Thailand: Village Society in Historical Perspective," *The Asia Pacific Journal of Anthropology* 2, no. 2 (September 2001): 114–134.

23. Anan Kanachanaphan, *Miti chumchon withikhhit thongthin wa duay sitthi amnat le kanchat kansaphayakorn* [The issue of community: how to think about locality in terms of rights, power and resource management] (Bangkok: Thailand Research Fund, 2001), 111.

24. Ministry of Interior, *Thiraluk khlai wan sathapana krasuang mahatthai* [Remembering Foundation Day of the Ministry of Interior] (Bangkok: Ministry of Interior, 1965), 256–258.

25. J. Alexander Caldwell, *American Economic Aid to Thailand* (Lexington, Mass.: Lexington Books, 1974), 57.

26. Ministry of Interior, *Community Development Bulletin* 1.2 (May 1962), 1.

27. Ministry of National Development, *Prawat lae ratchakan khong krasuang phattahanakan haeng chat* [History and work of the Ministry of National Development] (Bangkok: Ministry of National Development, 1964), 229.

28. Gunnar Myrdal, *Asian Drama: An Inquiry into the Poverty of Nations,* vol. 2 (New York: Pantheon, 1968), 1339.

29. J. S. Furnivall, *Colonial Policy and Practice: A Comparative Study of Burma and Netherlands India* (New York: New York University Press, 1956), 36–37.

30. Robert H. Taylor, *The State in Burma* (Honolulu: University of Hawai'i Press, 1987), 161.

31. Ministry of Interior, *Thiraluk khlai wan sathapana krasuang mahatthai* [Remembering Foundation Day of the Ministry of Interior], 260–261.

32. *Kitahara, The Thai Rural Community Reconsidered,* 30.

33. Anan Kanachanaphan, *Miti chumchon withikhhit thongthin wa duay sitthi amnat le kanchat kansaphayakorn* [The issue of community: how to think about locality in terms of rights, power and resource management].

34. Ibid., 113.

35. *Kanphattana naew watthanatham chumchon* [Developing community culture] comp. Kanchana Kaewthep (Bangkok: Catholic Council of Thailand for Development, 1995), 72.

36. Ibid., 74–75.

37. See Apichart Thongyou, "Thai NGOs and Rural Development: Formation, Growth, and Branching Out," in *The NGO Way: Perspectives and Experiences from Thailand*, ed. Shinichi *Shigetomi* et al. (Chiba, Japan: Institute of Developing Economies, Japan External Trade Organization, 2004), 157, 175, n14. Generally, Gandhi's ideas are under-researched and insufficiently recognized in Thai studies.

38. Gandhi's classic statement about the village *swaraj* is reproduced in Mahatma Gandhi, *The Essential Writings of Mahatma Gandhi* (Delhi: Oxford University Press, 1991), 358–360.

39. Mahatma Gandhi, *Village Swaraj* (Ahmedabad: Navajivan Trust, 1962), 63.

40. Chatthip Nartsupha, *Thrutsadi lae naewkhit setthakit chumchon chaona* [Peasant communities: economic theory and thought] (Bangkok: Withithat Project, 1998).

41. Chatthip Nartsupha, *Naewkhit setthakit chumchon kho sanoe thang thrutsadi nai boribot tang sangkhom* [Community economic thought: theoretical proposals in different social contexts] (Bangkok: Khrongkan Withithat, 2001), 12.

42. Chatthip Nartsupha, *The Thai Village Economy in the Past* (*Setthakit mu ban thai nai adit*), trans. Chris Baker and Pasuk Phongpaichit (1984; repr., Chiang Mai: Silkworm Books, 1999).

43. Robert E. Elson, *The End of the Peasantry in Southeast Asia: A Social and Economic History of Peasant Livelihood, 1800–1990s* (New York: St. Martin's Press, 1997), xix.

44. Chatthip Nartsupha, "The Village Economy in Pre-Capitalist Thailand," 69–70.

45. Ibid., 72.

46. Chatthip Nartsupha, "The Ideology of Holy Men Revolts" in ed. Andrew Turton and Shigeharu *Tanabe*, *History and Peasant Consciousness in South East Asia* (Osaka: National Museum of Ethnology Senri Ethnological Studies, 1984), 111–134.

47. Chatthip Nartsupha, *Prawattisat watthanatham chumchon lae chonchat tai* [History of community culture and the Tai races] (Bangkok: Chulalongkorn University, 1997), 99–103.

48. *Village Communities, States, and Traders*, ed. *Nozaki* Akira and Chris Baker (Bangkok, Thai-Japanese Seminar and Sangsan Press, 2003).

49. Properly speaking, the word should be "Tai-ness," since "Tai" here refers to the entire language family (Shan, Lao, Zhuang, Ahom as well as Thai), whereas "Thai" refers to the national language of Thailand and its speakers. Nicholas Farrelly, *Focus on the Tai Village: Thai Interpretations of the Shan along the Tai-Burma Border* (Canberra: Australian National University, Bachelor of Asian Studies Honours Thesis, 2003), especially ch. 3 and 4.

50. Chatthip Nartsupha, "The 'Community Culture' School of Thought" in *Thai Constructions of Knowledge*, ed. Manas Chitakasem and Andrew Turton, (London: University of London, School of Oriental and African Studies, 1991), 118–141.

51. Father Niphot's articles are collected in *The Idea of Community Culture in Development* (1988), which I have not been able to consult.

52. S. J. Michael Amaladoss, *Together Towards the Kingdom: An Emerging Asian Theology* at www.uni-tuebingen.de/INSeCT/wwide/asia-amaladoss.pdf (International Network of Societies for Catholic Theology) (Accessed on 19 August 2004).

53. *Kanphattana naew watthanatham chumchon* [Developing community culture], 71.

54. Reynolds, "Thai Identity in the Age of Globalization," 322–324.

55. Phittaya Wongkun, *Sang sankhom mai chumchanathipatai thammathipatai* [Building a new society: communitocracy — dhammocaracy], vol. 9 (Bangkok: Khrongkan withithat Local Knowledge Series, 1999).

56. Chairat Charoensinolan, *Watthakam kanphattana amnat khawamru khwamching ekkalak lae khwampenun* [Development discourse: Power, knowledge, truth, identity and otherness] (Bangkok: Center for Research and Textbook Production, Krirk University, 1999), 135–60.

57. Philip Hirsch, "Bounded Villages and the State on the Thai Periphery," in *The Village in Perspective: Community and Locality in Rural Thailand*, ed. Philip Hirsch (Chiang Mai: Chiang Mai University, Social Research Institute, 1993), 50; idem, "What Is *the* Thai Village?" in Reynolds, *National Identity and Its Defenders*.

58. Apichart Thongyou, *Simplicity amidst Complexity: Lessons from a Thai Village*, trans. James Hopkins (Bankok: Moo Ban Press, 1988), 39, 61, 131.

59. Andrew Turton, "Introduction," in *Civility and Savagery: Social Identity in Tai States*, ed. Andrew Turton (Richmond, Surrey: Curzon Press, 2000), 21–22.

Thammarat/Good Governance

in Glocalizing Thailand

In the summer of 1997, in the aftermath of the most severe financial crisis in Thai history, the term "good governance," conveyed by the IMF, was hastily reincarnated in the Thai language as the word "*thammarat.*" Although obviously prompted by the impending diktat of the global financial regime, its Thai inventor, Professor Chaiwat Satha-anand of the Faculty of Political Science at Thammasat University, and its chief public advocate, Thirayuth Boonmi, a lecturer in the Faculty of Sociology and Anthropology, explicitly stated that the intention behind the Thai coinage was to create a space for the interpretation of good governance in Thai cultural politics that was relatively autonomous from IMF meanings and policy imperatives.

Here I follow the reception of the word "*thammarat*" among different political groups in the Thai polity, including the authoritarian military establishment, the liberal corporate elite, and communitarian public intellectuals and activists. My intention is to highlight the ways in which debates about the meaning of "good governance" did indeed provide a space for different groups to negotiate with one another about the proper nature of the state, the market, and society more generally at a time when these concepts were being called into question. In fact, different political actors on the Thai scene staged debates through IMF language that went far beyond the wildest dreams of any IMF functionary.

Modern political history in Thailand has long been marked by explicit debates about the translation of foreign concepts. Successive generations of bilingual Thai intellectuals argued about translation as both an apparatus of capture of and also a buffer against Western-style modernity. Given Thailand's distinctive state-nationalized language, scripts, and sounds,

Western modernity has been consciously hindered from coming to the Thai public in its pristine, original, or direct linguistic forms. Thai intellectuals of all political persuasions have guarded these linguistic borders and the integrity of the Thai nation-state's "body cultural."[1] Each has tried to screen new translated lexical immigrants, turn away suspicious ones, or retranslate them in such a way as to civilize, harness, or domesticate them. Meanwhile, their unofficial counterparts incessantly sought to smuggle in and procreate illegitimate lexicons of their own unauthorized translations. Hence, the highly politicized nature of the process of translation-as-transformation through which key foreign political and ideological words were scrutinized, mediated, negotiated, contested, selected, modified, and kept under constant surveillance as they underwent their cross-cultural metamorphoses.

This process of translation-as-transformation was shaped by the Thai language itself: popular speech and literary genres emphasize end-sound rhyming. Thus, if new coinages were to gain wide circulation, they could not merely be transliterated from their native languages. They had to be *transformed* into Thai — that is, they had to be situated both within pre-existing structures of lexical meaning and aural aesthetics at the same time that they pushed the boundaries of these sociopolitical language norms. In simpler terms, they had to sound good to the Thai ear, which listens for and desires certain patterns of language, especially those of rhyme. The process of translation-as-transformation points both to the specific ways in which the entrance of foreign terms has been seen as an important site for political intervention by various official translators in Thailand and also to the flexibility and generativity of Thai rhyming genres.

A Nation of Rhymers

Rhymes allow us to say the same thing over and over again lengthily, verbosely, gracefully, powerfully, rhythmically, and rhymingly, making it easy to remember and recite or sing. Through their newly acquired musicality and sheer recitation, these words circulate and mobilize, sometimes conjuring hundreds of thousands of people to the streets and moving them to fight, to kill, and to die.

Rhyming is an everyday linguistic practice as well as the centerpiece of an ideology of culture, as attested to by two chief representatives from opposite political camps of modern Thai poetry: No.Mo.So., alias Prince

Phitthayalongkorn (1877–1945), a staunch royalist, and Intharayut, alias
Atsani Phonlajan (1918–87), a diehard communist. No.Mo.So wrote:

> Thailand Is a Nation of Rhymers. Siamese Thais are rhymers by habit.
> There are plenty of poets from the highest to the lowest classes. Some of
> them are scholars but many more are illiterates. The scholars who become
> poets may do so because of their literacy as well as disposition. But the
> illiterates do so purely on account of their disposition. If we are to publish
> a collection of all the verses composed by these illiterate rhymers in a year,
> it will take up a great many volumes. . . . If one is to estimate what
> percentage of the population of this country are rhymers, the figure should
> not be less than that of any other country in the world. We love rhyming so
> much that we versify not only in our own traditional genres, but also in
> those of other languages. And once we get hold of them, we do not follow
> their original version but modify them to suit our ears by adding rhymes,
> thus making them much more difficult.[2]

Intharayut puts it in more concise terms: "Thai people are rhymers by
habit. The sweet-sounding saying of rhymes is almost a commonplace, but
its content is another matter."[3]

Translated words were perfectly admissible and convenient candidates
for inclusion in Thai poetry for the simple reason that they were much
easier to rhyme with other Thai words than were their original foreign
equivalents. Not only could translated words be intentionally cast to fit
poetic genres, but they could also be cast to fit the politics of the translator.

One way to make sense of the Thai-style politics of translation is to
compare it with the start of a snooker game, in which a player hits a white
ball against a triangular formation of other balls so that, on impact, the
balls scatter and go their separate ways. It is as if, once imported or smuggled across linguistic boundaries, stripped of their original foreign script
and sound, made to incarnate Thai meanings, thrown into a new semantic
field, and then shoved into various Thai verse genres, those poor alien
words run into a virtual minefield of rhyming, syllabic, accentual, rhyth-
mic, and tonal rules that follow a totally disparate logic. They cannot help
but enter into a new pattern of multifaceted relationships with pre-existing Thai words, with etymological roots, denotations, connotations, and
associations completely unrelated to the original foreign words and absent
from their respective languages of origin. Crashing into these cultural
obstacles head on, they disintegrate on impact into free-floating political

signifiers, multiple signifieds, substituted referents, and incongruous practices, each going its own separate, mind-boggling, centrifugal way. The cultural and political travails of recollecting, reintegrating, reinterpreting, and redeeming these fragments are left for later generations of Thai intellectuals to carry out.

Official Neologisms: Translation as Politics

About six months after the overthrow of the absolute monarchy, in December 1932, Prince Narathipphongpraphan (alias Mom Chao Wan Waithayakon Worawan or Prince Wan),[4] the soon-to-be-appointed chairperson of the Rajbandittayasathan (the Royal Institute, which was the Thai equivalent of the British Royal Academy) and prolific Oxford-educated authority on modern Thai coinages, laid down what was to become the reigning principle of Thai official neologisms: "It is the Thai language that will guarantee the security of the Thai nation. This is because if we favor the use of Thai transliterations of Western words about ideas, we may walk too fast. That is, we may imitate other people's ideas directly instead of premodifying them in accord with our ideas. But if we use Thai words and hence must coin new ones, we will have to walk deliberately."[5]

During the four decades or so in which Prince Wan was involved with the work of the Royal Institute's Coinage and Dictionary editorial committees, he took on the coinage of Thai equivalents of Western words with enthusiasm. In his mission to stabilize the Thai nation amid the influx of Western modernity, as well as to tame and turn Western modernism into Thai-fied conservatism, the Prince managed to invent, along with hundreds of others, the following key Thai political coinages: *sangkhom* (society), *setthakij* (economy), *nayobai* (policy), *rabob* (system), *raborb* (regime), *phatthana* (development), *patiwat* (revolution), *patiroop* (reform), *wiwat* (evolution), *kammachip* (proletariat), *kradumphi* (bourgeoisie), *mualchon* (masses), *sangkhomniyom* (socialism), *ongkan* (organization), *sahaphap* (union), *watthanatham* (culture), *wiphak* (critique), *judyeun* (standpoint), *pratya* (philosophy), *atthaniyom* (realism), and *jintaniyom* (romanticism). With such a broad range of official terms, all modern political discourse in Thailand—of any political persuasion—draws on the lexicon of Prince Wan.

We can thus turn to translations as an important source for understanding Thai history. The following are examples of the politics behind—and beyond—some of these official coinages:

REVOLUTION : Prince Wan's coinage for revolution in Thai was "*pa-tiwat*," which literally means "turning or rolling back." It thus has a conservative connotation of restoration rather than denoting a radical break with the past or a progressive and qualitative change of affairs, as in the English original. Dissatisfied with the conservative connotation of Prince Wan's "*patiwat*," Pridi Banomyong,⁶ himself a democratic socialist revolutionary and leader of the constitutionalist revolution of 1932, coined the word "*aphiwat*" instead, which literally denotes "super-evolution."

COMMUNISM : Although Prince Wan did tentatively coin a couple of Thai words for communism as early as 1934, including "*Latthi niyom mualchon*" and "*Sapsatharananiyom*" (literally "Massism" and "Pan-Publicism," respectively), the transliterated version "*Khommunist*" has been universally adopted in both official and popular usages to this day. Sulak Sivaraksa, a radical, conservative royalist intellectual and noted cultural critic, has suggested that the reason for this might be to maintain the alien sound and appearance of the word and the idea — to deny it a legitimate place in the Thai language and keep it forever as the un-Thai Other at the lexical gate, so to speak. The radical leftists' subsequent attempt to coin a new Thai word for communism (such as Atsani Phonlajan's "*Latthi sahachip*," literally meaning "Unionism") failed to catch on.

DEMOCRACY : The present Thai equivalent of democracy is "*prachathipatai*," which, curiously enough, was coined by King Rama VI as early as 1912 to mean a "republic" (i.e., a government with no king). The shift in its meaning from "republic" to "democracy" followed from a compromise between the People's Party and King Rama VII during the revolution of 1932 when a constitutional monarchy was chosen in place of a republic. Thus, Thailand's present political system is characterized as "*rabob prachathipatai an mi phramahakasat song pen pramuk*," or, if one sticks to the original meaning of "*prachathipatai*," "republic with the king as head of state," an oxymoron made possible by the successful taming of a foreign-derived signifier.

BOURGEOISIE : Prince Wan chose a neutral-sounding and low-key translation of bourgeoisie as "*kradumphi*," literally meaning "the well-off" or "a householder." Atsani Phonlajan, alias Naiphi or "Specter" in English, a multilingual genius in the Thai language and etymology and probably the most erudite and sophisticated among Thai communist intellectuals,[7] re-translated the bourgeoisie as *"phaessaya,"* a Sanskrit-derived Thai word that has the notable double meaning of a "merchant class" or "a prostitute or bitch."

WORKER : A pioneering group of ethnic Thai labor-union activists and organizers in the 1920s deliberately chose to call their organization and affiliated newspaper *Kammakorn*, a Thai word with a residual meaning of "slavery and cruel punishment," as the Thai equivalent of "worker" in English. The authorities did not like its negative connotation and have waged a protracted war against the word *"kammakorn"* ever since. The official dictionary of the Ministry of Public Instruction published in 1927, as well as that of the Royal Institute issued in 1950, added an unusual note of caution to the entry specifically to explain that *"kammakorn"* was not a slave but should be thought of in a manner similar to the English "labour (labouring class)."[8] In 1956, General Phao Sriyanond, then the chief of police, bargained with delegates of the radical labor-union movement for a change in the Thai rendering of May Day from *Wan kammakorn* to *Wan raengngan* (or from Worker Day to Labor Day) as a precondition for allowing a public celebration on that date. More than thirty years later, General Prem Tinsulanond, the prime minister of Thailand from 1980 to 1988, again pleaded with labor leaders for the same nominal change!

PROLETARIAT : Prince Wan rendered "proletariat" in Thai as *"kam-machip,"* which translates literally as those who earn their living from laboring. Although they generally accepted this rendering, Thai radical leftist intellectuals and university students, many of whom are low-ranking and low-paid government employees themselves, fiercely—if confusedly—debated whether or not Thai government employees and tricyclists (or pedicab drivers) should be counted as members of the proletariat. Granted that, theoretically, the proletariat was supposed to consist of propertyless wage earners, the incongruity of the stituation lies in the fact that the former group, though relatively middle-class by station, were indeed salary earners employed by the state and did not own any means of production, while the latter, though dirt poor and toiling, nonetheless did own a piece of private property as means of production in their battered tricycles or pedicabs.

Subsequently, however, *"kammachip"* came to mean something other than "modern industrial workers" in actual political usage. If one looks at the top ranks of the Communist Party of Thailand (from 1942 to the mid-1980s), purportedly the vanguard of a Thai proletariat, one finds just a handful of Thai and Laotian industrial workers. The rest were mostly high-school-educated, Sino-Thai petty bourgeois, small and medium entrepreneurs, and shopkeepers and their apprentices, along with a few university-educated intellectuals. Hence, it turned out that their Chinese apprenticeship ethics of self-discipline, diligence, endurance, self-abnegation, parsimony, simple lifestyle, and so on, were identified as universal "proletarian characteristics and virtues" and became the prescribed model and hallmark of the Communist Party of Thailand's cadres and revolutionaries during the years of rural armed struggle.[9]

GLOBALIZATION : In the aftermath of the middle-class-dominated mass uprising that toppled the military government of Prime Minister General Suchinda Kraprayoon in 1992, "globalization" quickly became a buzzword in Thailand. Its first Thai avatar, "*lokanuwat*," which literally means "to turn with the globe," was coined by Professor Chai-anan Samudavanija, a maverick, colorful and versatile royalist political scientist turned public intellectual, and then widely and successfully propagated by *Phoojadkan Raiwan* (Manager Daily), a leading and very popular business newspaper of that period, together with its various sister periodicals. For a long while, "*lokanuwat*" became the talk of the town, making a ubiquitous appearance — oftentimes uncalled-for or not obviously pertinent — in press headlines, columns and news reports, radio phone-ins, TV talk shows, TV advertisements for all sorts of products including soy sauce, and even a birthday speech by King Bhumibol. With its seemingly progressive outward- and forward-looking connotations, the "*lokanuwat*" discourse was adroitly used by Chai-anan, *Phoojadkan Raiwan*, and the globalizers among Thai public intellectuals to culturally and politically push the military back to its barracks and challenge the legitimacy of the rising parochial, provincial mafia-type elected politicians by branding their respective rule "counterclockwise," "against the trend of the globe," and "falling behind the trend of the globe."

More ominously, the term was also used to signify an aggressive new national project of Thai capitalism with expansionist designs on its poorer neighbors. Symptomatic of this Thai expansionist trend was the decision of the Royal Institute to adopt — against Chai-anan's vocal opposition and much to his chagrin—a new coinage as the official Thai equivalent of "globalization" in place of the pre-existing "*lokanuwat*"—namely, "*loka-phiwat*," which literally means "to turn the globe."[10]

From Good Governance to *Thammarat*

The translation-as-transformation process also describes the coming of "good governance" to Thailand. The official website of the IMF explains that in 1996, the board of governors encouraged the Fund to "promote good governance in all its aspects, including by ensuring the rule of law, improving the efficiency and accountability of the public sector, and tackling corruption, as essential elements of a framework within which economies can prosper."[11] While the IMF was supposedly focused only on aspects of governance that relate to macroeconomic processes, its powers of surveillance to ensure "good governance" were nearly unlimited. "Good governance" could thus become a standard for measuring anything and everything, from industrial productivity to everyday corruption. Its definition, then, was mobile, unfixed, and extremely important in Thailand.[12]

The context was the world-famous "Tom Yam Kung disease,"[13] the most severe financial and economic crisis Thailand had ever faced in its modern history. In July 1997, the fixed exchange rate was abandoned, and the baht was effectively devalued, leading to a stampede of foreign capital out of the country.[14] Financially liberalized Thailand found its foreign-currency reserves depleted, and the government of Prime Minister General Chavalit Yongchaiyudh, then bankrupt of credibility, had no choice but to turn to the IMF for a rescue loan package.[15] This package came with the condition that the Thai government implement measures toward "good governance," a string commonly attached to loans in the 1990s as a result of the IMF's bleak view of the trustworthiness and efficiency of debtor countries. Almost immediately, Thai public intellectuals began discussing and strategizing about this "good governance."[16]

At that critical juncture, Chaiwat Satha-anand, who was then chairperson of the Faculty of Political Science at Thammasat University, convened a special faculty meeting to discuss what they, as a community of Thai political scientists, could do to help elucidate the volatile situation to a confused public. Chaiwat was concerned about the economic crisis and the coming of the IMF loan program with its "good governance" conditionality. His concern should be understood in a context in which academics had an established tradition of public intervention. Many of them took part in the popular opposition to military dictatorship during the 1970s; some participated in the rural armed struggle against it. Given their presumed knowledgeability and relatively secure and respectable social status, the Thai public generally expects scholars to be active as public intellectuals in addition to their normal teaching duties, more so even than it expects them to do research. Chaiwat is an exemplary figure: a Thai Muslim of Indian descent and the foremost scholar of peace studies and nonviolent conflict resolution in the country. (He is also a colleague and personal friend of mine.)

After some discussion, the meeting authorized the chairperson to issue a statement on behalf of the faculty that reflected the views aired in the meeting. In drafting that statement the following day, Chaiwat coined the term "*thammarat*" as the Thai equivalent of "good governance."[17] The statement was published as a full-page piece in a leading daily newspaper on 10 August 1997 under the title "Khosanoe waduai thammarat fa wikrit setthakij-kanmeuang (A proposal on good governance in the face of political economic crisis)."[18]

In a phone conversation the prior afternoon, Chaiwat told me the thinking behind his choice of the term "*thammarat*." "*Thammarat*" is composed of two words: "*thamma*," meaning righteousness, religious teachings, religious precepts, truth, justice, correctness, law and rules,[19] and "*rat*," meaning simply the state. In Thai Buddhism, "*thamma*" denotes (1) nature as it is; (2) the law governing that nature; and (3) the obligation of human beings to conform to the law of nature.[20] My uneasiness about the overt religious tone and moral absolutism of "*thamma*" led me to suggest such alternatives as "*thammabal*" (meaning the upholder of *thamma*) or "*thammasasna*" (meaning the teachings of *thamma*). But Chaiwat emphatically wanted the state to be grounded in moral terms. His idea was to make it possible to interpret "*thammarat*," or Thai-style "good governance," as the use of "*thamma*" (moral righteousness, truth, law, etc.) as the norm to control, regulate and discipline *the Thai state* and thus provide a legitimate ground for civil disobedience against it.[21] The faculty's *thammarat* statement emphasized three main expectations that would define whether the state was enacting "good governance": concern and care for the plight of the poor, the unemployed, and the disadvantaged on the part of the government, especially in time of crisis; the rejection of any government that might be installed by unconsitutional powers; and public administration based on the principles of justice, fairness, and righteousness.[22] The faculty thus wielded familiar terms in order to make a compelling case for radical, democratic reforms.

The term would also travel well in popular rhymes. According to the first Thai rhyming dictionary, in strict terms only a single Thai word — *kraen*, or dwarf — rhymes with a straightforward transliteration of "good governance," whereas 685 words rhyme with the translation, "*thammarat*."[23]

After a relatively quiet period of political gestation and organizational preparation, "*thammarat*" was picked up in January 1998 by Thirayuth Boonmi, a former student leader and guerrilla fighter but by then a suave and astute member of the Faculty of Sociology and Anthropology at Thammasat University. Thirayuth redefined the word in a broad manner as a tripartite self-reform of the state, business, and civil society for efficient and just public administration. He thereby inflected the democratic connotations of the term with more standard, IMF-derived tones, and because the term was now institutionally acceptable, he was able to build a consensus around this new definition. Thirayuth inaugurated a widely publicized national agenda and high-profile reform campaign, respectively called Khrongkan thammarat haeng chat forum (the forum on good governance of Thailand project) and Kanprachum haeng chat pheua thammarat haeng chat (National convention for good governance of Thailand), in the process recruiting some bigwigs to the "*thammarat*" cause, including Former Prime Minister Anand Panyarachun and the senior medical doctor and NGO activist Prawase Wasi.[24]

From that point on, "*thammarat*" inspired countless public meetings and panel discussions; a much vaunted agenda of government reform policy; numerous rules, regulations, guidelines, indicators, and committees of the Office of the Prime Minister, the Ministry of the Interior, the Office of the Civil Service Commission, various universities, local administrative bodies, and the Thai Stock Exchange Commission; quite a few well-funded research projects, many publications, a noisy bureaucratic slogan and ceaseless publicity campaign, a corporate mantra, an environmental governance project, and an active network of people's organizations against corruption.[25] The meanings and practices of "*thammarat*" were widely disparate and conflicting, even oppositional and incompatible. What follows here is my effort to unpack the meanings of *thammarat* that circulated in contemporary political discourse. In addition to its state-civilizing and national-consensus versions, I identify three other interpretations of "*thammarat*" as both word and model of governance.

Authoritarian *Thammarat*

The authoritarian version of *thammarat* made its first appearance in a public discussion that was part of the Forum on Good Governance of Thailand Project initiated by Thirayuth and co-organized by the National Economic and Social Development Board (the country's main technocratic development-planning agency) and King Prajadhipok's Institute (a political think tank affiliated with Parliament). At the event held at the army's auditorium in April 1998, General Bunsak Kamhaengritthirong, then the secretary-general of the National Security Council, presented *thammarat* from the point of view of the state security apparatus:

> *Thammarat* is precisely what I have in mind. *Thammarat means a state that runs on Thamma*. People in that state are intelligent. *This is exactly what the National Security Council is in charge of*. For when people are intelligent, society will be *united as one*. And the potential *enemy* wouldn't be able to do anything.
>
> If the Thais love Thailand, *know Thai-ness better*, and use their intellect, they will have the force and power to tell right from wrong, as well as a *harmonious and creative* style of management. In the end, *thammarat* will arise.
>
> As to the privatization of state enterprises, we need to consider it carefully. It is not that foreigners are taking over our country, but rather the practice of a theory that will improve it.[26]

Bunsak's speech is replete with conservative Thai watchwords, such as "united as one," "Thai-ness," "harmonious and creative," and "enemy." The general's speech captured the gist of Thai authoritarian thinking by attaching "*thamma*" to the state as its natural keeper. In this view, the state, through such government agencies as the National Security Council, would take charge of imparting *thamma* to the people so as to make them intelligent and achieve the proper Thai attributes listed earlier. The violence inherent in the position could also be read in the statement's invocation of an imprecise "enemy." Was this enemy internal or external? Such ambivalence justified the use of force both within and outside the borders of the nation-state.

Obviously, General Bunsak's top-down, *dirigiste* interpretation of *thammarat* was the exact opposite of Chaiwat's original radical intent, inasmuch as it reversed the power relations among *thamma*, the state, and the people that Chaiwat was hoping for. It also differed substantially from the liberal version of *thammarat*. What is striking, however, is that when it came to matters of economic policy during crisis, Thai authoritarian conservatism was at a loss for an "authentic" response and could only replicate and defend the neoliberal policy of privatization. Under free-market hegemony, even ardent nationalists had to accept the inevitability of the IMF's continued importance — its central role — in Thai political life.

Liberal *Thammarat*

If the enforced quiet of Thai law and order represented the authoritarian ideal of *thammarat*, its liberal counterpart was held to be open, diverse, clean (because uncorrupted and accountable), and clear (because transparent). At the same time, it was expected to be messy and deafening, as universal values — not merely Thai ones — were debated within the space of civil society. Such was the view of Cambridge-educated former Prime Minister Anand Panyarachun (1991–92), a favorite of the middle class. Taking an active, high-profile role in Thirayuth's *thammarat* campaign, Anand delivered the keynote address that formally launched the Forum on Good Governance of Thailand Project at the Faculty of Political Science of Chulalongkorn University in March 1998, thereby earnestly and willingly lending his high social stature and considerable political weight to it. On that occasion and in other addresses and interviews he gave on the issue, Anand aggressively advanced his own definition of *"thammarat,"* which in essence amounted to sound administration, transparency, fairness, efficiency, and the delivery of public services.[27]

Anand's version of *thammarat* accorded with most pronouncements on the issue from the corporate sector, with its emphasis on "efficiency and effectiveness" — that is, on management techniques rather than political fundamentals.[28] The general strategy of his discourse was to depoliticize *thammarat*, as was evident in his reply to a question raised following his keynote address on 25 March.[29] Pointedly queried as to how *thammarat* could avoid politics when it necessarily had to deal with the allocation of public resources, Anand insisted on conceptualizing *thammarat* as a matter of administrative process, not of power relations. As he had said in a talk to a group of intellectuals one month earlier: "'*Thammarat*' is translated from 'good governance.' What is *thammarat*? It is an efficient and fair government and administration in the public interest. . . . We can see that today political ideologies hardly mean anything. . . . At this point, political ideals hardly matter. . . . The answer doesn't lie in any doctrine but in the ability to govern and administer public affairs, and in the ability to manage private business to the satisfaction of the people."[30]

It thus logically followed from Anand's premise that no matter how a country was governed, be it by a dictatorship or democracy, and no matter what kind of power relations obtained between its rulers and people, be it centralized and monopolized or decentralized and evenly distributed, so long as that country was transparently, fairly, and efficiently administered and could deliver public services, it would represent *thammarat*. Anand went on to cite Singapore as an example of dictatorship with good governance.

Communitarian *Thammarat*

Anand's self-proclaimed a-political *thammarat* was the exact opposite of Prawase's reading. In his preface to Thirayuth's book, *Thammarat haeng chat* (1998), in which the author laid out his consensus-building liberal view of "good governance," Prawase argued that, "at present, every form of dictatorship, be it monarchical, military, or communist, is not considered good governance."[31] Hence, *pace* Anand, Singapore was automatically ruled out as an instance of "good governance." Only a democracy was eligible to qualify as a site of good governance. However, to win the title, it further needed to follow the prescription given by Prawase for an ideal communitarian society — namely, to link local communities together in a social network that would allow them to share their experience and knowledge and make use of their social capital and folk wisdom to strengthen themselves. It is through such networks, according to Prawase, that there would be bottom-up reform of the state, the economy, and society. This would make it possible to build the ideal *santi prachatham* society — a peaceful democracy within the bounds of *thamma*.[32]

The Five Meanings of *Thammarat*

The five different versions of *thammarat* are concisely summarized in Table 1. Focusing on the latter three contending versions of *thammarat* (Table 2), a series of observations can be made about the crucial differences among them.

ON THE ISSUE OF POWER : Authoritarian *thammarat* wanted to concentrate power in the hands of the state to unite the nation as one harmonious whole. Liberal *thammarat* wanted to limit, check, and balance state power, allowing for conflict as part of normal public life. Communitarian *thammarat* called for decentralization of power from the state and the corporate sector to local communities.

ON THE ISSUE OF THE MARKET : Authoritarian *thammarat* helplessly surrendered to and complied with free-market economic policy without any new economic platform of its own. Liberal *thammarat* began from the premise of the worldwide triumph of free-market capitalism over socialism and communism. Free-market capitalism was "the reality" that could not be denied or avoided and to which one had to adapt. As for communitarian *thammarat*, it began from the opposite premise of both the failure and injustice of free-market capitalism, as demonstrated by the ongoing Thai and East Asian economic crises. Consequently, it strove for a space for what the king had called a "sufficiency economy" as an alternative.[33]

ON THE ISSUE OF DEMOCRACY : Authoritarian *thammarat* sought a return to the good old days of "Thai-style democracy" (i.e., the absolutist military dictatorship of 1958–73).[34] Liberal *thammarat* distinguished *thammarat* and democracy as separate issues, whereas communitarian *thammarat* considers the two inseparable.

Conclusion

In the end, should one feel sorry for the towering Monsieur Michel Camdessus, managing director of the IMF from 1987 to 2000, because his forceful prescription for "good governance" had become completely and helplessly contaminated, bastardized, and transformed into this messy word "*thammarat*"?

Table 1. The Five Different Meanings of *Thammarat*

State-Civilizing *Thammarat*	National-Consensus *Thammarat*	Authoritarian *Thammarat*	Liberal *Thammarat*	Communitarian *Thammarat*
The use of *thamma* to control, regulate, and discipline the state, thus providing a legitimate ground for civil disobedience	A tripartite self-reform of state, business, and society—not just the state—for efficient and just public administration	The state imposes *thamma* on the people in a top-down manner	Orientation to management, efficiency and results plus depoliticization	Weaving social fabric together → generating social energy → pushing for national *thammarat* → building an ideal *santi prachatham* society
Chaiwat Satha-anand et al. (academic community)	Thirayuth Boonmi (pluralist political activist and strategist)	General Bunsak Kamhaengritthirong (military, National Security Council)	Anand Panyarachun (business leader, former prime minister)	Dr Prawase Wasi (royalist medical doctor, civic leader, and NGO sage)

Table 2. The Three Different Meanings of *Thammarat*

Issues	Authoritarian Version	Liberal Version	Communitarian Version
Power	State-centralized power over a monolithic, harmonious nation	Limitation, checks and balances of power; allowing for conflict	Decentralization of power
Market	Compliance with market forces	Taking as its premise the triumph of free-market capitalism	Taking as its premise the failure and injustice of capitalism; seeking space for a "sufficiency economy"
Democracy	Thai-style	Considering *thammarat* and democracy as two separate issues, the former being about administrative process, and the latter having to do with power relations; a country can have *thammarat* without democracy (e.g., Singapore)	*Thammarat* and democracy cannot be separated; hence, all forms of dictatorship, whether monarchical, military, or communist, are emphatically not *thammarat*

The Enlightenment belief in the universality of reason and transparency of the word–reality relationship has been shown to have been overly optimistic by the actual cross-cultural, cross-language motion of words and discourse. And yet this is no reason to hastily give up the noble dream of universal reason. One needs rather to understand that it is impossible to transport and transplant intact a fixed signifier with definite signifieds and unchanging referents from one culture and language to another, not least because there are no such fixed things in the first place. Having already disintegrated into semantic instability, "good governance" can come to other peoples only through a self-educating process in which they have to fight, experience, learn, improvise, invent, and reinvent *thammarat* themselves. Only through this concrete historical process can the free-floating signifier, the multiple signifieds, and the substituted referents that together constitute "good governance" be reintegrated in a new whole and its institutions be built and take roots. Even a generous attempt in good faith to come up with a universal definition of "good governance" can never replace that process. The only sustainable good governance is the one that people define and build for themselves, not the one decreed and then imposed on or offered to them by global power holders or well-wishers.

The world may therefore end up with many different good governances. Some we may envy; others we may disapprove of, to the point that we may not even want to call them "good governance." Certainly, *thammarat* falls far short of perfection, and we hope to change and improve many of its features in years to come. That is why the differences between our *thammarat* and the good governance of others are just as important as their common ground. For differences invite us to compare, contrast, and learn from one another's achievements and shortcomings. We need only open the vista of "good governance" beyond the purview of the IMF or any single site of power to seize the opportunity for open-ended dialogue. In the process, we may change their definition of "good governance," and they, in turn, may change ours. With no single universal definition of "good governance," the words can remain in motion as people talk and argue and learn to fashion their own versions of global concepts.

Notes

1. "Body cultural" is Prasenjit Duara's concept: see Craig J. Reynolds, "Identity, Authenticity and Reputation in the Postcolonial History of Mainland Southeast Asia," keynote speech given at the International Conference on Post Colonial Society and Culture in Southeast Asia, Yangon, Myanmar, 16–18 December 1998. See also Thongchai Winichakul, *Siam Mapped: A History of the Geo-Body of a Nation* (Honolulu: University of Hawaii Press, 1994), esp. 169–70.

2. No.Mo.So. (Prince Phitthayalongkorn), *Klon lae nakklon* [Rhymes and rhymers] (Bangkok: Sophonphiphatthanakorn Printing House, 1930), 1–2.

3. Intharayut (Atsani Phonlajan), "Wannakhadi kao kao" [Old literature], *Aksornsarn* 1, no. 11 (February 1950): 85.

4. Mom Chao is the title of the lowest royal rank, usually held by a grandson or granddaughter of a king.

5. Prince Narathipphongpraphan (Mom Chao Wan Waithayakon Worawan), "Pathakatha reuang siamphak" [A lecture on Siamese language], in *Chumnum phraniphon khong sassatrajan pholtri phrajaoworawongthoe krommeun narathipphongpraphan* [Selected writings of Professor Major-General Prince Narathipphongpraphan], ed. Songwit Kaeosri (Bangkok: Bangkok Bank, 1979), 416.

6. Pridi Banomyong (1900–83) was the top civilian leader and political strategist of the anti-absolute monarchy, constitutionalist revolution of 1932; key architect and minister of the subsequent constitutional regime; head of the underground Free Thai resistance movement against the Japanese occupiers during the Second World War; one-time prime minister; and the first royally conferred senior statesman of modern Siam. He went into exile in the aftermath of a right-wing, conservative-royalist military coup in November 1947, lived in communist China for the next two decades, then moved to Paris, where he stayed until his widely mourned death. See Vichitvong Na Pombhejara, *Pridi Banomyong and the Making of Thailand's Modern History* (Bangkok: Committees on the Project for the National Celebration on the Occasion of the Centennial Anniversary of Pridi Banomyong, Senior Statesman, 2001).

7. Atsani Phonlajan (1918–87) was a self-taught, rebellious, iconoclastic member of the Thai literati and one of the two foremost, most versatile, and finest communist Thai poets and literary critics, the other being Jit Poumisak. A lawyer by training and state prosecutor by profession, he was won over to communism by a leading *jek* (Thai of Chinese descent) Maoist intellectual and went underground to China for theoretical education in the 1950s. Subsequently, he rose to the upper echelons of the Communist Party of Thailand and worked in its theory department. When the communist-led rural armed struggle collapsed in the early 1980s, he refused to give himself up to the Thai government and went over instead to socialist Laos, where he died of old age a convinced communist revolutionary. See Kasian Tejapira, *Commodifying Marxism: The Formation of Modern Thai Radical Culture, 1927–1958* (Kyoto: Kyoto University Press and Trans Pacific Press, 2001).

8. *Pathanukrom krom tamra krasuang thammakan* [Dictionary of the Department of Textbooks, Ministry of Public Instruction] (Bangkok: Department of Textbooks, Min-

istry of Public Instruction, 1927), 13; *Photjananukrom chabab rajbandittayasathan* [The Royal Institute's dictionary] (Bangkok: Rajbandittayasathan, 1950), 18.

9. Pho. Meuangchomphoo (Udom Sisuwan), *Soo samoraphoom phoophan* [To the Phoophan battlefront] (Bangkok: Matichon Press, 1989), 74–75; Tejapira, *Commodifying Marxism*, 22.

10. The data and arguments in this section come from my dissertation and subsequent research: see Tejapira, *Commodifying Marxism*, 196–99; *Wiwatha lokanuwat* [Debate on globalization] (Bangkok: Phoojadkan Press, 1995), 17–39; "Signification of Democracy," *Thammasat Review* 1, no. 1 (October 1996): 5–13.

11. For an updated version, see IMF, Board of Governors, "The IMF and Good Governance," September 2008, available online at http://www.imf.org/external/np/exr/facts/gov.htm (accessed 3 December 2008).

12. At its inception in international development agencies in the late 1980s and early 1990s, the definitions of "good governance" as a policy agenda ranged from the technical Washington version (especially the IMF's) to the more political New York version (e.g., the United Nations Development Program's). For the neoliberal Washington consensus, "good governance" was read either as "a move beyond the Washington consensus" or "an extension of economic neoliberalism to the political sphere." Although these divergent meanings of "good governance" at its origins should be borne in mind, they need not restrict us here. For a survey of relevant studies, see Barbara Orlandini, "Consuming 'Good Governance' in Thailand: Re-contextualising Development Paradigms," Ph.D. diss., University of Florence, 2001, chap. 1.

13. Tom Yam Kung is a hot and spicy shrimp soup, flavored with chilies, lemongrass, and kaffir lime. Popular among Thais and well known with foreigners, it has become representative of Thai cuisine abroad. In the aftermath of the 1997 Thai economic crisis and its subsequent contagion effects around East Asia, its name was widely used in the Western media as a metonym of the economic ills and plague begotten by Thailand.

14. Taking advantage of cheap foreign loans made available through the opening of the country's capital account and the liberalization of the financial market under the Bangkok International Banking Facility program since September 1993, many big Thai companies borrowed extensively abroad (the total foreign debt of Thailand's non-financial private sector amounting to $85 billion at year end 1997) and channelled the easy money into mismatched investment on a grand scale. The devaluation of the baht (plummeting from 25 baht to more than 50 baht per U.S. dollar in late 1997) turned these foreign-currency-denominated loans into gigantic non-performing loans overnight at half the size of the Thai annual GDP. Thousands of companies folded; two thirds of pre-crisis private commercial banks went under and changed hands; 65 percent of the Thai capitalist entrepreneurial class went bankrupt; one million workers lost their jobs; and three million more Thais fell below the poverty line. The subsequent costs of restructuring the financial sector reached 42.3 percent of GDP. See Kasian Tejapira, "Post-Crisis Economic Impasse and Political Recovery in Thailand: The Resurgence of Economic Nationalism," *Critical Asian Studies* 34, vol. 3 (Septem-

ber 2002): 323–56; Richard Duncan, *The Dollar Crisis: Causes, Consequences, Cures* (Singapore: John Wiley, 2003), 34–42, 132–33.

15. For an informative and comprehensive account of the 1997 Thai economic crisis, see Pasuk Phongpaichit and Chris Baker, *Thailand's Crisis* (Chiang Mai: Silkworm Books, 2000). For its domestic political impact, see Kasian Tejapira, "The Political Lesson of the Thai Economic Crisis: A Critical Dissection of Electocracy," paper presented at the workshop "What Lessons We Learn from the Crisis?" International House of Japan, Tokyo, 14 June 1999; Tejapira, "Post-Crisis Economic Impasse and Political Recovery in Thailand."

16. Some early instances are Kasian Tejapira, "IMF kab anakhot khong ratthabal jew" [IMF and the future of the Chavalit government], *Matichon Daily*, 7 August 1997, 21; Chai-anan Samudavanija, "Good Governance (GG = Go! Go!)," *Matichon Daily*, 9 August 1997.

17. As a matter of fact and completely unknown to him, the word "*thammarat*" had already been coined for a different purpose before Chaiwat's utilization of it to translate "good governance." Some time after the bloody massacre of left-wing student protesters at Thammasat University and the subsequent military coup on 6 October 1976, a group of journalists published a weekly news magazine under the title *Thammarat*, with a Mr. Yongyudh Mahakanok as its publisher and Sriphanom Singhthong as chief editor. Short-lived and mostly forgotten, it carried the slogan "Pheua khwampentham khong sangkhom [for social justice]" from which its title might derive. This piece of little known information was unearthed and made public by Suchat Sawatsi, the omniscient "bookman" or literary critic of Thailand, so as to insert a jarring note into the brouhaha about *thammarat*. See his column under the penname Singh Sanamluang in "Roi pi haeng khwam hohiao [One hundred years of distress]," *Nation Weekender* 7, no. 319 (16–22 July 1998).

18. *Matichon Daily*, 10 August 1997, 2.

19. *Photjananukrom chabab rajbandittayasathan pho. so. 2525* [The Royal Institute's dictionary, B.E. 2525] (Bangkok: Rajbandittayasathan, 1995), 420.

20. Uthai Dullayakasem, "Sinlatham [Morality]," in *Kham: Rongroi khwamkhid khwamcheua thai* [Words: Traces of Thai thoughts and beliefs] ed. Suwanna Satha-anand and Neungnoi Bunyanet (Bangkok: Chulalongkorn University Press, 1994), 133.

21. Chaiwat's version of *thammarat* was invoked in a marathon protest by civic groups and NGO activists against the construction of the Myanmar-Thai Yadana gas pipeline that exploited Burmese ethnic minority forced labor and cut through a pristine forest in the border area. See Kasian Tejapira, "Huajai khong thammarat [The heart of *thammarat*]," *Matichon Daily*, 19 February 1998.

22. Thailand has one of the worst income distribution ratios in the world, a history of twelve successful military coups between 1933 and 2007 and a centralized, corruption-prone and repressive auto-colonial state bureaucracy schooled in anticommunist counterinsurgency mentality and practice.

23. Laong Misetthi, *Photjananukrom lamdub sara* [Rhyming dictionary] (Bangkok: Rungreuangsan Publisher, 1961), 669–701, 1022.

24. Thirayuth Boonmi, *Thammarat haeng chat: Yutthasat koo haiyana prathet thai* [National good governance: Strategy for salvaging Thailand] (Bangkok: Sai Than Publishing House, 1998); and Chedpong Siriwich, "Tour thammarat trip phises: Khwamreunrom phasom khwamkhid mai" [A special *Thammarat* tour: A mixture of enjoyment and new ideas], *Nation Weekender* 6, no. 301 (12–18 March 1998): 28–29.

25. For example, see Orlandini, "Consuming 'Good Governance' in Thailand," chap. 6; Bussabong Chaijaroenwatthana and Boonmi Li, *Tua Chiwad thammaphibal* [Indicators of good governance] (Bangkok: King Prajadhipok's Institute, 2001), 8–20, 38–47, 88–89; Thai Stock Exchange Commission, *Raingan kankamkab doolae kijjakan* [Corporate governance report] (Bangkok: Thai Stock Exchange Commission, 2001).

26. *Matichon Daily*, 22 April 1998, 20; emphasis added.

27. Anand Panyarachun, "The Tao of Good Governance," *Nation*, 18 February 1998, A2, A4–5; Anand Panyarachun, "Thammarat kab sangkhom thai [Good governance and Thai society] in *Mummong khong nai anand* [Mr. Anand's viewpoints]," ed. Sommai Parichat (Bangkok: Matichon Press, 1998), 25–32; Anand Panyarachun, interview on "Thammarat: Ik khrang khong songkhram khwamkhid [Good governance: Another round of war of ideas]," *Hi-Class* 15, no. 169 (June 1998), 40–42. See also Anand Panyarachun, *Mummong khong nai anand lem 2* [Mr. Anand's viewpoints, part 2] (Bangkok: Matichon Press, 2001).

28. See, e.g., Kiattisak Jelattianranat (then president of the Institute of Internal Auditors of Thailand), "Crisis Lends Urgency for Good Governance," *Nation*, 2 May 1998, B1.

29. The question was posed by Mom Ratchawong Prudhisan Jumbala, a political scientist from Chulalongkorn University. "Mom Ratchawong" is a title showing royal descent.

30. Anand Panyarachun, "*Thammarat* kheu aria? [What is *thammarat*?]," in Sommai, *Mr. Anand's Viewpoints*, 15–17.

31. Prawase Wasi, "Preface," in Thirayuth Boonmi, *Thammarat haeng chat*, 3.

32. Dr. Puey Ungphakorn, a top economic technocrat-turned-political dissident, and former rector of Thammasat University, has qualified the ideal of democracy by requiring *thamma*, lest democracy degenerate into the tyranny of the majority. See Prawase Wasi, *Kansadaeng pathakatha phises puey ungphakorn khrang thi 6* [The sixth Puey Ungphakorn memorial lecture] (Bangkok: Faculty of Economics, Thammasat University, 1998).

33. "Sufficiency economy" refers to an alleged universally applicable, peasant community-derived philosophy of moral economy under the Buddhist precepts of cautious moderation, which would avoid the worst excesses and risks associated with free-market capitalism, consumerism, and materialism. Reynolds in this volume translates the term as "the economics of enough-ness."

34. For an elaboration of Thai-style democracy, see Thak Chaloemtiarana, *Thailand: The Politics of Despotic Paternalism* (Bangkok: Social Science Association of Thailand and the Thai Khadi Research Institute, Thammasat University, 1979).

Notes on Contributors

Itty Abraham is the Marlene and Morton Meyerson Centennial Chair at the University of Texas, Austin. He teaches in the departments of Asian Studies and Government and directs the South Asia Institute. He is the author of *The Making of the Indian Atomic Bomb* (1998).

Mona Abaza teaches sociology at the American University in Cairo. She is the author of *Changing Consumer Cultures of Modern Egypt: Cairo's Urban Reshaping* (2006) and *Debates on Islam and Knowledge in Malaysia and Egypt: Shifting Worlds* (2002).

Partha Chatterjee teaches political science at the Centre for Studies in Social Sciences, Calcutta, and anthropology at Columbia University, New York. He is the author of several books, including *Nationalist Thought and the Colonial World* (1986) and *The Nation and Its Fragments* (1993). He is now writing a history of global practices of empire by focusing on the story of the Black Hole of Calcutta.

Carol Gluck is the George Sansom Professor of History at Columbia University. She is the author of *Thinking with the Past: Modern Japan and History* (forthcoming) and *Past Obsessions: World War Two in History and Memory* (forthcoming).

Huri Islamoglu teaches economic history and political economy at Bogazici University in Istanbul and at the Central European University in Budapest. She is the author of *Constituting Modernity: Private Property in the East and West* (2004) and editor, with Peter Perdue, of *Shared Histories of Modernity in Qing China, India and the Ottoman Empire* (2008). She is currently working on transnationalization trends in agriculture and property battles in Turkey, China, and India.

Claudia Koonz is Professor of German history at Duke University. She is the author of *The Nazi Conscience* (2003) and is now writing a book on the veil in contemporary Europe.

Lydia H. Liu is the W. T. Tam Professor in the Humanities at Columbia University. Her recent publications include *The Clash of Empires: The Invention of China in Modern World Making* (2004) and essays on literary theory and new media.

Driss Maghraoui teaches history in the School of Humanities and Social Sciences at Al-Akhawayn University in Ifrane, Morocco. He is writing a book on history, memory, and the culture of French colonialism in Morocco.

Vicente L. Rafael is Professor of History at the University of Washington. He is the author of *Contracting Colonialism* (1993), *White Love and Other Events in Filipino History* (2000), and *The Promise of the Foreign: Nationalism and the Technics of Translation in the Spanish Philippines* (2005).

Craig J. Reynolds is Adjunct Professor in the College of Asia and the Pacific, Australian National University. His most recent book is an edited collection of essays by the late O. W. Wolters, *Early Southeast Asia: Selected Essays* (2007), which includes an intellectual biography of Wolters.

Seteney Shami is an anthropologist and program director at the Social Science Research Council for the Middle East and North Africa Program and the Eurasia Program. Recent articles include " 'Amman Is Not a City': Middle Eastern Cities in Question," in the edited volume *Urban Imaginaries* (2007).

Alan Tansman teaches Japanese literature at the University of California, Berkeley. He is the author of *The Aesthetics of Japanese Fascism* (2009) and editor of *The Culture of Japanese Fascism* (2009).

Kasian Tejapira teaches political science at Thammasat University in Bangkok. He is the author of *Commodifying Marxism:The Formation of Radical Thai Culture, 1927–1958* (2001) and a frequent columnist in the Thai press.

Anna Lowenhaupt Tsing teaches anthropology at the University of California, Santa Cruz. She is the author of *Friction: An Ethnography of Global Connection* (2004) and *In the Realm of the Diamond Queen* (1993). Her current research follows global scientific and commercial connections involving matsutake mushrooms.

Index

'Abdu, Muhammad, 76–77, 81 n. 13
accountability: Japan, 101, 104 n. 6;
    Morocco, 121; Ottoman successor
    states, 274; public apology, 98;
    Thailand, 313, 317; Turkey, 274–
    75, 277–78, 283 n. 13, 284 n. 14;
    United States, 35–36
'ada (pl. *'adat*) [Arabic, "custom"], 3, 5,
    7, 13; affinity words, 67–68, 70;
    Egypt, 68–69, 76–80; Indonesia, 71–
    72; local practice, 47–48; Morocco,
    75–76, 79–80; origins, 13, 41–42,
    68. See also *adat*; custom; *'urf*
adat [Indonesian, "custom"], 3, 5, 7,
    13; affinity words, 71–72, 80; cul-
    tural nationalism, 43, 51–54, 59–60;
    Dutch colonial rule and *Adatrecht*,
    48–51, 72, 75–76; indigenous
    rights, 44–47, 54–60; *masyarakat
    adat*, 40–44, 46, 47, 59; origins, 13,
    41–43, 71–72; politics, 47. See also
    'ada; custom; indigeneity
Adatrecht. See *adat*
Algeria, 6, 81 n. 33, 112, 122, 178,
    181, 187, 191 n. 1, 257–58
Amazigh: Amazigh movement and
    secularism, 124–25; customary law,
    75; Egyptian census, 173 n. 46;
    literature, 170; Roman coinage, 128
    n. 38

Amazon: international coalition to
    protect, 43, 57, 64 n. 51; state
    expansion into, 31–33
analytic concepts. *See under* etymol-
    ogy; genealogy; scale; translation
anarchism: India, 244–50, 252; Thai-
    land, 286–87, 296; United States,
    25, 257
anticolonialism: Bandung, 51–53;
    Egypt, 171 n. 6; India, 242–43;
    Ireland, 250; Islamic world, 76;
    Morocco, 116–17, 122, 161–64;
    Philippines, 220–37
'aqalliyya [Arabic, "minority"]: Copts,
    151–71; Nubians and Sudanese,
    168–70; origins and affinity words,
    153–54, 156, 161–64. *See also*
    minorities
Arabic language: Amazigh movement,
    125; Copts, 155; cosmopolitan
    character, 13, 151; Islam, 47, 70–
    71, 125, 188; Nubians, 169; terms
    circulating in postcolonial Europe,
    174–75
Asian Development Bank, 41, 286
Asian Economic Crisis of 1997: Thai-
    land, 287, 289, 296, 299, 306, 313–
    14, 319, 324 nn. 13–14, 325 n. 15;
    "Words in Motion" project, 2, 4,
    12–13, 17 n. 2

167, 169; France, 175–78, 181,
185–91; India, 242; Indonesia, 43–
44; Japan, 94, 97–98, 102, 137–39,
144–45; Morocco, 125; Philippines,
230; Turkey, 276; United States, 25,
35, 53, 257

civilization: assertions of superiority
of Western civilization, 14–15, 59,
84–89, 119, 166, 210–11; China,
202; denials of superiority of Western civilization, 113, 136, 191 n. 1;
difference and identity, 40–42;
Egypt, 70, 167; France, 178, 182,
185, 191; Indonesia, 48–50, 59, 73;
Islam and Western civilization, 48–
50, 59, 70, 73, 113, 119, 178, 182,
191; Islamic civilization, 70–71,
123–24; Japan, 85–86, 88; Morocco, 113, 119, 123–24; natural
rights of indigenous peoples, 210–
11; Thailand, 307, 316, 320; units,
15; the word, 4, 15

civil society: Enlightenment and, 238
n. 11; France, 174–75; injury, 213–
16; Morocco, 119, 125; the term, 5,
12; Thailand, 315, 317

Cold War: ILO, 57–58; Islam, 62 n. 22;
post-Cold War, 6, 96, 175, 185;
security, 24–27, 29–30, 34–35, 257

colonialism: Algeria, 112, 122, 178,
181, 187, 191 n. 1, 257–58; Burma,
293; China, 201–5, 210–16; colonial language, 5, 14–15, 40, 174;
Egypt, 75–77, 153, 155–61, 168,
170–71, 173 n. 46; France, 174–91;
India, 14, 240–57, 260; Indonesia,
43, 47–60, 63 n. 29, 72–80, 81 n.
34; Islam, 67–80; Japan, 291; Middle East and Southeast Asia, 77–80;
Morocco, 75, 109–26; Philippines,
14, 219–28; postcolonial condition,
6, 53–54, 191, 201, 237, 254–55,

257–60; postcolonial critiques, 12,
215–16, 257, 291, 323 n. 1; Thailand, 325 n. 22

commission. See *komisyon*

communism: Bandung, 51–53; Brazil,
28–30, 33; Cold War, 24–25, 28–
30, 176, 257; community and, 286,
288; India, 244, 253–55; Indonesia,
44; Islamism and, 178; Thailand,
293, 288, 302 n. 17, 308, 310–12,
318–19, 321, 323 nn. 6–7, 325 n. 22

community: as aesthetic experience,
136–39, 144; affinity words, 287–
90, 295, 300–1; Arabic terms, 154,
156; Berber, 75; business, 275, 279;
conspiracy vs., 219; Copts, 160,
167–68, 171; custom and, 53, 75,
79, 136, 287; definitions of, 286–91;
disruptions, 152, 297, 300; economic development and, 286–87,
291–95, 326 n. 33; freedom, 116–
17, 167–68; Gandhi, Mohandas,
295–96; as governance word, 299;
Japan, 136–39, 144, 291, 297–98;
Marxist analysis, 288, 291; minorities, 152, 154, 160, 167–68, 171,
186; nations, 46, 100, 216; of
readers, 139; rights, 67, 117, 167–
68; security, 21; society vs., 288–89;
Thailand, 286–302; *umma* (Arabic,
community of all Muslims), 122–
23, 154–56, 286. See also *chumchon*

conjuración [Spanish, "conspiracy"]:
origins, 219–20, 223–24. See also
conspiracy

conspiracy: China, 248; community
vs., 219; India, 244, 248–49; international Islamic, 178, 186; Japan,
95; McCarthyism, 25; Philippines,
9, 14, 219–37, 248; September 11
attacks, 25; the word, 3, 6. See also
conjuración

constitutions: Egypt, 153, 157, 161, 164–66; Europe, 177, 258; France, 177, 183; India, 241, 248, 250, 254–55; Indonesia, 73; Japan, 91–97; the modern state and, 258; Morocco, 15, 115–17, 121, 123, 127 n. 10, 127 n. 23; Ottoman Empire, 266, 269; Thailand, 310, 323 n. 6; Turkey, 279; the word, 112

consultation [Arabic, *shura*]. See *shura*; parliaments

Copts: as minority, 9, 151–71. See also *'aqalliyya*

cosmopolitanism, 12–13, 15–16, 59; Arabic language and, 13, 151; Egypt, 158; Morocco, 109, 126; Muslim scholars, 48, 71, 79; Richard Wright, 52–53, 59

Couto e Silva, Golbery do, 28–31

custom: codification, 75–76; Egypt, 68–69, 76–80; Indonesia, 41–51, 59–60, 71; methodology of studying, 67–68; origins vs., 41–43; Philippines, 230; translations, 68; Turkey, 271; *'urf* vs., 48, 68–69; veil as, 175. See also *'ada*; *adat*; customary law; indigeneity; tradition; *'urf*

customary law: *Adatrecht*, 48–51, 72, 75, 76; Egypt, 68–69; Indonesia, 42, 44, 48–51, 72–75; Morocco, 75–76; Southeast Asia, 70–75, 77–80; *'urf*, 47–48, 68–69, 80 n. 9

de Man, Paul, 200

democracy: Brazil and Indonesia, 43–44, 59; Egypt, 166; France, 176, 178, 186, 267; India, 242–43, 254–55; Islam, 117–20, 124, 166, 178, 186; Japan, 94; liberal-democratic states, 213, 257–60; Morocco, 111–12, 117–20, 124–25, 127 n. 23; Philippines, 237; Thailand, 292,

310, 315, 318–19, 321, 326 n. 32, 326 n. 34; Turkey, 284 n. 24; the word, 4, 83, 112, 125, 237, 310

Derrida, Jacques, 103, 202, 238 n. 10

development: Bangladesh, 10 n. 4; Brazil, 28–33, 57, 59; Egypt, 158; Gandhi's village *swaraj*, 287, 295–97, 301; global South, 59; Indonesia, 41, 44–47, 51, 59, 73; ILO Convention 107, 58; Japan, 135–36; Marxism, 287–89, 291, 296–97, 301; Morocco, 113, 121; Ottoman Empire, 268–74, 281–83; Philippines, 237; Thailand, 286–88, 291–302, 310, 321, 324 n. 12; Turkey, 266, 274–83, 285 n. 28. See also Asian Development Bank; IMF; *segurança e desenvolvimento*; World Bank

Dillon, Michael, 22

diversity. See race and ethnicity

East and West: anticolonial movements, 52–53; assertions of superiority of Western civilization, 14–15, 59, 84–89, 119, 166, 210–11; assimilation of Western words, 5, 14–15, 84–89, 92, 94, 99, 103, 141, 200–1, 306–22; binary contrast between, 70, 113, 299; bureaucratic forms, 281; colonial contexts, 52–53, 59, 79, 85, 113–20, 153, 156, 191 n. 1, 200, 210, 216, 245–47, 291; counter-narratives, 5, 14–15, 59–60, 113–20, 191 n. 1, 216; denials of superiority of Western civilization, 113, 136, 191 n. 1; education systems, 113; essentialization of, 59, 70, 79, 299; fetishization of Eastern words, 202; Islam, 48, 59, 70, 79, 113–20, 122, 151; neologisms, 72, 84–88, 306–13; racial contexts, 52–

53, 257; resistance to foreign ideology, 14–15, 70, 113–20, 122, 151, 153, 306–13; revolutionary ideology, 245–47; social scientific categories, 158–59, 287–89, 309–13

education: development and, 292–94; fashioning of elites, 113–14; French, 177–78, 184–88; instrument of exclusion, 46, 114; modern, 75, 245; Muslim, 71, 113–14; secularization, 118, 121–22, 178; Western, 245–47

Egypt, 7, 9, 13, 127, 171 n. 8, 281; 'ada, 68–69, 76–80; anticolonialism, 171 n. 6; Berbers in census, 173 n. 46; body politic, 162–64, 170; Britain and, 76, 156–58, 160–62, 164–65, 168–69; Catholicism, 159–60; citizenship, 156, 160, 167, 169; civilization, 70, 167; colonialism, 75–77, 153, 155–61, 168, 170–71, 173 n. 46; constitution, 153, 157, 161, 164–66; Copts, 151–71; cosmopolitanism, 158; custom, 68–69, 76–80; customary law, 68–69; democracy, 166; development, 158; freedom, 161–63, 166, 167; Germany and, 157, 165; indigeneity, 157–59, 169–71; Indonesia and, 77, 79; intellectuals, 70, 79, 115, 152; Islam, 68–69, 151–71; Islamic modernism, 76–77; legal pluralism, 68–69, 80 n. 8; minority, 151–71; modernity, 70, 75–76, 151–53, 158, 163; Morocco and, 110, 115; nationalism, 151, 154–56, 162, 166–71; parliament, 70, 161; public vs. the state, 80, 151, 153, 162, 166–67, 170; race and ethnicity, 67, 70, 152–66, 168–70; republicanism, 151, 157–60, 171 n. 8; revolution, 158, 160; sovereignty, 166

encounter: civilization and barbarity, 210; community, 288, 301; cosmopolitan, 13; East–West, 70, 86; local–global, 12–15, 67, 299; sublime, 143

enemy. *See* internal enemy

environment: Brazil, 33, 57; environmental security, 21; global, 5, 31, 33, 57, 58; Indonesia, 43–45; Japan, 100–2, 104; security, 21, 57; Thailand, 287, 299, 315

The Essence of the National Polity (Kokutai no hongi): binding in, 135–41; expression of sublime, 136, 139, 144; modern product, 136–37; similarities with Ōgai, 137–38; "sublime turn" in self-abnegation to nation, 138–39; "sublime will of history," 139

ethnicity. *See* race and ethnicity

etymology, as analytic concept, 4, 111, 141, 199–200, 203–4, 308, 310

EU (European Union), 175–77, 180, 191, 267, 276, 282, 284 n. 24

Farias, Cordeiro de, 28–29

fascism: France, 186; Heidegger, Martin, 130; Japan, 8, 14, 129, 135–41, 145; Mussolini, 141

Fassi, 'Allal al-, 76, 116–18

filibusteros [Spanish, "subversives"]: ability to bewitch, 228; conspiracy, 223; foreignness and criminality, 225; origins, 223; use of to contain rebellion, 236. *See also* Rizal, José

First World War: Cold War and, 24; Indian revolutionaries, 244–47; Ottoman Empire, 274; war responsibility, 95

France: body politic, 180–81; Catholicism, 177–78, 182, 187; citizenship,

175–78, 181, 185–91; colonialism, 109–10, 122, 174–91; commissions, 267–68, 270, 272; constitutionalism, 177, 183; democracy, 176, 178, 186, 267; fascism, 186; freedom, 177, 180–81, 186–87, 189; Germany and, 178, 181; headscarf, 4, 6–8, 14, 174–91; identity, 174, 185, 190–91; Islam, 174–91; law, 176–78, 180, 185; private vs. public, 175, 179, 186, 190; public vs. the state, 175, 177, 179–80, 185, 187–89, 267; race and ethnicity, 175–78, 180, 182, 185, 187–89, 191, 192 n. 7; religion, 174–91; republicanism, 177–91, 268; responsibility, 96–97; Revolution of 1789, 178–79, 189, 240, 266–68, 281; secularism, 110, 112–13, 119, 122, 124, 175, 177–78, 183, 185, 188, 190–91; security, 267; sublime, 145; terrorism, 181, 187, 190, 258; universalism, 175, 177, 185–87. See also *hijāb*; *laïcité*; secularism: Morocco

freedom, 9, 200, 214–15, 240; China, 202, 208, 210–12; Egypt, 161–63, 166–67; France, 177, 180–81, 186–89; India, 242, 249–50, 252, 257–58, 260; Indonesia, 51–54, 63 n. 47; Japan, 84–85, 88, 92–93, 135; Morocco, 109, 115–18, 121–26; Philippines, 220–22, 229, 234–37; security, 22, 35–37. *See also* anticolonialism; democracy; revolution

genealogy, as analytic concept, 4, 40–41, 47, 52, 55, 85, 152, 230, 287–94
Gandhi, Indira, 255–57
Gandhi, Mohandas: India, 248, 250, 252–53; Thailand, 287, 295–97, 301, 304 n. 37

Germany: Britain and, 257; Egypt and, 157, 165; France and, 178, 181; India and, 244, 246; Japan and, 86, 94–99, 106 n. 46, 129, 130–36, 291; Philippines and, 222
globalization: citizens, 186; connections, 11–13, 41, 60, 61 n. 4, 151–52; environmentalism, 31, 33; indigeneity, 45, 56–57; market economy, 4, 266, 276, 282, 296, 301–2, 306; movement of terms, 85, 94, 100–3, 151; narratives of, 16, 41–42, 52, 60, 293; politics, 52, 214, 216; Thailand, 312–13; vocabulary of, 4–5, 12, 15–16, 41, 60, 312–13. *See* communism; IMF; transnational links: NGOs; UN; World Bank
governance: affinity words, 265; India, 242; Indonesia, 67; Ottoman Empire and Turkey, 265–67, 275–76, 278–79, 281–82; Thailand, community, 299. *See also* community; *komisyon*; *kurul*; *thammarat*

bai [Chinese, "injury"], 207
Hanafi, Hassan, 70
Hassan II, 120–22, 127 nn. 22–23
Havel, Václav, 102
headscarf: France, 4, 6–8, 14, 174–91; Turkey, 181. See also *hijāb*
Hertz, Neil, 130
hijāb [Arabic, "headscarf"], 4, 7, 8; affinity words and origins, 174–76; cultural essentialism and, 177; education and, 177–78, 184–88; French identity and Islamism, 176–79, 182–86; multiculturalism as universalism, 175, 177, 185–87, 190; Muslim immigrants, 174–83; politics of word choice, 174–75, 179–82, 185, 188, 190–91; private vs. public, 175, 179–82, 186, 190; secular citizen-

ship as universalism, 175, 177–78, 185–86, 190; Stasi Commission, 183–84. See also *laïcité*

Hirsch, Edward, 135

'ilmaniyya [Arabic, "secularism"]: Amazigh movement, 124–25; Islamists, 121–22; origins and affinity words, 110–12, 123; religious freedom, cultural diversity, and political Islam, 123–26. See also *laïcité*; secularism; *sécularisme*

ILO (International Labor Organization): Convention 169 on Indigenous and Tribal Peoples in Independent Countries (1989), 42, 44–46, 57–58; Convention 107 (1957), 45, 58

IMF (International Monetary Fund), 4, 6; Japan, 101; Thailand, 306, 313, 315–17, 319, 322, 324 n. 12; Turkey, 267, 275–82, 284 n. 25

India: anarchism, 245–50, 252; Britain and, 14, 240–60; citizenship, 242; colonialism, 14, 240–57, 260; communism, 244, 253–55; conspiracy, 244, 248–49; democracy, 242–43, 254–55; freedom, 240, 242, 249–50, 252, 257–58, 260; Germany and, 244, 246; governance, 242; indigeneity, 201; injury, 253; law, 247–48, 251–52, 256–57; modernity, 242; nationalism, 213, 241–43, 248–50, 252–55, 260; parliament, 254–55; public vs. private, 241, 245; religion, 246–47, 256; republicanism, 287, 295; revolution, 240–60; sedition, 201, 245–50, 254; sovereignty, 213, 240–60; the state, 248, 254–55, 257–58; terrorism, 5, 7, 9, 14, 201, 213, 241–60

indigeneity: Brazil, 30–31; India, 201; indigenous spirituality, 55–56, 63 n. 45; Indonesia, 40–64; theories of development, 295. See also *adat*; rights

indigenous peoples: Brazil, 31–33; Egypt, 157–59, 168–71; Indonesia, 40–64; international organization of, 55; Philippines, 230; South America, 43

Indonesia: Chinese in, 46, 73, 75; citizenship, 48–50, 59, 73; colonialism, 43, 47–60, 63 n. 29, 72–80, 81 n. 34; communism, 44; constitution, 73; custom, 41–51, 59–60, 71; customary law, 42, 44, 48–51, 72–75; democracy, 43–44, 59; development, 41, 44–47, 51, 59, 73; Egypt and, 77, 79; environmentalism, 43–45; freedom, 51–54, 63 n. 47; governance, 73; indigeneity, 40–64; intellectuals, 41, 79; Islam, 47–50, 59–60, 71–72, 77–80; modernity, 44, 50, 52–53, 59; nationalism, 43, 49–53, 63 n. 29, 74; public vs. state, 41, 51, 68; race and ethnicity, 45–47, 49, 51–54, 67; religion, 47–48, 52, 72, 74, 76, 78, 81 n. 27; science, 49–50, 73; sovereignty, 60; the state, 44–47, 59; tradition, 41, 42, 47–52, 55, 59, 70–71, 72–73. See also *adat*

injury, 4, 7; affinity words, 204; discourse of, 8, 199–201, 216; *hai*, 207; India, 253; liberal theory of rights and sovereignty, 213–16; Opium Wars, 14, 202–13; Philippines, 226; super-signs, 204–5; terrorism, 213, 215–16

insecurity: Cold War, 25; information insecurity, 31, 34–36; shadow of "security," 14, 21–23, 29–31, 36–38

22, 126, 176–79, 182–86; as multi-culturalism, 187; origins and affinity words, 110–12; separation of religious and scientific sphere, 112; translations, 111, 118; as secular citizenship, 175, 177–78, 185–86, 190. See also *hijāb*; *'ilmaniyya*; secularism; *sécularisme*

Lambarki, Mohammed, 123–24

law: colonial, 72, 75, 77; EU, 177; France, 176–78, 180, 185, 190; India, 247–48, 251–52, 256–57; international, 43–45, 54, 58, 84, 86–87, 95, 97–99, 207–8, 210–12; Philippines, 228, 231, 234; rule of, 4, 44, 47, 313; *shari'a*, 5, 13, 41, 46–49, 68–69, 71–72, 75–79, 80 n. 8, 122–23; Thailand, 290–91, 314, 317; Turkey, 270, 272–73, 276–79; universal, 41, 95, 119, 314. See also *'ada*; *adat*; customary law

Lin Zexu, 203, 205–12, 216, 218 n. 32

Locke, John, 199–200

Matheson, James, 202, 205, 207–12, 217 n. 15, 218 n. 32

minorities: Egypt, 4, 7, 9, 13, 98, 151–71; French universalism and, 175, 177–78, 185–87, 190; Indonesia, 43; Thailand, 325 n. 21; United States, 25, 43, 51–54. See also *'aqalliyya*

modernity: creative reinvention of Western modernity, 14–15, 50, 59, 88; Egypt, 70, 75–76, 151–52, 158, 163; India, 242; Indonesia, 44, 48, 50, 52–53, 59; Islam, 76–77; Japan, 14–15, 83–88, 90–91, 129, 131–36; modern "dread of unreason," 38 n. 3; modernization, 42, 120, 131–32, 158, 191 n. 1, 266, 269, 286; modern self, 90–91, 103, 129, 132; mod-

ern state, 6, 36–37, 135, 213, 215, 258; Morocco, 109, 111–14, 117, 120, 123–25; "native spirituality" and, 56; science and, 44, 70, 113; shadow words and, 41–42; Thailand, 286, 294, 306–7, 309; Turkey, 266, 269, 274, 281–83; words as products of, 6, 9, 22

Mohammed VI, 109, 121

Moniaga, Sandra, 45–46

Mori Ōgai, 131–35, 137–38, 142, 144, 146 n. 11

Morocco: *'ada*, 75–76, 79–80; anti-colonialism, 116–17, 122, 161–64; citizenship, 125; civilization, 113, 119, 123–24; civil society, 119; colonialism, 77–80; constitution, 15, 115–17, 121, 123, 127 n. 10, 127 n. 23; cosmopolitanism, 109, 126; customary law, 7, 75–76, 79–80; education, 113–14, 118, 121–22; freedom, 109, 115–18; intellectuals, 115–25; modernity, 109, 111–14, 117, 120, 123–25; nationalism, 8, 110, 114, 116–20, 122–23, 125–26; private vs. public, 111–12, 118; race and ethnicity, 122; religion, 109–26; republicanism, 111–16, 126; secularism, 5, 8, 13, 109–26; sovereignty, 115, 124; tradition, 113, 116

nationalism, 5; Arab, 125–26, 151, 155, 162; Brazil, 57; cultural, 43, 51–54, 58–60, 63 n. 43; Egypt, 151, 154–56, 162, 166–71; India, 213, 241–43, 248–50, 252–55, 260; Indonesia, 43, 49–53, 63 n. 29, 74; Islamic, 76–77, 119, 122–23, 167; Japan, 90, 99–100; Middle East, 116; Morocco, 8, 110, 114, 116–20, 122–23, 125–26; Philippines, 219–25, 228–31, 236–37; Thailand, 317;

race and ethnicity, 5, 7; body politic, 23, 25, 39 n. 36; Brazil, 23, 27; cultural nationalism, 51–54; Egypt, 67, 70, 152–66, 168–70; France, 175–78, 180, 182, 185, 187–89, 191, 192 n. 7; India, 246–47, 254–57; Indonesia, 45–47, 49–54, 67; Morocco, 122; Philippines, 220, 222–23, 231, 238 n. 14; postwar Europe, 177; Thailand, 298, 311, 325

religion, 5, 7, 8, 12; Britain, 212; China, 212; Egypt, 151–71, 177, 180; France, 174–91; India, 246–47, 256; Indonesia, 47–48, 52, 72, 74, 76, 78, 81 n. 27; Japan, 92; Morocco, 109–26; Ottoman Empire, 269–70; Philippines, 222–23; Thailand, 290, 299, 314; United States, 167, 172 n. 41. *See also* Catholicism; Islam

Renan, Ernest, 119

republicanism: Egypt, 151, 157–60, 171 n. 8; France, 177–91, 268; India, 287, 295; Morocco, 111–16, 126; Philippines, 227, 237; Thailand, 310; Turkey, 126, 268, 274, 283 n. 13; United Arab Republic, 158, 171 n. 8

responsibility, 6, 8, 14; board responsibility, 275, 280, 281; codification of *adat* into *Adatrecht*, 72, 75; fiduciary responsibility, 276, 283, 280; global movement, 84, 86–87, 97–100, 103–4; Hassan II as "Commander of the Faithful," 120; *Mitverantwortung*, 99, 106 n. 46; Opium Wars, 207; personal responsibility, 88–91; political responsibility, 86–87, 91–94; responsibility of the state, 257, 267, 269; revolutionary nationalism, 221, 237 n. 6; secularism, 122; social responsibility, 100–3; sublime, 133; Thailand, 293; United Nations and religious minorities, 168; vernacularization of, 87–91; war responsibility, 94–100; Zulu *ubuntu*, 103. *See also sekinin*

revolution: American Revolution, 209, 250; Britain, 283 n. 1; communist, 288, 296; Egypt, 158, 160; French Revolution of 1789, 178–79, 189, 240, 266–68, 281; India, 240–60; Iranian Revolution, 70; North Africa and Middle East, 115; Ottoman Empire, 268; Philippine Revolution of 1896, 9, 219–37, 248; revolutionary movements in Europe, 6, 84, 245–46, 250; secular, 118; Thailand, 302 n. 17, 309, 310, 312, 323 nn. 6–7; theories of, 29; Turkey, 269. *See also* anticolonialism; nationalism

rights: civil rights, 30, 179, 254–55, 257, 259–60; constitutional rights, 92–93, 183, 255; human rights, 4–5, 152, 166, 177–81, 187; indigenous rights, 40, 43–45, 48, 54–60, 63 n. 45, 67, 72–75, 125, 151; land rights, 43, 55–58, 72–73, 75, 81 n. 34, 269–74; minority rights, 125, 151–56, 162–65, 167, 189; natural rights (law of nations), 207, 210–16; neologism, 92; tension with national sovereignty, 33, 57, 60, 258; translation of term, 88, 92–93; women's rights, 69, 76, 98, 178–81, 184–89

Rizal, José, 221–23, 225, 228, 230, 236

saburaimu [Japanese, "sublime"]: erasure, 135; origins and affinity words, 129–31, 135–36, 144;

Snouck (Christiaan Snouck Hurgonje), 42, 49–50, 72–75, 77

sovereignty: the body and, 213–15; Brazil, 33, 57; China, 202, 211–12; Egypt, 166; India, 213, 240–60; indigenous peoples, 56–57, 60, 63 n. 47, 211, 215; Indonesia, 60; Japan, 85, 87; Morocco, 115, 124; national languages, 204; the people, 124, 254, 282; Thailand, 289; Turkey, 282

state: Egypt, 68–69; Engels, Friedrich, 288; France, 177; Germany, 222; India, 248, 254–55, 257–58; Indonesia, 44–47, 59; injury, 214–16; Japan, 84, 92–94, 96–98, 103, 132, 135, 141, 144; Morocco, 111, 116, 119, 123, 124; Ottoman Empire, 268–69, 272, 274; Philippines, 220, 223–25; security, 21–23, 28, 33–37, 316–17; Thailand, 291, 297, 300, 302, 307, 311, 314–19, 320, 321; Turkey, 269–74, 281–83, 284 n. 14. *See also* public vs. the state

subjectivity: modern, 91, 132, 201–2; national development and, 59; responsibility and, 84, 103

sublime: affinity words, 136–37; antinuclear left and, 141–43; blocking force of other words, 145; fascism and, 135–41; national identity and, 131–35; origins, 129–30, 144, 145 n. 1; semantic weight and evocation of, 129–44; vocabulary of, 129–31, 135–37; *yūgen*, 135–36. See also *saburaimu*; sublime turn

sublime turn, 130, 135, 137–38, 144; atomic bomb, 130, 141–43

subversives, 23, 30. See also *filibusteros*

Sudanese, 152–54, 159–60, 168–69, 173 n. 46

Syria, 115, 127 n. 10, 157, 159, 171 n. 8

terrorism, 5, 9; affinity words, 240; Algeria, 181; counter-terrorism, 36; France, 181, 187, 190, 258; India, 5, 7, 9, 14, 201, 213, 240–60; Indonesia, 49; injury, 213, 215–16; Iraq, 190; Islam, 49, 121, 181–82, 187, 190; the modern state and, 213, 257–60; Morocco, 121, 181; Pakistan, 256; origins, 240–41; September 11 attacks, 181–82, 215–16, 219

Thailand, 4, 5–8, 13, 15; accountability, 313, 317; anarchism, 286–87, 296; Asian Economic Crisis of 1997, 306, 313–14, 319, 324 n. 13; body politic, 307, 323 n. 1; capitalism, 295, 297–98, 302, 306, 312–13, 317, 319, 321, 324 n. 14, 326 n. 33; Catholicism, 298–301; civilization, 307, 316, 320; civil society, 315, 317; colonialism, 325 n. 22; communism, 293, 288, 302 n. 17, 308, 310–12, 318–19, 321, 323 nn. 6–7, 325 n. 22; constitution, 310, 323 n. 6; democracy, 292, 310, 315, 318–19, 321, 326 n. 32, 326 n. 34; development, 324 n. 12; environment, 287, 299, 315; Gandhi, Mohandas, 287, 295–97, 301, 304 n. 37; globalization, 312–13; IMF, 306, 313, 315–17, 319, 322, 324 n. 12; law, 290–91, 314, 317; modernity, 286, 294, 306–7, 309; nationalism, 317; parliament, 302 n. 17, 316; private vs. public, 311, 318, 324 n. 14; public vs. the state, 287, 294–95, 298–300, 306–22; race and ethnicity, 298, 311, 325; religion, 290, 299, 314; republicanism, 310;

Thailand (*continued*)
responsibility, 293; revolution, 302
n. 17, 309, 310, 312, 323 nn. 6–7;
security, 6, 309, 316; sovereignty,
289; the state, 291–94, 297, 300,
302, 307, 311, 314–19, 320, 321;
Turkey, 284 n. 14. *See also*
chumchon; *thammarat*

thammarat [Thai, "good governance"]: authoritarian *thammarat*,
316–17, 320, 321; departure from
IMF's term of "good governance,"
306, 319, 322; liberal *thammarat*,
317–18, 320, 321; communitarian
thammarat, 318; meanings, 320,
321; origins, 306, 313–16

thug [Hindi, "*thag*"], 8, 14; affinity
words, 204–5; origins, 201–2; anti-
Thug campaign, 201, 205; super-
signs, 203–5; terrorism, 247–48

tradition: Indonesia, 41–42, 47–52,
59, 70–73; Japan, 93; Morocco,
113, 116; Southeast Asia and the
Middle East, 68, 77–80; the word,
4, 41, 44, 70–71, 80, 112. *See also*
adat; custom

translation: *'ada*, 68; *adat*, 42, 43, 47,
49, 62 n. 17; as analytic concept, 4,
42, 88, 236, 265; anxiety of, 49;
'aqalliyya, 152; Benjamin, Walter,
on, 130–31; *chumchon*, 290–91; circulation and diffusion of, 8, 290;
colonialism and, 236; *conjuración*,
227, 236; cultural nationalism and,
52, 63 n. 45; of "economics of
enough-ness," 302 n. 5; etymology
and, 200; freedom, 92; *hijāb*, 175,
190; *'ilmaniyya*, 110; of indigenous
rights from Brazil to Indonesia, 43;
injury, 208; of ILO Convention 169,
44–46; imperialism and, 110, 115;
komisyon, 268; *kurul*, 274–75; *laïcité*,

111, 118; *masyarakat adat*, 41–47;
mistranslation, 105 n. 21, 203, 218
n. 32; non-verbal signs and, 15;
pacto de sangre, 236, 239 n. 38;
rhyming of, 15, 290–91, 306–7,
315; rights, 88, 92–93; routes of, 86,
88; *saburaimu*, 130–31; *segurança*,
30; *sekinin*, 85–88; *shura*, 125; stabilization of, 14, 46, 290–91, 302 n.
5; terrorism, 257; Thai politics and,
290–91, 306–13; *thammarat*, 313–
15; thug, 204; transformation and,
15, 264, 307–9, 313; transliteration
and, 86; transnational translations,
45, 53; as vehicles for modernity,
civilization, or Western ways, 85–
86, 88, 111, 115, 118, 152, 175, 190,
306–7; *yi*, 202–4, 218 n. 32

translingual practice: concept of, 15;
sekinin, 91; super-signs, 199–201,
203–5; thug, 204; *yi*, 204

transnational links: in the British
empire, 55; creation of meaning,
15–16; environmental movements,
31, 33, 43–45, 56–57, 102; indigenous peoples, 55–58, 75–77, 295;
intellectuals, 16–17; among Islamic
states, 115–17; legal discourse of
responsibility, 97–99, 102; material
aspects of language and, 15–16;
minorities, 165–68; national consciousness and, 33, 59; NGOs, 33,
43–44, 55, 102, 286–87, 294–95,
300–1, 325 n. 21; revolutionary
movements and, 244–46; social scientists, 68, 288, 294, 297–98; as
threat to sovereignty, 33, 43; transnational institutions as bureaucratic model, 266–67, 274–85;
UNESCO, 169, 295; unpredictability
of movement through, 9, 40. *See also*
anticolonialism; colonialism; cos-

Carol Gluck is George Sansom Professor of
History, Columbia University.

Anna Lowenhaupt Tsing is Professor of Anthropology, University of California, Santa Cruz.

Library of Congress Cataloging-in-Publication Data
Words in motion : toward a global lexicon /
edited by Carol Gluck and Anna Lowenhaupt Tsing.
p. cm.
Includes bibliographical references and index.
ISBN 978-0-8223-4519-0 (cloth : alk. paper)
ISBN 978-0-8223-4536-7 (pbk. : alk. paper)
1. Language and languages — Political aspects.
2. Language and culture — Political aspects.
3. Intercultural communication.
4. Globalization. I. Gluck, Carol, 1941–
II. Tsing, Anna Lowenhaupt.
P119.3.W58 2009
306.44 — dc22   2009013115

23337658R00206